The Vatican Versus
Horror Movies

The Vatican Versus Horror Movies

MATT ROGERSON

McFarland & Company, Inc., Publishers
Jefferson, North Carolina

Unless otherwise noted, all illustrations are by the author

LIBRARY OF CONGRESS CATALOGING-IN-PUBLICATION DATA

Names: Rogerson, Matt, 1976– author.
Title: The Vatican versus horror movies / Matt Rogerson.
Description: Jefferson, North Carolina : McFarland & Company, Inc., Publishers 2025 | Includes bibliographical references and index.
Identifiers: LCCN 2024056261 | ISBN 9781476695761 (paperback : acid free paper) ♾
 | ISBN 9781476654058 (ebook)
Subjects: LCSH: Horror films—History and criticism. | Exploitation films—History and criticism. | Motion pictures—Religious aspects—Catholic Church. | Segnalazioni cinematografiche (Rome, Italy) | Motion pictures—Censorship—Italy—Rome.
Classification: LCC PN1995.9.H6 R64 2025 | DDC 261.5/7—dc23/eng/20250118
LC record available at https://lccn.loc.gov/2024056261

ISBN (print) 978-1-4766-9576-1
ISBN (ebook) 978-1-4766-5405-8

© 2025 Matt Rogerson. All rights reserved

No part of this book may be reproduced or transmitted in any form or by any means, electronic or mechanical, including photocopying or recording, or by any information storage and retrieval system, without permission in writing from the publisher.

Front cover image: From a photograph by Josh Weiner of the 1973 film *The Exorcist* (Warner Bros. Pictures/Photofest)

Printed in the United States of America

McFarland & Company, Inc., Publishers
Box 611, Jefferson, North Carolina 28640
www.mcfarlandpub.com

Table of Contents

Preface	1
Introduction (The Vatican versus … Cinema)	9
1. It Started with a Bet (The Vatican versus … Gothic Horror and the Birth of Italian Horror)	21
2. Escluso per Tutti (The Vatican versus … the Birth of Modern Horror and the Giallo)	37
3. This … Is God! (The Vatican versus … the Slasher)	55
4. Dinah, Daughter of Jacob (The Vatican versus … the Rape/Revenge Film)	76
5. The Body of Christ … Amen (The Vatican versus … the Cannibal Film)	97
6. The Profane Resurrection (The Vatican versus … the Zombie Film)	117
7. Get Thee to a Nunnery! (The Vatican versus … Nunsploitation)	143
8. The Paradox of Memory (The Vatican versus … Nazisploitation)	165
9. The Power of Christ Compels You! (The Vatican versus … Satanic Horror)	193
Conclusion	213
Chapter Notes	221
Bibliography	239
Index	249

Preface

I became interested in the intersection between horror cinema and religion (and Roman Catholicism in particular) at a very early age. I was considered a quiet child, timid, anxious and easily frightened (due in part to a turbulent childhood), but I've never been scared of horror movies. To the contrary, I have always taken great solace in cinema's darkest of genres.

I was accidentally introduced to horror movies at the age of six, when I awoke one night and decided to sneak downstairs. In the living room of our modest terraced home in the very early 1980s, we had a number of VHS VCRs stacked in an alcove by the television. They were big, clunky early models (one of them a top loader that I distinctly remember had small operating levers rather than buttons), were all attached to one another and always seemed to be operating, a loud whirring permeating the house at all hours of the day and night. What they were playing and/or recording was, until that night, a mystery to me.

I climbed out of bed, silently tiptoed downstairs (my parents were fast asleep in their own bed, but nonetheless I made every effort not to stir them) and sat, in my pajamas, on the rug in the living room, facing what felt like an enormous, intimidating television set (in fact it was a 21-inch cathode ray tube, which any modern television screen would absolutely dwarf, but to me it was the biggest television there could possibly be). My tiny arm reached out, hit the switch and, as the television turned on I very quickly turned the volume dial counterclockwise to mute the sound. I then switched the channel dial to channel 9 (the VCR channel) and gasped in wonder at what I saw.

What I would later come to realize is that my dad was a VHS pirate. At a time when the UK was in the grip of the video nasties scandal, and various horror films were subject to bans, persecutions (from Mary Whitehouse and the National Viewers and Listeners Association to my grandmother, dad's mum, who sat on the local council's censor board and determined what could and couldn't be shown in Rochdale's cinema) and indeed prosecutions, my dad was an honest to goodness bastion of genre film, reproducing and distributing illicit copies of the films they were all trying to ban. When any of the residents of my local community got to see *The Driller Killer, Last House on the Left* or *Cannibal Holocaust*, it was thanks to my dad … and, because of my discovery that night, I would get to see them all before anybody else.

The film I saw that first fateful night was *Evil Dead*. Or, to be perfectly honest, I saw approximately 10 minutes of it. I remember the card game scene—*Two of spades! Jack of Diamonds! Jack of clubs!!! Why have you disturbed our sleep?!? Awakened us from our ancient slumber?!? You will die!!!* Transfixed, I grabbed a pillow and lay down on the rug to watch more … and within minutes I was asleep! I woke hours later, turned off the television and tiptoed back to bed.

My pilgrimages downstairs in the middle of the night became a regular occurrence. I saw a film called *Zombi* next—not a video nasty but a supposedly uncut version of an American film called *Dawn of the Dead*. It featured zombies leaping forth from an elevator and one in particular having the top of its skull whipped off by a helicopter rotor blade.

I vividly recall being spellbound by its supposed sequel—Lucio Fulci's *Zombi 2*. I remember watching in awe the scene where a zombie had an underwater fight with what I thought must have been *Jaws*, and the zombies that climbed out of the earth with maggots and worms in their eye sockets. *Zombi 2* captivated me, and on subsequent expeditions downstairs I would see Joe D'Amato's *Anthropophagus*, Mario Bava's *A Bay of Blood* and a film about Nazis (I couldn't honestly tell you which one) that had naked ladies in it.

So I wasn't just introduced to horror movies at that tender age. I was introduced to what were considered at the time the sickest, most depraved horror movies in existence. Zombies and ghouls and cannibals, committing foul, graphic violence on the various unfortunate protagonists, feasting on human flesh. I also recall seeing various evil creatures doing particularly gruesome things to eyeballs, which I *loved* (although to this day I'm happy wearing glasses because laser eye surgery is not for me. I won't even wear contact lenses because my eyes are not to be touched or messed with. Make of that what you will).

It was the Italian films that stuck with me the most. The films of Lucio Fulci, Dario Argento and various others just had something to them, a visceral quality that the American entries couldn't quite match for me. Even at six years old I preferred Fulci's living dead to George A. Romero's, and that has never changed. But, for close to a year, I avidly snuck downstairs and watched the sickest films imaginable and was never once scared, shocked or traumatized. I was, in fact, at peace. They provided me with hours of solace and comfort. I understand now that they were my safe space.

The only thing that scared me was getting caught. If I was ever discovered, I knew I would be in trouble. But not in trouble with dad, the kind of trouble that might mean my toys were temporarily taken away or I might, if my crime was especially egregious, get smacked.

No, I would be in GOD trouble.

I grew up in the Roman Catholic Church. Neither of my parents were actively religious (my mum was from a Protestant family but not really raised in observance of faith, and my dad didn't really believe in anything), but my aforementioned grandmother, the family's matriarch, was staunchly Roman Catholic, which meant that's how I was to be raised. My parish church, which still stands (St. John the Baptist in Rochdale) was a grandiose, blisteringly cold and intimidating, inhospitable place, with a triptych of giant mosaics behind the altar depicting Judgment Day. The centerpiece illustrated the Second Coming of Christ, the left-hand piece showed Heaven, the angels and a beautiful rainbow ... but it was the right-hand image that always drew my eyes and my attention. The scene featured wretched souls writhing in the sulfur fires of Hell, while demons overhead delighted in their suffering. It was a terrifying image, far scarier than any film, mostly because every Sunday I was reminded by the priest's sermons that those flaming pits would be my destiny if I sinned. The church also featured tablets featuring the 14 Stations of the Cross (essentially the world's first torture porn, a story of violence that as a child I was expected to learn, to recite and to be able to draw from memory before receiving the sacrament of holy communion for the first time) hanging on its pillars.

Though I couldn't appreciate it at the time—how could I, a mere child—there was an incredible irony there. My devoutly religious grandmother (the family used to joke that God would sit beside *her* throne in Heaven), who was heavily involved in both the church and the local council, wanted me to learn all about the terrifying horrors of Hell, and of Jesus' torture, crucifixion and death. This was fine, apparently, and the real sin was watching horror movies.

Eventually, my luck did run out. One night I snuck downstairs, watched whatever film my dad was making copies of at the time, and fell asleep on the rug in the living room. This time, I did not awaken until my dad came downstairs in the morning and discovered me there. He did not punish me, which surprised and confused me. He and my mum were concerned what effect watching these films might be having on me, but stopped short of leveling any of the usual childhood sanctions, I suppose because they themselves felt a sense of guilt that I was even able to watch these films, and watch them unsupervised in my own home.

It was around this time, as I turned seven, that I took the sacraments of confession and communion. These were a big affair, the preparation for which dominated weeks of my schooling as well as church activity. My Roman Catholic primary school, St. John's, was a parish school that occupied the same property as the church, and any Roman Catholic schoolchild will tell you that the line between school and church is somewhat blurred (and I feel I'm being generous here).

In school, I learned the 14 stations of the cross until I could not only recite them but also accurately depict them with pencil and Crayola (I still consider this a bizarre and unhealthy task to be given as a child, but it was one we were quickly taught not to question), learned the prayers and songs that would be part of the ceremony, and the correct way to receive the body of Christ (Amen). It was also impressed upon me that my confession was equally important. For my first confession, I was to consider what was the greatest sin, observed but unpunished by God, that I had committed in my seven short years of life. What had I done that I should feel most guilty about and seek God's forgiveness for?

The answer I came to was, of course, my midnight horror film watching activities. And let me tell you, dear reader, that was *a mistake*. I confessed to my priest, Father O'Driscoll, that I had been sneaking downstairs at night to watch X-rated movies (they were in fact unrated, but I didn't know the difference at the time). I also confessed that when caught by my parents I was not punished. Father asked if these were my dad's movies, and I explained that dad was making copies of them to give to his friends.

And the jig, as they say, was up.

The first thing the priest did was seek out my nana, our matriarch, and tell her. There was, of course, a confrontation with my dad, the details of which were never revealed to me, but as a result all video nasty distribution activities stopped immediately, never to be resumed.

I do recall that dad never did punish me, even after I dropped him in it at confession. In fact, when I was a little older (11, arbitrarily, was the age he decided upon) dad allowed me to resume watching horror films. He set up a membership in my name at the local video rental store, and instructed the owner (a lovely man whose name I forget, but who was friends with my father) that I had parental permission to rent out 18-rated horror movies but no pornography.

And I did, at a rate of one a week. *A Nightmare on Elm Street* and its sequels were among those I most enjoyed, as was a little Spanish horror movie called *Anguish*, which featured the lady from *Poltergeist*, hypnosis, multiple bewildering layers of reality and lots of eyeball-related violence! Although I must have watched every 1980s horror title available in that small store, I did notice that none of my favorites were there. They were, of course, still banned in the UK, and would be for another 15 years or so. It was not until the British Board of Film Classification (BBFC) began to relax their position that certain boutique DVD labels such as Vipco began to release the films of Lucio Fulci et al. for me to enjoy all over again, this time as an adult.

Once they were available, I bought and rewatched lost treasures and sought out my favorite video nasties, mostly Italian but sometimes Spanish, English or American, and so often they took me back to my childhood, to those precious moments at home where I felt truly safe and protected from the world. After my father passed away a few years later, these films became my surrogate for his love and protection, my everlasting link to his memory.

But where the younger me had enjoyed these horror films purely on an aesthetic level, now I was beginning to notice more. I began to recognize how sacrilegious they were, filled with the sacred and the profane, with quasi-religious symbolism and iconography, in many cases, outright criticizing the Church. MY church. Roman Catholicism and its headquarters, the Vatican.

I started to realize that the directors of these films, films which had been banned and taken from me by my nana, the church and moral panics, were also Roman Catholics who had conflicted feelings about church and faith. Lucio Fulci (forever my favorite) depicted priests as abusers of children, showed us zombies as resurrected Christian soldiers and depicted Judgment Day and Hell unleashed upon earth. The cannibals of Ruggero Deodato and Umberto Lenzi weren't just eating people, they were taking part in a subversive version of my first holy communion. Ken Russell excoriated the Church's past with gleeful sacrilegious abandon, while William Friedkin and Damiano Damiani showed priests as flawed humans, as equally questioning of their faith as their parishioners. There was, I began to realize, an entire subgenre of films devoted to showing the horrors of the Nazis and their fascist allies, regimes that I would later learn had been propped up by MY Church (funnily enough this aspect of Roman Catholic history was never taught in the mandatory Bible study classes I had to take in school throughout my formative years).

Not only was my dad an unlikely working-class hero, crusading against censorship through piracy, the directors whose films he distributed were also unlikely heroes, crusading against the crimes and hypocrisy of the Roman Catholic faith through their transgressive art. I felt a great swell of pride as I began to realize this, a tremendous sense of satisfaction, of justice, and wished to explore this further, through studying and writing about film. In many ways, this exploration has become my life's work.

Much like the Italian genre filmmakers that so incensed the Vatican, whose apostatic journeys were explored through their work and are examined in this book, I underwent my own conscious uncoupling from the Church, beginning at age seven, in the form of introspection and reflection on who or what I truly believed God to be, and whether I could reconcile that with the fear instilled in me by the Church. At age ten I stopped attending church on Sundays. At age 12 I refused the sacrament of confirmation. My church and school pressured me, even gave me multiple detentions as punishment in efforts to make me change my mind, but I held fast. My nana hated this, which was just fine by me. She made efforts of her own, and even my dad made halfhearted attempts to change my mind (no doubt under her orders), but ultimately I made up my own mind. My resolve remained, and I continued to separate from my faith during my adolescence and early adulthood. A number of things continued to contribute to my own apostasy; my relationship with religion is damaged beyond repair, and I'm okay with that. Honestly, it was over the day they took my horror movies away.

There is, of course, an argument that religious trauma never leaves you, and that even if you can successfully and truthfully say you no longer believe in God, you're still afraid of His wrath. I would say I'm firmly in that category and always will be. I haven't been to church in decades but I still wear rosaries. I never pray but, at times, I still fear.

This book is the product of all of the above. The subject is horror and exploitation film where it stands directly at odds with the Church (specifically the Roman Catholic Church). It aims to explore matters of the sacred and profane, the quasi-religious symbolism and iconography of various subgenres of horror and exploitation, and determine exactly what it was about these films that made them so evil in the eyes of the Church. My research took me first to the content of the films themselves, to search out and analyze the above aspects and gain an understanding of the elements of Roman Catholicism in horror and exploitation film and why they were put there by the filmmakers in question. From there, I researched Roman Catholicism itself, its history, the most controversial and salacious aspects of the religion's past and present, and in particular how the religion's influence waned in the latter half of the 20th century during what has become known as the new secularization, with more and more Catholics drifting from the church and experiencing apostasy. This led me to a discovery: the Centro Cattolico Cinematografico (Catholic Film Center), an institution set up in the infancy of the film medium, as the Vatican realized film's potential power and sought to control it. Ultimately, my research into the CCC led me to the *Segnalazioni cinematografiche* (Film Signals), the regularly produced and distributed film review pamphlet that the Vatican used to exert its control over what films were shown in the cinemas of Italy. I sought out as many issues of the journal as I could find, from trips to Italian libraries and bookshops to late nights scouring Italian eBay and niche online booksellers, amassing a collection ranging from the 1930s to the 1990s. I began to learn to read and write in Italian, something that took several years but proved invaluable in translating content from the journal, which had never been published in the English language.

As a result of my research, this book presents a rich and contextualized dissection of Roman Catholic themes, symbolism and iconography present in the gothic horror of the late 1950s and early 1960s, of the development of the horror film, the rise of the giallo and of subgenres including the slasher, rape/revenge films, zombie films and cannibal films, nunsploitation, nazisploitation and satanic horror. It catalogs these films' symbols and themes and juxtaposes them with the reviews, moral judgments and censure of the Centro Cattolico Cinematografico, as well as the history of the Catholic church, in an attempt to determine precisely how the Vatican views each subgenre and how damaging it considers them, both to the moral good of the human race and to itself as an institution. Throughout the book are a number of original illustrations, highlighting the films under discussion. These illustrations are based on images from the films themselves and/or their promotional materials, and each is intended to emphasize one or more of the following: any pertinent symbolism, iconography or subtext present in the film; the political, social or historical context behind the Vatican's opposition to it; and the incumbent pontiff at the time of the film's release.

While my writing maintains a critical stance with regard to the religion I was born into, the true mission of this book is to celebrate the power of genre film. Horror cinema is often revealed to be more prescient and revolutionary than its critics give it credit for, and certain subgenres of horror and exploitation film in particular have proven to have been a thorn in the side of the Roman Catholic institution for over half a century. In the world of narrative cinema, the work of criticizing the Church had begun as early as 1911, when Italy's very first feature film was an adaptation of Dante's *Inferno*, the Italian poet's own exploration of his faith and apostasy as he broke away from the Church. Due to the "fictional" nature of their art, subversive writers and directors often (but not always) find themselves relatively free to create narratives that criticize the Church indirectly and, over subsequent decades, both high art cinematic poets and transgressive genre stalwarts alike have woven Roman Catholic themes into their works. This criticism sometimes came from cinema's greatest poets, but often it was the directors of transgressive genre film that proved themselves to be the true agitators.

The Church would always fight back, through censorship and prosecution, as it sought to "protect" its flock from such subjects in the cinema that provoked its ire (only to indulge freely in and then cover up multiple evils in real life and ruin countless lives in the process). While the influence of Roman Catholicism would lead to the prohibition of many genre films across Europe, and the prosecution of their directors and producers, the agitators of genre cinema did not relent: instead they pushed harder and harder at this most powerful of targets and tore down barrier after barrier erected in the name of "decency." Many of the most popular films in horror and adjacent genres that would embrace sacrilege in order to shock and appall on the surface (while pushing, through subtext, a scathing narrative not just of religion, but of precisely *this* religion) are covered in the chapters of this volume.

More than anything, this book celebrates the *tenacity* of genre film. For decades, the Church fought a war against genre film that it would ultimately lose. As papal power waned and more and more members of Roman Catholicism's congregations began their own apostatic journeys, the horror film only grew in power and influence, producing box-office success and infiltrating mainstream society to the point where a new generation would come to worship the likes of the resurrected Freddy Krueger and high priest Pinhead instead of God the Father, God the Son and God the Holy Spirit.

Finally, this book is an exploration of cinema's greatest gift to us: its rich history. The current generation(s) of horror fans have over a century of macabre feature films to indulge in, and to examine the influence of a particular film or films over a period of time is a joy that I know anybody reading this will understand. I have made my best attempt at making the most of this opportunity: to reframe the familiar films of the modern horror genre and examine their critical potency using the lens of the Vatican via its own film review pamphlets, the *Segnalazioni cinematografiche*. What you now hold is the first of what I hope to be a series of books on the subject of my favorite horror and exploitation directors and their transgressions against the Church, and how the Church attempted to fight back.

This is the Vatican versus horror movies.

—Matt Rogerson, 20 December 2023

Introduction

(The Vatican versus ... Cinema)

Since the first public audience in Paris viewed the moving pictures prepared by the Lumière brothers in December 1895, the film industry has become a universal medium exercising a profound influence on the development of people's attitudes and choices, and possessing a remarkable ability to influence public opinion and culture across all social and political frontiers. The Church's overall judgment of this art form, as of all genuine art, is positive and hopeful. We have seen that masterpieces of the art of film making can be moving challenges to the human spirit, capable of dealing in depth with subjects of great meaning and importance from an ethical and spiritual point of view.[1]

The above quote comes from Pope John Paul II, in an address made in 1995 to the Plenary Assembly of the Pontifical Council for Social Communications to commemorate the centenary of cinema. The Vatican marked the occasion by creating the Vatican best movies list: 45 films rated for their contribution to religion, values and art. An unusual move for an institution that had often sought to oppose commercial cinema, the list included such classics as Ingmar Bergman's existential masterpiece *The Seventh Seal*, Steven Spielberg's heart-wrenching war drama *Schindler's List* and Roberto Rossellini's *Rome: Open City*, the 1945 tale of the underground resistance in German-occupied fascist Italy that became a landmark of Italian cinema's neorealism movement.

The list also featured a single horror movie: F. W. Murnau's 1922 vampire classic *Nosferatu*. The Vatican praised the silent expressionist classic for its "eerie portrayal of the vampire in images which seem to personify evil and dread in a movie even more remarkable for having been filmed mostly on location rather than in the controlled confines of a studio."[2]

On March 17, 1995, Pope John Paul II addressed the plenary assembly of the Pontifical Council for Social Communications to commemorate 100 years of cinema and reveal the Vatican Film List of 100 important films from cinema's first centenary. *Nosferatu* (1922) was the only horror movie included on the list. Illustration by the author.

This very progressive, permissive move by the Church was celebrated by the movie world, especially as the endorsed films reflected a wide range of cinema, rather than focusing solely on narratives based upon Roman Catholic scripture. The Pope's address, however, carried with it a caveat, a familiar refrain that had been heard many times by Italy's filmmakers and public over the previous century:

> Unfortunately though, some cinema productions merit criticism and disapproval, even severe criticism and disapproval. This is the case when films distort the truth, oppress genuine freedom, or show scenes of sex and violence offensive to human dignity. It is a fallacy for film-makers to do this in the name of free artistic expression.[3]

John Paul's argument punctuates the Vatican's attempts to censor and censure film production since it began to take hold in Italy around the turn of the 20th century. Though the Pope did his best in 1995 to reassure the industry that "the Church is not seeking to limit creativity but to liberate creative talent and challenge it to pursue the highest ideals of this art form,"[4] those with longer memories would know that the Holy See had always considered itself to have an obligation to adopt a paternalistic stance with regard to cinema: to assess the moral quality of what the Vatican believed to be "the most immediately influential of all art forms"[5] and only allow those films with "the moral vision which gives genuine content and inspiring expression to this art"[6] to be seen by the Roman Catholic public, in Italy and elsewhere.

By the time of the release of Italy's first feature-length film—Francesco Bertolini, Adolfo Padovan and Giuseppe De Liguoro's 1911 Dante adaptation *L'Inferno*—the Vatican had already made its first decree with regard to the medium, and would issue several more over the coming years. The Church had become quite suspicious and fearful of cinema's influence as it spread across Europe, entertaining and delighting the masses with its fantastic celluloid stories. The Vatican's first decree on film, issued in 1909, forbade the clergy from attending any public film screenings whatsoever. This was followed by a second decree in 1918, which prohibited the screening of any films in churches.[7,8] This fearful opposition to the new media in Italy would continue, and it would come not just from the Church but from the state as well.

Benito Mussolini's Partito Nazionale Fascista marched on Rome in 1922. This coup d'état was successful and King Victor Emmanuel IV transferred power from the incumbent prime minister to Mussolini.

In Germany at the time, Hitler's Nationalsozialistische Deutsche Arbeiterpartei carried out its führer's orders to rule not just the people's public behavior but their private thoughts and opinions. A German under Hitler's rule could not be critical of the Nazi regime even in the company of their own family for fear that they would be reported to the government and arrested for their opposition.⁹ The use of cinema for propaganda had been planned for several years prior to the party taking control of Germany. Under Hitler and Goebbels, any filmmaker who did not wish to work producing propaganda for the Reich would be forced to leave the country: soon after, some 2,000 directors, producers, cinematographers, editors and actors were either deported or fled to the U.S. to work in Hollywood.¹⁰

But in Italy, Mussolini's dictatorship was not a totalitarian but an authoritarian one. Il Duce sought only to control people's outward behavior in order to crush any opposition they may have toward the government; people were somewhat free to develop their personal thoughts and opinions in private. Rather than deport the country's intellectuals, Mussolini allowed them to continue to live and work in the country.

Mussolini sought to control the means of film production, distribution and exhibition. He would create L'Unione Cinematografica Educativa (LUCE) in 1925 to promote the making of educational (read: propaganda) films and documentaries. In 1933, he passed laws to preserve the integrity of Italian films and the Italian identity through cinema. These laws stated that Italian films screened abroad could not be dubbed into foreign languages, while all foreign films broadcast in Italy must be dubbed into Italian at the cost of the production house, not the government. Mussolini would use the proceeds from the government savings to reinvest in domestic cinema film production.¹¹ He went on to create the Direzione Generale per la Cinema, a state-funded and controlled censor board run by Luigi Freddie; set up the professional film school Centro Sperimentale di Cinematografia to train the country's future filmmakers; and establish Cinecitta Studios for the production of movies with Mussolini-approved messages.¹² The film industry of Italy would function in service of the fascist ideal of civilization, presenting audiences with "cheerful and reassuring dreams"¹³ that would serve to placate and distract audiences from anything that might breed criticism or contempt of Il Duce's rule.

This, of course, meant restrictions on what films could be made domestically, or imported from other countries: films with any kind of socialist dialogue would be banned from exhibition in Italy, as would almost any film set in prerevolutionary Russia (Mussolini would reportedly become alarmed by any film that featured characters with Russian-sounding names).¹⁴ In addition, war films would be banned, as would all horror films. After 1911's *L'Inferno* (which, though it was an adaptation of classic literature, of course featured Hell, Lucifer and all his demons in a number of grand, fantastical and horrific sequences) and Eugenio Testa's 1920 *Il Mostro di Frankenstein* (an adaptation of Mary Wollstonecraft Shelley's classic novel, now believed to be lost), horror films would not be exhibited in Italy until long after Mussolini was ousted from power, and the Italian domestic industry would not produce another horror movie itself until 1957's *I Vampiri*, directed by Riccardo Freda and Mario Bava.

The incumbent Pope at the time of Mussolini's rule, Pius XI, produced the Encyclical Letter Divini Illius Magistri in 1929 demanding that Catholics exercise vigilance against "these most powerful means of publicity, which can be of great utility for instruction and education when directed by sound principles, are only too often used as an incentive to evil passions and greed for gain."[15] In 1936, Pius followed this up with Vigilanti Cura, an edict that called upon Catholics across Italy and the world to help in the fight against "unhealthy" films. Pius praised the conservative U.S. Christian pressure group the League of Decency (which battled vociferously and effectively in the U.S. for the censorship and outright banning of controversial films, leading to the infamous Hays Code) for its work and sought to replicate it in Italy.[16]

In 1933, Cardinal Secretary of State Eugenio Pacelli (who would go on to become the next Pope, Pius XII) signed a concordat with the Reich, proclaiming Roman Catholicism the recognized religion in Germany and ensuring it remained free to exercise its will in Italy under Mussolini. The concordat of course proved controversial, seemingly giving moral legitimacy to the Nazi regime soon after Hitler had acquired quasi-dictatorial powers through the Enabling Act of 1933 (itself facilitated via the support of the Catholic Center Party). Pacelli/Pius XII would become known as "Hitler's Pope,"[17] was heavily criticized, and was labeled a Nazi sympathizer for his silence during the Holocaust. It is now known (thanks to the recent unsealing of Vatican documents) that Pius XII was aware of the mass murders being committed by the Nazis from

Volume 1 of the *Segnalazioni cinematografiche* (1934–35), the Vatican's film review journal. Photograph by the author.

the very beginning, and neither spoke publicly nor made any private pleas to Hitler to reconsider the deaths at Auschwitz and the other sites where the Holocaust took place (despite various clerics pressing him to do so).[18] By turning a blind eye to the genocidal atrocities of the Nazis, Pius XII ensured a relationship between Church and state that would go on until after the fall of the Nazis and the removal of Mussolini from power in Italy in 1944.

In 1934, The Vatican established the Centro Cattolico Cinematografico (CCC), its own censorship organization, a separate entity from Mussolini's Direzione Generale per la Cinema. Now aligned directly with Hitler and Mussolini, the CCC served to police the moral and religious content of all cinema produced or exhibited in Italy, allowing the Vatican's power over cinema without causing friction between it and the state. It did this through a number of tools, one of which was the *Segnalazioni cinematografiche*.

The *Segnalazioni cinematografiche* took the form of a fortnightly publication (later collected and published in biannual editions) for the classification and pastoral critique of every film released in Italy in the corresponding period. A number of individuals provided reviews, overseen by a pope appointee: often a member of Opus Dei, the controversial and far-reaching Church institution with a mandate to "foster the search for holiness and the carrying out of the apostolate by Christians who live in the world, whatever their state in life or position in society."[19] The *Segnalazioni cinematografiche* was distributed to Roman Catholics far and wide, not just via the clergy and at Church but via "an incredibly widespread network of organisations, associations and clubs."[20]

Angeli notes that "the power and influence of Centro Cattolico Cinematografico publications was enormous, as they could determine a film's success, or lack thereof, at the box office."[21] The *Segnalazioni cinematografiche*'s reviews showed that the Vatican intended to use that power and influence. Many of Italy's theaters were parish cinemas, firmly under the control of the Church, and if those that weren't strictly under the Vatican's control employed Catholic operators or projectionists, they would often make a moral decision as to whether to show films granted release by the state but subject to an ecclesiastical ban. The first modest pamphlets contained no fewer than 66 condemned films, and the judgments passed were swift and merciless. As previously explained, domestic filmmakers in Italy under Mussolini could only produce "cheerful and reassuring dreams,"[22] and any foreign imports would need to fit similar criteria. While films of the burgeoning horror genre (birthed by the German Expressionists in the 1920s and subsequently led by Hollywood's Universal Studios and their stable of gothic monsters throughout the 1930s and '40s) were filling cinemas in the U.S., UK and across Europe, they would not get a foothold in Italy until Il Duce was firmly in the country's rearview mirror. Instead, Italian cinemas were filled mostly with friendlier imports from Hollywood (due to Mussolini's restrictions on the sorts of films Italian filmmakers were allowed to produce, which in fact dissuaded filmmakers despite Il Duce's efforts to create a successful but tempered production system).

The first issues of the *Segnalazioni cinematografiche* were produced in 1935 and were reasonably crude in format to begin with. Films were rated A (suitable for all, with or without cuts) to D (unsuitable for all), and the Vatican's negative verdicts were very brief and dismissive.

Even before the advent of the horror film in Italian cinema, the Vatican still had much to guard its flock against, judging by the pages of the very first issue of *Segnalazioni cinematografiche*. Of Paramount Studios' noir thriller *Crime Without Passion* (starring Claude Rains, who had already starred in Universal's *The Invisible Man*), the first issue of the journal noted: "Apart from any other consideration on the plot's immobility, the scrupulous lesson that this film teaches, about how to avoid leaving evidence and escape the penalty of a crime, is enough to exclude it."[23] This simple, short criticism would see the film hamstrung at the Italian box office.

Columbia Pictures and David Burton's romantic musical *Let's Fall in Love* was damned for "the vast immoral content of the story and the environment in which it takes place (which) makes the film not advisable."[24] Twentieth Century–Fox and Alfred L. Werker's historical picture *The House of Rothschild* similarly met with the disapproval of the Holy See, which described the film as "outside of the educational concepts of the cinema as understood in a Christian way."[25] This was a particular form of censure that became synonymous with the *Segnalazioni cinematografiche*, as the Vatican sought to ensure that any historical events presented on-screen for the Italian public's consumption carried no messages that conflicted with sanitized historical records ratified by the Church.

MGM and Victor Fleming's musical *Reckless* was condemned with just three words: "film not recommended."[26] In a mere six syllables, Fleming's film would be effectively banned; it opened to empty auditoriums as Catholics were ordered to stay away and largely obeyed.

Warner Bros. and Robert Florey's drama *House on 56th Street* was simply described as "morally inadmissible."[27] and that was that; with an ecclesiastical ban, the film was doomed to failure in Italy. Even much-revered auteur Cecil B. DeMille did not escape the Vatican's ire, as his Paramount epic *Cleopatra* was "absolutely not recommended"[28] and failed at the Italian box office as a result.

The Holy See reserved its real ire for domestically produced projects, especially those that sought to include matters of Church and faith and had not been fully ratified by the Holy See. Mario Camerini's comedy *The Three-Cornered Hat*, adapted from 19th-century Spanish novelist Pedro Antonio de Alarcón's novella, came in for scorching criticism from the *Segnalazioni cinematografiche*, which condemned the film for "the mouth-watering plot, the equivocal situations and the inappropriate presence of religious people (that) make the film not recommended."[29] This criticism is particularly prescient, as it would be echoed time and again in subsequent publications of the journal whenever subversive cinema (particularly horror) featured religious figures or themes.

The Vatican would continue to exercise its power over cinema for decades to come, long after the fall of Mussolini and fascism. Over time, the *Segnalazioni cinematografiche* grew into a more sophisticated publication. For each film reviewed in the pamphlet, the basic personnel details (director, producer, screenwriter and principal cast) were listed, followed by a summary of the plot, a brief note on any cultural value of the film, with the main portion of the entry devoted to the pastoral evaluation, a moral critique of each film's content that would determine the film's classification.

Films were classified in the following way:

P	for parish halls (usually documentary films featuring parochial teaching and Catholic lectures)
T	viewable by all
Tr	viewable by all, with reservations for the very young
A	viewable by adults only
Ar	viewable only by adults of a certain moral maturity (a purposefully nebulous term, which essentially aided the Vatican in avoiding any accusations of hypocrisy: its scholars would still watch those films it had forbade its flock)
S	not recommended for anyone
E	forbidden for everyone

The ramifications of a negative review in the *Segnalazioni cinematografiche* continued to be significant for filmmakers. In the decades that followed, Roman Catholicism witnessed a massive expansion at home and abroad. By 1950 almost all of Italy's citizens identified as Roman Catholic, and 70 percent were regular churchgoers.[30] The Church was present in every facet of society: in the country's schools; health and social care institutions; union offices; parish priests would even make the final recommendations for local employers looking to hire workers.[31] Every city, town and village felt the influence of the Vatican, and these fortnightly pamphlets were disseminated through every available communication channel. The power of the *Segnalazioni cinematografiche* was such that, even if the state censor deemed a film permissible, if the owner or projectionist of your local cinema was Catholic, it was highly likely that film would not be screened if censured by the Vatican. For domestic directors, a negative rating could not only spell box-office disaster: filmmakers would soon receive a stern visit from a senior member of the Church, or even be summoned to a court appearance as Church figures gathered with local magistrates to engineer prosecutions (a range of domestic directors were frequently tried under various obscenity laws, from celebrated artist Pier Paolo Pasolini to genre journeyman Ruggero Deodato).

From 1958–1978, Italy experienced what Angeli calls "The New Secularisation,"[32] a period where Italy's population underwent a massive apostasy, and this was reflected in the country's art and media. This period arguably began with the Second Vatican Council (1962–65). This ecumenical council of the Catholic Church, more commonly referred to by the Vatican as "aggiornamento" (bringing up to date)[33] and known to the outside world by the very film-like title of "Vatican II" was convened by Saint John XXIII, who wished to oversee the "modernization of the Church after 20 Centuries of life."[34] Saint John XXIII considered it "necessary (for the Church) to keep up to date with the changing conditions of this modern world"[35] and the result was a renewal of Catholic life in almost every aspect, from the theology of the Mass to the role of the laity in engaging with the secular world and with other religions (which itself prompted the Church to make greater use of mass media to spread its message). This approach to reform would lead to a number of controversial changes in ecumenical policy, such as more permissive attitudes toward "the plague of divorce,"[36] birth control, abortion and same sex relationships.

In the modern era it is widely considered that the council precipitated a "Catholic Crisis"[37] that resulted in an "ever increasing confusion"[38] in Roman Catholic peoples, who organized petitions of "theological doubts"[39] to the College of Cardinals by its own members and directed hostility toward not just the council but all successive Popes since.

Vatican II was not the only reason behind the waning influence of the Holy See over the coming decades. The Vatican's alliance with Mussolini's Partito Nazionale Fascista, its complicity in the actions of the regime at home (and Pius XI's collusion with the architects of the Holocaust) had damaged its reputation irreparably and led to a crisis of faith. How could the Italian public's belief in its spiritual leaders not be damaged, after 20 years of living under an oppressive shadow, one that killed millions of people, one which the Vatican had allied itself with? How could the flock still believe in the integrity of the Church, in its position of spiritual shepherd and moral arbiter, after it had done little to fight or even criticize the atrocities that would be recorded as the most defining moment in humanity's history?

As the modern era began, the guardians of the Catholic Church's flock would have their work cut out for them. The neorealism movement that populated and popularized Italian cinema post–World War II was led by communists and intellectuals, ensuring that many of the films they produced were critical of the Church and the role it played in Italy's darkest period. These films, which despite being subversive in content were tremendously popular not just domestically but internationally as well (with the films of Federico Fellini, Vittorio De Sica and Elio Petri becoming Oscar winners in Hollywood), would contribute toward a desire to create a more permissive cinema that pushed boundaries. Thanks to Mussolini's Centro Sperimentale di Cinematografia (CSC), many of Italy's leftists and cerebral creatives had completed apprenticeships in cinema, and their attitudes would begin to populate all domestic film production, from the high art of Fellini to the transgressive horrors and thrillers of Lucio Fulci and Umberto Lenzi. Much to the chagrin of the Vatican, a more permissive era of domestic cinema had begun, and was set to take over the world. For the first time, Italy's cinemas were open to more than just the "cheerful and reassuring dreams"[40] they had been fed for decades. Instead, they would soon be home to the horror, exploitation and sleaze of genre cinema.

This book will focus on a period of time from the 1950s (the decade that saw the first international horror films screened in Italy, leading to the birth of the country's domestic horror genre) to 1990, when the Vatican's influence had waned to the point that the moral judgments of the *Segnalazioni cinematografiche* no longer had any material effect at all on the Italian public's screening and viewing habits.

Looking at first at the birth of the Italian Gothic horror film in the 1950s, this text will then turn to 1960, the year of the release of Alfred Hitchcock's *Psycho*, the film that "changed the genre"[41] and gave birth to modern horror, a genre built not upon classic romantic literature and creatures that inspired fear and empathy in equal measures, but on subversive, sociopolitical content designed to shock modern cinema audiences and constantly push the boundary of what is acceptable in film. Subsequent chapters will then turn to exploitation subgenres with a specific Italian identity, such as the giallo, slashers, cannibals, zombies, rape/revenge films, nunsploitation, nazisploitation and satanic horror. Various films produced within each of these subgenres, often made by Italian directors, will be examined for quasi-religious symbols and iconography and themes of the sacred and the profane, to establish where apostate Italian directors sought to criticize their Church and their faith through their subversive art. Themes and narratives in the *Segnalazioni cinematografiche* reviews of these films will be interrogated, juxtaposed with articles of wider context such as international critical opinions and global current affairs at the time of the films' release as well as the Vatican's own documented troubles, controversies, hypocrisies and scandals as relevant to the films in question. Ultimately, the meaning behind the Vatican's responses to those acts of celluloid sacrilege produced by recusant Italian artists will be determined and summarized within these pages.

In Mario Bava's 1960 directorial debut, *Black Sunday*, Princess Asa Vadja (Barbara Steele) is about to be tortured to death with a contraption known as the Mask of the Devil as a likeness of Pope Pius XII holds the device to Asa's face. Illustration by the author.

1

It Started with a Bet

(The Vatican versus ... Gothic Horror and the Birth of Italian Horror)

I wish to join the Legion of Decency, which condemns vile and unwholesome moving pictures. I unite with all who protest against them as a grave menace to youth, to home life, to country and to religion. I condemn absolutely those salacious motion pictures which, with other degrading agencies, are corrupting public morals and promoting a sex mania in our land.... Considering these evils, I hereby promise to remain away from all motion pictures except those which do not offend decency and Christian morality.[1]

The above passage forms a pledge made by members of the Catholic Legion of Decency, an organization founded in 1933 in the U.S. (but championed by Roman Catholic institutions at all levels, including the Vatican) and dedicated to combating "objectionable" content in motion pictures. The legion worked closely with the secular forces behind Hollywood's Hays Code, which brought strict censorship to motion pictures in the United States from its inception in 1934, censorship that other Catholic countries would soon align themselves with. Essentially, if a film was deemed to be objectionable, obscene, or even critical of the Church, any Catholics who wished to see the film would do so under threat of mortal sin. The 20 million Catholics in the United States at the time were being threatened with eternal suffering in Hell, all for watching the wrong movie. It would be the Legion's influence and its early success stories abroad that inspired the Vatican's own movements into censorship of the medium.

Prior to the influence of the Legion, and the introduction of the code, directors and producers in the U.S. and across Europe were relatively free to create subversive and shocking art in order to provide the public with escapism from the very real horrors of life, from World War I to the Great

Depression. Robert Wiene's expressionist masterpiece *The Cabinet of Dr. Caligari* (a film often credited as being the first progenitor of the horror genre) was brought to North America by producer Carl Laemmle, who went on to become a mainstay at Universal Studios as they established the on-screen versions of the literary "Monsters" that would popularize horror as a cinematic genre. Alexandra West also documents the nihilistic content of such films as MGM and Tod Browning's *Freaks* (1932) and Paramount and Rouben Mamoulian's *Dr. Jekyll and Mr. Hyde* (1931), which brought (according to their conservative, Catholic critics) an element of social decay and unhealthy attitudes to the cinema screens of the United States.[2]

While many of these films found popularity in the U.S. and across Europe, thanks to Mussolini's fascist regime and the complicity of the Church, none of them played on screens in Italy.

The Hays Code was successful in its censorship of Hollywood output from 1934 until 1968, when film production had increased to the point where it was no longer possible to keep up with the slates of new pictures and enforce the conservative Catholic values. Throughout the late 30s and 40s, the subversive content of horror films was sufficiently watered down that filmmakers were unable to successfully mirror the impact or financial success of the expressionist horrors of the 1920s and Universal's Monsters in the early 1930s.

It would not be until the late 1950s that the horror film made a serious comeback, earning success at worldwide box offices and the ire of censors and moral guardians. That its comeback would be spearheaded by a nation where horror movies had previously been banned outright was something of a surprise.

In the home of the Roman Catholic Church, a combination of fascist rule and Vatican interference had left the entire country under a gloomy shadow. Like just about every other component of Italian life, the cinema industry had been effectively hamstrung by Mussolini's regime, but the end of World War II and the fall of the dictator had initiated changes in the country's demeanor. The country's artists and poets (many of whom had trained at the Mussolini-established Centro Sperimentale di Cinematografia, which provided opportunities to build their cinematic storytelling skills even as other elements of the dictator's rule stopped them from ever really using them) responded with what would become known as neorealism: a cinematic movement inspired by French poetic realism, the tenets of Marxism and Christian humanism. Beginning with Luchino Visconti's 1943 neorealist noir *Ossessione*, the movement was characterized by its stories set among the working classes, analyzing the difficult economic and moral condition of Italian lives following the fascist rule

In Universal Studios' 1941 monster movie *The Wolf Man*, the titular Wolf Man (Lon Chaney, Jr.) holds the unconscious body of Gwen (Evelyn Ankers) while Captain Montford (Ralph Bellamy) threatens with a large crucifix held overhead. Illustration by the author.

and what was seen as the Church's betrayal of its people in aligning with fascism. Neorealism quickly grew to worldwide significance, birthing the careers of Visconti, Roberto Rossellini, Vittorio De Sica and Federico Fellini (among others) and directly influencing the cinema of France (the Nouvelle Vague), Brazil (Cinema Novo) and Iran (Iranian New Wave). The movement propelled its directors to popular acclaim, their films garnering multiple awards both on the European continent and beyond. They did so in spite of the Vatican (which of course disapproved of these politically incendiary films with their anti–papal messages). It also led other directors and producers to dream of what was possible in Italian cinema with the country freed from the grip of fascism. Outside of the neorealist poets, many directors had trained at the CSC were looking to make their own mark on cinema, and had begun to notice horror films being passed by state censors for broadcast in Italian cinemas.

It had taken several years following the 1943 fall of Mussolini's regime for Italy's cinemas to screen movies featuring the same monsters, madmen and creatures that had been entertaining audiences elsewhere for decades. Since the inception of Italian cinema, the only Italian feature films to feature creatures and demons had been adaptations and parodies of Dante's *Inferno*. Universal Studios was one of the first to take a chance at distributing the movies featuring its revered Monsters in 1949, setting up a distribution deal first for its relatively tame "team up" entries *House of Dracula* (1945) and *Abbott & Costello Meet Frankenstein* (1948), before following up with its earlier classic *The Wolf Man* (1941), starring Lon Chaney, Jr.

In the decades following the film's release, the Wolf Man would become known as a (rather kindly) metaphor for the Nazis: an otherwise well-meaning man is transformed into a vicious killing animal who chooses his next victim based on them having the symbol of a pentagram (an emblem aesthetically similar to the Star of David) on them. This takes root in the now rightly dismissed Good German trope that many Nazis were just soldiers doing a job they had been forced to do. In fact, screenwriter Curt Siodmak based the film's script on his experiences in Nazi Germany: just as it was for the film's protagonist, Larry Talbot, Siodmak's life was thrown into chaos almost overnight (in this case, as the Nazis took control of the country) and he had to go on the run, ending up in the U.S.

The term "werewolf" already carried Nazi connotations: Werewolf was the name of a Nazi plan to create a resistance force to disrupt the advancing Allies, drawing inspiration from the creature of folklore. In 1945, national radio broadcasts urged German civilians to join the Werewolf movement, fighting the Allies and any "traitorous" German collaborators:[3] "I am so savage, I am filled with rage, Lily the Werewolf is my name. I bite, I eat, I am not tame. My werewolf teeth bite the enemy."[4]

The Holy See reviewed Siodmak's film and stopped short of excluding it entirely, instead considering it permissible for adults. "The work does not contain situations or episodes, acts or words (that are) contrary to morality, but some scenes, likely to arouse disgust or terror, impose a reservation. The film ... is allowed only for adults."[5]

That the film (one of the very first true horror films to be screened in Italy) was not given a full ecclesiastical ban is of interest. The reviewer had either not picked up on or had chosen to ignore any subtextual themes. In 1950 the *Segnalazioni cinematografiche*'s discussions were not as in-depth and intellectual as they would become over time. Pronouncements were still short but sweet, either permitting or condemning films in short order.

There is the likelihood that, at this early stage, the Vatican was unsure precisely what to make of horror films, their artistic value and any threat of moral corruption (or criticism of the Church) they might pose. While it would become clear to a later audience that writer Curt Siodmak imbued *The Wolf Man* with anti–Nazi subtextual messaging, at the time the film was chiefly viewed as another fun outing from Hollywood's monster factory. For the time being, the artistic power of the horror film was an unknown entity. The *Segnalazioni cinematografiche* had not even used the term "horror" to describe the film's genre; it was so unused to the term that it considered *The Wolf Man* to be a fantasy adventure film. Up until 1950, the Vatican's writers had considered dramas, thrillers and comedies (the main genres Italy's own artists worked in) to be the most dangerously influential of films, those that carry the most subversive of messages and were therefore of the biggest threat to the innocence of the flock.

It would be a few years until this changed, when domestic horror had slowly become a regular feature at Italian box offices. The Vatican eventually recognized horror's influence and began to forbid Italian Catholics from viewing any such genre films that made it past state censors and into the country's cinemas.

And it all began with a bet, made by journeyman director Riccardo Freda.

While 1911's Grand Guignol adaptation of Dante's *Inferno* canticle could certainly be said to contain horror elements, and 1921's *Il mostro di Frankenstein* was based on Mary Shelley's classic gothic horror (a lost film, we know little else about it, but it was likely an adventure film, shorn of the dark flourishes of the Universal movie), the rise of Mussolini and the stranglehold fascism and the Vatican had over Italy's cinematic output meant that horror as a genre did not really exist in the Italian cinematic lexicon. Yes, Universal Studios had in recent years begun to bring its monsters from gothic literature, the celluloid creatures that spearheaded cinematic horror, to Italy's screens, but there had never been a true Italian horror film. Freda sought to change that.

Freda approached his regular producers Ermanno Donati, Luigi Carpentieri and Goffredo Lombardo and placed a bet that not only could he make an unprecedented Italian Gothic horror movie, but he could shoot it in 10 days and on a shoestring budget, without troubling domestic film censors.[6] The result was *I Vampiri* (1957), which is now almost universally considered to be Italy's first true horror film.

Freda knew how he would do it. The Christian Democrat party (in power in Italy since the fall of fascism and ideologically aligned with the Church) had passed laws to boost Italian filmmaking and gain a control over the country's cinematic output that was more benevolent than Mussolini's. By heavily taxing foreign imports at source, Italy accumulated a funding stream for domestic directors to take advantage of. Add to this a mandatory quota that ensured films made within the Italian industry would show in cinemas for at least 80 days of the year, and there was suddenly a burgeoning industry that could embrace everything from small genre fare to the likes of Fellini's *La Dolce Vita*.

Freda himself remained very proud of his accomplishment, stating, "I have always liked to be the first in filmmaking. *I Vampiri* was born in quite curious a way. I was in Donati and Carpentieri's office, we were thinking about some stories to bring to the screen, and I somewhat casually proposed to make a horror film.... I agreed to shoot the movie in about 10 days, demanding only Gianna Maria Canale as lead actress, Mario Bava as cinematographer and Beni Montresor as production designer."[7]

I Vampiri was green-lit and funded by the state, and Freda went to work on the film with cinematographer and special effects maestro Bava (who finished the film for Freda, when the director left the project before its completion). It was turned around in a few short weeks, from a preapproved screenplay that ensured it would not be troubled by censors. The film was presented as a dramatization of the legend of Countess Elizabeth Báthory de Ecsed, and therefore considered by the state to have historical and cultural value. Its plot would later be cheekily altered by Bava, with the cinematographer's addition of more elements from the likes of Universal's Dracula and Frankenstein films.[8]

Freda's approach to the state had proven a smart one, as the finished film found itself shielded from the moralizing of the Vatican (at least partially). *I Vampiri* appeared to have blindsided the Church's film critics, who were still becoming used to the changing relationship between Church and state and the modern goals for film production, and somehow stopped short of petitioning Italy's first horror film be banned altogether, instead recommending that it only be shown "to adults of full

In Riccardo Freda's 1957 film *I Vampiri*, Lorette (Wandisa Guida) lies in a casket with a glass lid. Illustration by the author.

moral maturity."⁹ The *Segnalazioni cinematografiche* even offered the film some critical praise, declaring that "the director creates, with a certain skill, a nightmarish atmosphere."¹⁰

I Vampiri carried with it a social commentary discussing the fears of modernization (something that was beginning to trouble the Italian public, as the country rose from fascism's ashes and began to embrace decadence, and had already been explored by a number of directors working in the neorealism movement) as well as enough expressionist shadow, blood and murder to fully embrace the concept of the horror film. Freda's mixture of the Dracula and Frankenstein mythos certainly confronts fears about modernization—the presentation of an up-to-date clinical laboratory built in a very gothic space is quite jarring, the juxtaposition of past and future creating a very unsettling mise-en-scène. As the plot develops and the vampiric Countess Du Grand is revealed (in the film's spin on the aforementioned Countess Elizabeth Báthory) to be using blood transfusions to transform herself into a creature of youthful beauty, it is science that the film's monster has employed, not mysticism, to continue her evil reign. Beyond the obvious parallels with the *Dracula* plot, the film itself offers a more optimistic statement about modernization. Freda and Bava's careers were, essentially, the product of the fall of fascism and the subsequent golden age in Italy. As recently as 15 years before, such a film would never have been funded or green-lit, whereas now the director and his cameraman were proving to be trailblazers in bringing the horror genre to Italian domestic film. In fact, what Freda and Bava's film did manage was something quite exceptional, considering that Italy had not produced a horror film in over 40 years of filmmaking. Their template would not only kick-start the horror genre at home, but contributed to a global resurgence of cinematic horror and romanticism not seen since the Universal Monsters.

In the 1950s, science fiction films had largely filled the void left by the disappearing horror trend. The U.S. and Japanese markets led the way, with much of their output featuring social commentary critiquing the use of the atomic bomb in World War II (and seemingly voracious appetites to use them again). A riposte to the annihilation of Hiroshima and Nagasaki in Japan, and the growing Soviet threat following the end of World War II, films such as Ishirō Honda's *Godzilla* and Robert Wise's *The Day the Earth Stood Still* used science fiction narratives to craft stark warnings and cold war commentaries, communicating humanity's fear of nuclear Armageddon through tales of fantasy.

In the UK, Hammer Studios had known domestic success with Val Guest's Nigel Kneale adaptation *The Quatermass Xperiment* (1955) and Leslie Norman's *X—the Unknown* (1956) but neither had brought the studio the commercial and critical successes it desired. Producer Anthony Hinds and director Terence Fisher (along with screenwriter Jimmy Sangster) turned their attention to the literary heavyweights, the characters that had helped see cinema become a boom business some decades before ... the Monsters. In order to avoid the ire of Universal Studios' lawyers, Hammer ensured their monsters were different in both appearance and character—gentlemanly but explosive, erudite yet barbaric ... so very, very British.

Fisher's *The Curse of Frankenstein* was the first to be released, screening in UK cinemas only a month after *I Vampiri* saw its debut in Italy. Thanks to a combination of effects design and shooting the film in Eastmancolor, not the traditional black and white, the action was striking, the gore effects were unprecedented and, crucially, the monster (played by Christopher Lee) was suitably enough removed from that of James Whale's earlier film as to not provoke litigation. *The Curse of Frankenstein* had a great impact domestically and crucially abroad. Fisher's film would lead to six sequels and a global spotlight on the British studio.

But it was *Dracula* that proved Hammer's biggest success. The producer-director-writer team from *Frankenstein* went on to release *Dracula* the following year, with once again enough changes to revitalize the property, make it their own, and avoid litigation from Universal. The film would star Christopher Lee as the titular count (a charming, well-spoken aristocrat far removed from the character Bela Lugosi portrayed) and Peter Cushing (as a dynamic, swashbuckling version of Van Helsing), and its success would lead to the boom period the British studio had been longing for.

The *Segnalazioni cinematografiche* considered Hammer's output to be "made with superficiality and ostentatious in (its) bad taste,"[11] asserting that "it is difficult to view so many horrible things, so many disgusting scenes, acts of sadism and superstition united in a single film"[12] and forbidding the Italian public from watching this new, richly colorful, blood-soaked approach to horror.

The gothic horror was alive again. In the U.S., Roger Corman and American International Pictures (who by now had a deal to distribute the films of Mario Bava in the United States) began a cycle of films based not on the same classic monsters but on the similarly gothic literature of Edgar Allan Poe. Corman would bring seven productions based on Poe's short stories to the screen over the course of four years, beginning with *The Fall of the House of Usher*, starring Vincent Price. Sensing that horror was beginning to become a profitable genre, one which would cause frequent headaches for the teachings of the Church, the *Segnalazioni cinematografiche* was as damning of Corman's cycle as it was Hammer

Studios, lamenting that Usher's story "seems to affirm that evil, at a certain point, becomes indestructible and its power inevitable. The characters live in an atmosphere and condemnation which they cannot escape; even love is ineffective."[13] The very present notion in Poe's works (carried onto the silver screen by Corman) that evil is undefeatable proved too much for the Vatican, who ordered all but adults of a moral maturity stay away.

If the Vatican was concerned that the sudden global surge in the popularity of the horror film might affect domestic cinema output, it was right to be. By the time Roger Corman began his Poe cycle, the gothic template had proven a big hit among Italian filmmakers, and something of a cottage industry had begun.

Freda and Bava would collaborate again, this time on a gothic/science fiction hybrid (that owed much to Hammer's *The Quatermass Xperiment*) called *Caltiki: The Immortal Monster*. This tale of an ancient evil discovered in a Mayan temple saw Bava's role expand under his mentor, as he not only supplied the stunning black-and-white photography but created the special effects and directed all of the film's action sequences. Essentially an adventure film involving daring archaeologists and suitable helpings of western romance, by the final act (as Bava takes over) the film changes in tone, delivering stunningly gory set pieces as the blob-like titular monster attacks the cast, putrefying their limbs and leaving behind nothing but bones and goo. A showdown with the army pulls out all the stops to deliver a thrilling finale to the film.

With the influence of foreign money (Caltiki was coproduced by Climax Film of France) and the success of Hammer's Quatermass film on the production, it becomes apparent that *Caltiki* was made with the foreign markets of Europe and the U.S. in mind. This was just as well, as the Vatican labeled the film "ridiculous and gruesome"[14] and imposed reservations upon the God-fearing public because of the film's "repulsive scenes ... and sensual attitudes."[15] All but the most intellectually mature flock were forbidden from seeing the film when it opened in Italian theaters on 8 August 1959. Subsequently, *Caltiki* fared no better than *I Vampiri* domestically, managing to take only 94 million lire from its theatrical release.[16] The film visited the U.S. the following year, where it found an audience on drive-in circuits alongside the likes of *The Quatermass Xperiment* and its sequels, the atomic-horror films of Jack Arnold and several early Roger Corman productions.

Italy had taken note of Freda and Bava's experiments, and it was not long before various other domestic productions were on the way. Tireless satirist Steno had already moved from writing six or seven screenplays per year for his colleague and friend Mario Monicelli to directing more than 20 films in the difficult postwar period, and his career was showing no signs of slowing down.

In 1959 he cowrote and directed *Tempi Duri per I Vampiri* (Hard Times for Vampires), a comedy that married neorealism themes with the new gothic template to tell the tale of a hard-up member of the bourgeoisie, forced to turn his ancestral castle into a guest house in order to pay off his debts. When he receives a visit from his uncle, a real-life vampire, the down-at-the-heels Baron is forced to try to protect the hotel guests that now occupy his family chateau. With little actual horror in it, Steno's film showed the Italian satirist at his comedic best, effortlessly exploiting and sending up genre movies in his inimitable style.

Along with Dino Risi, Mario Monicelli and Pietro Germi, Steno shaped the era's comedy films, which came to be known as *commedia all'Italiana* (comedy, Italian style). Essentially a comedic cousin to the neorealism genre, these films satirized Italian social issues of the time, such as poverty, sex and sexuality, the emancipation of women through contraception and divorce, and, of course, the traditional religious influence of the Catholic Church. Steno reveled in normalizing cultural and social taboos and advancing the liberalization of Italian society. This, of course, led the Vatican to put his films under the microscope frequently.

On this occasion, the pastoral verdict of the Church was resoundingly negative. The Vatican panned this "superficial film"[17] and its "improper scenes and situations"[18] in a strict verdict that reflected both the rise of the horror film in Italy and Steno's existing reputation as a subversive influence in domestic cinema. Catholics were forbidden from seeing the film outright. Despite the verdict of the Holy See, Steno's film proved more successful than *I Vampiri* and *Caltiki* combined, grossing 385 million lire and marking Hammer Studios star Christopher Lee's first appearance in an Italian production.

Renato Polselli was one of a number of directors who embraced the burgeoning horror genre and proved something of a pioneer himself. Considered an author of "the most original, hallucinatory and sleazy low budget productions in the genre"[19] and of making the best use of a simple formula of "eroticism, sentiment, vulgarity and a happy ending,"[20] Polselli was an innovator of the lowbrow and the transgressive, his exploitation oeuvre containing a singular internal logic and often exhibiting the reversal of some of the most traditional clichés of the genre.

Seeing the success of Terence Fisher's very erotic Hammer horror hit *Dracula* and the viable prospect of duplicating it in Italy (thanks to Freda's *I Vampiri*), Polselli and screenwriter Ernesto Gastaldi took what they considered to be a workmanlike script by Giampaolo Callegaris and fashioned it into the dreamlike, erotic horror *L'Amante del Vampiro* (The Vampire's Lover; also known as The Vampire and the Ballerina). Filming took place over Christmas in an Italian castle owned by the Borghese family of noble and papal lineage, and featured various semi-nude turns from busty damsels (the girlfriends of the director and his backers). Borrowing liberally from Fisher, from Freda's *I Vampiri* and from the expressionist nightmare of Carl Dreyer's *Vampyr*, Polselli's film took the gothic template, steeped it in askew imagery and existential dread and ramped up the eroticism, creating a hallucinatory and sleazy quality that marked the country's first truly transgressive horror film.

The Vatican was certainly unimpressed, lambasting Polselli's "macabre scenes alternated with improper dances and skimpy clothing"[21] and branding the film "morally unacceptable (and) excluded for all."[22] Italian horror had, for the first time, caused something of a furor in the Church and provided the genre with a genuine provocateur. Polselli would continue in the same vein, combining the gothic template with risqué dance sequences, nudity and hallucinatory qualities again and again: in 1964's *Il Mostro dell'Opera* (The Monster of the Opera, an experimental adaptation of the Gaston Leroux novel *The Phantom of the Opera*); the surrealist fetishism and sexual violence of his 1972 seedy masterpiece *Delirium*; the censor-baiting 1973 erotic tableaux of *Riti Magie Nere e Segrete Orge nel Trecento* (Black Magic Rites and Secret Orgies of the 14th century).

Anton Giulio Majano's *Seddok: Erede Di Satana* (or The Atom Age Vampire) would again take its cue from *I Vampiri* and include a mix of horror and science fiction that did not actually feature any vampires in the traditional sense. *Seddok* is the tale of a doctor living in post–Hiroshima Japan who develops a serum for restoring living tissue and the vain but disfigured chanteuse he falls in love with (and kills for). The film tips its hat to *Quatermass*, to *Caltiki* and the nuclear horrors of Jack Arnold, and the various filmic incarnations of *Dr. Jekyll and Mr. Hyde*. Majano blended his many influences expertly, even weaving in detective thriller elements in an attempt to appeal to as wide an audience as possible. When he learns that the effects of his serum are only temporary, the doctor realizes he must kill in order to create more, and has a crisis of conscience. In order to overcome his moral quandary, he injects himself with a raw version of the serum, knowing that it will turn him into a monster, unafraid to kill. The resultant monster (the titular Seddok) goes on a murderous rampage, killing innocents to extract their tissue for the serum that, ultimately, will never fully work.

Majano's film was shot in a neorealist style and featured elements of melodrama and tragedy that separated it from the rest of the vampiric content unleashed upon the Italian cinema-going public. The Vatican's view was certain, stating that the film's "complacency with which macabre scenes and gruesome situations are presented" along with "striptease and other sensual scenes, ambiguous female characters with inappropriate attire and dialog make the film morally unacceptable."[23] Catholics across Italy were prevented from seeing the film.

Giorgio Ferroni was a somewhat well-traveled filmmaker, figuratively speaking, when he helmed his sole horror film in 1960: *Il Mulino delle Donne di Pietra* (Mill of the Stone Women). A director of documentaries, comedies and neorealist works, he was already garnering a reputation as a stylistic director when the gothic horror trend took hold, and like many domestic filmmakers he would willingly work wherever the production budgets were. Ferroni's film, the first Italian horror film released in color, was one of the highlights of Italy's early gothic period. Rather than following the *I Vampiri* template, it featured a relatively original story about a sculptor whose stone figures of Dutch heroines turn out to be a front for a series of murders, as he keeps his beautiful daughter alive with their blood. Like Polselli, Ferroni drew influence from Carl Dreyer's 1932 Danish experiment in expressionism and surrealism *Vampyr*, adventure from the Peplum films of which the director was already fond, and combined them to create a lurid and hallucinatory movie. The Vatican delivered a suitably damning review of the film, claiming that *Mill of the Stone Women* "does not present any morally acceptable element, having been made for the sole purpose of creating a hallucinatory atmosphere, apt to upset the viewer."[24]

At this point the Vatican was beginning to have concerns that the horror genre was a corrupting influence on its flock (especially when these films were being produced by domestic, Catholic directors), and would more often pronounce such films as wholly morally unacceptable. *Mill of the Stone Women* was excluded for Catholic audiences but, while it was not a huge hit, the 164 million lire it made domestically was better than most of the Italian horror films released the same year. The lure of the country's first full-color horror feature was too much for audiences to resist, and the Church confessionals were likely very busy following opening weekend.

Piero Regnoli, Freda's screenwriter on *I, Vampiri*, would himself make a directorial addition to Italy's burgeoning horror industry, with *L'ultima Preda del Vampiro* (translated as *The Vampire's Last Victim*, though more commonly known as *The Playgirls and the Vampire*). The film (which he also wrote) featured a troupe of exotic dancers who take refuge in Count Gabor's castle after encountering a ferocious storm. One by one, the dancers fall under the spell of a vampire. One of the reluctant dancers becomes the object of affection for both Count Gabor and the vampire when it turns out she resembles the vampire's long dead wife.

Like Renato Polselli, Regnoli recognized the potential of combining gothic horror with lots of scantily clad pinup girls and sexy scenes. His finished film, while grossing only 72 million lire at home, was picked up by American producer Richard Gordon, who repackaged it as an adults-only

In Mario Bava's 1960 film *Black Sunday*, Princess Asa Vadja (Barbara Steele) is bound by rope at the wrists and waist as a likeness of Pope John XXIII approaches wielding a heavy mallet. Illustration by the author.

attraction for the U.S. grind house circuit. Unlike Polselli, Regnoli's film did not feature the same expressionist flourishes or hallucinatory atmosphere. It was apparent that Regnoli's talent was on the page rather than behind the camera, and there was little artistry in the film other than in how Regnoli managed to shoehorn in so many scenes of women in various states of undress. The horror element was barely present, with the bawdy eroticism placed front and center as the film's main calling card.

Perhaps the most interesting point to be made about *The Playgirls and the Vampire* is that its director, a screenwriter of over 100 scripts covering virtually every genre known to cinema, was the former film journalist of Vatican newspaper *L'Osservatore Romano*. It was through Regnoli's pen that the Church's critical message had flowed on neorealism masterpieces such as de Sica's *The Bicycle Thieves*. Regnoli had been given free rein to criticize the anticlerical sentiment of the postwar cinematic movement, and to passive-aggressively note that de Sica's film offered an offensive portrayal of the faith of the Italian people, presenting it as superstitious and ignorant. In his malignant attempt to influence censure while still maintaining a moral high ground, Regnoli had piously declared that somebody ought to "express a judgment on the actions of those who approved such a film, and gave it access to the public. But we prefer to abstain from doing so. At least for the time being."[25]

When the time came, the Vatican certainly did not abstain from passing judgment on Regnoli's film, stating that "the director has made a banal, superficial film, in which … not infrequently the story slips unintentionally into the ridiculous."[26] The *Segnalazioni cinematografiche* review continues, remarking upon "the absurdity of the story of reviving corpses, of vampires that survive for years in their graves… (and of) complacent and frequent performances of nudity."[27] The Vatican's verdict was damning and final: "The film is to be considered excluded for all."[28]

As various filmmakers adopted and adapted the gothic template laid down by Freda and his cinematographer, Mario Bava would find himself moving out from under his mentor's wing. After his ability to complete the unfinished movies of other directors (Freda's *I Vampiri* and *Caltiki*; Jacques Tourneur's *The Giant of Marathon*) was noticed by Galatea Films, Bava found himself promoted to full-time director and given the opportunity to helm a film of his own. Already a fan of the fantastic because of the influence of his father (a special effects genius) and his work on the two Freda films, Bava sought to advance Freda's vision and create a gothic horror that would stand out among the various *I, Vampiri* copycats and rival the recent successes of Hammer Studios in the UK.

Black Sunday (1960; original title: *La Maschera del Demonio*) was Bava's first feature as sole director, and has become known as the film that finally popularized the production of horror movies in Italy as an export to audiences around the world. The story, a mix of the vampire mythos and Nikolai Gogol's short story "Viy," sees Princess Asa Vadja (Barbara Steele), an accused witch and servant of Satan, put to the stake by black-robed priests for her apparent crimes. The titular Mask of Satan (an Iron Maiden–type contraption) is placed on her head and hammered home by a burly executioner, causing blood to spray as the spikes penetrate her brain and kill her. Two hundred years later, an inquisitive (and foolish) traveling doctor wanders into Asa's tomb, cuts his hand on broken glass and allows his blood to drip onto Asa's dead face. This, of course, awakens her, and it is up to the doctor's younger companion Gorobec (John Richardson) and

Asa's identical descendant Katia (also Barbara Steele, in the other half of a mesmerizing dual performance) to stop Asa before she can awaken her dead consort and drain Katia's life force to grant herself immortality.

The film does indeed build upon the earlier *I Vampiri*, with Bava using his excellent cinematography in combination with Giorgio Giovannini's stunning crumbling crypts and mist-covered moors to fantastic effect, creating visually arresting sequences with a sense of atmosphere clearly superior to that of its predecessor. By adding more scenes of horror (the horrific opening sequence; the monstrous visage of the reincarnated Asa and her lover; Asa's body revealed to be a fleshless skeleton in the final act), Bava manufactured a genuinely terrifying gothic piece to rival anything Terence Fisher was doing in the UK, and ensured himself a long, fruitful career as director in the process.

Unsurprisingly, the Vatican did not look upon the film kindly. *Segnalazioni cinematografiche* opined that "the absurdity of the dark story, enriched by superstition and shocking scenes, leads us to consider the film completely unacceptable."[29] The pastoral verdict was in, and the film was of course given an ecclesiastical ban. The criticism itself represents a relatively mild condemnation by a Church that appeared to want to write off Bava's film as lowly and worthless, rather than obscene and damnable.

If there was anything to truly threaten the Church in the film, it was contained not in the domestic release of *La Maschera del Demonio* but in the film's U.S. release. For the North American market, Bava's film was reedited, redubbed and retitled by distributor American International Pictures (beginning a long and mostly fruitful relationship with Bava). Christened *Black Sunday*, the film is instantly shorn of the suggestion of gothic melodrama, replaced by an Antichrist message as it subverts the notion of Easter Sunday and of the Resurrection.[30] A narrative voice-over suggests, "One day in each century, it is said that Satan walks the earth. To the God-fearing, this day is known as Black Sunday." This, coupled with the resurrection of the long-dead witch Asa Vajda (Barbara Steele in a breakout role), reinforces the ominous weight of the film's new title.

The evil of Bava's film, however, is represented not as a force of Hell but as a monster of sexual threat and very human transgression. Nevertheless, *Black Sunday* does play with the Resurrection and Antichrist mythos (even if this element was somewhat muted for its Italian release), illustrating the influence of the Church and religion in the Italian horror genre, an influence that would continue in the decades to come.

Where Black Sunday differed substantially from Freda and Bava's earlier genre movies (and the majority of the films that had been rushed into cinemas since) was in its reception. Domestically it did well enough in what was proving to be a crowded market (it was one of three domestic horror films released in just one month, *Atom Age Vampire* and *Mill of the Stone Women* being the other two), grossing 139 million lire upon its release in August 1960. A modest domestic success would be followed by overseas sales: picked up by American International Pictures (AIP), the film subsequently earned an impressive $14,750 in its very first week in a single U.S. theater, before playing in drive-ins and grind houses across the land, making steady money for the distributors for close to twenty years.[31]

The film performed well in almost every territory it was released in, was lauded by critics and caused a stir in the UK, where it was banned until 1968 due to its violent content. *Black Sunday* would go on to influence the industry for the next fifty years, often considered one of the greatest horror films of all time, and an inspiration for the works of many lauded directors, including Francis Ford Coppola's 1992 gothic adaptation of Bram Stoker's *Dracula* and Tim Burton's 1999 fantasy *Sleepy Hollow* to name but two.[32]

It was the gothic template of Freda's *I Vampiri* and Bava's *Black Sunday* that opened the floodgates for European horror. In between Freda setting the precedent and Bava providing the first genuine global cinematic success of Italian horror, a cottage industry had been formed, with screenplays written overnight and filming turned around in a couple of weeks on various pictures, using existing sets of crumbling castles, dark crypts and fog-covered moors to depict various battles to save young virgins from ancient mistresses of evil. American International would, following their purchase of *Black Sunday*, become very interested in Bava, and in other Italian genre directors, the U.S. outfit's financing and distribution deals proving a boon to the Italian industry. Thanks largely to Bava, the Italian Gothic had finally proven a success, putting the country's burgeoning horror industry on the domestic and international map.

Despite *Black Sunday*'s success, the template set by Freda and Bava was unfortunately becoming quite restrictive, the output predictable: low-budget gothic melodrama and late romanticism, using the same archetypes, set in historical and foreign contexts, recycling sets and locations and featuring chaste damsels versus evil aristocrats. Though they had attempted to carve out a path for home-grown horror, thanks in part to the looming shadow of the Church censors, Freda and Bava's gothic model was now lacking in bite. Italian filmmakers had a newfound freedom to experiment with horror alongside their American and British counterparts, but it also ensured that their productions were not particularly challenging or transgressive at all when compared to a new wave of horror films coming from elsewhere. Just as Italy had caught up with (and even inspired) the rest of the world with its first foray into the horror genre, its product was becoming fairly homogenous.

Thankfully, a new boom period of horror, featuring a very different type of celluloid monster indeed, was on the way.

2

Escluso per Tutti

(The Vatican versus ... the Birth of Modern Horror and the Giallo)

It is commonly recognized that the second horror era began in 1960 with four seminal films from four directors. The British Film Institute lists Alfred Hitchcock, Michael Powell, Georges Franju and Mario Bava as the directors in question, whose faces would be "etched in granite on the mountainside" of a Mount Rushmore–style monument to celebrate the fathers of the modern horror film, were such a thing to exist.[1]

Nineteen sixty was indeed a "year of exquisite vintage"[2] and Bava had made his mark with *La Maschera del Demonio/Black Sunday*, but while he was still working within the gothic horror template established by himself and Riccardo Freda three years earlier in 1957, the other three directors in question had given something much different to the world: psychosexuality; realism; tactile brutality; the killer next door, all qualities related to social convictions of the time that left audiences feeling vulnerable.

By the time of Alfred Hitchcock's long-celebrated *Psycho*, the landscape for horror cinema was already shifting. After an initial wave that had been very reliant on the gothic, romantic classics of Mary Wollstonecraft Shelley, Bram Stoker, Robert Louis Stevenson and Victor Hugo (among others), and a second wave effectively hamstrung by the Hays Code, a new surge of gothic horror was finding success in Europe, thanks largely to the advent of the new *gotico italiano* movement of Italy, Hammer Studios in the UK and the Corman/Poe cycle in the U.S. Three decades after the term "horror film" had been coined, the likes of Dracula and Frankenstein still very much ruled the landscape, although not for long.

Hitchcock, already a celebrated director of such suspense films as *The Man Who Knew Too Much* (1934; 1956), *Suspicion* (1941) and *Vertigo* (1958), effectively birthed the modern horror movie with his 1960 adaptation of Robert Bloch's terrifying novel. By adapting this contemporary text, taking horror away from the gothic and the supernatural and instead into

In Lucio Fulci's 1972 giallo *Don't Torture a Duckling*, tragic witch La Maciara (Florinda Bolkan) haunts priest Don Alberto (Marc Porel) as he clutches the young child Malvina (Fausta Avelli) to his chest. Illustration by the author.

the realm of charming killer next door Norman Bates (and perhaps most importantly adding a psychosexual element that would titillate and terrify in equal measure), the master of suspense reinvented the genre by significantly broadening its scope.

At roughly the same time as Hitchcock, another storied British director turned from his usual oeuvre to make a very modern horror film, one involving a mentally scarred young man who would lure women to his home and then murder them. But this man was no psycho ... he was just a Peeping Tom.

Sadly, Michael Powell's similarly psychosexual tale of lady-killer Marc Lewis and his camera did not (at least not at the time) give the director infamy in a new genre. While *Psycho* proved (thanks to some expertly manipulated shock and controversy) a box-office hit and cemented Hitchcock as one of cinema's greats, *Peeping Tom* was buried by UK critical reaction and served only to ruin Michael Powell's legendary movie career. The creator (alongside producing partner Emeric Pressburger) of classics such as *Black Narcissus* and *The Red Shoes* would effectively never work again.

In retrospect, *Peeping Tom* and *Psycho* are comparable in just about every way. Each was created by a recognized master of cinema, and executed flawlessly: Hitchcock making use of the expressionist flourishes afforded to black-and-white filmmaking to create a great sense of suspense; Powell moving from his trademark Technicolor to the grungier Eastmancolor, retaining a vibrancy to the palette that recalled the lush color of *The Red Shoes* while creating impenetrable shadows alongside the beautiful textures. Both films deal with emotionally disturbed central characters created, to a degree, by their parents. Norman Bates suffered an emotionally abusive relationship with his domineering mother Norma, who taught him that all sex was sinful and delivered to him both a mistrust of and psychopathic tendencies toward women. The relationship lasted long after his mother's death, with Norman assuming her character as a symptom of dissociative identity disorder (a condition often borne of severe emotional trauma suffered during childhood). In *Peeping Tom*, Marc reveals to his tenant Helen (through the screening of a series of old home movies) that his psychologist father would manipulate him into a state of terror in order to photograph the results. The emotional scarring led Marc to grow into what is often termed the cycle of abuse—the ongoing, repeating pattern, where the victim becomes the abuser in later life. Like his father, Marc films his victims in a state of absolute terror as he kills them.

In Italy, horror films were finally beginning to be allowed certification to screen in cinemas across the Roman Catholic territory (much to the Vatican's chagrin). The country was still somewhat naive to the darkest of cinematic genres when *Psycho* and *Peeping Tom* were released. Both

Hitchcock's masterpiece and Powell's own ill-fated modern horror experiment were far removed from what the staunchly Catholic country was getting used to, and this opened them up to some very damning criticism and censure from the Church.

Much has been made of why *Psycho* succeeded and *Peeping Tom* failed. Interestingly, the critics of the *Segnalazioni cinematografiche* treated *Peeping Tom* with significantly more consideration than they did *Psycho*. The film was judged to be made by an expert in his craft, and Powell's technical artistry was noted even in this lowest of genres. The *Segnalazioni cinematografiche*'s review noted, "It is a well-made film... (with) appreciable photography, color, acting, some noteworthy cinematography."[3]

With both films, it would be the psychosexual elements and lurid murder scenes that would cause the Vatican to consider them unsuitable for all audiences. Even then, the *Segnalazioni cinematografiche*'s judgment upon *Peeping Tom* was not quite as swift and condemnatory as might be expected, the journal stopping to consider the themes and messages of Powell's film before issuing its damning verdict:

> To the large group of psychoanalytic films with a sexual background, we add this work which deals with the *psycho*pathic case of a young man suffering from "scopophilia" (the morbid need to peep), with directorial manias and pseudoscientific interests. The sole positive element is the love between the protagonist and the girl, but it is not a decisive element. The faults of the fathers, the responsibility of the environment and family education are the background to the narration, dotted with inadmissible episodes of violence, of numerous erotic scenes ... sometimes sought with malice. The viewing of the film is excluded for everyone.[4]

Meanwhile Hitchcock's decades of experience in the medium was more or less dismissed out of hand by the Vatican's critic, with no such consideration of *Psycho*'s technical and thematic merits featuring in the pastoral review. Instead, the *Segnalazioni cinematografiche* was far quicker to pour scorn on the director's efforts:

> Contrary to the other Hitchcock films, this one, even if it contains scenes of authentic suspense, does not manage to interest entirely because of the excessive psychological capacity of the performance and some long dialog sequences that end up boring.[5]

The Vatican's reviewers went on condemn "the excessive reality of some macabre sequences that end in the most vulgar 'Grand-Guignol' manner" in *Psycho* and branded it as follows: "Wrong from its very base ... the film, in presenting its misdeeds, lingers to describe, with an excess of macabre details, some criminal actions which...[lead us to] advise against viewing the film."[6]

Ultimately, The Vatican's verdicts ensured that many Italian theaters would screen neither movie. Those that did would find many of their seats empty as Catholics had been effectively ordered to stay away. Despite this, *Psycho*'s success in the UK and U.S. made Italian cinemagoers curious, and it did see some interest in the *terzia visione* theaters. (The term "third season" was used at the time for second-run cinemas, movie houses out of the way of societal centers, many in the country's rural, pastoral South, where the long arm of the Vatican might not always reach but its shadow still fell.) *Peeping Tom* had no such luck, and was a flop in Italy as it was in the UK and U.S.

In Georges Franju's 1960 film *Les Yeux Sans Visage*, Christiane (Edith Scob) is depicted as the Virgin Mary. Illustration by the author.

Irrespective of the box office, the decision of the *Segnalazioni cinematografiche* to point out the artistry and explore the psychoanalytical nature of *Peeping Tom* suggests something about the maturity of Powell's vision, at least in the Church's eyes, as opposed to that "most vulgar 'Grand Guignol' manner"[7] of *Psycho*.

Georges Franju's *Eyes Without a Face*, also released in 1960, dealt with a horribly disfigured daughter, an obsessive father, and a string of brutal, bloody murders. *Les Yeux Sans Visage* in its native France, this French-Italian coproduction was based on the novel by Jean Redon and tells the story of Cristianne (Edith Scob), whose face was horribly disfigured in a car crash, and her plastic surgeon father Dr. Génessier, who is determined to restore her face to its former beauty. He sends his lover (Alida Valli) out to befriend young women, who are drugged and brought to his home surgery so he can remove their faces in order to create a new one for his daughter.

While grisly, the face-removing and subsequent killing and burial of the drugged women are not the only horrors contained in the film. Like *Psycho* and *Peeping Tom*, *Eyes Without a Face* tells the story of an abusive parent-child relationship, with Cristianne locked away in the family home, unable to join society or have any kind of a life, simply existing to be the subject of her father's experiments. When Dr. Génessier meets his eventual fate, Cristianne is completely unmoved by his death, because in truth she has not lost a loving father. She has lost nobody but the architect of her imprisonment and suffering.

Franju had began his career as a documentary maker, whose early works were influenced by the Nazi occupation of Paris. *Eyes Without a Face* was only his second fictional narrative. As Hoberman suggests, the film is "enriched by free-floating allusions to then-recent European history. It takes no stretch of the imagination to … see the coldly psychopathic Génessier as a Nazi scientist."[8] Add to this the inclusion of Alida Valli, the sweetheart of fascist cinema dubbed "the most beautiful woman in the world" by Mussolini,[9] who Franju casts as an ally to his pseudo-Nazi mad doctor Génessier, and there is much to consider. The film indeed appears to carry a postwar social commentary, critical of the fascism that started a war that ravaged Europe.

The Vatican considered Franju's film "yet another attempt to make a story based in sadism serve spectacular ends" and determined that "the macabre tale, even if scarcely convincing, makes the film morally negative."[10] The *Segnalazioni cinematografiche* stopped short of totally forbidding the viewing of the film but graded it S—not recommended for anyone.

What is clear here is that the Vatican's writers did not hold the director in similar esteem to Hitchcock and Powell, who both had several decades experience making entertaining movies that captured the hearts of audiences in Hollywood and across the world. Nor did it consider Franju's cinema to have quite the same corrupting influence as the most recent films of the Englishmen.

The Church had, for some time, experienced difficulty dealing with the films of the Italian neorealist directors, many of which criticized not only fascism but the Church's role within the regimes in both Italy and Germany. It had sought to ban the films of De Sica, Rossellini, Visconti and Fellini, condemning the now classic *La Dolce Vita* in the strongest of terms and trying hard to secure a state ban upon the film's release in 1960. Given Franju's past in documentary realism, working with themes critical of the fascist movement the Church had allied itself with, and his anti–Nazi sentiment here, perhaps the writers of the *Segnalazioni cinematografiche* recognized Franju as another such agitator. Nonetheless, horror was moving on from the gothic template, into something far more realistic and visceral.

It would be three years later that Mario Bava gave his own answer to Hitchcock's *Psycho*, Franju's *Eyes Without a Face* and Powell's *Peeping*

2. Escluso per Tutti

In Francesco Barilli's 1974 film *The Perfume of the Lady in Black*, Silvia (Mimsy Farmer) and young Silvia (Lara Wendel) fall under the glare of many eyeballs. Illustration by the author.

Tom. That came in the form of 1963's *The Girl Who Knew Too Much* and, from the following year, *Blood and Black Lace.*

In the former, Leticia Dean plays Nora, an American tourist in Rome who witnesses a murder and, when the body goes missing and the authorities don't believe her story, decides to investigate matters herself. Bava would mix the noir of Hitchcock with the expressionist shadow of the West German *krimi* film (in turn borrowed from the Weimar era of Fritz Lang, F. W. Murnau and the other pioneers of cinema's early movement), took the gimmick-laden plot devices of the lurid yellow-jacketed pulp novels from which the giallo takes its name (Bava's film features a number of murders following a pattern, tied to a decade-long string of killings of victims chosen in alphabetical order) and added liberal amounts of sex, murder and morbidity. At the center of Bava's first giallo was a vulnerable woman: an outsider, stranger in a strange town, a picture of delicate beauty about to be shattered. Inspired by the shocking death of Janet Leigh's Marion Crane in *Psycho*, the destruction of beauty would become a powerful tool, central to Bava's gialli.

The Vatican was largely untroubled by Bava's slickly stylized and somewhat sophisticated Hitchcockian effort, considering it to be nothing more offensive than "a clumsy detective story set in Rome." Recognizing that "given its nature, and some gory details, reservations are needed,"[11] the Vatican stopped short of forbidding the viewing of the film, instead allowing it to be seen by adults of moral maturity.

Bava's 1964 clash of murder and glamor in an haute couture fashion house depicted a series of models dying in increasingly inventive ways at the hands of a masked killer. This stylish, psychosexual murder mystery saw an increased concentration on the female form—established as the essence of sexuality, then punished with violence—married with beautiful imagery, technical mastery and realistic violence. While *The Girl Who Knew Too Much* is credited with birthing the giallo movie, *Blood and Black Lace* was the first of the auteur's movies to marry all the elements of the yet-to-be-named movement in one movie. The film contained all the established tropes of Bava's previous effort, including the amateur sleuth, black-clad killer, uninterested, incompetent police, Lastly, Bava added the terrifying atmosphere of Franju's *Eyes Without a Face* (and his own *Black Sunday*) and a grungy, lurid color palette that was redolent of Powell's *Peeping Tom*. There is also an ironic sense of the abstract in the film. By day, the world is a rational, logical place; by night, things change—symbolized by opulent color, by shadows that transform the physical places that had seemed so familiar and innocuous into foreboding labyrinths.

With *Blood and Black Lace*, the giallo was officially born and the era of cinematic horror in Italy fully established. Before long the giallo was popularized in Italy, with audiences flocking to the country's smaller, *terzia vision* cinemas to see these subversive films that the Vatican did its best to keep out of the nation's major theaters.

It is nigh on impossible to have any sort of in depth discussion about the giallo without at least attempting to describe the *filone* system of Italian cinema. A term often misinterpreted as to mean genre, filone more accurately describes the flexibility and fluidity of the film industry in Italy, and its willingness to branch off in different directions in response to whatever was popular at any given moment. Genre is a word that is not as meaningful to Italian cinema as it is to cinema in the U.S. or UK, as it has too many limitations (an action film will always be an action film; a comedy will always be a comedy, though either may differ in tone and sometimes feature elements of the other). Filone is a term that carries much more nuance and provides a bigger sandpit for Italian filmmakers to play in. A filone is a typical yeast bread that originated in Calabria and Tuscany but that you will find all across Italy. A filone is a strand or thread, perhaps found in a necklace. A filone is the primary vein found in igneous rock, from which a network of pegmatitic-aplitic veins crosscut through its structure. A filone is a current in the water.[12] These definitions, confusing at first, do provide the essence of detail: the filone system represents a fluid stream of films, each influenced by their forbears but moving in the current of popularity.

In each of the above descriptions, the one uniting characteristic is that filone describes a thread originating from a certain place. You can buy filone bread anywhere, but it will always have originated in Calabria and Tuscany. You can find various veins in minerals, but they will always lead back to that primary vein or thread. Therefore, in film, filone describes works that are in the tradition of something, but what that particular something is doesn't have to be as rigid as when using the term "genre."[13] Whichever description makes most sense to you, a genre is all the movies of a same type together, while a filone is more complex and less transparent.

The giallo is often described as a filone, essentially because its films all descend from the lurid yellow paperback thrillers published in Italy since the 1920s. What began as the circulation of the works of Edgar Wallace and Agatha Christie would soon be exploited by Italian authors writing under anglicized pseudonyms and ensuring these books contained typically lurid content—often very violent and sometimes quite sexually titillating and misogynistic. It is this content that is woven through the giallo film ... and yet, the giallo can itself (and indeed does) branch off in many different directions. Giallo directors would take elements created by Bava for *The Girl Who Knew Too Much* and *Blood and Black Lace* from the main body of "water" and allow various currents (from the works of Fritz Lang to those of Alfred Hitchcock, to the West German *krimi* and beyond) to take hold and drive these films in different directions: courtroom dramas (Duccio Tessari's *The Bloodstained Butterfly*), nonlinear thrillers (Aldo Lado's *The Short Night of Glass Dolls*, Duccio Tessari's *Puzzle*), explorations of psychological trauma (Francesco Barilli's *The Perfume of the Lady in Black*, Luigi Bazzoni's *Footprints on the Moon*), pornography (Enzo Milioni's *The Sister of Ursula*, Mario Gariazzo's *Play Motel*), even looping back around to gothic horror (Emilio Miraglia's *The Night Evelyn Came Out of the Grave* and *The Red Queen Kills Seven Times*).

Across three decades, hundreds of domestic films were labeled gialli, yet each was quite distinct. Whatever the streamlet being navigated, the giallo managed to hold a mirror up to many of the existential problems plaguing the Italian people. Koven suggested that the giallo came to reflect the brewing resentment that lay beneath the social upheaval that modernity brought to Italian culture in the 1960s, discussing "issues pertaining to identity, sexuality, increasing levels of violence, women's control over their own lives and bodies, history, the state—all abstract ideas, which are all portrayed situationally as human stories in the giallo film."[14] The directors of giallo films were keen to use their stories to pull back the glitzy curtain on liberal, permissive society and reveal the aching heart beneath, the pained husk of an organ left behind by fascism.

Francesco Barilli's 1974 giallo *The Perfume of the Lady in Black* is a film dedicated to exploring issues relating to women's control over their own lives and bodies in a patriarchal state. Burfield notes that modern Italy "remains a country whose very culture is sown with sexism and fundamentally unequal power dynamics,"[15] highlighting a hostile environment toward social equality where men have exerted dominance over women in many ways over the centuries. Burfield evidences this in several ways, from the "complete exclusion of female authors from the canon of Italian literature"[16] to the pressures placed on women to conform to traditional societal expectations of femininity: to be lovers, housewives and mothers, and little else. Those pressures have, of course, largely been encouraged (even enforced) by the Church, the ecclesiastical sphere (being entirely patriarchal in nature) that has sought to limit women's prospects to serving the family.

Barilli's film tells a tale of Silvia Hacherman (played with a fragile, detached and ethereal quality by the always excellent Mimsy Farmer) who is gaslit into believing she has lost her mind by all those around her. Silvia's character is clearly a riposte to Italian patriarchal traditionalism: she is an industrial chemist, a woman in a position traditionally inhabited by men, who remains unconcerned that her job affects her relationship with her boyfriend Roberto (Maurizio Bonuglia). She is liberated and has agency, happy to maintain a sexually active relationship without letting it interfere with her passion for her work.

Silvia attends a party with Roberto, held by an African professor and his wife. Here, discussion turns to witch doctors, cults and human sacrifices. This scene appears to serve a dual purpose: it serves as a foreshadowing of Silvia's tragic fate in the film, but it also comments on the Roman Catholic Church's views of the African continent and its people, heathens and savages who need to find God and be tamed (via its many missions to the continent).

Silvia is soon plagued by visions of her childhood (visions that suggest an extremely traumatic episode that she has likely dissociated from in the intervening years) and visited by an angelic child who may be her younger self, or may not exist at all. As the visions begin to unravel Silvia's delicate psyche, all those around her (from Roberto to her friends to complete strangers in the town) appear to be in cahoots to gaslight her, to make her doubt her sanity—as pointed out by Ellinger and Deighan, virtually every other character in the film is presented as a suspect, as having an ulterior motive and not to be trusted.[17]

Silvia's gradual but total psychological breakdown follows, as she is plagued by her own abandonment issues and the specters of her past. After reliving the trauma of her childhood, and realizing there is nobody in her adult life she can turn to for solace, Silvia takes her own life. It is only at this point, in a stunning final reveal, that we understand that Silvia's psychological breakdown has been an entirely managed one. That the African professor's cult story was in fact true, and that Silvia was being groomed by those around her to be a human sacrifice. From Roberto to the strangers in the town, all were preying upon Silvia from the very start, their actions coordinated, and they proceed to gather and ravenously devour her fresh corpse.

That the villain of the film is a voodoo cult is pertinent, as this represents a quasi-religious antagonist that has sought to undermine and control Silvia since the start. Her every action is questioned by the cult, which essentially wishes to divorce her from her independence. Janisse notes that at the core of Silvia's trauma is an irrepressible paternal figure—her mother's lover, the man at the center of Silvia's traumatized past[18]—and while this is entirely correct it doesn't stop at the man in her visions. Silvia's entire surroundings are the manifestation of an irrepressible paternal figure: the Italian patriarchy itself. Considering Burfield's assertions, Silvia represents everything the patriarchy in Italy does not want her to be: she is a leading woman in a male-dominated professional field, and has no interest in merely being a wife to Roberto and mother to his children. Thus, she cannot be allowed to *be*, and by the film's end her independence has been sacrificed and she has been (quite literally—the film ends with an act of cannibalism) swallowed by patriarchy, and by the Church.

Given that it was almost four decades after the film's release that it was fully dissected, by the likes of Ellinger, Deighan and Janisse, it is unlikely that the Vatican's writers would have picked up on the complex subtext in Barilli's work, nor that they would understand the "issues pertaining to identity, sexuality, increasing levels of violence, women's control over their own lives and bodies ... portrayed situationally (in the film)."[19] Nonetheless, the *Segnalazioni cinematografiche* was damning of the film, summarily dismissing it as "a work devoid of bite and suspense, despite the abundance of truculent and unhealthy elements that reach the apex of bad taste in the cannibalistic final sequence,"[20] and Italian Catholics were forbidden from viewing the film.

There would be entries into the giallo filone that were *openly* critical of Italy's institutions, and genre directors invested in telling incendiary stories of power, corruption and abuse in both Church and state. Mario Bava had, in his initial gialli *The Girl Who Knew Too Much* and *Blood and Black Lace*, introduced the concept of the destruction of beauty: modern, attractive, confident and sexually liberated women becoming targets of the killer in the giallo. As the filone developed, so did some directors develop this trope and change it into something even more potent: the destruction of innocence.

Taking the notion of innocence and "preserving it" by killing a child (or children) before the many vices of humanity can take hold is a device that appears to have grown out of the coda of the giallo and spread across to the *poliziotteschi* (Italian police thriller), to horror, and into serious drama, while picking up elements from elsewhere along the way. This device takes the innocent (often female) childhood and subjects it to the whims of depraved (usually male) adulthood. The notion of innocence is, in the antagonist's mind, preserved by killing the child before the many vices of humanity can take hold, thus ensuring their passage to Heaven.

The trope feeds on parental fear; namely, the desire to keep children as "little ones" and resist their attempts to grow up and establish their own (often sexual) agency. Where it both differs from and mirrors the existing giallo trope of the destruction of beauty, or the modern horror trope of sex = death, is that it looks to those whose innocence is corrupted, specifically by moral guardians and usually by sexual assault or murder, rather than punishing those who are using their own agency to explore their own sexuality. Therefore, the antagonists of these films are often priests or other members of the clergy, sometimes teachers, even parents. The Church being the ultimate parental figure, it feeds that parental fear, expressing constant caution, emphasizing that the innocence of children will be corrupted by the agents of the world, which introduce them to sin. In genre film, that corruption comes in one of two ways: either through the literal destruction of innocence by an evil (again, almost always male) antagonist who preys upon the young (consider *A Nightmare on Elm Street*'s Freddy Krueger, or Pennywise the Clown from Stephen King's *IT*, for instance) or through a more realist position where a paternal antagonist takes to killing children in the name of preserving their innocence and saving them from their own inevitable sexuality.

While a constant theme in horror, the destruction of innocence was explored regularly in the giallo throughout the 1970s. The idea had really captured the zeitgeist and tapped into parental fears in Italy at the time. One real-life fear was of children being abducted, abused and murdered by the growing sex-trafficking industry. According to Bonilla and Mo, there were as few as seven organizations worldwide that focused their operations on sex trafficking prior to 1970. From 1970 onward, an average of four

2. Escluso per Tutti   49

new sex-trafficking organizations were founded per year, as the practice became big black market business worldwide.[21]

A second real world influence on this theme in films, and a particularly pertinent one here, was the growing allegations of sexual abuse by members of the clergy. Though not officially reported on until decades later, the 1970s are now considered to have been the "peak" years of child abuse activity within the Church, with as many as 1 percent of the 500,000+ ordained Roman Catholic priests worldwide thought to have been abusers, and as many as 5.3 percent of priests in the United States alone accused of abuse, according to just one study.[22] In Italy, the global home of the Roman Catholic Church, the country was already experiencing a mass apostasy from its faith for a number of reasons, and its liberal artists (from poets to filmmakers) were suspicious of the Church and its agents.

In 1972, this suspicion would be explored in the gialli of Aldo Lado and Vittorio De Sisti (*Who Saw Her Die?*) and Lucio Fulci (*Don't Torture a Duckling*). Both films featured members of the clergy as their child-murdering antagonists, and each was vociferously condemned by the Church upon release. Lado and De Sisti's murderer of young girls is revealed to be Don James, a cross-dressing priest whose own mother was a prostitute.

In Fulci's *Don't Torture a Duckling*, as the bones of her dead baby are unearthed from the ground, La Maciara (Florinda Bolkan) screams in anguish. Illustration by the author.

His revenge for the trauma he suffered would be to prevent young girls growing up in vice by killing them with their innocence intact. Fulci's priest Don Alberto had seen the young boys of his peaceful parish corrupted by prostitution (in this case via voyeurism) and wished to ensure them eternal life in Heaven by killing them before their innocence could be extinguished by a sinful world. In each case, the misguided preachers (proxies for the Church itself) romanticized their mission, "saving" the innocence of children from a life of sin.

Lado, De Sisti and Fulci recognized the furor their films would cause within the Church. Lado had served as an apprentice under Italian agitator Bernardo Bertolucci, while Fulci had studied under Luchino Visconti at Rome's premier film school, Centro Sperimentale di Cinematografica. Fulci in particular would irritate the Vatican with several of his films, and found himself in court on more than one occasion accused of various improprieties. *Don't Torture a Duckling* was one such occasion. Fulci was accused of exposing young boys to the naked body of actor Barbara Bouchet on set, and the director had to explain in court how he had used doubles to keep the child actors safe from the "harm" of observing a naked female form. While there is no way to prove the Church's involvement in bringing Fulci to court, it is somewhat suspiciously ironic that Fulci pointed his finger at the Church and laid bare its complicity in decades of child abuse, only for him to be accused of committing child abuse in making his film.

Meanwhile, in the pages of the *Segnalazioni cinematografiche,* Lado's film was accused of having "poor technical skills at the service of a confused and artificial film."[23] The director's work was lambasted for "deceiving the expectations of the audience ... and in disturbing them spiritually by means of a horrifying sequence of sadistic scenes or erotic sequences."[24] Riposte to Fulci's film came from Catholic newspaper *Il Giorno*'s critic Morando Morandini. Morandini accused the film of "dishonesty in the use of suspense, abuse of horrifying details, sadomasochism with both hands, disdain of logic."[25] Both *Who Saw Her Die* and *Don't Torture a Duckling* were deemed unacceptable, and Catholic audiences were forbidden from watching either.

In accusing Lado and De Sisti of disturbing cinema audiences spiritually and forcing Fulci to appear in court on child abuse charges, it was clear that the makers of both films had hit their intended target. The directors had sought to explicitly criticize the Church, to highlight very real suspicions held by the Italian public, and in doing so they had incensed the Vatican a great deal.

At the same time, Massimo Dallamano began his "schoolgirl" giallo trilogy with *What Have You Done to Solange?* (1972). This would be followed by 1974's *What Have They Done to Your Daughters?* and concluded in 1978's *The Red Rings of Fear* (although this third film was in fact directed by

Alberto Negrin, not Dallamano). These films would also probe the theme of the destruction of innocence, this time with schoolgirls falling prey and an entirely different set of moral guardians shown to be failing their children.

The first (and best) of Dallamano's triptych is one of the finer examples of the core giallo film. It sees a series of violent murders at a Catholic girls' school. A professor at the school who has been having an affair with one or more of the girls is at first suspected, but later cleared, as it turns out the girls were part of a sex club and another patriarchal figure entirely is responsible for their deaths. If there is any weakness in Dallamano's film, it is in the director's lack of resolve when it comes to what would otherwise have been as controversial a reveal as Fulci or Lado managed: Dallamano's killer is thought to be an actual member of the clergy but turns out to be a man who merely dresses as a priest.

Dallamano's second film on the subject concerns an underage prostitution ring, which police officers happen upon while investigating the case of a girl found hanged. Unlike the earlier giallo, this film sees Dallamano take the device and change not so much the setting as the filone, bringing elements of the Italian *poliziotteschi* film together with the tools of the gialli, having Claudio Cassinelli's embattled Commissioner Silvestri involved in a tense investigation that leads into darker and darker territory. The central theme is not just the murder of these young girls but the destruction of their innocence, through predators who have insinuated themselves into positions of power. It is, in fact, more than a theme—it is an accusation. The on-screen notes at the end of the film assert that 8,000 girls go missing in Italy each year, 8,000 daughters who will have their innocence destroyed by the very people who are supposed to help them keep it intact. The *Red Rings of Fear* would be Dallamano's third schoolgirl giallo (at least until he passed away and Alberto Negrin was brought in to direct the installment) and features a trafficking racket, this time supplying schoolgirls for parties.

Though Dallamano's films all dabble in exploitation, they treat their characters seriously. In each film, the girls are not presented as wretched or nymphomaniac temptresses; the promiscuity of one 15-year-old girl is presented as a simple matter of fact, and not destructive to her innocence at all, compared with the external forces that either guide or force many like her down a dark path. In the case of each film, it is the adults around the children who all let them down, their safeguarding failures leading to the girls' losing their innocence and their lives.

The *Segnalazioni cinematografiche* had opinions on Dallamano's films, and surprisingly they weren't all negative. The Vatican's review of *What Have They Done to Your Daughters?* begins with a quite sober consideration "that the trafficking of minors is a serious problem in today's society and, in order to fight it or take care of it, it is essential that the voluntary cooperation of the entire citizenship be joined with the police forces—this film proclaims it loudly and rightly."[26] Here the Vatican agrees with what it perceives to be the message of the film: that each adult plays a role in keeping the children safe, and that those moral duties have lapsed in modern society. It was, in fact, in the organizations of the Church and the state that those moral duties had long since lapsed, and filmmakers such as Dallamano, Lado, De Sisti and Fulci were rightly pointing their fingers.

"Conversely, the work largely neglects the analysis of the psychological and socio-cultural causes of the disaster: in this way there is a reason to doubt its educational effect. What are the true roots of evil? Why is there so much moral disintegration in society and in the youth? What should parents or educators need to prevent and safeguard the very young victims?"[27] The *Segnalazioni cinematografiche* appeared to be engaging with Dallamano on a different level, and it has to be assumed that, were Dallamano to have been brave enough to point a more direct finger at the Church (as Fulci, Lado and De Sisti had done) then the discussion would have been a different one.

In his 1975 film *The Suspicious Death of a Minor*, Sergio Martino was not shy in pointing his finger at the very organizations within society that were believed to be culpable in the crimes of child abuse and child trafficking, either actively or through apathy. From an Ernesto Gastaldi script that manages a deft filone tightrope act throughout (the film is part macabre thriller, part police procedural and part comedy, and the balance is struck superbly), Martino's film sees maverick cop Paolo Germi (Claudio Cassinelli) investigating a child murder that leads to a human trafficking ring involving some powerful figures. The premise is dripping with shadow and intrigue, action and humor … but nonetheless is another dark and accusatory tale of the abuse of vulnerable children at the hands of predators.

Like several of the gialli that bear the destruction of innocence theme, *The Suspicious Death of a Minor* was at least partly inspired by horrors of the real world. Human trafficking was (and remains) a problem in Italy, with the need for migrant workers used as a cover for trafficking women and minors from countries such as Nigeria for sexual exploitation.[28] Martino's film perhaps is most reminiscent of Dallamano's *What Have They Done to Your Daughters?*: not only does Cassinelli play a cop determined to put a stop to the deaths of underage girls; he uncovers a sex trafficking ring that has been turning the lives of precocious young girls into tragedies. The deepest, darkest thread of Martino's film understands, just as Dallamano's did, the horror and poignancy of this subject, and the director wants to use his influence and his skills to shine a light on it.

> The story, put together through the looting of a hundred Italian and American works on the same subject, does not lack references to sad news on the enterprise

of evil and repeats certain simplistic statements on the roots of the abandonments of minors and on the radicalness of organized crime in high spheres. However, the superficiality of the discussion and the evident purely commercial interest of the film prevent it from qualifying as a civic document. Furthermore, basing its spectacle on the smug description of evil as such, the film contains numerous scenes of raw violence and shameless sensuality. Consequently, it is a product that is anything but educational. Unacceptable/negative.[29]

A number of the *Segnalazioni cinematografiche*'s reviews suggest that the Church considers the giallo filone no more than a vehicle for exploitation. Perhaps the Vatican considers these films as neither deserving nor capable of presenting serious social or political commentary. What is more likely, and will be highlighted on several occasions throughout subsequent chapters, is that when genre directors highlight the very real crimes of the Church in their subversive art, the Vatican chooses to respond in the most aggressive of ways, censuring these transgressive films and attempting to punish their directors.

That the Vatican goes some way to criticizing supposedly spurious insinuations about corruption in high places is quite galling in retrospect, considering that at around the same time, the former Masonic Lodge Propaganda Due (P2) fully transformed into a criminal organization populated with people in high places, including senior politicians, Vatican figures, army and police officials, bankers and mafiosi.[30] Originally founded by in 1877, the Lodge had been suppressed by Mussolini, reactivated again following his downfall, and would for a decade function as a secretive state within a state, only ceasing operations when it was finally publicly exposed in 1981, leading to the resignations of Italian prime minister Arnaldo Forlani and his entire cabinet.[31,32] The leftist Italian intelligentsia had anticipated such a thing, via its poetry and art, since the fall of fascism. Suspicion of such cabals was so widespread among the general public that the directors of genre cinema would readily criticize the secretive relationship between Church, State and the criminal fraternity relationship through their subversive art, in some cases (such as Martino's film here, and Lucio Fulci's 1972 erotic satire *The Eroticist*, a film that received a state ban after secret screenings attended by politicians and clergy were held in the Vatican[33]) directly accusing the Church of being part of a deep state, a conspiracy theory that, as would later prove to be the case, was in fact true.

In 1970, Dario Argento burst onto the scene and caused a different kind of storm. His template was to go back to Bava, and indeed to Bava's influences, ramping up the glitz while removing the subtextual commentary to create a series of stylistic thrillers that would see him earn the nickname "Italian Hitchcock."[34]

Argento succeeded, with a trio of gialli dubbed his "animal trilogy" (*The Bird with the Crystal Plumage, Cat O' Nine Tails, Four Flies on Grey Velvet*), which would propel him to success and longevity. With Argento, the writers of the *Segnalazioni cinematografiche* found themselves with an inner conflict: wanting to praise the cinematic style and vision of a bold and skilled young director while profoundly disagreeing with the immoral content of his films. Argento's gialli would, of course, be rendered unacceptable, but not before a deal of deliberation within the pages of the *Segnalazioni cinematografiche*.

Four Flies on Grey Velvet was characterized as "made with remarkable technical skill and ability to create suspense" despite its "unpleasant scenes, vulgarity ... and some horrifying details."[35]

There is something interesting about the conflict here for the writers of the Vatican's film pamphlet, and it is one that goes back to the initial interest of the Church (and the state) in the medium. The Centro Cattolico Cinematografico had ostensibly been set up to aid the film industry in Italy, as had LUCE and Rome's Cinecittà Studio, and was dedicated to the promotion of domestic Italian cinema. However, the *Segnalazioni cinematografiche* was a tool of censorship; in classifying each commercial film released in Italy, it exerted its control over who was actually able to see them. As a result of this conflict of purpose, the Vatican's writers do occasionally take pause to note the style, the skill and the craftsmanship of certain domestic directors (and foreign ones), even if they are to censure the same director/film in the very next sentence. This is particularly evident in its reviews of Powell's *Peeping Tom*, and in the early films of Argento.

Subsequently, because of their apparent sophistication and artistic skill, Argento's gialli were not always forbidden by the Church but after much deliberation of the director's technical skill and hand-wringing over the salacious content were usually reserved for adults of a particular intellectual and moral maturity. This was the closest the Vatican's writers could come to openly considering these films as acceptable viewing.

Argento established himself as a giallo director at a time when the filone was beginning to morph into something else entirely. The template set by Bava in 1963–64 would be replaced by something darker, more violent and with a meaner, nastier edge, something that would influence horror directors in the U.S. and create an entirely new subgenre of horror, one that would become big business at box offices throughout the '70s and '80s and remains popular today.

Italian genre directors like Argento, Sergio Martino and, of course, Mario Bava would be at the forefront of what was to become known as the slasher film.

3

This ... Is God!
(The Vatican versus ... the Slasher)

One of the most enduring and durable additions to the modern horror pantheon was the rise of the slasher film, a high-concept horror subgenre with a simple template that almost guaranteed success: a marriage of the whodunit murder mystery, confined or remote setting, a crazed and charismatic antagonist and a high kill count (including increasingly inventive murder set pieces) proved to be popcorn fodder in the making.

In recent years, a favored pastime of the horror fan has been to discuss certain subgenres, the film or films that officially birthed them, and their progenitors. In no subgenre of horror has there been more fervent discussion of this than the slasher film. The concept of the slasher film as a specific subgenre of horror did not come about until after John Carpenter's seminal 1978 film *Halloween*. It is in this film that most agree the formula of the subgenre was fully realized.

Hunter describes genre histories as malleable, with dates and information points that alter as they become better informed by contemporary knowledge of early films. Others believe that genres begin when they are named. The term "horror" was not used as a descriptor until inspired by 1931's *Frankenstein* and *Dracula* movies from Universal Studios; therefore, to those with a rigid sense of genre history, the horror genre began in 1931. There is, of course, a paradox in accepting that a film genre only begins when it is first named: if no such examples of the genre existed, how did it begin? How was it named? A film or films must have inspired the act of naming the genre in the first place. If *Frankenstein* and *Dracula* inspired the term "horror film," then surely the films that informed *them* must be a part of that canon. Furthermore (according to Hunter and those who agree with him), acceptance of *Frankenstein* and *Dracula* as horror films must in turn allow us to use our contemporary knowledge to reappraise those that went before, those that first produced the characteristics or tropes that directly influenced the Universal movies, as having contributed to the recognition of the genre.[1]

In John Carpenter's 1974 proto-slasher *Halloween*, as Laurie Strode (Jamie Lee Curtis) navigates the streets of Haddonfield, an ethereal Michael Myers (Nick Castle) watches over her. Illustration by the author.

3. This ... Is God!

It is the above paradox that provides film fans, writers and historians with the opportunity to talk of progenitors. These are the films that inspired the term, the films that existed before the canon, yet are intrinsically linked to the genre or subgenre in discussion. The progenitors of the slasher film sit largely (but not exclusively) within the giallo filone. Mario Bava, Sergio Martino and Dario Argento are all considered to have directed movies that helped first establish the coda adopted in the slasher template.

This chapter discusses those progenitors, examines their influence on the slasher subgenre that would follow, and looks at the *Segnalazioni cinematografiche*'s reviews of both the progenitors and the slasher canon proper, not just to find out the Vatican's opinion of them (it will come as no surprise to learn that, on the whole, the Vatican found the slasher film to be *inaccettabile*) but to ascertain if the Holy See understood what was unfurling before its eyes; the cultural shift and creative experiments that led to the creation of a new, somehow more transgressive (and incredibly popular) subgenre of horror very much birthed from the domestic filone of Italy.

When it comes to the proto-slashers, Alfred Hitchcock's *Psycho* has to feature heavily in any conversation, just as it does when it comes to discussion of the birth of modern horror in its entirety. In retrospect, *Psycho* is widely considered to have birthed modern cinematic horror and had a significant influence on the slasher film.

Brueggemann is certainly not wrong when he suggests that "there are few films that have had the impact of this one. Written by B-movie horror writers and made for a Blumhouse budget, it was more than a financial success; it changed the kinds of films that filmmakers and actors would make, and informed the language of cinema around the world."[2]

Brueggemann can easily say this in 2020, 60 years after the film was released. However, even with the film's initial financial success, audience reactions, controversy and drama, were you to suggest in 1960 that *Psycho* would change the visual language of the medium forever, you would likely be accused of hyperbole. In the modern age, film writers, critics, historians and keen fans alike have the privilege of having seen history unfold, of watching the scores and scores of movies that would adopt the coda of *Psycho* over the next six decades. What Brueggemann has rightly recognized is the impressive effect Hitchcock's masterpiece mixture of expressionist framing, film noir stylings and subversive psychosexual content has had on an entire medium across over half a century—but it is done with the benefit of much hindsight.

Pioneering, template-breaking movies such as Hitchcock's tend not to make their impact all at once. As has happened with such films over the last 130 or so years, at the time *Psycho* sent out only ripples into the rest of the horror filmmaking community. At the time, many critics had much to lament about the film, including *Time* magazine, which stated that "the experienced Hitchcock fan might reasonably expect the unreasonable—a great chase down Thomas Jefferson's forehead, as in *North by Northwest*, or across the rooftops of Monaco, as in *To Catch a Thief*. What is offered instead is merely gruesome. The trail leads to a sagging, swamp-view motel and to one of the messiest, most nauseating murders ever filmed. At close range, the camera watches every twitch, gurgle, convulsion and haemorrhage in the process by which a living human becomes a corpse."[3]

On the other side of the Atlantic, English critic C. A. LeJeune started her review with the assertion that "a new film by Alfred Hitchcock is usually a keen enjoyment. Psycho turns out to be an exception."[4] LeJeune would also go on to describe "one of the most disgusting murders in all screen history. It takes place in a bathroom and involves a great deal of swabbing of the tiles and flushings of the lavatory,"[5] called the mystery surrounding the film's presentation to critics "stupid"[6] (critics were denied advance screenings, instead made to watch the film with a "normal"

Norman Bates was played by Anthony Perkins in Alfred Hitchcock's groundbreaking 1960 modern horror *Psycho*. Illustration by the author.

audience, as Hitchcock took a leaf out of horror super-producer William Castle's gimmick book) and stated of the film that "it is difficult, if not impossible, to care about any of the characters."[7]

Hitchcock's films had been very popular in Italy, but, as noted in Chapter 2, the *Segnalazioni cinematografiche* also appeared to struggle with reconciling its evaluation of *Psycho* with its opinion of the celebrated director's works to date.[8]

The Vatican's review is interesting here for a particular reason: this is one of a number of times (occurring with such frequency that a cynic may call it an editorial tactic) where the writers attempt to convey a sense of disappointment and boredom in a film—the same film it is telling its congregation it is unsuitable for them to view—rather than the dismay or dismissal tactics it usually stuck to. Across the pages of the *Segnalazioni cinematografiche* it becomes apparent just how very purposeful the publication's editors were, and how seriously it took the role of censor (as well as critic). Here, the Vatican wants to give the sense that it is untroubled by the film's corruption, such is its belief in the strength of the Lord. But is the Holy See's real aim to avoid giving the film any free press? In contributing to a film's controversy, it is also possible (and, in some cases, highly likely) to inadvertently contribute to its success.

Soon enough, though, the mask slips and the awkward mock-boredom of the reviewer dissipates. Normal service is resumed, with a stern, dismissive tone: "Wrong from its very base … the film, in presenting its misdeeds, lingers to describe, with an excess of macabre details, some criminal actions which…(lead us to) advise against viewing the film."[9]

Ultimately, the Vatican's verdict ensured that Catholic-owned/operated theaters would need to choose between a potential box-office smash that would put food on the table and the decree of its religion. The patriarch had spoken, and usually this was enough to limit a film's run in theaters. Despite this, however, *Psycho*'s success in the UK and U.S. made Italian cinemagoers curious, and it did enjoy similar success in Italy (much to the disapproval and consternation of the Church).

The slasher was still (officially at least) almost two decades shy of being born, but we have now had the privilege of seeing the Hitchcock effect on this particular type of film as it developed over the years and decades that followed. Just as the language of Hitchcock's undeniable masterpiece inspired the next, viscerally subversive breed of horror auteurs, so did its influence slowly infiltrate what would eventually become the most popular genre property of the '70s and '80s.

In 1963, in between his popular string of Vincent Price–starring Poe adaptations and numerous other projects, American B-movie mogul Roger Corman mentored a young Francis Ford Coppola on his first feature, *Dementia 13*. The film was made over 11 days in Ireland with a crew of nine and a budget of $30,000 (while Corman simultaneously shot a second film in nearby Liverpool, England, called *The Young Racers*).[10]

Coppola's film takes the Agatha Christie *Ten Little Indians* template (a family reunites at their remote ancestral castle home, all with the matriarch's last will and testament on their mind, and a series of murders begins, with the various family members each in the frame) and marries it with the popular gothic aesthetics of the time. The family of the film (which includes Luana Anders, Patrick Magee, Bart Patton, and Eithne Dunne as icy matriarch Lady Haloran) is sketched broadly by Coppola's screenplay, which allows us to get involved in the mystery, to take in the framing of the looming Irish castle that represents the threatening effect of the matriarch (instantly redolent of Hitchcock) and to welcome the subversive and the risqué undertones that this quite base (but very effective) thriller takes from Hitchcock's seminal 1960 film. It has a single, isolated (if grandiose and bourgeois) location. The scares come pretty often for a film of *Dementia 13*'s time, from a series of creepy toy dolls (that would be equally welcome in Charles Band's *Puppet Master* franchise or WWE superstar Bray Wyatt's *Firefly Funhouse*) to the film's brutal axe murderer and his first kill, a half-naked, waterborne Anders, all of which was clearly an attempt to outdo the subversive content of its predecessor.

Apparently Coppola, then a second unit director in Corman's employ, promised his mentor "a gothic knockoff of Hitchcock's *Psycho* with a lot of axe murders and sex,"[11] and that appears to be exactly what he got. The film features a family gathering at a remote location, a mystery killer and a series of set piece murders, all signs that the tropes of a genre (or filone!) are beginning to gather.

Though the *Segnalazioni cinematografiche* afforded cinematic master Alfred Hitchcock's *Psycho* a fairly reasoned critique, it was not going to do the same for this 24-year-old who had previously worked principally as an assistant on sex films. However, nor did it shine its spotlight quite so keenly on the film as it had on *Psycho*. The journal's critic considered that "the mediocre and cumbersome work seems to have the sole purpose of offering, to an audience of poor pretensions, a rapid succession of shots, without however worrying about making the narrated story credible."[12]

With this damning comment, the Vatican's writer appears to insult not just the film but anybody who might wish to go and see it, characterizing any potential audience of the film as having shallow pretensions (to enjoyment and fulfillment). The *Segnalazioni cinematografiche* would go on to determine that "the complacency and the insistence with which the film presents macabre scenes and the amorous ambiguity of some sequences impose, despite the harmlessness of the imaginative and incredible plot, clear reservations."[13]

The Vatican takes the stance that the content of the film is incredible, but this is a superlative of incredulity, not a compliment. The writer means that the film is an unbelievable fantasy, and therefore less harmful due to its convoluted plot. Because of its view of the work's mediocrity, the *Segnalazioni cinematografiche* considers it not as potent as Hitchcock's *Psycho* and imposes a verdict of "For adults with reservations"[14] rather than an outright ban, meaning adults could essentially make their own decision as to whether to view the film or not (but would do so with the knowledge that they were being judged on their decisions).

Meanwhile, in Italy, Mario Bava was doing almost exactly the same thing as Coppola and Corman. His racy 1963 thriller *The Girl Who Knew Too Much* began the cinematic giallo genre in Italy and inform its coda, but it was very much informed by Hitchcock. Nineteen sixty-four follow-up *Blood and Black Lace* was the film that codified the elements that would become the giallo blueprint: the series of murders (often elaborate and theatrical); the mystery, which can only be solved by an outsider; the killer, dressed in black, often masked and with a gimmick weapon; beautiful women; lurid color; a sense of irony; a sense of the abstract. One trait that was missing from both *The Girl Who Knew Too Much* and *Blood and Black Lace*, that would be integral to the slasher film, was a vein of uncompromising cruelty not seen since Hitchcock's seminal 1960 film.

But Bava soon caught up.

The director's later, more gruesome giallo entries *Hatchet for the Honeymoon* and *A Bay of Blood* would see the coda of the giallo transform into something far more cruel and aggressive, something more akin to what would later be termed the tenets of the slasher. *Hatchet for the Honeymoon* was derided at the time as a mediocre effort from the director, largely because of the sense of style and sumptuous visuals eschewed from his past work and the crueler streak adopted in its stead. Bava's 1970 tale of a man who feels compelled to murder young brides in order to recall details of past trauma features a string of elaborately staged bloody deaths, a series of murderous tableaux created by a director beginning to realize that the deaths of characters needn't be mere shocks within the film: they could become *the entire point*. *Hatchet* also features a charismatic killer with a gimmick (whose character mirrors *Psycho*'s Norman Bates in a number of ways) and a final girl in Dagmar Lassander's Helen Wood. Each of these elements would take this latest film farther away from Bava's gialli and into the realm of a subgenre of horror film yet to be named.

The *Segnalazioni cinematografiche* was as dismissive of Bava's film as could be reasonably expected, dispatching its critique swiftly and without mercy. "A highly morbid atmosphere, the absolute immorality of the characters and the unscrupulousness of the scenes and dialogs make the film completely negative."[15]

Judging by the Vatican's reaction, Bava's blueprint was indeed changing, from that of the traditional cosmopolitan giallo that didn't particularly bother the Church to a cruder cousin yet to be born, one intended for the voracious appetites of horror audiences. *Hatchet for the Honeymoon*'s influence can be seen in subsequent U.S. horror films such as Armand Mastroianni's 1980 slasher *He Knows You're Alone* and in Mary Harron's satirical slasher *American Psycho* (2000).

Bava would follow *Hatchet for the Honeymoon* up with 1971's *A Bay of Blood*. This latest film would trouble censors so much that it became a part of the UK's video nasty hysteria, earning itself prosecutions and a place on the infamous list of banned films under the 1984 Video Recordings Act. It would also provide yet more inspiration for the slasher film in the U.S. *A Bay of Blood* features a remote, isolated setting (a family mansion on the edge of a great lake) and a series of characters that are introduced for no real reason other than to raise the film's body count in new and interesting ways. The film eschews the traditional giallo whodunit by introducing multiple killers (a trope Bava had already experimented with in his 1964 *Blood and Black Lace*) and has a clear dedication to making its rising body count and inventive murder set pieces the focal points of the film.

Among writers and genre fans alike, *A Bay of Blood* has become known as the film that perhaps informed the birth of the Slasher more than any other. As Lowenstein suggests, the "all-encompassing frenzy of violence subsumes questions of motive and mystery."[16] Nastasi would agree, asserting that "[Bava's] plot about a familial inheritance drama exists only to propel us to the next kill. A Bay of Blood is often categorized as a giallo film, and it bears a few hallmarks of the genre (red herrings and a glimpsed black-gloved killer), but what Bava has created here is an early prototype for the slasher film."[17]

Beyond the above, *A Bay of Blood* is widely recognized not just as a precursor to the slasher film but as a major influence on one of the slasher's biggest franchises. Two of Bava's murder set pieces (a coitus interruptus double impalement; a billhook to the face) would be reused in Sean S. Cunningham's 1980 Halloween cash-in *Friday the 13th* and its 1981 sequel. While Cunningham has refused to admit the film had any influence on him, the evidence would suggest otherwise. *A Bay of Blood* shared many Grindhouse double billings with *Last House on the Left* (1972, dir. Wes Craven), a film produced by Cunningham. At some of these showings, *A Bay of Blood* was marketed as "Last House Part 2." Given that Cunningham would do all the publicity for his films himself, and even drive the reels to the drive-in theaters personally, it would follow that he knew Bava's film well. Martin Kitrosser, script supervisor on *Friday the 13th* and its sequels, was himself massively influenced by Bava (such a fan of the director that he named his son "Mario Bava Kitrosser"!). Kitrosser loaned Cunningham and screenwriter Victor Millor his own personal print of *A Bay of Blood* for them to study as they developed *Friday the 13th*.[18]

As was frequently the case, where Bava went, others followed. Sergio Martino soon responded with his own cruel giallo, 1973's *Torso*. In the early 1970s, Martino was becoming something of a master of the giallo himself. The Roman director (in collaboration with his producer brother, Luciano) would tap into virtually every current in the filone across five years and six films, with *Torso* being his fourth giallo in three years.

Given the provocative alternative title of *The Bodies Bear Traces of Carnal Violence*, the film makes its statement early; using voyeuristic POV sequences in each transgressive scene of sexual violence. Martino maintains this shooting style throughout, partly to keep the identity of his killer a mystery, but mostly to challenge the viewer by making us complicit in the violence. POV shots have become a horror staple, particularly in the found footage subgenre, as they invite the audience to live vicariously through a character: we see what they see, we do what they do, and we are no longer innocent bystanders but the player in the act.

Torso is essentially a transgressive manifesto, offering its audience the most violent and fetishistic content a giallo had produced to date, a celebration of (sexual) violence in art. In a series of gruesome set pieces, a number of sexy coeds are picked off by the murderer, a masked killer with a gimmick: he strangles (with a silk scarf), stabs and molests his victims (in that order) before gouging out their eyes. The unflinching violence and liberal sexuality of Martino's film are absolute precursors to the slasher, as are its isolated setting (a cliffside villa) and very pronounced use of what would become the "final girl" trope. Suzy Kendall's virginal Jane is the only one of the (otherwise promiscuous, sexually liberated) girls to make it to the end and unmask the killer.

Nastasi agrees that *Torso* too is a progenitor of the slasher, asserting, "*Torso*'s focus on repressed sexuality, centered on a killer whose childhood trauma has twisted his psychosexual mind, influenced the hormonal American slasher genre…. *Torso* takes place in a secluded setting … champions a final girl … indulges in visceral thrills."[19] The writer goes on to draw more parallels with *Friday the 13th*, this time between *Torso*'s moralizing killer and Pamela Voorhees.

The Vatican appeared to be picking up on the move from the traditional giallo coda to a crueler, cruder filone, noting in its review that "the film, in which the narrative structure and the psychologies of the characters are almost non-existent, limits itself to showing, in a disgusting sado-masochistic crescendo, but also with frequent falls into the grotesque, scenes of cruelty and sex (deviant or otherwise)."[20] The film would receive an ecclesiastical ban and, like Mario Bava before him, Martino would look beyond Italy to find an audience for his boundary-pushing transgressive vision. *Torso* was picked up by Joseph Brenner Associates for distribution in the U.S., where it would play America's drive-ins and grind houses to larger and more avid audiences than it was allowed to find on home soil.

That the *Segnalazioni cinematografiche* wasted little time in dismissing the film as little more than a series of sex scenes and murders, and proclaiming it unacceptable for the Roman Catholic public without risking drawing any curious attention to the film, is interesting. The critique takes a moment to recognize what the Church considers to be "deviant"[21] sex, such as the graphic lesbian and group sex sequences (this is to be expected; it is not news that the Vatican and the Roman Catholic religion has a homophobia problem, as well as viewing any sex outside of monogamous marital heteronormative sexual activity to be morally unacceptable) but clearly seeks to draw a swift line beneath it and give this very transgressive film no more air than is absolutely necessary.

It would appear, then, that the Vatican had begun to notice a transition, from the recognizably domestic giallo template to something more transgressive, something darker and crueler. Of course, how could it not: genre cinema had, in roughly the space of a decade, already moved on from the suggested violence of Hitchcock's shower scene (with its 78 camera set ups and 52 edits intended to trick the viewers' eyes into believing it was seeing real violence take place) to stark, graphic, drawn-out sex and murder scenes. The sight of Janet Leigh's shoulders and calves in the shower was considered racy in 1960; in 1973's Torso, the sequence of disrobing, strangling, sexually assaulting, eye gouging and stabbing that establishes its own visual language by the time of the swampland murder of Carol (Conchita Airoldi) is borderline pornographic, as is the sex being had at the hippy party she visits moments before her death. The same transgressive sequence is repeated across the killer's murders, an extended, bloody ritual, each time with the same reverse POV shots to establish killer and victim POV and use the predatory male gaze to inform any emotional response to the sequences.

Dario Argento's *Profondo Rosso* (1975) is by now accepted as one of the standout entries in the giallo canon, and one of the legendary Italian director's classics. It is also a film that sought to remold the genre's template but in a slightly different way than recent entries by Argento's peers had reflected. The maestro wished to keep the murder mystery element

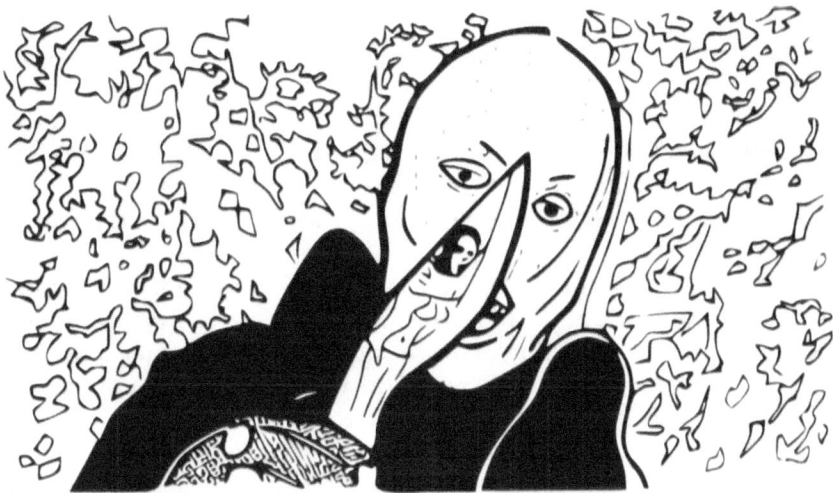

In Sergio Martino's 1973 giallo *Torso*, the masked killer Franz (John Richardson) stands, knife in hand, as his semi-naked victim Carol (Conchita Airoldi) is seen reflected in the blade. Illustration by the author.

in his film, but instead used technical and aesthetic means to stylize (and therefore draw more attention to) certain aspects of his giallo. Dario Argento would become known as "The Italian Hitchcock" and not without cause: there was an unmistakable style to his feature films (which would translate well to the horror film when Argento eventually fully made the jump, with the 1978 horror masterpiece *Suspiria*) as well as a psychosexual element that would grow in prevalence across his oeuvre as it developed. Argento was always shooting and editing inventively, exploring new techniques, codas and other components of the visual language of cinema.

Argento's interest in the psychosexual would ensure that alternative notions of gender and sexuality were pushed in an almost matter-of-fact way, challenging audiences and critics alike with the inclusion of marginalized people and a progressive view of matters deemed deviant by the Church. *Profondo Rosso* featured a queer transgender character, and Argento's later film *Tenebrae* would feature lesbian and bisexual women in polyamorous relationships as well as a transgender actress in a cisgender role. In addition, his gialli were getting darker, just like those of Bava and Martino. Set piece kills had a crueler streak, and *Profondo Rosso*'s killer enjoyed a particular gimmick: a remote-controlled doll on a tricycle, striking terror as it races across a room toward its victim and certainly an influence on James Wan's 2004 movie *Saw* (and its sequels) as well as Christopher Landon's 2017 neo-slasher *Happy Death Day*.

The *Segnalazioni cinematografiche*, despite previously looking somewhat favorably on the director, was damning of Argento's latest from the start, asserting that "even a superficial examination of the plot reveals a lack of logic and many consistencies, which are accompanied by psychologies that do not go beyond a schematic sketch."[22] The Italian Hitchcock was not afforded the same praise for his technical skill he had earlier enjoyed, instead lambasted for "images bordering on sadism"[23] that "offer the recipient the questionable 'pleasure' of leaving them with their heart pounding."[24]

Of most interest about the Vatican's review of the film was that the reviewer had appraised the film well enough to recognize that they were not dealing with a giallo film in the classic sense but something quite different. The *Segnalazioni cinematografiche* ensured to point out that "the director, preferring artifice to fantasy and surface reaction to truthfulness, has aimed exclusively at creating an atmosphere of continuous obsession: the provocation of anxious sensations. Consequently, if the general layout of the film follows the rules of the classic giallo, not infrequently the individual scenes make use of ingredients of the horror film."[25]

Where it was often quick to censure without further interrogation, the Holy See here opted to discuss what it saw as the development of something. This was no longer the cosmopolitan giallo of the 1960s. Nor was it akin to the political protest gialli adopted by the likes of Lucio Fulci and Massimo Dallamano to attack the Church directly. The films of Bava, Martino and Argento were becoming meaner, sleazier and more transgressive, bringing several darker traits to cinema screens, and the Vatican was beginning to understand that the modern Italian thriller was becoming something else entirely. For the most part, the extent to which the giallo influenced the slasher is something that has been recognized and documented by critics over the course of several decades after the fact, with the same hindsight that Brueggemann has when discussing Psycho's influence 60 years after its release. That the writers of the *Segnalazioni cinematografiche*, usually concerned only with censure and censorship, were among those documenting the gradual change from giallo to slasher *as it happened* is impressive.

It was only a matter of time before filmmakers in North America began to take notice of Bava, Martino and Argento. Two directors in particular, one from Canada and one from the United States, would take the elements gathered in *A Bay of Blood*, *Torso* and *Profondo Rosso*, combine them, add something of their own and codify the elements to make the finished product: the slasher film.

Bob Clark's *Black Christmas* (1974) features Margot Kidder, Olivia Hussey and John Saxon in a thriller that was subversive yet sophisticated, using the "killer in the house" template to create an engaging murder mystery that was nonetheless something more transgressive than much that had gone before in North American horror.

More than that, *Black Christmas* explored controversial subjects (unwanted pregnancy and abortion; the toxicity of traditional gender roles and expectations; alcoholism) in a mature and balanced way, and arguably finalized the template that we associate with the slasher film, at least in North America: a confined location (a sorority house); an unseen killer (hiding within the house); inventive kills (including a suffocation, impalement on a hook and Margot Kidder stabbed to death with a glass unicorn head); and even a final girl of sorts in Olivia Hussey (though not chaste, she is presented as smart, mature and level-headed). Several of these bear resemblance to the key tropes of the giallo, whereas others can be recognized as having come from Hitchcock's *Psycho* and from Coppola and Corman's *Dementia 13*. To these, *Black Christmas* adds, for the first time, the notion of the killings taking place on a holiday—something which of course would become a focal part of the coda, with a holiday featured in almost every subsequent entry's name, from *Halloween* to *April Fool's Day* via *Friday the 13th*.

At the time, the *New York Times*' A. H. Weiler called the film "a whodunit that begs the question of why it was made."[26] *Variety* was also unimpressed, asserting that the film was "a bloody, senseless kill-for-kicks feature, exploits unnecessary violence in a university sorority house.... Its slow-paced, murky tale involves an obscene telephone caller who apparently delights in killing the girls off one by one, even the hapless house-mother."[27]

While the *Segnalazioni cinematografiche*'s verdict was ultimately a conservative one, it was preceded by a reasonably thoughtful review. "These are 'thrillers,' which the unexpected conclusion is not enough to make different from the typical products of the genre. Although amidst inconsistencies and illogical elements that are also glaring, the mechanism of suspense never loses steam."[28] The Vatican's critic appears to be somewhat invested in the development of these thrillers, already recognized as moving away from the Italian giallo, becoming something else, something new.

The film's suspense is lauded by the Holy See's agent, even as the film is rendered unacceptable. "It works so well, indeed, that the whole story is immersed in a more unhealthy atmosphere, made even more turgid by the serious obscenities.... Unacceptable/negative."[29] Ultimately, the film appeared to be a little too effective for the Vatican; so potent is Clark's ability to build a tense atmosphere that the finished film involves too many negative elements for the *Segnalazioni cinematografiche* to condone.

If *Black Christmas* appeared to finalize the template for the slasher, it would be John Carpenter that would use the same coda and his own ideas to not only consolidate the template but create the most successful film of its kind since *Psycho*. In the end, it was Carpenter and cowriter/producer Debra Hill that created something so memorable it officially birthed a subgenre of horror. Nineteen seventy-eight's *Halloween: The Night He Came Home* began one of the most popular, profitable periods in the horror genre's history.

Carpenter's film took only the very best from everything that had gone before: the tension and once-in-a-lifetime shocks from Hitchcock's *Psycho*; the sleazy sex = death trope and the virginal final girl from Martino's *Torso*; virtually every successful element from Bob Clark's film, including the one Clark had added (the film is set on a national holiday, something that would become a firm part of the Slasher film coda). Carpenter even sought to include a visually arresting antagonist, taking cues from the various gialli of Bava, of Martino and Argento.

Roger Ebert praised *Halloween* for its ingenuity and its effectiveness. He also made the link to a certain film that, after 18 years, came home again, describing *Halloween* as "an absolutely merciless thriller, a movie so violent and scary that, yes, I would compare it to 'Psycho' (1960). It's a terrifying and creepy film about what one of the characters calls Evil Personified."[30]

Ebert would award Carpenter's film his rare four star review score (rarer still for horror films). Conversely, the *Washington Post*'s Gary Arnold was less enthused, stating that "this plodding exercise in sham apprehension would (not) look impressive even if one felt starved for morbid stimulation. Now at area theaters, 'Halloween' is far more proficient at torpor than terror."[31]

Meanwhile, the *Segnalazioni cinematografiche* appeared perturbed by the point of such a film, considering that "once again one wonders what such films can serve: morally lacking; typical scenes that are unhealthy and sadistic."[32] As it had with Martino's transgressive *Torso*, the Vatican kept its condemnation of Carpenter's film brief. It was swift and damning, not wanting to draw too much attention to something it considered so unhealthy as to have a potentially corrupting influence.

Of course, the film would receive that attention with or without the Vatican's endorsement. Though it may have divided critics, Halloween brought in a $70 million worldwide haul from a $93,000 budget.[33] Carpenter and Hill created a film that would capture the imagination of a generation, have people hiding behind their sofas at home and frightened to answer the door on Halloween night, and become the de facto figurehead of the movement that followed. The slasher film became hugely popular, graduating from drive-ins, grind houses and fleapits to sold-out marquee showings as well as taking advantage of the lack of regulation in home video releases. A slew of inspired auteurs, impresarios and imitators released their own low-budget, holiday-themed, utterly transgressive slasher films upon audiences only too willing to lap them up.

In August of 1980, Sean Cunningham released *Friday the 13th*. As already discussed, the film took inspiration from Halloween and from *A Bay of Blood*, and brought us the tale of vengeful Mrs. Voorhees and (in the sequels) her undead son, Jason.

Interestingly, in Italy the film's heritage was noticed immediately. The Catholic newspaper *Il Giornale*'s Massimo Bertarelli called Cunningham's cash-in a "rough and creepy 'giallo' with horror outlines, which overflows with blood and naivety, yet it has an undeniable suspense"[34] but assured the cinema-going public that "fans will risk jumping on the armchair from start to finish. The killer? The average spectator unmasks them in ten minutes, the police in an hour and a half, just long enough to fill the cemetery."[35] Already highlighted by the Vatican's own writers, it was slowly becoming clear to the critics of Italy that the slasher film was essentially the bastard child of the giallo.

The Vatican was not so upbeat about this latest addition to the canon, with the *Segnalazioni cinematografiche* damning Cunningham's template of "sex and violence repeated in an 'escalation' of crimes, of paradoxical and hallucinating situations. The film that lives in this unhealthy atmosphere cannot be accepted ... unhealthy."[36]

The *Segnalazioni cinematografiche* gave its verdict, but, of course, the film's killer would not stay dead, and nor would the box office. *Friday the 13th*'s success spawned a sequel immediately and, by 1984, a further two. The Vatican remained unimpressed by the slew of successful sequels for a film that it believed held no value and could only be considered unhealthy. The Holy See would continue to censure this franchise which, it asserted, contained "continuous references to the previous episodes of 'Friday the 13th' (that) unfold without a real plot; it is all a succession of murders, brutalities and lakes of blood where, paradoxically, the spectator does not even have time to get caught up in suspense."[37] Like the rest of Italy's Roman Catholic critics, the *Segnalazioni cinematografiche* noted and lamented what the slasher had forgotten from the giallo (even if the giallo was not exactly the Holy See's favorite filone). The Vatican's critics would emphatically state that *Friday the 13th* franchise was "a product to forget, without regrets. Unacceptable/heinous."[38]

In Canada, Nelson McCormick's *Prom Night* would be added to the slasher conveyor belt, with the *Segnalazioni cinematografiche* considering the Jamie Lee Curtis and Leslie Nielsen–starring slasher as "affected by a coarse direction that abruptly passes from one floor to the other without any stylistic justification and is resolved in the search for situations that fill the sterile story and dilate the duration of the film."³⁹ The Vatican lambasted the film for its "totally amoral atmosphere where all the characters sink (into the mire)."⁴⁰

John Carpenter's *Halloween* had kick-started what was becoming a phenomenon. Dino De Laurentiis, never shy to cash in and exploit another's success, would ensure *Halloween 2* went into production quickly. The resultant sequel would be criticized by the Vatican for having "little bite, little suspense, but above all without that critical and provocative charge

In Wes Craven and New Line Cinema's *A Nightmare on Elm Street*, Freddy Krueger (Robert Englund) stands before a stained glass window in a church, mocking Christ. Illustration by the author.

that films of this genre, if done well, possess."[41] The Vatican's writers still don't have a name for the slasher film but by now accept it as a new genre, something derived from but no longer related to the giallo. Here, the Vatican shows its exasperation with the popularity of the slasher film, complaining that this new template was becoming quite stale: "the direction cannot give it depth of story and of reasons that are not worth to justify the abundance of means used and special effects used."[42] The *Segnalazioni cinematografiche* determined that *Halloween 2* was not only unacceptable, it was "questionable/silly."[43]

By the time of William Lustig's disturbing, transgressive *Maniac* (1982), the *Segnalazioni cinematografiche* had entirely wearied of the slasher film phenomenon, of a template it now considered stale, and of the unhealthy content of these vicious serial killer films, complaining that "the film has its own stylistic coherence within the genre to which it belongs ... progressive tension, gloomy atmospheres and scenes of butchery. Everything, always according to the rules of the game ... doctrinally (the film) says nothing and the tensions are restricted to the disturbing scenes for the mixture of sex and sadism. Unacceptable/unhealthy."[44]

The truth is that the slasher template *was* becoming predictable and stale, with a number of cash-ins and sequels churned out quickly for the grind house and home video markets by producers who wanted to make a quick, easy buck. That the Vatican's writers could see this and wished to comment on it shows that the Holy See's critics were proving to be quite knowledgeable about the subgenre and sought to offer a more in-depth criticism than just to censure individual films. The *Segnalazioni cinematografiche* had followed and commented on the development of the slasher film from the gialli of Bava, Martino and Argento to the franchises of Carpenter and Cunningham, and clearly had an understanding of the horror subgenre, its roots, its coda and the fact that it was beginning to run out of steam.

In 1984 Wes Craven decided to turn his hand to the slasher subgenre and, in doing so, completely revitalized it. With the right inspiration (we know the stories by now: the Cambodian boy who tried to evade his dreams until one night, they killed him; the disfigured homeless man in the dirty hat and sweater that eleven-year-old Craven had seen from his bedroom window one night; the highly publicized child molestation cases in California) he begin to draft what would become *A Nightmare on Elm Street*. Bob Shaye of fledgling studio New Line Cinema picked up the script after others passed on it, the film was shot in 32 days for $1.8 million and made most of that back in its opening weekend.[45]

The tale of horrifically burned, supernatural child molester Freddy Krueger would take in more than $25 million at the box office in total,[46] refresh the subgenre and help Bob Shaye make a success of his New Line venture. It would also do something much more significant, something that a horror film had not done for a number of years.

For the first time since the Universal Monsters of the 1930s, *A Nightmare on Elm Street* created a movie character who would become legend, bigger than the transgressive, fringe subgenre that produced it, bigger even than cinema. Freddy Krueger would capture the imagination of the public via comic books, lunchboxes, MTV appearances ... and even intrigued the Vatican!

Catholicism looms large in *A Nightmare on Elm Street* and its sequels. Freddy Krueger himself is a perverse resurrection, returning as a dream demon after his murder at the hands of the Springwood parents to harvest the souls of their children. Later episodes (parts 3 to 5 specifically) introduce a wise nun who gives advice to our protagonists, with holy water, crucifixes and consecrated burials offered as the solution to killing him for good, as well as a showdown in a cathedral.

The pastoral evaluation of *A Nightmare on Elm Street* waxes lyrical like rarely seen in the Vatican review's pages, praising this horror film's "continuous succession of pitfalls, shots and breath-taking atmospheres"[47] and declaring it "a great show from start to finish."[48] The review was not done there, offering the film several compliments: "It is all a tension for the spectator who cannot relax for a moment. From this point of view the director was skilled and the film is flawless."[49]

Craven's film had clearly captured the imagination of the Vatican writer, whose review would continue to delve deep, discussing what the Holy See considered to be the film's artistic flaws: "the boundary between dream and reality is too indeterminate, the ruthless nightmare assassin chases people and nothing seems to save them, not even the constant recourse to prayers and the crucifix."[50] There was yet more from the *Segnalazioni cinematografiche*, as it examined the film for subtext: "The bad deed (the lynching of Freddy) performed by the parents falls on the children: the remorse felt by the guilty ones. Does it condition the young people to the point of creating these unbearable nightmares? The answer is not in the film; everyone interprets the story as he believes, given that (we think) it is intentionally ambiguous."[51]

The *Segnalazioni cinematografiche* would engage more fully with *A Nightmare on Elm Street* than it had virtually any other horror property to date, providing a thoughtful and nuanced review to rival that of any mainstream critic. It did, of course, eventually turn to the film's "pathological-morbid mood"[52] and declare it "unacceptable/unhealthy"[53] for Catholic audiences, but not before doing its best to engage the mind of the reader with a thorough and considerate review of the film and its components.

With *A Nightmare on Elm Street*, the *Segnalazioni cinematografiche* had responded not with vitriolic disgust or with empty-handed dismissal but with one of the most impressed and impressive statements on the horror genre in its half-century publication history. The Vatican's film pamphlet even discussed the effectiveness of the film's horror and gore effects, offering its consideration that "it is undoubtedly a film that disturbs and anguishes the spectator, which continually offers violent, unpleasant and gruesome sequences (repellent gashes, impressive wounds and burns, hideously disfigured faces, rivers of blood)."[54]

Over the rest of the decade, *A Nightmare on Elm Street* became a super-franchise, a behemoth that would go on to gross half a billion dollars.[55] Freddy became a cross-pollinating pop culture figure, getting his own TV show and action figures, appearing on MTV and leering from children's lunch boxes during the years he captured the attention of the wider world. As he became more popular, the films became less about making original scary horror movies and more about new gimmicks to power the million-dollar merchandising of the *Elm Street* venture.

The *Segnalazioni cinematografiche* was with the franchise all the way, carefully dissecting each film in its review and granting the series more time and energy that it did any other horror franchise.

On Jack Sholder's *A Nightmare on Elm Street Part 2: Freddy's Revenge*, the *Segnalazioni cinematografiche* would continue its praise of the technical merits and effectiveness of the horror, and did its utmost to engage with the text and the subtext, and evaluate whether serious topics could ever be fully explored by the low genres, considering that "a somewhat shrewd spectator will have to ask themselves what such productions are targeting, as the film in question ... so as to exorcise the fears ... tackles (sometimes with passion: for example, the fundamental theme of fear and of the many evil and terrifying drives that ... proliferate in the soul of man) serious topics, which would deserve a much more thoughtful and disturbing work."[56]

Though the *Segnalazioni cinematografiche* is criticizing the film in its dual roles of critic and moral guardian, its writer is clearly engaged with the film and intent on exploring it fully, opining that "these are certainly not easy, often rather arduous, issues that upset and leave [us] thoughtful for all their implications on the psychophysical, human and moral level. It is not a film of horrors, of bloody furrows on the epidermis of repugnant victims of other similar "happy events" that can be drawn from the top of scientific credibility, or intellectuals."[57] The Vatican's critic examines both the possession aspect of the film and the mechanism of "love's kiss" to free Freddy's poor teenaged host (which together of course imply the now widely understood subtext of the film that Freddy = repressed homosexuality): "to tell us in conclusion that Evil dwells within us, here indeed portrayed as an irreversible half-stasis and, moreover, he knows. The kiss meant for the boyfriend, young Jesse, given to the perverse and perverted demon who has now taken possession of the body of their beloved, far from making us remember the fairy tale of Beauty and the Beast ... tries to smuggle the usual happy ending."[58]

Once more, the Holy See is ultimately disapproving of the film but is also specifically disappointed by the director and his apparent dereliction of moral duty: "Very ready to make us believe in the simple idea that the Devil exists, however, we are trembling and credulous before the hypothesis that in the cellar of our house there is really a powerful monster, visiting our nightmares and making us liars and potential killers. A symptom of extreme spiritual frailty and, after all, also a nice alibi for any future eventuality."[59]

While this is quite a strong criticism of the Jack Sholder sequel, the Vatican's issue appears to be that the film essentially asks us to believe in great evils and then cannot provide a realistic good power to fight this evil, and that this is immoral and something the Christian flock would be vulnerable to, were the Church not there to protect them. It also considers that the film might provide an alibi or defense for anybody whose "future eventuality"[60] might involve becoming so spiritually corrupted by the film that it leads them to violence themselves. The review appears to be regurgitating the same arguments made earlier in cinema's history by the National Legion of Decency and, during the recent video nasties era in the UK, the National Viewers and Listeners Association—that horror movies are immoral and that the violence portrayed in these movies is certain to influence real-life violence.

That the critic does not dismiss these films but engages with them on an intellectual level and seeks to expertly pick apart exactly what is morally wrong about them perhaps suggests not only an appreciation of the artistry within them but that the Vatican has by now realized the reach and influence of this franchise, and of the slasher film in general. *A Nightmare on Elm Street* was becoming a global phenomenon, reviving a flagging horror subgenre, and the Vatican would have to work hard to convince potential audiences that these films that come complete with toys and other merchandising are in fact of a spiritual danger to them. Perhaps there is also a sense of hope that, by engaging in reasonably good spirits with the films, it might be seen as a more progressive institution and tempt the hip younger generation of apostates to return to the fold if they see the Church wants not to censure their favorite transgressive cinema but to engage with it intellectually.

Whatever the *Segnalazioni cinematografiche*'s intention, its critics' adulation for this particular franchise was in danger of giving them away. The writer signed off with a rather witty note about the future of the franchise, seemingly in anticipation of Chuck Russell's *Dream Warriors*, which would be rushed into production soon after: "The undaunted director then bursts out in the final snicker: his demonic Krueger is not dead even this time, he is incombustible, non-deformable, stainless and threatening. And, since there is no two without three, let's get ready—alas!—to new brutalities, to sulfurous flashes, to more chilling prostheses and to laughter."[61]

This admission that Freddy Krueger is not yet dead and will return once more continued throughout the *Segnalazioni cinematografiche*'s reviews of the Elm Street series but with a difference: changing from a knowing wink and a nod to, ultimately, a sense of weary resignation. Noting of Renny Harlin's fourth entry in the series that it makes "reference to the existence of an inescapable evil, precisely because he resurrects after each apparent defeat,"[62] it becomes apparent that the Church is not just lamenting the irrepressible nature of Freddy Krueger but by extension that of this hugely successful modern form of horror cinema and the Church's apparent failure to convince its flock of the moral peril of indulging in the Elm Street franchise.

It is in the Vatican's reviews of the slasher genre, and particularly the Elm Street franchise that we identify something of a grudging respect, combined with what could be an admission of defeat. In the 1980s, the mass apostasy of Italy, this new secularization fueled by the ineluctable facts of history (the Church's past alliance with fascism; its involvement in the shady deep state power cabal Propaganda Due in the intervening decades) was reaching hitherto unseen levels and causing the Vatican to further reflect on the spiritual distance between the Church and its flock. In this respect, there were bigger battles for it to fight than this one, against genre cinema. The modern horror film, the slasher, and its greatest icon, Freddy Krueger, had become inevitable, indefatigable and irresistible. It felt as though, in the Vatican's never-ending war on cinematic evils, this particular battle had been determined, and the slasher film had won.

4

Dinah, Daughter of Jacob

(The Vatican versus ... the Rape/Revenge Film)

There are few examples of genre film that have courted controversy quite like the rape/revenge film. From The *Virgin Spring*, Ingmar Bergman's tale of the rape and murder of an innocent girl and her father's violent revenge (itself based on a 13th-century Swedish ballad, *Töres döttrar i Wänge / Töre's Daughters in Vänge*) to Meir Zarchi's grungy and oft-censured '70s grind house classic *I Spit on Your Grave*, these are regularly the most brutal of films that appear to revel in male excitement at the physical and sexual subjugation of women. They personify the negative power of what Laura Mulvey coined as "the determining male gaze"[1] in her psychoanalytical breakdown of representation of genre in cinema, a "world ordered by sexual imbalance"[2] that commodifies women.

The subject has been repeatedly examined in depth, notably by Clover in 1992 and Heller-Nicholas in 2011, with the links between women's bodies and male pleasure closely observed, and the motivations of a number of directors discussed in a decades-long attempt to determine whether the rape/revenge film must be dismissed as an exploitative and sensational whole, catering to a demographic that perhaps it shouldn't with a message that is so easily misread as to perhaps be cynical and deliberate, or whether the themes within the work challenge that viewpoint and present transgressive but powerful stories that have worth to society.

In Heller-Nicholas' more recent analysis, the author would assert that "rather than dismissing rape-revenge as a single, unified phenomenon, it is time to ask what the significance of these films is—not despite but because of their complexities and contradictions."[3]

In the UK, the video nasties controversy of the early 1980s (and subsequent introduction of the 1984 Video Recordings Act that saw many genre films successfully prosecuted and banned) was peppered with examples of the rape/revenge film. No fewer than 13 of the 39 films prosecuted under the act featured scenes of brutal sexual assault among their objectionable

Scenes from Abel Ferrara's 1980 film *Ms .45*. Depicting Thana (Zoë Lund) in her nun outfit, gun in hand, and ready to shoot. Illustration by the author.

content: *Love Camp 7* (1969); *Night of the Bloody Apes* (1972); *Last House on the Left* (1974); *Exposé/House on Straw Hill* (1976); *Island of Death* (1976); *The Beast in Heat* (1977), *Gestapo's Last Orgy* (1977); *Axe* (1978); *I Spit on Your Grave* (1978); *Night of the Demon* (1979); *The House on the Edge of the Park* (1980); *Evil Dead* (1982); *Tenebrae* (1982). Roughly half of these films adopt an outright rape/revenge template for their narratives, and many would be subsequently banned across other territories, with some still banned or censored as of the time of writing.

Rape/revenge *is* a subgenre that looks to be moving in a more palatable direction. After decades of these films being largely written and directed by men, the subgenre has received an injection of feminist social commentary in recent years, with women's voices taking the traditional male-focused narrative and turning it into something more prescient. Writers and directors such as Leah McKendrick and Natalia Leite (*M.F.A.*, 2017), Coralie Fargeat (*Revenge*, 2017), Jennifer Kent (*The Nightingale*, 2019), Isabella Eklöf (*Holiday*, 2018), Melanie Aitkenhead (*Revenge Ride*, 2020) and Emerald Fennell (*Promising Young Woman*, 2020) have joined what was previously a very narrow field comprising Virginie Despentes and Coralie Trinh Thi (*Baise Moi*, 2000) and Janet Greek (*The Ladies' Club*, 1986) as authentic voices with the ability to create something both prognostic and entertaining within the form of the rape/revenge narrative.

A number of critical women voices have welcomed the change. Billson praises the films, in particular Fargeat's *Revenge*, for "asking us to look at (the protagonist's) ordeal through her own eyes"[4] ensuring that this "replaces the male gaze with the female one."[5] McAndrews goes further, highlighting Kent's *The Nightingale* and McKendrick and Leite's *M.F.A.* for resisting the urge to "revel in male pleasure"[6] and focus instead on the women's experience, noting "moments of detachment in both … (that) serve as foils to previous representations of rape in the rape-revenge genre."[7]

These films, and the discussion points around them, have altered somewhat since the rape/revenge subgenre gained popularity half a century ago.

Though Ingmar Bergman's 1960 drama *The Virgin Spring* arguably inspired the rape/revenge exploitation narrative, it would not be until the 1970s that the subject matter was taken up by a number of subversive directors in the lower genres and given transgressive life. Wes Craven's 1972 film *The Last House on the Left* is often credited as the first, the fledgling director marking his intent upon modern genre film by teaming with drive-in distributor Sean S. Cunningham to deliver a shocking shot in the arm to horror cinema that was very much based on Bergman's art-house classic.

Of course, others came between Bergman and Craven. The landscape between the art cinema legend and the doyen of darkness-in-waiting is not without scenery, with several notable examples of cinema using rape as inciting incident, and revenge as resolution. In the U.S., Russ Meyer was on his way to huge financial successes with his "mondo" skin flicks, and 1965's *Motor Psycho* exploited the act of rape purely for titillation purposes, prior to his (much-improved) follow-up *Faster, Pussycat! Kill! Kill!* In Italy, Giulio Petroni's 1967 western *Da Uomo a Uomo* (Death Rides a Horse) is a tale of one man's violent revenge upon the gang that raped and murdered his mother and sister at the outset but one firmly set within the spaghetti western filone. Burt Kennedy would continue this emerging trend with his 1971 film *Hannie Caulder*, a western starring Raquel Welch, Robert Culp and Ernest Borgnine, in which Welch's titular frontier wife is gang-raped, learns the ways of the gunslinger, and takes violent retribution upon her tormentors.

Perhaps the most interesting entry from the early days of the subgenre is Sam Peckinpah's 1971 release *Straw Dogs*. No stranger to transgressive cinema, the director would break from the western genre that was home to some of his most interesting works to adapt Scottish author Gordon Williams' psychological horror *The Siege of Trencher's Farm*. In the film, Dustin Hoffman's writer and pacifist abhors society's savagery, only to unleash his own capacity for violence when attacked in his remote country house by a gang of miscreants that includes his wife's rapist.

The film courted controversy upon release, with the same critics who had lauded Peckinpah's deconstruction of the western genre *The Wild Bunch* calling his latest film "a major disappointment"[8] and concluding, "Peckinpah's theories about violence seem to have regressed to a sort of 19th-Century mixture of Kipling and machismo."[9]

In Italy, the Vatican also had much to criticize Peckinpah for. The *Segnalazioni cinematografiche* considered that *Straw Dogs* "confirms the undoubted mastery that the director has of the profession"[10] but with a number of substantial caveats. First, it noted the "proposed metaphors" of the film's subtext were "obscured by grand guignol effects and sequences."[11] Second, the Vatican considered this study of vigilante violence to be a pessimistic thesis, built on morally shaky ground. "The film tends to demonstrate how violence is part of human nature (and that) it also overwhelms the people who, by character and education, should be the least willing to use it."[12] In the end it was "the pessimism of this thesis (alongside) the crude realism of some sequences of violence, the morbidity of scenes, situations and humour"[13] that justified the Vatican's judgment that *Straw Dogs* was not acceptable viewing for its domestic flock.

Already, the Holy See was starting to take a keen interest in this type

Looking detached and distant in Sam Peckinpah's 1971 film *Straw Dogs*, Amy (Susan George), wife of David (Dustin Hoffman), is reflected in the glass fragments of her husband's shattered spectacles. Illustration by the author.

of film, in its themes and in what effects they may have on impressionable minds, especially when wielded by intellectual directors. However, also of significance is that the Vatican's writer appears to completely ignore the brutal and controversial rape sequence (where Susan George's character at first resists her attacker, then appears to become aroused, Peckinpah giving the viewer the impression that what started as violence has somehow become a consensual sexual act). Of all the transgressions noted in Peckinpah's film, the central rape sequence is not mentioned by the Holy See's critic at all, an interesting omission.

In September 1972, John Boorman's *Deliverance* was released in cinemas. Craven's *The Last House on the Left* actually preceded it by one month but, because Boorman was an established director and a part of the "New Hollywood" gang of filmmakers, his film received wider distribution and was seen by far more eyes upon its initial release, as Craven's film reached audiences via a slow crawl across rural drive-in theaters.

Deliverance turned a tense survival thriller into a shockingly brutal affair as Ned Beatty's character became the victim of graphic male rape. The film would be released to both critical and commercial success, with even the *Segnalazioni cinematografiche* praising elements of Boorman's film "such as the originality of the story and the setting, the virtuosity of the canoe scenes, the expressiveness of the color photography, the adherence of the actors to the characters entrusted to them."[14] The Vatican's reviewer had particular praise for Boorman's apparently cynical thriller, stating that "as tragic as a story and bitter as a philosophy, the director's speech is stimulating: nature cannot be crushed or suffered, it is a character with whom it is necessary to (have) dialog. A similar balance is necessary on the part of every man and every group towards society, if brutish and destructive forces are not to be unleashed."[15]

Because of its narrative of man versus nature, the Vatican saw the film's merits and allowed it to be viewed, though not without noting that "unfortunately, the film also contains a very disturbing scene of homosexual violence"[16] and reserving its viewing to only adults of full emotional and moral maturity. Something that is of interest here (and that will be picked up on later in this chapter) is the Vatican's use of the term "homosexual violence." The *Segnalazioni cinematografiche*'s writer again appears reluctant to use the word "rape" (although here the act is at least mentioned, not ignored completely). This could be because the Church views all homosexual activity as sin: it would therefore mean little to the Vatican writer to make the distinction between consensual homosexual sex and sexual violence. What is perhaps just as notable is that the Vatican appears to view rape as an act of sex: it is widely considered that rape should *not* be referred to as an act of sex but an act of violence. The motive behind rape is never about sexual attraction or gratification: it is about power, about exerting such dominance over a victim that the aggressor can defile them in the most repugnant of ways. This is, however, an attitude that has developed over time, and perhaps was not as prevalent in the 1970s, which may account for the Vatican's consideration in its writing on the film. As this analysis of the *Segnalazioni cinematografiche*'s reviews of rape/revenge films continues, the Vatican's true attitude toward rape will perhaps become more apparent.

The Last House on the Left, Wes Craven's genre debut, shocked and appalled censors, earning its X rating as it kick-started the rape/revenge horror subgenre proper with a subversive twist on the 1960 Bergman film it was loosely based on. This nihilist tale of escaped convicts who kidnap, torture, rape and murder a pair of teen girls, only to unwittingly seek refuge in the house of the family of their 17-year-old victim Mari Collingwood (Sandra Peabody), was initially described by Roger Ebert as a "tough, bitter"[17] film and it shocked drive-in audiences expecting a less traumatizing experience than that which the director served up to them.

Wes Craven was raised by a God-fearing matriarch with a strong will. A Baptist pessimist, Craven's mother was strict, vigilant and ever suspicious. Craven was instilled with the fear of God (a familiar phrase to apostate Roman Catholics and a central cause of what Winell calls "Religious Trauma Syndrome"[18]—the serious and pervasive after-effects of religious indoctrination that remain even after the break from religion and require similar treatment to other forms of PTSD) from a young age, and carried it through to adulthood. Craven would admit, "I had so much rage as a result of years of being made to be a good boy.... I think when you're raised to be within such rigid confines of thought and conduct, what that does to a person is you think you are terrible if you violate the rules. It makes you crazy. Or it makes you angry. I'm surprised I never climbed to a tower and [shot people]."[19]

As an adult, Craven rejected the ideas of his childhood and began to lead a bohemian life. When he established a partnership with producer Sean Cunningham (beginning work as an editor on Cunningham's grind house exploitation films) Craven sought to hold a mirror to the world he knew. The director wanted to reflect the harsh reality of the Vietnam conflict that was being fed back to Americans on the television. He also felt the urge to finally rebel against his mother, pondering that "maybe Last House was just flying in the face of my Mother's judgment. You want to see violent? You want to see sick? Here it is!"[20]

Craven found Bergman's *Virgin Spring* an ideal source of inspiration, and soon crafted his relentlessly tense and anxiety-inducing study of pointless violence that introduced him to horror audiences. Sean Cunningham hand delivered it to theaters on the U.S. drive-in/grind house circuits, and the film itself genuinely shocked critics and audiences alike. Roger Ebert recognized the power of the film's philosophy, praising it for its realism in depicting the evil of men: "And there is evil in this movie. Not bloody escapism, or a thrill a minute, but a fully developed sense of the vicious natures of the killers."[21]

The film was something of a scourge in the UK, being refused a cinema certificate twice before having its home video release successfully prosecuted under the 1984 Video Recordings Act and becoming part of the infamous video nasty list. In rejecting the film, BBFC censor Stephen Murphy wrote that "we can find no redeeming merit, in script, in acting, in character development, or in direction, which would lead us to feel that this muddly [sic] film is worth salvaging."[22]

In Italy, the film proved incredibly popular among genre filmmakers because of its unflinching nature, and soon the *sfruttamento* (the system of exploitation that drove the video nasties) took hold and *Last House* inspired a filone. Many imitators and derivatives followed; some in an attempt to cash in on the film's notoriety, others simply to bring this daring, transgressive content to the home of the Holy See. Mario Bava's *A Bay of Blood* (1971), though already released and not a rape/revenge film at all, was soon repackaged as "Last House Part Two" and saw success on the same U.S. circuits as Craven's film thanks to international distributors AIP and, at one point, Cunningham, as both films would be screened as a double bill in some locations. Pasquale Festa Campanile's crime drama *Hitch Hike* (1977); Franco Prosperi's *Last House on the Beach* (1978) and Ruggero Deodato's video nasty *House on the Edge of the Park* (1980) all contributed to what became a strong current in domestic genre film but not before Aldo Lado's 1975 exploitative and heartbreaking *Night Train Murders* put a very Italian stamp on the nihilism of Craven's original.

Aldo Lado took to the notion of the destruction of innocence in *Last House on the Left* and exploited the earlier production perfectly. The subtext to Craven's film had essentially been to hold a magnifying glass to events of the Vietnam War, exploring the futility of violence and how it makes monsters of us all. In Italy, its themes would be adopted into messages that meant more to domestic audiences. Just like Craven, Lado sought to make the audience complicit in viewing the rape, torture and senseless death of innocent children, changing the setting to a deserted night train and, in doing so, preying very specifically upon the fears of Italian parents and grandparents who remembered life in the country under fascism. Travel was policed heavily under fascism, with Italian trains regularly patrolled by armed Nazis who, as well as looking to capture and punish anyone who might be attempting to flee the country, would routinely attack and sexually abuse young women traveling alone.

The *Segnalazioni cinematografiche* considered Lado's film to be "trivially expressed, scripted with little respect for logic and verisimilitude" and suggested it was "based on the naive little thesis that society is the victim of a violence that is generated by itself and from which he would not be able to defend himself if not using it."[23] The Vatican critic stops short of specifically mentioning "an eye for an eye,"[24] the tenet featured in the Books of Exodus and Matthew, referred to by Jesus in his Sermon on the Mount, but it is clear that it is this to which he refers: Christian critics of Judaism often point to this as an apparent example of the vengeful nature of justice in the Hebrew Bible, and refer to Jesus' teaching of turning the other cheek as a more palatable form of justice.

The Vatican saw nothing of worth in Lado's cynical exploitation, suggesting it was "committed more to painting the exploits of the hallucinating and aberrant trio (of antagonists), than to demonstrating his assumption. The director has overburdened the film with brutality and beastliness. Unacceptable/abhorrent, and badly copied from many films."[25]

For Craven's film that inspired Lado, the *Segnalazioni cinematografiche*'s review showed a slightly more philosophical bent, albeit one no less censorious. The Vatican tended to reserve its real ire for home-grown subversion, usually brutally paternalistic in its damnation of any Italian directors who sought to provoke or offend, while sometimes making an attempt to actually explore the themes and craft of their U.S. peers. The Vatican's critic suggested that "the story [of Last House on the Left] … shows that in today's world everyone is a potential murderer and that where the law of the jungle reigns, justice becomes a private affair"[26] before making "an absolutely negative judgment. Unacceptable."[27] The Vatican's writer notes that Craven's film does at least carry a message (a courtesy not extended to Lado's follow-up).

The outcome was very much sealed—Craven's was viewed as unsuitable for the country's Catholics, and Lado's home-grown effort was buried alongside it. That both films were deemed inadmissible by the Vatican was not the only aspect they shared: in each case, the *Segnalazioni cinematografiche*'s critic focused on the revenge aspect of the narrative and did not mention the rape aspect at all. Just as it had with Peckinpah's *Straw Dogs* (though not Boorman's *Deliverance*) the Holy See pondered on man's capacity for violence when faced with evil, but refused to engage directly with the abhorrent rapes that act as inciting incidents in each film.

Given that, in the case of both films it was the rape elements that led to the films' censure in other territories, it seems unusual that the Holy See would not condemn these sequences of visceral sexual violence. To gain an understanding as to why this might be the case, one must take in contextual matters not related to cinema at all but to the general attitudes of the Church toward rape.

The Roman Catholic Church has, of course, been beset by a number of scandals with regard to sexual violence. While its complicity in covering up the molestation and rape of thousands of children over several decades by many of its clergy is perhaps the most public it is not the only instance

4. Dinah, Daughter of Jacob

In Michael Winner's *Death Wish* (1974), Paul Kersey (Charles Bronson) holds a pistol, ready to unleash vengeance as his wife, Joanna (Hope Lange), is held by a freak (Jeff Goldblum) during a home invasion. Illustration by the author.

of the Vatican having a problematic view of sexual abuse. As explained by Hobbs, Church sermons on divorce highlight the existence of rape culture within Christianity, which portrays marital sex as compulsory, an obligation on the part of the wife to succumb to her husband's desires.[28] Hobbs dissects the influential factor of the Church sermon in determining men's beliefs and attitudes toward sex, to marriage, and indeed to women in general, explaining that "while many factors influence the formation of these beliefs, few discursive events are as important ... as the weekly sermon. Though biblical texts are undoubtedly viewed as the most trusted and valued sources of truth about how to live as a believer, the sermon is where the Christian audience can have these texts explained to them."[29]

That is not to say that Christianity's teachings on rape are entirely archaic and without nuance. The catechism of the Catholic Church teaches that "rape deeply wounds the respect, freedom, and physical and moral integrity to which every person has a right. It causes grave damage that can mark the victim for life. It is always an intrinsically evil act."[30] This modern teaching not only suggests that rape is a mortal sin; it also asserts that no victims are responsible in any way for what has happened to them or that they are in any way morally corrupted by having been abused[31] (although it stands at odds with the Church's stance on marital rape). It requests that they be provided support and counseling and that efforts be made to bring the perpetrators to justice. These teachings even usurp the Church's position on conception and abortion, asserting that any "woman who is a victim of rape has the moral right to prevent the pregnancy"[32] because the rape is an act of aggression, not love, and "the woman is not responsible for the action, and thereby has the right (to termination)."[33] Serpa notes that "at least nine women ... were canonized because they chose death over rape. They are considered patronesses of purity (and) patronesses of rape victims."[34] These teachings do suggest a more progressive attitude from the Church toward women and rape than that suggested by Hobbs.

Clearly there are contradictions in the Church's attitudes toward rape. The truth that rape "is always an intrinsically evil act"[35] cannot be easily reconciled with Hobbs' assertion that Christianity dictates an obligation on the part of the wife to succumb to her husband's desires (making marital rape permissible in the Church's eyes).[36] These contradictions are difficult to navigate from a moralistic point of view. Could it be this, then, that leads the writers of the *Segnalazioni cinematografiche* to remain tight-lipped on the subject of rape when critiquing a series of films for which rape not only features but is the inciting incident that the entire narrative arc hinges upon? To provide nary a mention of the plight endured by the protagonist, whether it be in order to condemn the director of transgressive cinema for using rape as a mechanism to titillate audiences, or even to enter into a discussion about whether or not the revenge aspect of these films could or should be justified? In discussing rape, and its celluloid depiction, does the Holy See risk inviting criticism of its own contradictory attitudes toward rape and its attitudes toward women specifically (remember that rape *is* at least tacitly mentioned by the Vatican's critics when it happens to a man: the "disturbing scene of homosexual violence"[37] in Boorman's *Deliverance*). While there is no dearth of topics upon which the Church could be credibly accused of hypocrisy should it attempt to censure them in film, rape may be the most serious, and therefore one that the scholars of the *Segnalazioni cinematografiche* might seek to actively avoid addressing.

We can consider the Church's views with regard to rape in different settings, and the contradictions implied, in order to make suggestions as to the reasons the rape portion of rape/revenge films is not given the attention we might expect by the writers of the *Segnalazioni cinematografiche*. When it comes to the revenge element, clearly given much more focus by the Vatican's clerics in their reviews, the reason is somewhat easier to determine: "Do not take revenge, my dear friends, but leave room for God's wrath, for it is written: 'It is mine to avenge; I will repay,' says the Lord."[38]

The seven capital vices (known more commonly as the seven deadly sins), are, in Christian teaching, abuses or excessive versions of one's natural faculties or passions, which give rise to greater immoralities that, in turn, can commit a soul to Hell. As articulated by Pope St. Gregory the Great, the seven sins are: pride, avarice, lust, envy, gluttony, wrath, and sloth. Vengeance is the embodiment of wrath; in fact. wrath is specifically described by Pope St. Gregory as "the inordinate desire for revenge."[39] Further example of Christianity's attitudes toward both rape and revenge can be seen in the story of the Defiling of Dinah in the Book of Genesis.[40] The parable tells of the rape of Dinah, daughter of Jacob, at the hands of a Hivite prince. In an attempt to make amends, the rapist's father asks that her hand be given in marriage (the implication being that, if Dinah marries her rapist it negates the act of rape), and her brothers later wreak revenge upon not just the rapist but every man in his city, forcing each to be circumcised before murdering them. Even in her own story, Dinah is not the focus; in fact she is barely present in the story, as an object. The majority of the 31 verses focuses on her brothers, describing how the revenge is plotted and carried out, and then Jacob's regret that his sons' acts of vengeance have proven effectively pointless and will only cause more problems for their family.

The Church is very specific in its teachings about anger and revenge, noting the difference between wrath and what it calls righteous anger, or anger about injustice in the world that leads one to seek to address the issue and restore justice. In the eyes of the Church, wrath offends against justice, since a person seeks not to right a wrong but to meter out a punishment (revenge). Wrath is often considered to be man's quickest route to Hell. St. Catherine of Siena said, "There is no sin nor wrong that gives a man such a foretaste of Hell in this life as anger and impatience."[41] The teachings of Christ guard against wrath and forbid vengeance by anyone other than God. Thus, the *Segnalazioni cinematografiche*, in its examination (and condemnation) of rape/revenge films, focuses not on rape but on what it sees as the glorification of revenge, a cardinal sin from which the flock must be protected at all costs.

It focuses on wrath.

Michael Winner's *Death Wish*, and indeed Winner's career on the whole, is something of an enigma. After the sly advertising satire *I'll Never Forget What's'isname* (1967) and war comedy *Hannibal Brooks* (1969) ensured Winner captured Hollywood's attention for a short while, the director took on this Dino De Laurentiis production, written by Wendell Mayes from a book by Brian Garfield. Originally intended for Sidney Lumet, *Death Wish* was produced and released in good time to at least attempt to join the same gritty but mainstream conversation as Scorsese's *Taxi Driver*, Friedkin's *The French Connection* and Don Siegel's *Dirty Harry*, as Briton Winner attempted to gate-crash the New Hollywood Renaissance with his own bleak, violent melodrama.

Through genre glasses, this Charles Bronson revenge vehicle was more of a violent action thriller than an exploitative shock picture, and might not necessarily be considered a straightforward rape/revenge movie (although there is a vicious sexual assault at the core of the film's inciting incident). But just as Aldo Lado, Franco Prosperi and Pasquale Festa Campanile had used the filone method to take the formula of Wes Craven's 1972 film in several different directions, so too did Italian producer De Laurentiis, who expected Winner and screenwriter Mayes (whose credits stretch back to 1957's Billy Wilder suspenseful aviation biography *The Spirit of St. Louis*) to provide something that would make a return on a modest budget and be redolent of recent films from other territories. *Death Wish* uses the shock value of its inciting incident to justify the absurdly hyperbolic violence that closes the film's vengeance arc. The film is not without social commentary, although it is not subtext; it is an overt message hammered home: Wes Craven's screenplay was informed by his own mindset as a conscientious objector to the Vietnam conflict; in Winner's film, Charles Bronson's character Paul Kersey is an objector (and combat medic) during the Korean War, as well as an architect and family man. Like in Craven's film, Kersey's angel of vengeance is not the original victim of violence;

rather, it is Joanna and Carol, his wife and daughter, who are brutalized (in graphic, cinema verité style), and Joanna later dies from her injuries; patriarch Kersey is the one who finds his justice in perpetuating the cycle of violence, which is written (surely deliberately) in a way that it could be a commentary on toxic masculinity and man's capability, or it could be explicit machismo intended to excite teen boys and young men in audiences. Watching Winner's film in the present day, it appears as though his and De Laurentiis' aim may have been to capture both audience demographics; to have its subversive, violent cake and eat it.

The *Segnalazioni cinematografiche* took a similarly curious view of this film that gleefully stepped either side of the line between thoughtful neo-noir and cynical exploitation. Upon watching *Death Wish*, the Vatican's critic heaped praise upon Winner, exclaiming, "The expert job of the director ensures his film a spectacularly compelling and highly elegant configuration, full of suggestive scenes and good characterizations (among other things rendered by excellent generics and a sure protagonist)."[42] The Vatican was intent on delivering "an objective evaluation of the work,"[43] but its praise eventually gave way to familiar criticism, as the review lambasted the film's "exasperated narrative approach"[44] when it came to the subject of vigilantism, citing "that private justice is the only means of curbing crime is a very dangerous affirmation, since it would lead society to excesses of violence typical of primordial life forms,"[45] asserting that any intellectual conclusion "is lessened and becomes both an invitation to greater public responsibility for the police and a call for the latter to an attitude of force."[46] Once again, the rape element of the film goes entirely ignored. It is the subsequent wrath and vengeance that stirs both the Church's interest and its ire.

Unlike other entries in the filone, Winner's film was regarded as "questionable"[47] but not outright unsuitable for Roman Catholics of a moral maturity. Once more, an overseas property appears to have been treated less harshly than domestic films with similar content.

It is quite perplexing that the Holy See was more forgiving of international cinema than homegrown efforts in this particular case. There is a clear attempt on the part of the Vatican's critic to engage with the film and judge it on its own terms, in stark contrast with the rest of the critical world. Roger Ebert described *Death Wish* as "a quasifascist advertisement for urban vigilantes."[48] The *New York Times*' Judy Slenfsrud noted that "the moviegoers ... don't just sit there in their seats calmly munching popcorn. They applaud and cheer wildly whenever Charles Bronson ... dispatches a mugger with his trusty 32 pistol,"[49] and the headline from Vincent Canby's review read "'Death Wish' Exploits Fear Irresponsibly."[50] Somewhat perversely, the *Segnalazioni cinematografiche* offers the least damning verdict of Winner's film. Could it be suggested that the writers of *Segnalazioni cinematografiche* were beginning to act not as paternal censor but growing as art critics and engaging with these exploitation nasties on a level hitherto unseen? Had the popularity of this subgenre, which featured strong, unpalatable messages about the deadly sin of wrath at its core, spurred the Vatican's writers to try to truly understand the material in order to give a parochial view that might influence cinemagoers? Or was the Holy See simply falling into a trap, naively accepting a bad faith argument indulged by many of the film's supporters? That director Winner sought not to exploit but to pose a moral quandary similar to those posed by Schrader and Scorsese (*Taxi Driver*) and Friedkin (*The French Connection*) to be considered by his audience in some depth? For whatever the reason, the Vatican appeared to be making an attempt to properly critique at least some of these controversial films of low genres, rather than just damning them outright.

Meir Zarchi's 1978 film *I Spit on Your Grave* has stirred up more controversy than most in the subgenre, and perhaps with good reason. Banned in several countries both at the time of release and on several subsequent occasions (and as recently as 2010 in Ireland[51]), *I Spit on Your Grave* is noted as a nadir both in the subgenre and in horror as a whole. Ebert asserted it to be "a film without a shred of artistic distinction. It lacks even simple craftsmanship. There is no possible motive for exhibiting it, other than the totally cynical hope that it might make money."[52] Though a variety of opinions on this most infamous rape/revenge movie have been added since, the original (and more censorious) critical voices are not without merit: the film contains a brutal depiction of sexual violence (a sequence with an entire half hour of screen time devoted to it) and carries a muddled moral message (the film strips an attractive female not only of her clothes but her agency, humiliating and denigrating her in the process, only to then empower that same woman to respond in a very simplistic and traumatic way—through a perpetuation of the violence committed upon her by the males).

I Spit on Your Grave soon found itself labeled a video nasty in the UK and prosecuted under the Video Recordings Act. It would not be successfully released in the territory until 2001, and even then only after seven minutes of cuts were made.[53]

The film has since been rediscovered and reappraised by (among others) Heller-Nicholas and McAndrews, and has come out with its reputation somewhat improved, but the subject of Mulvey's male gaze remains the crux of the film's controversy even now. Heller-Nicholas considers the film to be absent of male gaze, with the direction supposedly suggesting that the film wants its audience to identify with the woman at the film's center, not with her attackers.⁵⁴ McAndrews contradicts this assessment, asserting that from the outset, cinematographer Yuri Haviv's camera lingers on the body of Jennifer Hills (Camille Keaton) as a petrol attendant eyes her up and down, replicating the gaze with a lyrical movement designed to "paint a picture of male desire."⁵⁵ These conflicting views, both of which carry merit, open the film to a contextual contradiction: when we first meet protagonist Jennifer, she is shown to us both as an empowered young woman and as prey. Is it, perhaps, on the audience to look inward and reflect on ourselves, based on our perception of Jennifer during the violent assault that follows? Do we see her merely as prey, as an object waiting to be defiled? And, if we do, does that say more about us than it does about the film? *I Spit on Your Grave* is by no means an entertaining film, and nor is it meant to be; it is a grueling ordeal that dares its audience to try to survive to the end alongside the film's protagonist. With the above in mind, it

In a twist on the story of the rape of Dinah, daughter of Jacob, from the Book of Genesis, Jennifer (Camille Keaton) stands naked and defiant before the Shechemites in Meir Zarchi's *I Spit on Your Grave* (1978).

may well have been Zarchi's intention to present us with a moral choice, and see what appeals to our base instincts, in order to reveal something about each and every one of us and then silently judge us for the choice we have made.

That this debate continues even at the time of writing, over forty years after the film's release, is testament to *I Spit on Your Grave*'s lasting impact in the pantheon of extreme cinema.

In Italy, the film was not met with the same ponderous critical opinion that *Straw Dogs* and *Death Wish* had been. The *Segnalazioni cinematografiche* considered *I Spit on Your Grave* to be a "Truculent film"[56] filled with "abject violence ... episodes and moments of real brutality."[57] It also had plenty to say about heroine Jennifer "bonding, in the name of revenge, with horrific methods and instruments of death."[58] Note that, once more, the Holy See glosses over the rape sequence, not acknowledging it by name; instead describing it merely as one of a number of moments of grim but nonspecific violence. The Church is more concerned with how unpalatable Jennifer's wrath, her revenge, is. The Vatican also suggests that the film carries a "well-known message, which wants the American citizen to be more confident in doing justice for himself."[59] Here, the Church is (correctly) asserting that vigilante justice, something that is heavily romanticized in American society, is indeed a corrupting influence.

That the *Segnalazioni cinematografiche* asserts the picture's message is intended for American audiences is telling: in doing so, it is determining that this film is not meant for the Italian Catholic palate. Before pronouncing the film "Unacceptable/heinous."[60] the Vatican's pastoral review includes a wonderfully parochial parting shot, noting that "amidst violence, furious torture and the very limits of 'horror,' a beautiful river and the thick forests remain impassive: the only appreciable thing about the film."[61] In this tale otherwise bereft of moral value, the Holy See notes that the beauty of God's wondrous creations cannot be corrupted by the film's evil.

One can only spend so long dissecting controversial exploitation fare without considering Abel Ferrara; the Pasolini biographer, pornographer and famously cantankerous schlock auteur who has aggrieved censors more than most directors, who approached the rape/revenge subgenre in 1981 with *Ms .45*. It would be this film, and this Roman Catholic director, that would provoke a somewhat surprising review from the pages of the *Segnalazioni cinematografiche*.

Ferrara's film was perhaps the first in the canon since Craven's *Last House on the Left* to be truly appreciated by critics. Ferrara was already known for "working the gutter no-budget beat—a correlative to New York's no-wave punk music of the period"[62] his films derided by some, adored by others, but always engaging, with their ethic of obnoxious, intrusive art that has something to say and doesn't much care how it says it. Ferrara was considered a quasi–Warhol, with his visual art drawing frequent parallels to the music and other cultural elements of his home city.

Ms .45 tells what begins as a tragic tale but soon becomes a fable of catharsis and redemption. At the outset, mute seamstress Thana (Zoë Lund in an emotionally wrought central performance) is raped not once, but twice after leaving work one evening. First, a masked assailant drags her into an alleyway and forces himself onto her. Then, as she arrives home, traumatized by the event, she discovers a burglar in her apartment. The burglar forces her to undergo a further ordeal, and it is this one that proves too much. This time, Thana manages to fight back, bludgeons her attacker with an iron and places his corpse in her bathtub. Shock and trauma have overcome Thana, fracturing her psyche, and awakening within her a second persona, a dissociative identity that undertakes a killing spree on the streets of the Bronx, murdering any man who exhibits misogynistic tendencies. The violent narrative that follows culminates with Thana, dressed in a nun's habit at a party, wreaking bloody havoc on all the men gathered there.

Thana's arc is one of death and rebirth. Her name is an abbreviation of Thanatos, the Greek God of death, and it is clear that the multiple attacks Thana suffers at the film's outset have destroyed her, taking her innocence, her optimism, every positive trait she possesses. Her wrath, her revenge, is her rebirth; brought back from tragedy as a nemesis, a deity of destruction (the film's alternative title is *Angel of Vengeance*). Though Thana delivers violent vengeance, at no point does she seem akin to the male, patriarchal agents of retribution in *Straw Dogs, Last House on the Left* and *Death Wish*, nor does she mirror Jennifer of *I Spit on Your Grave*. Even in the film's most bloody and brutal moments, there is the clear presence of the feminine in Thana, and indeed of feminism.

That Thana wears the robes of a nun in the finale is no accident; the vestiges represent femininity, spiritual purity and, of course the mantle of martyr, as worn by the real-life nuns forced into abuse and sexual slavery within the Roman Catholic Church. Many instances of sexual abuse of nuns by the clergy are now known to have taken place across decades, even centuries, a systemic abuse problem that was covered up by previous pontiffs and finally acknowledged by Pope Francis in 2019.[63] The pontiff admitted the complicity of his predecessors, and even that these sexual abuse crimes were likely still going on. This subject will be discussed in more depth in the chapter on nunsploitation films, but the systemic sexual abuse of nuns from within the Church is worth noting here as it adds yet more complexity and contradiction to the teachings of the Church regarding rape. If Roman Catholicism teaches that rape is "always an intrinsically evil act,"[64] and that survivors of rape should be centered and provided support and healing, the cover-ups of a number of rape scandals by the Church cry hypocrisy and leave the Vatican on very shaky moral ground indeed.

It is likely that Ferrara, an Italian-American Catholic, was already aware of the many allegations of rape perpetrated on nuns when he started out as a filmmaker. Ferrara described being "raised in the middle of it, in a southern Italian family. My mother being Irish also thought I should go to church. We went to a Catholic school with 15 kids in a class (taught by nuns)."[65] Though it wasn't admitted publicly by the pontiff until 2019, the systematic abuse of nuns was common knowledge among Western Catholics, in countries such as the UK, Ireland and the U.S. (and of course in Italy). Priests believed that women became nuns simply to serve them, that they were effectively their property, and though they largely let it happen without intervention (in part due to the fear invoked by the power dynamic between clergy and flock), Catholics understood what was going on. As noted in this chapter and elsewhere, the Catholic directors of Italy, unable to criticize state and church directly for fear of prosecution, would often use their art to point a finger at these institutions and highlight their wrongdoings. As a Catholic director in the United States, a provocateur and enfant terrible, Ferrara would regularly feature Catholic iconography and point out the hypocrisy in Catholic teachings in his films.[66]

Ferrara as director is considered "faith-haunted."[67] He certainly understands the complexities and contradictions in Roman Catholic teachings, like those discussed in this chapter. He believes that religion should not be oversimplified and couched in exclusively negative or positive terms, and his films suggest a spiritual faith thrown into turmoil, frequently holding a mirror to the perverted beliefs of some Catholics that they can commit wrongs and remain unimpeachable if they do so in the name of their God.[68] In 1992's *Bad Lieutenant*, the titular corrupt, transgressive, sexually violent cop played by Harvey Keitel claims, "No one can kill me, I'm blessed. I'm a fucking Catholic."[69]

In interviews, Ferrara speaks wryly and provocatively of nuns being regarded very much as sex objects, describing one as "the spitting image of Angelina Jolie"[70] and asserting that "you'd have a field day if you got into that (sex with nuns) as a fetish thing."[71] Ferrara appears to be recalling the nuns in his school in the typical way an adolescent schoolboy might: sexualizing and fetishizing attractive women who were likely the only female company Catholic boys got to experience up close (Catholic boys and girls would often be kept apart, and sometimes still are, attending separate schools entirely). It is also worth bearing in mind that Ferrara is ever the provocateur, and fully aware that he is describing the nuns as objects, not as people in their own right: he is representing them as they were (and still are) considered by many priests within the Church.

At the time of release, *Time Out* praised Ferrara's "slick visual sophistication"[72] and commended the director for allowing "a coherent, if extreme, feminist position to emerge"[73] from his narrative. More recently, *Ms .45* has been reviewed and readdressed by a number of critics. Susan Wloszczyna considers the film to be "less concerned about exploiting the act of rape and more about a young woman fighting back."[74] Sheila O'Malley praises "the transformation she (Thana) goes through physically ... she's set free by violence."[75] Wloszczyna posits that, in the selection of her victims (Thana brutally murders any man who so much as irritates her), the film discusses the notion that rape victims are "asking for it"[76] by dressing provocatively or having an awareness of their own sexual potency. In Ferrara's film, it is the men who are asking for it and *Ms .45* is duly happy to oblige. If Ferrara was drawing attention to the objectifying and sexualizing of nuns in his interviews, in this film he is clearly empowering the protagonist to strike back against her abusers and oppressors.

In its initial consideration of the film's worth, the *Segnalazioni cinematografiche* was predictably damning of Ferrara's offering, asserting that "the film consists of the description of the executions. Any psychological in-depth analysis is missing."[77] Peculiarly, just like Wloszczyna and O'Malley, the Holy See's review fixated on the film's protagonist Thana's transformation. "The suspicion that Thana's madness is born, described without the minimum ironic detachment, is not an exclusive young protagonist illness"[78] states the Vatican's reviewer, asserting that Thana was driven "crazy because of the violence suffered. Something exploded in her after those tremendous experiences."[79] Though the reviewer describes it as a madness, what it is recognizing is a form of post-traumatic stress disorder brought on by Thana's ordeal, which is to blame for her dissociative episode and the reason why she follows her torment with a spree of seemingly meaningless violence. The Vatican's writer has, like Wloszczyna and O'Malley, watched *Ms .45* and been just as confronted and disarmed by the portrayal of Thana's character. Whether he wants to admit to the existence of any "in-depth analysis,"[80] the Vatican's writer has clearly been affected by Thana's ordeal and subsequent transformation, because half of the review is devoted to discussing it. This is a striking contrast to the reviews of all the previous films discussed in this chapter, where the *Segnalazioni cinematografiche* has shown little interest in the degraded survivors of rape at all; its concern more focused on the (usually male) agents of vengeance rather than the well-being of the (usually female) victims.

Perhaps this should be seen as some small cause for celebration: after concerning itself only with the cardinal sin wrath, with the brutal revenge portion of the rape/revenge film, the Vatican finally appears to have shifted, to have been confronted by the moral message, to have seen *Ms .45* from the woman's point of view and to have been touched by the experience of its protagonist, something missing in its experiences of other films, from Wes Craven's *Last House* to Meir Zarchi's *I Spit on Your Grave*. Rather than pontificate on man's propensity for vengeful violence, the writer of the *Segnalazioni cinematografiche* offers us a crude psychoanalysis of Thana, rooting her "madness"[81] in the trauma she has undergone. While it does not address Thana's suffering by name (once more, the word "rape" does not feature in the review at all), it is made clear that her bloody revenge is brought about by the trauma of her sexual assault.

This offers a catharsis of sorts that, after eight years and dozens of reviews, the Vatican eventually found itself capable of watching a rape/revenge film and seeing it from the woman's point of view. An exploitation genre film, made by a provocative and intellectual Catholic filmmaker from abroad, had stopped the Vatican's critics in their tracks. Finally, after so many errant critiques, it was at least tacitly acknowledged by the Church's publication that rape is a traumatic and destructive act, deserving of as much attention and consideration as the wrath and murderous revenge it instigates. Abel Ferrara achieved something his peers were unable to: to have his audience, his critics, and even the Vatican identify with the woman at the film's center.

It is therefore almost moot that the *Segnalazioni cinematografiche* condemns the film for even attempting to tackle such dark matter. "But you don't try even to touch the mystery of that improvisation of total alienation,"[82] it warns, before taking aim at the director, who "takes the inspiration (from the alienating event of multiple rapes) and packages the show with a series of situations that are repeated according to a unique cliché with a repetitively predictable outcome: the bad taste of a special repugnance."[83] The Vatican would go on to call the film "Questionable/violent. Crazy, evidently"[84] and of course render it completely unacceptable for the Italian public (who, by 1982, were growing increasingly disobedient and flocking to see these films in spite of parochial guidance to the contrary).

However, after the revelation offered in the body of its review, the final verdict is of less importance. What is of greatest significance is that, after decades of ignoring even its existence, the Roman Catholic Church appeared by the 1980s to finally be acknowledging the horror of rape (at least in the movies).

5

The Body of Christ ... Amen
(The Vatican versus ... the Cannibal Film)

> And he took bread, gave thanks and broke it, and gave it to them, saying, This is my body given for you; do this in remembrance of me.[1]

A common schoolyard taunt aimed at Christians by atheists is the accusation that they are cannibals, a status obtained via the Eucharist, as transubstantiation means the wafer and wine received during the Sacrament actually becomes the body and blood of Christ. It is a matter of historical fact that, during its early years, members of the Christian Church were persecuted by the Roman empire, and that this accusation was first levied in the second century.[2] Early Christian philosopher and apologist Justin Martyr confirmed in his *First Apology* that the Romans accused Christians of atheism (because they refused to worship the pantheon of ancient Roman gods), incest (the Christian concept of being united as "one family in Christ") and, because of the belief in the real presence of Christ in the Eucharist, cannibalism.[3] This persecution would form the basis of anti–Christian rhetoric throughout history. During the French wars of religion in the 16th century, Protestant and Catholic writers clashed often over the Eucharist and whether the eating and drinking of the body and blood of Christ was to be interpreted literally or figuratively.[4] There have been other such accusations, from the early years of Christianity through to the present day, each time refuted by Christian scholars and practitioners alike, but they are accusations that the Christian Church has never quite managed to escape from.

It is therefore no surprise that cannibalism in movies dates back to Italy in the 1960s, already highlighted as the time of the Second Vatican Council, which precipitated an unprecedented mass apostasy. The landscape in Italy was changing. A previously family-orientated, God-fearing society was entering what would become an extended period of existential crisis, and Catholicism no longer defined the country's social attitudes.

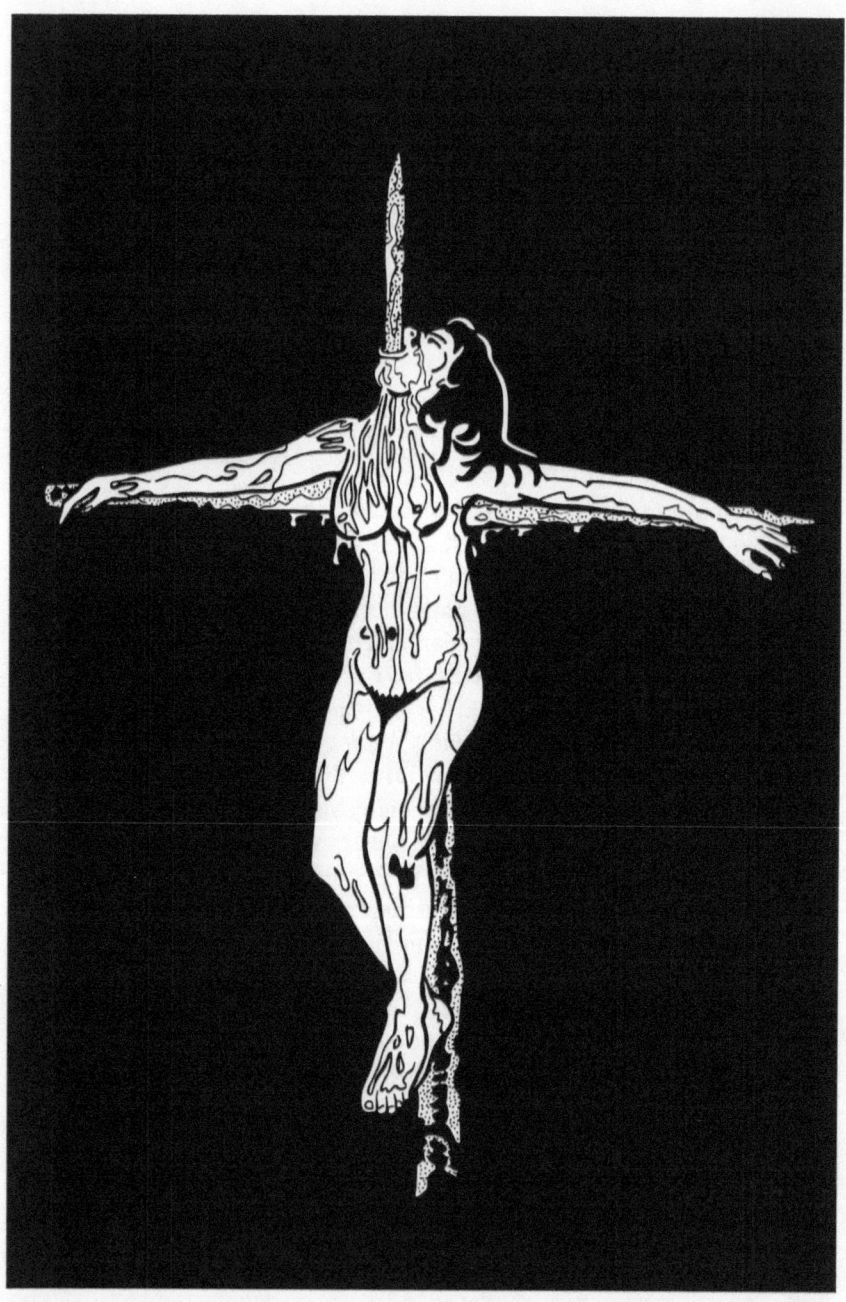

In Ruggero Deodato's infamous video nasty *Cannibal Holocaust* (1980), an unnamed victim's corpse is impaled on a spike and crucified. Illustration by the author.

5. The Body of Christ ... Amen

During this period, many of Italy's artists, both its most celebrated creatives and those working in low genres, would explore their apostasy through their work.

It is not unreasonable therefore to consider the act of cannibalism in Italian genre film as a corruption of the Eucharist. If the Sacrament could be considered cannibalism through transubstantiation, then the act of cannibalistic violence in genre film is the perversion of the Eucharist: not the body of Christ but that of humans (denoting the absence of Christ, and of God by extension); not given freely so that it may absolve us of venial sin, but taken from the unwilling in a celebration of transgression.

This chapter will examine the Italian cannibal film (and its direct predecessor, the mondo film) in the context of Catholicism, considering the cannibal film as perversion of the Eucharist. It will also consider the narrative critique that exists in cannibal films of the invasion and colonization of the Third World by white Christian missionaries. By doing so, and interrogating the Vatican's own reviews of cannibal films in the *Segnalazioni cinematografiche*, perhaps a greater substance than that previously ascribed to these low-genre video nasties will be evidenced.

It is *Mondo Cane*, directed by Gualtiero Jacopetti, Paolo Cavara, and Franco E. Prosperi, that is credited as the most direct and immediate ancestor of the cannibal film. Catt describes mondo films as "documentaries that downplay factual documentation in favor of sensationalistic exploitation. They are typically gross and violent, and they are often offensive to any number of different cultures."[5] Such films often feature racist portrayals of foreign cultures and staged sequences of death, murder and cannibalism. Jacopetti, Cavara and Prosperi birthed the genre with their film, its title a Tuscan colloquialism roughly translating to "it's a dog's life."[6]

Mondo Cane offered a whistle-stop tour of rituals and practices from around the world that were designed to titillate and revolt European audiences, including: the cannibalism and bestiality of a New Guinean Chimbu tribe (including a woman seen breastfeeding a pig); dogs in Taipei butchered and skinned before being sold for food; an Easter ritual in southern Italy where people beat their legs with glass shards and spill their blood on the streets ahead of a procession.

While the *Segnalazioni cinematografiche* noted that the film was "made with skill and a frank, journalistic narrative bite,"[7] it was ultimately decided that *Mondo Cane*'s substance was unacceptable, with "a cruelty in the film" and a "questionable inclination to the macabre and the horrid."[8] Nonetheless, the film took box offices by storm and the mondo film would become something of a global phenomenon, with dozens of productions over the course of the next 30 years.

As the mondo film's staged exposé of cannibalistic practices was taking root around the world, controversial Italian Pier Paolo Pasolini would borrow from the genre in his latest cinematic work of sacrilege.

A champion of taboo-busting sexuality, extreme political cynicism and casual blasphemy, Pasolini had clashed with both political and papal authority since his arrest in 1949 for "corruption of minors and obscene acts in a public place,"[9] a charge lacking in detail but thought to be punishment for his open homosexuality. Controversy would continue to dog both his personal and professional life, not least with his 35-minute film *La Ricotta* (a chapter of the collaborative anthology film *Ro.Go.Pa.G.* released in 1963). *La Ricotta* saw Orson Welles appear as an American filmmaker directing an adaptation of *The Passion*. Considered to be quite savage in its attacks on Catholic tradition, the film led to a suspended prison sentence for Pasolini on charges of insulting the religion of the state.[10]

Pasolini's 1967 film *Porcile* (Pigsty) tells two stories in parallel: In one, an isolated man (Pierre Clémenti) perpetrates increasingly barbaric acts of cannibalism in a volcanic hellscape, first killing then eating a soldier before becoming the leader of a group of rapists and cannibals. In these actions he finds freedom, joy, and a purpose. In another, the son (Jean-Pierre Léaud) of a wealthy industrialist and former fascist hides away from his family and from human relationships, choosing instead to lie with pigs. As his father first goes to war with a competitor then later becomes their ally, the son is eaten by the pigs he has tried to have relations with. In these two tales of transgression, Pasolini dissects the moral rot at the heart of the corrupt world he lives in, and nobody escapes his ire: whether Nazis, capitalists or the Church, all are denounced as monsters by the pessimist Pasolini. That he uses the tropes of the mondo film (the human/pig relationship brings to mind the New Guinean Chimbu woman breastfeeding her piglet) is both important and meaningless—Pasolini was an artist and poet who often brought elements of the low genres into his higher art and elevated them by crafting powerful political messages out of them. Clearly he has become aware of the mondo film and considers it to have tools worth using, but he merely raids the genre as he might any other for useful elements to provoke and incite audiences.

If Nietzsche proclaimed that God is dead, Pasolini asserts that we have eaten Him. Italy's greatest modern creative uses cannibalism to make this very point, thus it is the Eucharist, or at least a perversion thereof. The body of Christ (Amen).

The *Segnalazioni cinematografiche* considered *Porcile* "a film that goes beyond the limits not only of morals but of good taste and tolerability."[11] As often proves to be the case in its examination of Pasolini's films, the Holy See at least appears to express exasperation and apathy in equal measure, and when it suggests that "the author himself felt it necessary to explain the film's allegory ... through a sterile and paradoxical symbolism, mostly uninspired" it becomes apparent that the reviewer wants to explain Pasolini's controversial art away as being impotent, meaningless. However, that the *Segnalazioni cinematografiche* does this time and again with Pasolini suggests that there is a deeper frustration with the artist than the Church is willing to admit in its writings. The continued battles fought against Pasolini, the attempts to ban his works and to prosecute him through the courts (as well as the implication of Church and state involvement in Pasolini's murder in 1975—see the nazisploitation chapter), suggest that what the Church felt toward Pasolini was not apathy but anger and a modicum of fear. Pasolini was Italy's most verbose and influential poet at a time that the entire country was experiencing apostasy, shepherding yet more of God's flock away from Roman Catholicism, just as the Church scrambled to find ways to keep them.

The *Segnalazioni cinematografiche* condemned *Porcile* as a "completely negative"[12] film "with a tone between the grotesque, coarse and the elementary."[13]

While arch-provocateur Pasolini used tropes from the mondo to fuel his own interrogations of fascism, consumerism and Catholicism, the mondo film would stay true to its low-genre roots as more and more exploitative films about the nature of relations between man and beast (featuring liberal helpings of racism and cannibalistic overtones) were produced.

One such film was Antonio Climati and Mario Morra's *Savage Man Savage Beast* (1975). The narrative of Climati and Morra's film was one of animal/human interaction and featured various hunting sequences, many of which were (as was already the mondo way) staged but presented as authentic. Two scenes in particular (the first showing a lion attacking a tourist in Namibia and the second the murder of an indigenous South American man by a group of mercenaries) have gained notoriety as purportedly genuine footage of human death.

Both Climati and Morra had previous experience working in exploitation film in other capacities when they decided to direct a film together. Climati had served as director of photography on *Mondo Cane*, while Morra had worked chiefly as an editor on a number of genre films, including Fernando Di Leo's subversive war thriller *Red Roses for the Fuhrer*. Their film would earn them sufficient notoriety that they would go on to make a further two films in the same vein: *This Violent World* (1976) and *Sweet and Savage* (1983).

What is most notable about *Savage Man Savage Beast* is that it marks a waypoint in the development from the mondo genre to the cannibal film.

While *Mondo Cane* featured a wide range of unusual footage (including a parade of the "Life Savers Girls Association" in Sydney, Australia, and a massage parlor for drunk men in Tokyo), Climati and Morra made the decision to lean away from this sort of content and focus on hunting and murder, showing a brutal, cynical streak that was missing from some films of the mondo genre.

If the *Segnalazioni cinematografiche* had noticed the cruelty in the earlier *Mondo Cane* and all but dismissed the film's symbolism as "elementary...(and) sloppy,"[14] the overt cynicism of Climati and Morra's film was immediately apparent to the Holy See's critics, who hit out at the production in very robust terms. The "undoubtedly remarkable photography sequences"[15] were briefly appreciated before lambasting the film's "very evident search for the sensational, rather than the didactic, carried out with extreme cynicism and with no respect for the viewer."[16] The reviewer also highlighted the film's racist overtones, recognizing that "the constant reference and parallel between the degeneration of the art of hunting and the religious spirit of the peoples is not only anti-scientific, but also of a visceral and evil demagoguery."[17] The Vatican was clearly quite incensed by Climati and Morra's apparent lack of journalistic ethics, explaining in no uncertain terms that, in their determination to present some of the on-screen atrocities, the directors "leave at least the suspicion of complicity or partial co-responsibility: if, as the work claims, certain types of hunting are condemnable, this way of conceiving the cinematic hunt for aberrant images is even more so."[18]

Meanwhile, in the United States, a pair of young directors would unleash their own cannibalistic terrors upon the world for their sophomore releases. After inauspicious starts, both Tobe Hooper and Wes Craven turned to the horrors of a different kind of savage, home-grown cannibal clans based very much on real-life legends.

In 1974, Tobe Hooper directed one of the most influential and emulated movies of the last 50 years, a tale of a group of counterculture-influenced young adults traveling across the Texas plains, soon captured, trapped and tortured by the secluded Sawyer family. Draped in human skin and wielding chain saws and meat hooks, the film's antagonists captured an image that reflected the most visceral fears of a certain cross section of America at the time.

At the time of *Texas Chain Saw*'s release, the crimes of American Ed Gein and other serial killers were very much at the forefront of the public consciousness. Paul John Knowles (the Casanova Killer) was tied to the deaths of 18 people between August and November of 1974, before he was captured by Vietnam War veteran David Clark, handed over to the Georgia Bureau of Investigation and later shot to death when he allegedly attacked his captors. Both Ted Bundy and Dennis Rader (the BTK Killer) committed their first murders in 1974. John Wayne Gacy committed his second. Carl "Coral" Eugene Watts (the Sunday Morning Slasher) murdered an estimated 90 young women in an 8-year spree that began ... in 1974. There were, of course, other traumas in the minds of Americans in 1974 as well. Vietnam was ongoing; a global arms race was in the news; the Watergate scandal was about to topple President Richard Nixon.

While very much an American production with American influences, substituting bohemian teens for Christian missionaries, *The Texas Chain Saw Massacre* was a film clearly influenced by the mondo flicks of Jacopetti, Cavara and Prosperi, and of Climati and Morra. There were nods to that same narrow view of indigenous peoples as savages. The name and practices of chief antagonist Leatherface was certainly meant to reflect the customs of Native American and Inuit tribes, who would both create and wear masks and dolls made of animal hides.[19] Hooper used handheld cameras and grimy 16mm film stock to achieve a cinema verité style that lent an element of realism sufficient enough to see the film banned in several territories, gaining a notoriety in horror that had not really been seen before, and would not be matched until the early 1980s and the advent of the video nasty era. Like Craven's *Last House on the Left*, in many ways this shocking piece of exploitation surpassed all that had gone before to become the ultimate modern horror progenitor, still credited today as among the most sadistic, censor-baiting films ever made.

Tobe Hooper's unrelenting and all too realistic movie massacre very much nailed the zeitgeist, and was rewarded for it to the tune of $30 million from the domestic box office—a pretty good return from its $140,000 budget. Hooper's film managed this feat despite being pulled from many theaters due to complaints about its violence and gore. It would go on to be banned in 10 countries (Brazil; France, West Germany, Australia, Finland, Norway, Great Britain, Sweden, Singapore, Iceland) yet still managed to draw a staggering $235 million worldwide. While Hooper's film wasn't outright banned in Italy, *The Texas Chain Saw Massacre* did come in for some heavy criticism by the Vatican.

The *Segnalazioni cinematografiche* considered that "this hallucinatory story ... is so inhuman that it is not credible at all. The monotonous and obsessive work describes itself with an extreme abundance of macabre and aberrant details. The lack of plausibility and appreciable justifications, either psychological or social, leads us to think that it is a show of bad taste, conceived and created for the benefit of abnormal people to be definitively plunged into the abyss of dehumanization."[20]

These were strong words, even for the Vatican. In a rare reversal, the Holy See's writers were more damning of this American horror than they

In Tobe Hooper's 1974 shocker *The Texas Chain Saw Massacre*, Leatherface (Gunnar Hanssen) stands in his prize room, skulls and bones hanging around him. There appear to be a number of crucifix formations. Illustration by the author.

were anything similar coming from domestic directors. To suggest that anybody willing to see this movie is essentially inhuman, and destined only for "the abyss"[21] (a common synonym for biblical Hell) shows the strength of the Holy See's fervor for this shocking, visceral film. For the Vatican to equate seeing this movie with mortal sins (the only infractions that would instantly condemn a soul to Hell's eternal fire) represented either an incredible exercise in hyperbole or the reflection of the visceral terror that the Vatican felt upon viewing Tobe Hooper's grind house masterpiece.

After starting his directorial career with the rape/revenge cult classic *Last House on the Left*, Wes Craven continued to work in supplying genre films to the grind house circuit before his sophomore feature, 1977's *The Hills Have Eyes*. Craven's tale of survival and revenge was partly inspired by Hooper's earlier cannibal horror masterpiece but also loosely based on a true story—the mountain-dwelling cannibal family that wreaks havoc on the caravanning all–American Carter family was partly inspired by Alexander "Sawney" Bean, the feral Scotsman who (along with his 14 equally depraved children) killed and ate anybody unlucky enough to cross paths with him in 16th century East Lothian.[22] In Craven's movie, the setting is updated to the present day Nevada desert, with Papa Jupiter (James Whitworth) and his children representing Bean and his clan. The Jupiter clan lived in caves near a nuclear bomb testing site, the implication being that radiation had mutated them and turned them into cannibals.

Once again, bohemian Craven was concerned by the Vietnam War and its chilling effects on the American people. In the U.S., the events of the war had left Americans in a period of intense introspection, wondering about their place in the wider world, and the government's treatment of its own people. The young director juxtaposed this feeling, of a people alienated by its own government, with the horrors of the country's colonial history, and of the first settlers and their wars upon the indigenous peoples of North America. Craven added a third element to his film, incorporating personal experiences on the road into his narrative. On a motorcycle road trip, the erudite and conservative Craven had stopped in the Nevada desert to eat and refuel. Here, Craven had come under attack, as a trio of young local men in a pickup truck fired arrows that narrowly missed him, before threatening to murder him. According to Zinoman,[23] this altercation provided a seed of inspiration for what would become *The Hills Have Eyes*.

In *The Hills Have Eyes*, Jupiter's wild cannibal clan steals the Carter family's infant child (a plot device taken from John Ford's schismatic western *The Searchers*, just as *The Last House on the Left*'s plot had essentially been borrowed wholesale from Bergman's *The Virgin Spring*) and it is up to the everyman Carters to tap into their own savage side in order to defeat their foes and rescue their infant. Craven's film was a resounding critical and commercial success, winning the International Critics' Jury Prize at the Sitges International Fantastic Film Festival Catalonia and earning $25 million from box offices against its $300,000 budget,[24] adding to evidence that the young director had a knack for tapping into prescient fears and creating modern horror that went over well with bloodthirsty genre audiences while echoing the themes of classic mainstream and art house cinema.

The Vatican took aim at the prizewinning film, warning that "the film's advertisement announces: 'first prize at the Sitges Film Festival and judged best film of the year at the Horror Film Academy' ... we have no reason to doubt this news, but are obliged to translate it into a warning: given the nature of the film, one might think that the Sitges Festival and the Horror Academy are welcomed by amateurs of the worst that cinema can possibly put into images; only in this way is their enthusiasm understandable."[25] In an attempt to undermine the film's achievements and clever marketing campaign by criticizing the institutions that celebrated it, the review went on to dismiss *The Hills Have Eyes* as "an anthology of bad effects, of inhumanity, of low butcher details, of stomach-turning figures and actions"[26] and the Vatican's writers considered of Craven that "the director, as well as screenwriter, editor and producer (all Craven), will also be a genius in the subject he prefers; but we do not believe that this matter can be in any way pleasant for the common spectator and we are sure that one cannot participate in this cruelty and remain immune from dehumanizing reactions. Unacceptable/heinous."[27] As it had with Tobe Hooper's *The Texas Chain Saw Massacre*, the Vatican had censured Craven's film with even more fervor than it had the domestic productions of Climati, Morra et al., an unusual step given its usual preference for judging homegrown genre filmmakers much more harshly than their American counterparts. With *The Hills Have Eyes*, as with *The Texas Chain Saw Massacre*, the Holy See saw a "heinous"[28] film that was not just unacceptable but "dehumanizing,"[29] something Italian audiences must be protected from at all costs.

The mondo genre would continue to flourish, and the success of Hooper's *The Texas Chain Saw Massacre* and Wes Craven's *The Hills Have Eyes* helped give birth to the cannibal filone proper, which quickly spread across Italy and beyond. Joe D'Amato would combine the cannibal film with the softcore pornography Emmanuelle series in 1977's *Emmanuelle and the Last Cannibals*. Sergio Martino's 1978 *The Mountain of the Cannibal God* would crack the U.S. market by using household name and Bond girl Ursula Andress to appeal to North American audiences. In Spain, cult super producer/director Jesús Franco would also get in on the act, churning out both *Devil Hunter* and *Mondo Cannibale* in 1980. While the filone was proving popular enough with genre audiences both in Italy and the U.S., it would not be until 1980 that it would truly leave its mark upon the world, with a director and a film whose names remain synonymous with extreme and controversial cinema.

Ruggero Deodato, a stalwart of the video nasty era in general, would direct three cannibal exploitation pictures over the course of a decade, beginning with 1977's *Jungle Holocaust*. The first two of Deodato's three entries featured what is now considered to be the genre canon: a documentary style (the audience is led to believe that it is viewing "real" footage, recovered after genuine expeditions); a narrative critique of the invasion and colonization of the Third World by white Christian missionaries (characterized by various "native tribes" of remote lands who practice cannibalism and who view their white interlopers with suspicion that later turns to anger and violence over a threat, abuse or sacrilege); sexual violence; animal cruelty (sadly, while the other elements of the cannibal genre film are sensationalized fiction, the animal suffering presented on screen is real, and many creatures were tortured and killed needlessly in the name of entertainment).

Cannibal Holocaust remains one of the most notorious films ever released. A centerpiece of the UK video nasties controversy and prosecuted by the courts, it was banned in the UK from its 1980 release until 2001, and was denied certification in several other countries (including the U.S., Australia, Norway and Singapore).[30] The film is rich in transgressive, pseudo-religious symbolism. Though superficial in execution, *Cannibal Holocaust* levels an anti-imperialism criticism at the invading white characters. The audience is asked to consider who are the real savages here, the cannibalistic South American tribe or the white filmmakers who invade their lives and treat them as less than human. When the indigenous people turn on the white interlopers, it becomes clear that their cannibalism is indeed a perversion of the Eucharist—it is the consumption of Christian flesh that takes place, although their bodies are not offered freely but taken in an act of transgression. In addition to the corrupted Eucharist, one of the film's most powerful single images—a tribeswoman impaled on a wooden spike—itself functions as a bastardized crucifixion.

In Deodato's home country of Italy, the film earned both itself and its director even more notoriety than abroad. Ten days after its Milan premiere, the movie was confiscated by authorities and Deodato was arrested and charged with murder.[31] Due to the documentary style of the film, authorities believed it to be a snuff movie, and Deodato was forced to prove his innocence in court: the actors who played the "murdered" characters had to appear in person to prove they were, in fact, very much alive, and Deodato had to demonstrate how he had achieved realistic practical effects such as women impaled on spikes.[32] Though he escaped the murder charge, Deodato received a suspended jail sentence for obscenity[33] and the film was banned in Italy due to the on-screen animal cruelty.

Deodato did his best to continue to provoke, directing home invasion/class war parable *The House on the Edge of the Park* (another film that

Inside a skull, a cannibal tribeswoman devours human entrails in *Cannibal Holocaust*. Illustration by the author.

made the UK's video nasty list) the same year, but *Cannibal Holocaust* had significantly harmed his career prospects and he saw few opportunities in other filones. In 1985 he returned to the movie that earned him his reputation, in an attempt to recapture his past glory, when his producers requested a sequel to *Cannibal Holocaust*.

Inferno in diretta (Cut and Run) follows a reporter (Lisa Blount) and her cameraman investigating a war in the jungles of South America between drug cartels and a cannibal army led by a Jonestown survivor turned army colonel. As an exercise in Deodato-level gore, *Cut and Run* offered a smörgåsbord of grisly delights, from realistic beheadings to bodily dismemberment, rape and torture. The film also works as a commentary on the relationship between rich and poor parts of the world, offering analysis on the exploitation of the poor nations of South America by rich white interlopers while striking a note of caution by way of the visceral violence outsiders may be subjected to if they stray too far into the unknown. Where the film differed from Deodato's previous cannibal entries was that it was not particularly shocking fare at all. Where *Cannibal Holocaust* used a cinema verité style and sequences of stomach-churning animal cruelty to successfully give it that sense of realism that fooled audiences, censors and state authorities alike, *Cut and Run* was a slickly produced, ostentatious attempt to embrace the violent, over the top action vehicles of the 1980s (while stealing heavily from *Apocalypse Now*) that set it worlds apart from what is still considered one of the most shocking movies ever made. As a result, the film represented, unfortunately, a death knell. Deodato directed only four more films in the 1980s, all low in budget and quality (including the comically execrable 1988 fantasy film *The Barbarians*) before his output became much more sporadic. Despite being probably Deodato's most technically excellent film, *Cut and Run* was a sign of an exploitation provocateur willing to exploit his own past glories in order to stay in work.

Because *Cannibal Holocaust* had quickly secured an enduring state ban in Italy, there was neither requirement nor need for the *Segnalazioni cinematografiche* to review it. In the case of *Cut and Run*, however, the Holy See had lots to say about the film's contents, which "exude chilling cruelty from every effect and... (are) literally studded with gruesome atrocities, very often gratuitous."[34] The *Segnalazioni cinematografiche*'s censure of *Cut and Run* does not seem commensurate with the content and quality of the film: though it was a graphically violent offering, by the mid–1980s the Vatican had seen more than its share of violence and gore, and tended not to waste too much time indulging this type of content. Here, the Vatican's critic seemed almost to be giving his opinion not on *Cut and Run* but on the director's earlier cannibal content, positing that Deodato's on-screen cruelty was "so much as to make Jack, the London Ripper, turn pale"[35] and pronouncing the film as not just unacceptable but "heinous."[36] Having been denied the opportunity to speak out on Deodato's most infamous film due to its state ban, the Church was making up for it by censuring Deodato now.

It is worth noting that, despite his reputation, the Vatican stopped short of condemning Deodato quite as strongly as it had Climati and Morra, even Hooper and Craven. Could it be that, unlike the courts who accused Deodato of murder, the Vatican had come to understand that these cannibal films were works of fiction, as opposed to the earlier mondo entries which were very clearly and deliberately sold to the public as documentaries of real-life events? As a result, did the Holy See view the domestic cannibal film as significantly less harmful to its flock than the barbaric pseudo documentaries of the mondo genre?

Entirely absent from the *Segnalazioni cinematografiche*'s critique of the cannibal genre so far is any mention of cannibalism as a perversion of the Eucharist, or of the anti–Christian missionary narrative present in these films. In some instances what the Vatican does not say in its reviews can be as revealing as what it does, but here this appears not to be the case. Beyond the criticisms of Pasolini's allegorical content and the accurate accusations of demagoguery in the mondo films, there are no depths to explore, no subtexts to reveal in the *Segnalazioni cinematografiche*'s criticisms of the filone. Are the Vatican's writers choosing to ignore the commentaries on Western Christianity's crusades, on the myriad missions the Church has made around the world to force a white Jesus upon indigenous peoples and change their ways of life by coercion? Or is it that there is not enough substance within the filone for the Holy See to acknowledge and therefore warrant a response?

Whatever the reason, one director's work would change that, creating what many consider the definitive Italian cannibal film (even above Deodato's *Cannibal Holocaust*) and the one such genre production that would not just clearly point its finger at the Church: it would provoke a response.

By the time Deodato had achieved infamy with *Cannibal Holocaust*, Umberto Lenzi had already made waves in the genre with 1972's cannibalistic adventure film *The Man from Deep River*. Unlike Deodato, Lenzi spent the decade that followed directing a dozen or so films across a number of filones and genres, becoming celebrated for his gialli, war films and especially his crime dramas.

Lenzi was a graduate of Rome's Centro Sperimentale di Cinematografia (Italy's most prestigious film school, staffed by the likes of Roberto Rossellini and Luchino Visconti and with alumni ranging from Michelangelo Antonioni and Pietro Germi to Lucio Fulci). A disciple of Pier Paolo Pasolini, he had cut his teeth in the 1960s and early 1970s on adventure films, spy thrillers and spaghetti westerns before turning to darker material.

Lenzi had made inroads into the cannibal genre with 1972's *The Man from Deep River*, a slightly more mature adventure film that mixed elements of the western genre (most notably Elliot Silverstein's 1970 film *A Man Called Horse*) with the graphic sensationalism of *Mondo Cane*. By the time Lenzi returned to the genre in 1980, Deodato and others had already popularized the cannibal exploitation filone. Lenzi's 1980 film *Eaten Alive!*, about a young woman (Janet Agren) who is searching for her sister after her abduction by a cult in the jungles of New Guinea, employed all the developed tropes to add to the pantheon, but it was 1981's *Cannibal Ferox* that took things to the next level. The film is about anthropologist Gloria Davis (Lorraine De Selle), who travels to Colombia to prove her belief that cannibalism is a racist myth, only to encounter other white interlopers who want to exploit the indigenous people for emeralds and cocaine. The native tribespeople turn on their intruders, hunt them, and of course indulge in displays of savage torture and cannibalism (including a vomit-inducing castration sequence).

Bitel asserts, "*Cannibal Ferox* fully deserves its reputation as one of the genre's toughest watches,"[37] and it is hard to disagree. Lenzi's film is presented as a circumscribed reality: not quite the "found footage" style of Deodato's *Cannibal Holocaust* but definitely presented in that cinema verité style, documentary at least until it becomes sensationalized and exploitative itself.

"My thesis claims that cannibalism as an organized practice of human society does not exist, and historically has never existed. Let's say it was an invention of racist colonialism which had a vested interest in creating the myth of the ferocious subhuman savage fit only for extermination. The mythical lie of *Cannibal Ferox* was only an alibi to justify the greed and cruelty of the conquistadores."[38]

There is a sense in the above passage from the film that Lenzi wants to have his cake and eat it. It's important to the director (who also wrote the screenplay) that cannibalism is acknowledged as a myth, invented by

In Umberto Lenzi's shocker *Cannibal Ferox*, Gloria (Lorraine De Selle) is bound as a tribesman force-feeds her human flesh in a perversion of the Eucharist. Illustration by the author.

white Christian colonizers to dehumanize the indigenous peoples they sought to exploit. However, he himself continues the exploitation by portraying the indigenous people of Colombia as savage cannibals despite his own assertions otherwise.

Primarily though, Lenzi has the Catholic Church in his sights. His use of Latin in the film's title is a very deliberate signal to the Church and one that the writer of the *Segnalazioni cinematografiche* picked up on: "When science stumbles upon cinema outside the rigorous documentary, it proves to be trouble for everyone: for science, for cinema, and for the audience. No exception to this almost absolute rule is a film which, from its half–English, half–Latin title, reveals the double hit of foolishness and ridicule."[39]

The review notes Lenzi's use of Latin, the mother tongue of Roman Catholicism, and ridicules his directorial hypocrisy. However, in unpacking Lenzi, the reviewer accidentally reveals the Church's own attitude toward indigenous peoples. The *Segnalazioni cinematografiche* determines that anthropologist Gloria's assertion that cannibalism is a racist invention is naive and based on underwhelming evidence. The reviewer explains that "cannibalism is one of the most universally documented practices by Homer, to Strabo, to Pliny, San Girolamo, up to the travelers, explorers and anthropologists ... of neighboring countries in present day."[40] Here, the Holy See is essentially defending Christianity's view (and treatment) of indigenous peoples throughout the ages. By accusing them of still indulging in cannibalism "in present day,"[41] the Church attempts to justify its view that even now the indigenous peoples of South America are indeed savages who need to be tamed by white Christianity.

Finally, after Deodato, after Climati and Morra and all the others, it is Lenzi, the classically trained disciple of Pasolini, who manages to tease an admission from the Church, a tacit acknowledgment of its view of indigenous people around the world (which is exactly what each of these Italian directors, all of whom are part of a country undergoing mass apostasy, are attempting to address in the cannibal film).

The genre would continue into the late '80s, with notable entries including Mario Gariazzo's 1984 film *Amazonia: The Catherine Miles Story*. In an extra layer of exploitation, the film carried the alternative title of *Cannibal Holocaust 2* in an attempt to entice fans of Deodato's controversial cult film to watch what was actually more melodramatic love story than horror movie. The film's protagonist (played by Elvire Audray) is the teenage daughter of wealthy plantation owners who flaunt their privilege and entitlement by taking pleasure cruises along the Amazon to celebrate the young debutante's graduation from an English boarding school. Catherine is abducted by an indigenous tribe and forced into sexual slavery, where she develops a bond with her captors before eventually enacting her revenge on the tribesmen who beheaded her parents and took her captive.

Gariazzo's film, like Deodato's before it, makes an attempt to convince us that we are watching true events unfold. Perhaps learning from Deodato's legal troubles, he does so not by presenting the footage as real but by inserting a bridging sequence that shows Catherine on trial for murder, suggesting that we are seeing a dramatization of a true story (which this is not—the film is entirely fictional).[42] The majority of the film is an excuse for exploitative eroticism, occasional violence and very little else, and it is a disappointing entry in an otherwise highly controversial and shocking filone. This is highlighted in the *Segnalazioni cinematografiche*'s pastoral review, which dismisses the film's content out of hand by calling it "90 annoying minutes of eroticism and crudely packaged truculence."[43]

Toward the end of the filone's glory days, Antonio Climati returned to the genre he helped birth with his 1988 entry *Green Inferno*.

Climati's latest was another film given the alternative title of *Cannibal Holocaust 2*. As with Gariazzo's *Amazonia* (and, while we're counting, Massimo Tarantini's 1985 film *Massacre in Dinosaur Valley*), Climati's producers hoped to cash in on the notoriety of the most infamous entry into what was now a dying filone. In fact, it wasn't just the cannibal subgenre that was struggling—the still largely state-funded Italian film industry had taken severe financial hit after severe financial hit due to the political and economic turmoil the country had experienced during the Years of Lead (1968–1988) and the P2 scandal and was about to collapse entirely.

Green Inferno looks at first as though it is following in the footsteps of Deodato's *Cut and Run* rather than *Cannibal Holocaust*, looking and feeling for all intents and purposes like an '80s action film as four friends steal a plane to head into the Amazonian jungles to find a missing professor and a legendary indigenous tribe said to be in possession of a great treasure.

Once the quartet reach their destination, however, Climati's true intention kicks in. The Italian title of the film is *Natura Contro*, or "against nature," and it is the American interlopers' crimes against nature (and nature's very successful attempts to defend itself) that occupy the majority of the run time. Local man Don Pedro, who captures animals from the region and ships them to zoos around the world, convinces the group to catch monkeys for him in return for gasoline, and it is their attempts to do so that provoke the ire of the indigenous tribes (although not before an electric eel swims up their guide's anus and bats attack their camp, both clear indicators that these western invaders are not wanted here).

Captured by tribespeople, the group are caged and one is covered in red ants as a form of torture. Later, after it becomes apparent that the tribe has been attacked and slaughtered by gold prospectors, a three-way battle ensures between the protagonists, gold prospectors and indigenous tribespeople with much slaughter and bloodshed. The professor is eventually found and recovered, and the group learn that the tribe is in fact not the same tribe they were looking for. Ever the exploiters, they decide to return to America and lie about finding the tribe in order to secure their fame and fortune.

The most notable aspect of the film is Climati's documentary style, carried over from his previous mondo films with Mario Morra. Goodwin notes that "an oddly harmonious documentary air evokes an unusual authenticity; a heightened reality which strengthens the screenplay,"[44] while Woods opines that "the *Green Inferno* displays as much if not more so of the spirit of Werner Herzog as it does Umberto Lenzi or Ruggero Deodato"[45] The *Segnalazioni cinematografiche* also takes time to praise the director's filmmaking skill before offering critique of his film's content, much as it had with Climati's earlier mondo films: "The director is a valid documentary maker, the genre is certainly the one he does best: the images of nature are in fact very beautiful, wild, and the photography is always evocative."[46]

It also notes Climati's attempts to instill valid themes, both ecological and humanitarian, in the film: "The author certainly wants to say that nature must not be violated, whose beauty he exalts.... Then there is a clear condemnation of cruelty against defenseless and peaceful populations, decimated out of greed by the highly civilized 'conquerors.'"[47] Noteworthy here is that, when the conquerors in question are not Christian missionaries but American atheists with their own personal agendas, the Vatican suddenly understands the greed and cruelty of the interlopers and is critical of it.

Finally, attention is turned to the cruder content of the film, the review considering first that "unfortunately the film lacks the strength necessary for the message to be effective...[with] crudeness in many sequences ... the director presents gruesome images"[48] before determining that Climati had struck a balance and taken care to handle the cruder elements of the plot maturely, noting that "certain situations, which could have become scandalous, such as the night-time encounter between the girl and the solitary man, are resolved with delicacy. Acceptable reservations/crudeness."[49]

Talk about how this speaks a lot about the filone, and how it has lost its edge... From Climati's early mondo entries, whose content incensed the Church so much that it had accused him of directorial and journalistic atrocities, to the badland horrors of *Texas Chain Saw* and *Hills Have Eyes* to the video nasties of Deodato and Lenzi, the cannibal movie had embraced the extreme and gone about as far as it was possible to go, which meant latter entries had nowhere to go in terms of horrific content. The filone had become, it appeared, sufficiently grown up to the point where the Vatican no longer had such issues with these films, and was content to permit their viewing with "acceptable reservations."[50]

Now the cannibal movie had lost its edge. There were no more controversies to elevate it beyond squalid exploitation, no suggestion of real-life murders, no more animal torture (thankfully) and no message to send to the Church. It would be three decades before a new generation of filmmakers, such as Julia Decournau (*Raw*, 2017) and Luca Guadagnino (*Bones and All*, 2022) embraced the filone to tell an entirely different kind of story, this time using cannibalism as a metaphor for puberty and teenage sexuality. But back during the cannibal film's heyday, a message *had* been sent, from the Italian people to their church via Umberto Lenzi, to condemn the Christian "missionary" expansions to tame and indoctrinate indigenous peoples, practices that had contributed toward the decimation of a number of innocent peoples and their environments.

An array of zombies, representing (rear) *Dawn of the Dead* and (front, l-r) *Zombie Flesh Eaters*, *City of the Living Dead*, and *Tombs of the Blind Dead*. Illustration by the author.

6

The Profane Resurrection

(*The Vatican versus ... the Zombie Film*)

There is no creature in all of horror, at least in terms of smart, complex storytelling, sociopolitical commentary and rich, varied history, quite like the zombie.

The shuffling ghouls that would later become synonymous with the films of George Romero (later still with the comic books of Robert Kirkman and the television of Frank Darabont) began their undead lives a racially coded archetype based on Haitian folklore of the 17th century (where West African slaves were taught that the penalty for committing suicide would be to exist in perpetuity as walking corpses, rather than return to their African homeland).[1]

The zombie was first brought to the silver screen when United Artists sought an answer to Universal's all-conquering Monsters. That answer came to them in the form of director and producer duo Victor and Edward Halperin's *White Zombie* (1932), the Bela Lugosi–starring tale based on American explorer and occultist William Seabrook's 1929 novel/travelogue *The Magic Island*. When the zombie myth was first transferred to the silver screen, it was as this folklore version, or an approximation: enslaved Black men, put in a state of perpetual trance by voodoo, forced to toil the land for their white master. Sadly for United Artists, *White Zombie* did not bring the studio the same fortunes that *Dracula*, *Frankenstein* and all their macabre literary pals had brought to Universal. It would not be until three and a half decades later that zombies would really begin to leave their mark on the horror genre.

Over the intervening years, the shuffling corpses of the undead visited various studios, including the smaller production houses of the 1930s dubbed "Poverty Row" (perhaps Hollywood's first foray into exploitation cinema, these studios sprang up from nowhere, made a fast buck on low-budget B movies before disappearing into the ether) and RKO and Val Lewton's classy experiment in macabre melodramas such as *Cat People*,

The Leopard Man, Ghost Ship and *Bedlam*. Lewton's apprentice director Jacques Tourneur's *I Walked with a Zombie* (1943) retained the slaves-as-zombies narrative, daring not only to address the very obvious subtexts of colonialism and the slavery of Black people by the United States of America, but also the fetishization of Black men by white women and the idea espoused by white men that Black men were sexual predators and wanted integration in order to "steal" white women and be with them sexually (a notion that would see many innocent Black men and boys lynched, perhaps the most famous being the 1955 lynching of Emmett Till, the 14-year-old child accused of making improper advances to a white woman, Carolyn Bryant).

Despite this relatively rich history, mention the word "zombie" to someone and the first name to reach their lips is unlikely to be William Seabrook. It is unlikely to be Victor Halperin, Bela Lugosi, Val Lewton or Jacques Tourneur.

It is, however, highly likely that the first name you will hear is George A. Romero.

That is because, to horror fans of a certain age, the golden age of zombie film is synonymous with two things, both borne of Romero's classic zombie trilogy (*Night of the Living Dead*, 1968; *Dawn of the Dead*, 1978; *Day of the Dead*, 1985). First, the Romero cycle displayed some of the most impressive, repulsive splatter and gore effects in all of horror (thanks to the now legendary effects artist Tom Savini). Second, those same films contained smart sociopolitical messages as subtext, each holding a mirror up to the United States of America at the time of its making.

To the Church, and to the apostate Roman Catholic filmmakers and audiences of Italy, however, the zombie has a very specific connotation: the profane resurrection.

Sage discusses the term, speaking of gothic literature such as Mary Shelley's *Frankenstein*, explaining that "the narratives of the Gothic are often shaped by the threat of a Profane Resurrection of the Body, an explicit taboo reinforced in [Christianity]."[2] Sage goes on to explain that the notion of the undead is something that has fascinated the public imagination since the 18th century.

Thrower goes further, explaining, "It's hardly surprising that Italy, a country under the desiccated thrall of Catholicism, should have produced the most dedicated and compulsive volume of zombie films."[3] Thrower understood that "a zombie in Italian Cinema carries an iconoclastic connotation. It is explosive; able to fragment realism by inferring the implacable presence of something supernatural yet stubbornly corporeal: and it is philosophical, beyond good and evil; parading the flesh without the much-vaunted spirit."[4] When you consider that, for Roman Catholics, the body is a temporary corporeal form that the soul excretes when it passes from this world and enters Heaven, the zombie offers us the perverse opposite. It is often inferred in the zombie film that those whose corporeal materials later become zombies have not successfully completed their passage to Heaven but instead found their souls in limbo or worse, something exemplified in Romero's *Dawn of the Dead*: "When there is no more room in Hell, the dead shall walk the earth."[5]

This phrase, and indeed the narratives of several films within the modern zombie canon, suggest that when the dead walk the earth it is because the end times are upon us. Hell is full, Judgment Day has befallen the earth and the ungodly resurrections that walk are those who have no place in Heaven. DeCou expands upon this notion of the zombie as part of the imagery of Judgment Day, asserting that the theological zombie is a tenet of divine absence that is evidence of the spiritual abandonment of humans by their creator.[6]

The zombie therefore represents the most heinous of creatures to the Church. It is at once a perversion of both the host body and the spirit, a creature that diverted from the teachings of Christ in its original life on earth, committing the mortal sin that condemns the soul to eternal suffering in Hell upon death, only to have the sinful flesh resurrected to roam the earth and commit more mortal sins. But more so, the zombie is sacrilege on the part of the artists who created it: a statement writ large that God does not exist, that He is either dead, or has abandoned us.

Religion and the zombie are, as Thrower has implied, irreconcilable. Everything about the zombie screams profanity to the Church, from its mere existence to the way it moves. When zombies rise from the grave they do not function like the people they once were. Without a soul, these lifeless husks instead move in a shuffling, undulating way, limbs swaying, rising and falling in choreographed repetition, a perverse dance. LaMothe, investigating the relationship between religion and dance, notes that resistance to dancing by religious patriarchy "implies that dancing represents a threat to their ability to distinguish 'religion' from the rest of life."[7]

To the Vatican, everything in society must be dictated by the Word of God and the teachings of Christ, including dancing. And so, the seemingly innocuous, rhythmic movement of the corporeal form causes an odd reconciliation between the sacred and profane in which "the body that will be resurrected can [also] prance seductively."[8] And so, the zombie offers its own profane seduction, its slow, deliberate, rhythmic movements that both terrify and entice us at the same time, a notion taken to its logical conclusion with the dancing zombies of director John Landis's Grammy Award–winning video for Michael Jackson's "Thriller."

When Romero's landscape-changing film *Night of the Living Dead* was released in 1968, it provoked a level of horror and disgust from critics that would be difficult to top, yet audiences lapped it up, and flocked to see it in droves. The zombie of Romero was a new creature, one we had not seen before. Where Seabrook had talked of men turned into mindless slaves, Romero and his screenwriter John Russo imported elements of the Grand Guignol and Artaud's Theater of Cruelty into the legend and reimagined the zombie as the resurrected corpse of the recent dead, brought back to life to roam the earth with no apparent purpose other than to consume the living, their rotting cadavers spilling entrails out onto the ground even as they attempt to eat more.

What Romero and Russo also brought to their zombie epic was a biting political commentary. The film operates as a discussion of Vietnam and American racism, both on its own shores and in the disproportionate amount of Black first line infantry sent to that country to kill and to die. While this would be discussed and celebrated a great deal in the coming years, at the time of release it was overshadowed by the more gratuitous elements. *Night of the Living Dead* featured more violence, blood and gore than any film produced so far, and would leave an impact on the genre that, perhaps to this very day, has not been matched.

Variety's response to the film contained such vitriol that it effectively functioned as free publicity for the film in the United States, the critic protesting that "until the Supreme Court establishes clear guidelines for the pornography of violence, 'Night of the Living Dead' will serve nicely as an outer limit definition by example. In a mere 90 minutes this horror film … casts serious aspersions on the responsibility of its Pittsburgh-based makers, distributor … the film industry as a whole and [exhibitors] who book [the picture], as well as raising doubts about … the moral health of filmgoers who cheerfully opt for this unrelieved orgy of sadism."[9]

Variety did not hold back on its censure of director George A. Romero, asserting that he was "incapable of contriving a single graceful set-up,"[10] that the production overall was "amateurism of the first order," the screenplay "a model of verbal banality," and that lead actors Duane Jones and Judith O'Dea were "sufficiently talented to warrant supporting roles in a backwoods community theatre."[11]

The film would go on to rack up $30 million globally, almost 264 times its $114,000 budget.[12]

When *Night of the Living Dead* was released in Italy at the start of 1971, the *Segnalazioni cinematografiche*, perhaps surprisingly, had some positive things to say about the film, specifically about Romero's sociopolitical subtexts. The Vatican considered it "a horror film whose content seems to overshadow a certain sociological-political theme: from the consequences of technological progress that gets out of hand to the power

6. The Profane Resurrection

In George A. Romero's *Night of the Living Dead*, a likeness of Pope Paul VI's face lurks in the face and hair of a sinister-looking zombie child. Illustration by the author.

that promotes it, to the inability of the white man to react in any other way than with repression or fear. The same conclusion of the story, which sees the only man (a Black man) who has found the courage to face reality, carelessly killed by whites, seems to have an anti-racist meaning. Realized with evident poverty of means, the work alternates sequences in which an unnecessary verbosity prevails with others in which it reaches, as far as suspense is concerned, its undoubtedly rough efficacy."[13]

Despite the consideration and praise, the Vatican's reviewer went on to lambast what were seen as the film's negative aspects: "The aforementioned themes do not appear with such evidence that they can be understood without difficulty [and] the most grim and grand-guignol aspects of the horrific story may have quite another influence on the viewer."[14] The *Segnalazioni cinematografiche* considered the film's "scenes of cannibalism, made with macabre, disgust realism"[15] to be unacceptable for the palate of its flock.

It is interesting, to say the least, that the Vatican found a number of elements of the film worthy of intellectual discussion and offered some reserved praise where the supposedly more liberal critics in the U.S. had dismissed the film out of hand as violent pornography. Not only had the scholars of the Centro Cattolico Cinematografico, so used to condemning genre movies, picked up on the film's subtextual messages and wished to discuss them, but they had also highlighted a subtext not commonly discussed elsewhere, then or now.

So does George A. Romero's film discuss "the consequences of technological progress"? Certainly, *Night of the Living Dead* offers a wide-ranging critique of contemporary American society, including, as we already know, the Vietnam War and the systemic racism within the country that sadly continues even today. With regard to technological process specifically, much of the film is spent with the cast holed up in a remote country farmhouse, watching and listening in terror as television and radio broadcasts theorize that the reanimation of the recent dead is occurring due to radiation from a space probe that exploded in Earth's atmosphere on the way back from Venus. Here we have what could be determined as a message regarding the dangers of technological progress. Man's attempts to explore outer space have wrought its apparent destruction, a postnuclear, shuffling yet inevitable Armageddon.

It is this element that, along with the racially charged killing of Duane Jones' Ben by a white lynch mob, is picked up on by the Church and discussed in depth prior to the *Segnalazioni cinematografiche*'s ultimate dismissal of the film. That the Vatican's review is concerned with such subtext in a lowly horror film is quite remarkable and goes some way to show that the Centro Cattolico Cinematografico did at least intend its publication to operate on the level of artistic evaluation as well as acting as a censorship tool (even if it did not often regularly strike the balance as well as it does here).

The success of Romero's film would, as noted in previous chapters, further change the face of modern horror (and indeed modern cinema as a whole) and spark the imaginations of an entire generation of transgressive filmmakers and willing audiences. The zombie film was resurrected, and it would not take long for the influence of *Night of the Living Dead* to spread.

6. The Profane Resurrection

Much like Romero's seminal film, Amando De Ossorio's 1972 film *Tombs of the Blind Dead* sought to create a new, original zombie myth. In this Spanish/Portuguese coproduction, the zombies are neither Haitian slaves nor are they the recent dead brought back to life by radiation from outer space. Instead, the film draws upon material familiar to the Spanish people, the works of 19th-century Spanish author Gustavo Adolfo Bécquer.[16]

Ossorio adapted from Bécquer's tales of the Knights Templar a fictionalized version of the real-life order that was disbanded by France's King Philip IV in the 14th century. In the film, the Templar Knights are said to have returned from the Crusades having swapped Christianity for the occult, and due to their practices of witchcraft and heresy, they were excommunicated and hanged. A local legend warns of a town on the Spain/Portugal border where the corpses of the Knights (blind because their eyes were pecked out by crows at the gallows) rise from their graves at night, thanks to one of their earlier occult rituals. Ossorio's zombies were also physically different from both the classic model and Romero's: essentially reanimated sacks of bones and dust (as one would expect of 600-year-old corpses), yet they still ride on (zombified) horseback and carry the array of weaponry they had fought with in the crusades.

Stylish, original and genuinely chilling, the film was very successful, and Ossorio beat Romero to the claim of first genuine zombie franchise: three sequels were produced over the next three years, before the series was laid to rest due to diminishing returns.

The *Segnalazioni cinematografiche* called the film a "silly story ... conducted on a line of narrative inconsistency, approximate interpretation and slow pace, adding boredom to annoyance."[17] The Vatican's critic dismisses the film quite quickly, pronouncing it unacceptable due to its "immoral situations"[18] and essentially accused de Ossorio of being no more than a hack, trying in vain to thrill and horrify audiences (something that said audiences would disagree with, given the film's reasonable success and slew of sequels). The "line of narrative inconsistency"[19] in question is that of Bécquer's Knights Templar, which the Vatican's writers clearly saw as a distasteful and morally corrupt portrayal, a caricature that is both a mockery of the Church and potentially harmful to its reputation. That these noble, holy Christian soldiers might have returned from the Crusades having abandoned Christianity for the occult is clearly a source of anger here and what leads to the simultaneous accusations of boredom, silliness and immorality. De Ossorio's movie could not be met with anything short of full condemnation, and that is exactly what it received.

The following year, Argentine León Klimovsky directed his own take on the shuffling undead with *Vengeance of the Zombies*. Klimovsky's zombies were the corpses of murdered women (all victims of the same idiosyncratic serial killer), but otherwise his premise drew more from the original, Haiti-inspired legend of the zombie. The killer's victims are brought back to life by the supernatural practices of an East Indian shaman named Katanka who wishes to create an army to do his bidding. The film, as well as being genuinely disturbing, carried a significant erotic element, something synonymous with Spanish-language horror in the 1970s.

The *Segnalazioni cinematografiche* considered there to be "nothing more foolish and sad than this blood orgy where, at the extreme misery of the narrative and the direction, a perverse taste is reflected from this low butcher."[20] The Vatican clearly found both Klimovsky and his film very distasteful, calling his profane resurrections "inhuman and pagan," "unacceptable [and] aberrant."[21] The insult of "butcher"[22] carries with it a double meaning: the Vatican is not only attempting to highlight Klimovsky's supposed ineptitude as a filmmaker (butchering his material); it also refers to the profession of butcher, suggesting he is uneducated and uncultured, lacking in intellect and therefore to be denigrated. A typically classist (and classless) jibe from the Vatican that shows exactly what it thinks of its flock, which will of course feature many a butcher from across the land.

Most notable among the rest of this Spanish branch of the new zombie filone is Jorge Grau's 1974 film *The Living Dead at the Manchester Morgue*. Another coproduction, this time between Spain and Italy, the film was a mainstay on the U.S. drive-in circuit for a number of years, as many European horror productions at the time were used as the "B" picture in double features with American horror films such as *Last House on the Left* and *Texas Chain Saw Massacre*.

Grau's film, like Ossorio's earlier *Tombs of the Blind Dead*, takes the zombie creature and fashions another original premise around it in the form of a technological development in the agriculture industry. Ultrasonic radiation, used as an experimental pest control method, reawakens the dead, and they promptly roam the English countryside murdering the living. It is closer to Romero's both in origin story (rooted in science fiction and the resurrection of the deceased, rather than the occult) and in terms of it carrying a serious message: *The Living Dead at Manchester Morgue* is about ideological war, pitting the authorities against the counterculture movement at a time when England was on the cusp of the punk movement (it would formally begin the following year), as Generation X began to protest the authoritarianism of the prior generations. Though modestly popular at the time (and in its subsequent home video releases), the film has grown in stature in recent years, with some critics considering it the most important addition to the modern canon not directed by George A. Romero.

As Navarro states: "In between [Romero's *Night of the Living Dead* and *Dawn of the Dead*] was Jorge Grau's *The Living Dead at Manchester Morgue* ... years ahead of *Dawn*, therefore free to forge its own path[;] Grau borrowed Romero's concept of ... bold social commentary through a zombie lens to craft one of horror's greatest zombie films of all time."[23]

Despite recognizing a message it believed the film shared with Romero's predecessor, the *Segnalazioni cinematografiche* had reservations about the film's suitability for mass consumption, considering it "a typical horror film, hidden behind the semblance of a message, which is, among other things, superficial and obvious: do not violate nature with technology because you could be victims of a consequent disorder of forces. The reality of the film is constituted by a succession of macabre killings, acts of cannibalism, details of a vampiristic and Grand Guignol nature. Unacceptable/macabre."[24]

The Vatican alternated between disgust and dismissal in its considerations of the Spanish zombie filone, certainly not affording the Spanish films the same generosity as it had Romero. In previous chapters it has been suggested that the Holy See's condemnation of Italian genre film and directors appears to be harsher than its reaction to foreign product, and here we see an ire similar to that usually reserved for domestic genre film being leveled at productions from Spain. Building on Thrower's earlier assertion that the zombie is irreconcilable with Roman Catholic beliefs, Russell considers that the ire toward the Spanish genre product is unsurprising, given the country's Catholic population and its proximity to the Holy See's city-state in Rome. He asserts that the "Catholic fascination with the flesh certainly informs the mechanics behind this philosophical-spiritual-religious questioning."[25]

This goes some way toward determining the popularity of the zombie film in the cinema of Spain (and, later, Italy) and its imagery of profane resurrection. Consider also the imagery of the Italian cannibal film as perversion of the Eucharist. More so, it also helps explain why the *Segnalazioni cinematografiche*'s censure of Italian (and now Spanish) directors was so heavy-handed. It is not because it is domestic product; it is because it is *Catholic* product. The Vatican was able to give the work of atheists from other countries the benefit of the doubt—there is a chance that, through their ignorance of the scripture, they don't truly understand the significance of the sacrilege they are committing by routinely resurrecting the dead and having them perform feats of cannibalism. But those directors from the home of Roman Catholicism (and its nearest Catholic neighbor) fully understand and appreciate the religious significance of the zombie (and the cannibal), they are fully aware of the profanity they create; indeed, that is the point. The reason these filones, with their quasi-religious symbolism, were so popular among filmmakers raised in Catholicism is because they functioned as a form of protest. These artists, working at a time of mass apostasy and great anger toward the Church (for its complicity in fascism) were using symbolism of the sacred and the profane as a tool to attack the Holy See, and the Vatican understood this. This is, most likely, why the writers of the *Segnalazioni cinematografiche* fought back so hard against domestic genre films and their directors.

Spain wasn't the only territory getting in on the zombie act. Canada's Bob Clark directed a pair of zombie films in the 1970s, namely *Children Shouldn't Play with Dead Things* (1972) and 1974's *Deathdream*.

While *Children Shouldn't Play with Dead Things* is essentially a very broad horror comedy, Clark's later zombie effort is an entirely different affair. As with Ossorio and Grau, Clark (and screenwriter Alan Ormsby) opts to follow Romero's lead, by forging his own path, drawing from the world events around him and creating perhaps the most singularly interesting zombie yet. When Andy Brooks, an American soldier in Vietnam, is shot by a sniper and dies, he appears to telepathically "hear" the voice of his mother calling out to him. Back home, his family learns of his death and begins to grieve, until he arrives home, in the middle of the night, in full uniform and seemingly very much alive. As the plot progresses, it is revealed that Andy is indeed one of the undead, brought back to life by nothing more than the heartfelt desire of his mother to see him return home safe. Andy needs the blood of others for his undead form to survive, pitching him halfway between zombie and vampire, and kills local people in order to obtain it.

The film keeps the setting intimate and dramatic, focusing on Andy's family's attempts to deal with their son's strange behavior, and the message is quite clear: like Romero, Clark seeks to comment upon the Vietnam War, with the Canadian drawing upon the psychological effects of the war on those soldiers who returned home. Andy is a metaphor for those who survived the war physically but not psychologically, those who returned to their families stripped of their humanity and dealing with the post-traumatic stress disorder provoked by the horrors of war.[26]

A combination of the nature of the war, the trauma the soldiers suffered and the drug use many of them turned to as a coping mechanism "changed their sense of identity and perspective of society,"[27] and Clark's film explores this in a very effective manner, so much so that the thought-provoking film was later preserved by the American Film Institute in its catalog of important films from the first 100 years of cinema.[28]

The Vatican certainly recognized something in Clark's film that it had not seen since *Romero's Night of the Living Dead*, noting, "The film possesses qualities of originality in the screenplay and technical skills in

In Bob Clark's 1974 Vietnam drama cum zombie horror *Deathdream*, Andy Brooks (Richard Backus) wields a syringe and choppers blanket the killing fields of Vietnam with napalm as soldiers look on, defeated and forlorn. Illustration by the author.

the realization."[29] Of course, the Vatican's critics were not in the habit of heaping praise upon horror films without reservations, and the *Segnalazioni cinematografiche* had a number of them. The Vatican recognized Clark's "allegorical basis: the morbid matriarchy and the dehumanization brought by the war"[30] but considered that "starting from the point of the 'zombie' [the director] has only managed to confuse [his message]."[31] This was enough for the Holy See to conclude that "ultimately, the film falls into those that cause ambiguity through the macabre scenes and the tensions created, so are unable to positively impress. Questionable/Morbid."[32]

The *Segnalazioni cinematografiche* stops short of damning Clark's film, suggesting instead that it is suitable for adults of moral maturity. The Vatican is clearly uncomfortable with Clark's use of the zombie, that creature of perverse resurrection, as his allegorical tool, but will not outright censure him for it asClark (being North American) is not considered to fall under the shadow of the Holy See in the same way that Italian and Spanish directors are. With this approach, the Vatican continues to draw an indelible line in the sand between zombie films from what it considers to be atheists and those made by the Catholics of Italy and Spain.

The father of the modern zombie, George A. Romero, would return to his creation after a 10-year hiatus so as not to be pigeonholed as director of a single zombie film (an effort that would, sadly, largely fail: his later years as a filmmaker would be defined by each subsequent entry into his series of films featuring the undead). *Dawn of the Dead* (1978) would be his second zombie film, shot primarily in Monroeville Mall, Pennsylvania, and taking place the morning after his previous film's zombie apocalypse began (at least artistically—it is never outright stated, and it is in fact clear that years have passed between *Night*'s Vietnam era and *Dawn*'s timeline). Once more, Romero's film carried a sociopolitical message, this time drawing our attention to inner-city violence, heavy-handed policing and the looming shadow of race war, all under an overarching critique of American consumer culture.[33]

Romero's film would of course reset the zombie genre once more, be lauded by critics (Roger Ebert gave great praise to *Dawn of the Dead* and awarded the film his very rare four star rating) and since its release has regularly featured in greatest horror movies of all time lists. There is little to say about the film here that has not been said elsewhere, except to reiterate that while in preproduction the project garnered the attention of Dario Argento. The Italian director, along with his producer brother Claudio, offered to cofinance the film in exchange for European distribution rights and a certain level of creative input. Romero would consult Argento during the screenwriting stage and would write and direct enough additional material to enable the Italian to assemble his own cut of the film specifically for the European market.

By the time of *Dawn of the Dead*'s release in Italy, shepherded by Dario and Claudio Argento, the Holy See had bigger problems than the influence the film might have on cinemagoers. Assembled into a cut that was particularly palatable to Italians, it was not only successful at the box office but had a profound influence on the nation's genre filmmakers. If 1968's *Night of the Living Dead* was the film that gave license to directors around the world to remake the zombie mythos as they saw fit, *Dawn of the Dead* was the film that saw an explosion in the zombie subgenre in Europe. The filone system would go into overdrive, in Italy and across the continent, producing a plethora of perverse religious symbolism to aggravate the Church.

The most infamous of the films that followed Romero's *Dawn of the Dead/Zombi* was the cheekily titled *Zombi 2* (the film was released with alternative titles in various territories, including: *Zombie; Zombie Flesh Eaters,* and *Voodoo—The Zombie Island of Terror*), directed by one Lucio Fulci. The Italian was soon to become known principally as a horror

6. The Profane Resurrection

director by English-speaking audiences, thanks largely to this production and his "Gates of Hell" triptych of films that followed it. *Zombi 2* was in fact Fulci's first horror film: he had spent close to two decades as a screenwriter and director of comedies, then entered his self-proclaimed "genre terrorist"[34] phase, where he moved between satirical comedy, drama, western, giallo and even family adventure films for another decade before being offered the opportunity to direct a screenplay, written by Elisa Brigante and Dardano Sacchetti, that Italian action director Enzo G. Castellari had turned down. In a wonderful example of Italian exploitation fashion, producer Fabrizio de Angelis slyly marketed the finished film as a direct sequel to Argento's version of Romero's own zombie sequel.

Fulci's film, despite hitching itself to the success of *Dawn of the Dead/ Zombi*, is perhaps the most interesting European zombie film in terms of influences and how it used them. Fulci's film begins and ends in Manhattan, with a zombie invasion that is sure to decimate the city's human population (much like Romero's film, which was largely set in Philadelphia, another large U.S. city completely overrun with the undead).

The Romero influence ends there, however, as the narrative tracks the origin of the zombies to a remote (and fictional) Caribbean island called Matul. Here, Fulci, Brigante and Sacchetti pay tribute to the origins of the zombie myth: to William Seabrook, to Victor and Edward Halperin, to Val Lewton and Jacques Tourneur. Fulci would, of course, also insert some anti–Catholic commentary into *Zombi 2*.

As the film's heroes (Tisa Farrow's Ann Bowles and Ian McCulloch's Peter West) battle zombies, they stumble upon a conquistador graveyard, where yet more corpses reanimate and overcome their human opposition. Fulci's conquistador zombies were a nod to de Ossorio's *Tombs of the Blind Dead* and its long-dead Templar Knights in more ways than one. By the mid–1530s, Francisco Pizarro and other Spanish adventurers had completed a series of expeditions to the Americas and seized control of the civil war–ravaged Inca empire in South America.[35] Pontiff Julius II and the Spanish monarchy embraced the evangelization of the newfound continent and dispatched priests to convert the conquered Incas. Spanish Catholic conquistador Hernán Cortés and his men landed their ships at Veracruz, Mexico, on Good Friday 1519 "with multiple objectives, chief among them the conversion of the indigenous peoples to the Catholic faith."[36] A man of deep, pious faith who told his men, "Brothers and companions, let us follow the sign of the Cross with true faith and in it we shall conquer,"[37] he laid siege to what Roman Catholics deemed the "grotesque and barbaric"[38] Aztecs and erected an altar and cross in their temple. Later, non–Catholics were forbidden from settling in the Spanish colonies in the Americas. The Incans and other Native peoples were forcibly converted to Christianity and indigenous religions were outlawed. The conquistadors had spread Roman Catholicism to the Americas, and Fulci was surely commenting on this. His own zombified conquistadors rise from their graves to continue their mission, to visit more of what they had really brought upon the region: assimilation, or death.

In addition to all of the above, Fulci also brought his experience working with special effects, creating a horrific and wholly original zombie and one that would, in turn, be adopted by virtually every zombie film that followed. Fulci's "walking flowerpots"[39] were extras caked in clay and oatmeal, giving them a horrifically rotting, subhuman look. Finally, zombies were *monsters*, far removed from Halperin and Tourneur's hypnotized Black men, removed even from Tom Savini's blue-faced zombies in Romero's *Dawn of the Dead*. Fulci's zombies wore the rotting, decomposing flesh of those whose souls had long since left or perished. They exemplified the "body as mere waste product"[40] in accordance with Catholic beliefs, yet these rotting forms had returned to life and escaped their graves just as Jesus was risen after three days in the tomb. Fulci's zombies were the reincarnated Christ but corrupted, distorted. They were beings only in terms of physicality and not of spirituality.

Zombi 2 became his biggest success yet, and by a significant margin, earning £3 million from its £410,000 budget.[41] Fulci would go on to find further success in the horror genre, and continued to use zombies as his primary antagonists for many years, always in a religious context. So, when modern audiences sarcastically refer to Easter Sunday as "Zombie Jesus Day" it is the perversions of Lucio Fulci that first entertained this notion.

The *Segnalazioni cinematografiche*, perhaps unsurprisingly, had a lot to say about Fulci's film:

> In a piece of dialog, the film attempts to validate the theory of "woo-doo" (the living dead) and does so with the extravagant appeal of a mixture of Christianity—brought to the Caribbean Sea by the conquistadors—and the pagan beliefs of its indigenous peoples. But the solution to the mystery, entirely imaginative (even if the film has tried to stay faithful to "White Zombie," directed by Victor Halperin in 1932), was not the objective of Lucio Fulci, who aimed exclusively for horrible, grand-guignolesque special effects. Only an intensely masochistic spectator can enjoy the sight of monsters who, having torn off shreds of live meat from the unfortunate [humans], face each other in the foreground with disgusting faces full of worms. Unacceptable/Horrible.[42]

Clearly, the Vatican's writer picked up on Fulci's use of what had once been Christian forces as his zombies. The review would not outright entertain any ideas of the zombie's profane link to the resurrection of Christ beyond this (perhaps so as not to put the notion in the heads of any impressionable audience members who might not otherwise pick up on it), but the disapproval and consternation with regard to Christian soldiers used in such a transgressive and subversive way is palpable. The *Segnalazioni cinematografiche*'s review is interesting in that it notes the film's influence as being *White Zombie* rather than *Dawn of the Dead*, and much like the reviews of *Night of the Living Dead* and *Deathdream*, shows that the Vatican's critics have been engaging with the zombie film on more than just an aesthetic level, providing more than just censure. It is becoming more and more apparent that the *Segnalazioni cinematografiche*'s writer(s) engaged with this filone on an intellectual level, tracking not just the films' tropes but the subtexts and even the history of this subgenre that was such an obvious perversion of the Christian canon. What is more surprising is that the Vatican has engaged this way with a film in the subgenre made by an Italian genre director, rather than writing its domestic directors' output off in a couple of short, pithy sentences (although normal service would resume shortly).

The zombie filone would explode both domestically and across Europe. Not only was the zombie suddenly popular in Italy, but Fulci's film showed that Italian directors could be successful on a global scale within this filone, as the subsequent films to come out of Italy had as many (if not more) similarities to *Zombi 2* as they did to Romero's film, or indeed any other movies featuring the shuffling undead.

Bruno Mattei's *Virus/Hell of the Living Dead* used a chemical leak as its mechanism for creating zombies, and crafted a narrative around a team of commandos and group of ecoterrorists, who have taken hostages inside the U.S. embassy in Barcelona. The terrorists have one demand: that the chemical research facility (in Papua New Guinea) be shut down before it causes untold damage to the earth. Of course their plot is thwarted, only for the commandos to later be sent to the facility to investigate what turns out to be the zombie contagion, which spreads beyond the island and soon sees hordes of zombies in city parks in the developed world.

Mattei's film carries an ecological message. This is important, as one of the defining characteristics of the Romero zombie film is that the narrative is a metaphor for something else: Vietnam in *Night of the Living Dead*; rampant capitalism and consumerism in *Dawn of the Dead*. While Fulci's film dispensed with Romero's subtextual element, Claudio Fragasso and José María Cunillés' screenplay takes it forward into the Italian zombie filone. Mattei clearly takes influence from *Zombi 2* in the look of his walking dead, though. They are closer in appearance to Fulci's walking flower pots than any other zombie aesthetic.

The film's attempt at an ecological message did not help it when it came to the Holy See. The *Segnalazioni cinematografiche* opined that "the implicit ecological apology is an absurd and macabre representation of quartered bodies, disembowelments, horrendous meals of human offal."[43]

The review goes on to contend that the "uses and customs of primitive populations concerning funeral rites and the cult of the dead are exploited with a reprehensible and unhealthy taste."[44] It also criticizes Mattei's cinematic style (borrowed from the similarly popular cannibal filone), stating that "the tourist-documentary filming does nothing to help the viewer suffocated by the macabre insatiability of ruthless hordes of vampires and cannibals."[45]

Finally, the critic expresses his exasperation at Mattei's picture, noting the lack of originality in the work, and signing off with typical Vatican snark as he asserts, "The film is not even original as an idea, as it refers to the work of G.A. Romero's *The Night of the Living Dead*, with the aggravating circumstance that zombies are unleashed both night and day here."[46]

The film was branded "unacceptable [and] unhealthy"[47] and doomed to a limited domestic run in *terza visione* theaters domestically, although the success of Fulci's *Zombi 2* paved the way for it and others to be picked up for the U.S. drive-in circuit as well as see decent returns from home video markets.

Umberto Lenzi would call his film *Nightmare City* a "radiation sickness movie"[48] rather than a zombie film, and, while the film's "zombies" are indeed created by a radiation leak, these mutated ghouls share many similarities with zombies (and Piero Regnoli's screenplay behaves in much the same way as Romero and Argento's *Dawn of the Dead* screenplay and those of its Italian imitators, just as his mechanism for creating the zombies shares similarities with Romero's *Night of the Living Dead*). There are notable differences: Lenzi's zombies are quick and aggressive, the first of the modern zombies to abandon the shuffling gait of Romero's and of Fulci's; their look is different, as they have the appearance of living people with chemical burns rather than the resurrected dead.

While Lenzi's film is not considered to be among the strongest of the filone (it was widely panned by critics) it carries a definite antinuclear and ecological message, proving that Lenzi had learned from Romero and knew to insert a political commentary into his film. Unlike Fulci, Lenzi opted not to attack the Church directly (he would save that for his cannibal movie *Cannibal Ferox*) but still proceeded with the knowledge that the zombie, in Roman Catholic Italy, was a perversion of faith.

The *Segnalazioni cinematografiche* gave the domestic director's film short thrift, asserting that Lenzi's narrative served only to "drag the viewer from violence to violence, from horror to horror to the end, with obsessive repetitiveness: massacre in TV studios, massacre at the hospital, massacre...[of] the armed forces ... [and] massacre of family members ...

without sparing hideous spectacle."[49] The film was branded "unacceptable [and] unhealthy."[50] with its antinuclear message gone either unnoticed or ignored, a sign that, whatever the Vatican's critics' interest in the earlier films of the filone and the messages they carried, as zombies became commonplace in Italian cinemas, the Church was only interested in condemnation of this cinematic plague.

The patience of censors and self-designated moral guardians elsewhere was also being tested. The zombie film, and specifically the Italian zombie film, helped stir up one of the biggest controversies in the history of the medium, the video nasties scandal in the UK. Just like rape/revenge and cannibal movies, this particular filone of horror proved too much for censors and moral guardians alike and featured heavily in the list of films drawn up for prosecution under the UK Video Recordings Act.

Lucio Fulci saw two of his zombie films successfully prosecuted under the act, *Zombi 2* and *House by the Cemetery* (1981), as was Charles McCrann's *Toxic Zombies/Forest of Fear* (1980). A further five zombie films were not prosecuted but still made it onto the official list: Fulci appeared again with *The Beyond* (1981); Gary Sherman's *Dead & Buried* (1981); Frank Roach's *Frozen Scream* (1980); Bruno Mattei's *Virus* (1980); Jorge Grau's *The Living Dead at the Manchester Morgue* (1974) all became fully fledged video nasties. A substantial number of zombie movies were hitting the home video market in a short space of time, and many of them were products of the Italian filone system that followed hot on the heels of Fulci's *Zombi 2*.

If Fulci's first zombie film had leaned into criticism of the colonial march of Roman Catholicism across the world and inspired his fellow Italians to explore the notion of the profane resurrection, his follow-up films *City of the Living Dead* (1980) and *The Beyond* (1981) would be absolutely overt in sacrilegious content.

Christianity teaches that all will stand to be judged by God at the Second Coming of Jesus Christ. Fulci's *City of the Living Dead* represents a profane reading of the Second Coming. *City of the Living Dead* opens with a priest committing suicide (in doing so, guaranteeing his judgment will result in eternity in Hell), but Fulci isn't just killing a priest—the act represents the death of religion. What follows is all the former residents of the fictional town of Dunwich rising to be judged. However, when they rise, their bodies have dwindled and decayed. In Fulci's Second Coming it is not Jesus but the priest that is resurrected, and those that rise around him are zombies, an army of the dead that the priest uses to thwart any that oppose his perverse redemption and Fulci's sacrilegious Judgment Day.

Emboldened by the commercial success of his *Zombie Flesh Eaters* and of the proliferation of the zombie filone, Fulci took the anti–Catholic theme of his previous horror (that the zombies were the resurrected corpses of the conquistadors who had arrived in the Caribbean on a mission to oppress and indoctrinate) and built upon it for *City of the Living Dead*. His zombie epic perverts the notion of the resurrection, the Second Coming and Judgment Day.

The Vatican's pastoral evaluation completely ignored the sacrilegious elements of the film, focusing instead on its excessive gore, on the "crescents of blood, in scenes of repugnant realism, which force the viewer to hold back not the breath, but the vomit."[51] The film is noted as abandoning suspense in favor of more transgressive shocks, and branded "unhealthy" for Catholics.[52] The Holy See's review, sadly, offers little in way of insight into the film, suggesting only that the writer did not wish to engage with Fulci's use of the Book of Revelation as the grounding for his screenplay, his perverse Second Coming and Last Judgment being ignored entirely. It is perhaps worth considering that, by 1980, Fulci had already seen himself in hot water with the Vatican on a number of occasions, from his 1969 nunsploitation drama Beatrice Cenci (which critiqued and censured the corruption of the Vatican's past) to his 1972 comedy *The Eroticist* (a very scathing, satirical critique of Italy's secret deep state power cabal, of which senior Vatican figures were revealed to be a part) and giallo *Don't Torture a Duckling* (which prodded at the systematic abuse of children by Roman Catholic priests). It could, therefore, be that once the director moved on from criticizing the institution directly, the Holy See chose not to let his sacrilegious horror content push its buttons. Though not censured in depth, the film was branded unhealthy for the Church's flock because of its content.

The second of the director's loose "Gates of Hell" triptych followed, narratively speaking, the end of the world in *City of the Living Dead*: a literal descent into Hell, with the titular beyond featured as a vast, frozen landscape, similar in presentation to the lake of Cocytus in Dante's *Inferno*, an endless wasteland that occupies the lowest level of biblical Hell, where Lucifer himself dwells, consuming the anguished bodies of those banished to his realm. From the opening credits through to the final moments, there is the distinct suggestion that the flames of Hell have risen to consume the earth, and that the fates of the film's protagonists are sealed from the outset.

In moving from directing in several genres to working almost exclusively in the horror genre, Fulci was utilizing the fantastic to explore the Book of Revelation on-screen. The genre terrorist didn't stop there though, opting to feature the notion of the profane resurrection not just thematically but literally. *The Beyond* opens with the crucifixion of a suspected warlock, Schweick, who is then sealed in the wall of the Seven Doors Hotel

6. The Profane Resurrection

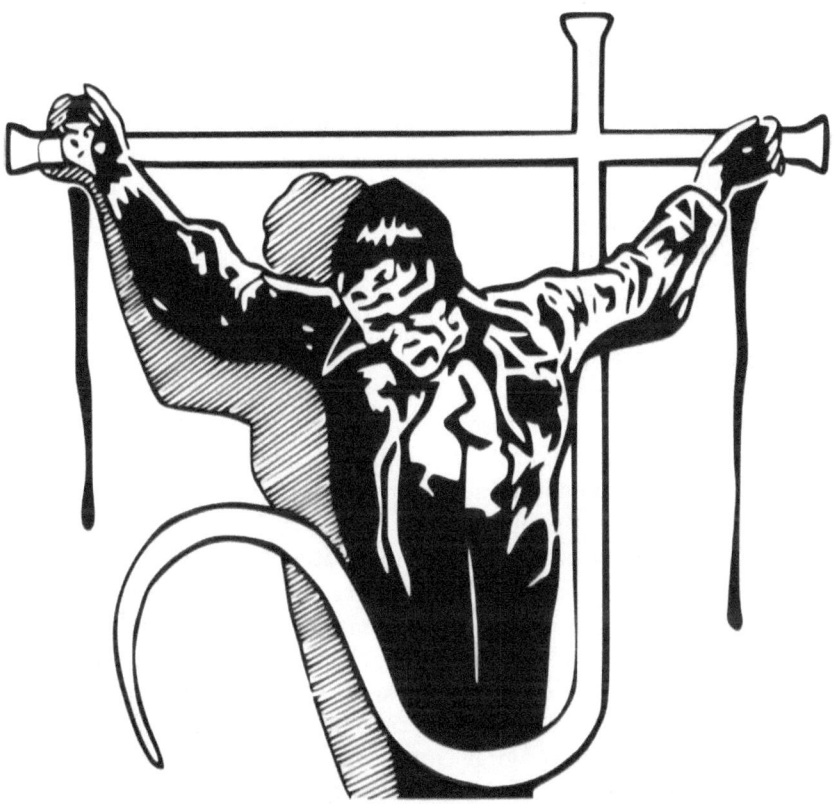

In Lucio Fulci's plotless zombie masterpiece *The Beyond*, zombie warlock Schweick (Antoine Saint-John) is crucified entwined in the pseudo-crucifix symbol from the Book of Eibon. Illustration by the author.

in Louisiana in 1927. As the story leaps forward to the present day, Schweick's corpse is discovered in the bowels of the building by renovators, still occupying the same pose, nails through his palms just as they had been driven through the palms of Jesus Christ. Schweick is resurrected and goes on to lead the army of zombies that take over the world (or the portion of it that Fulci chooses to show: *The Beyond* is set in New Orleans, and he never takes us outside of it, but it becomes clear that what is happening here is the end of times). Fulci holds nothing back in this chapter of his horror opus, bringing not only the rapture to the silver screen but serving us up a perversion of Christ, the crucified and resurrected Son of God, through a deplorable lens.

That Fulci is so overt in his quasi-religious iconography makes it almost frustrating that the Vatican's writers still don't want to rise to the bait. Perhaps the common thread to be found in the *Segnalazioni cinematografiche*'s condemnations of decades of zombie movies so far (other than its refusal to treat Italian schlock auteurs with anywhere near as much intellectual interrogation as their North American counterparts) has been an almost willful ignorance of the theme of the profane resurrection, choosing to disregard the sacrilege and focus instead on the aesthetic and violence, on those many "quartered bodies, disembowelments, horrendous meals of human offal."[53] In its review of *The Beyond*, the Vatican continues this theme despite the clear bait offered by Fulci, expressing that "what grows, as the story progresses, is not the tension but the disgust. The imagination of the screenplay and direction, in fact, is entirely exhausted in the search for the macabre and the horrifying."[54]

Fulci's film was deemed "unacceptable and unhealthy"[55] and dismissed out of hand, with no mention given to its theme of the biblical rapture or blatant tableaux of profane crucifixion and resurrection.

The critical and financial success of zombie films continued unabated. The zombie remained a popular filone in Italy, with films such as Andrea Bianchi's *Burial Ground* (1981) and Pupi Avati's *Zeder* (1983). Across the European continent, zombie films were increasing in number and popularity. Shuffling ghouls would return to Spain, in the form of Jesús Franco's *The Abyss of the Living Dead* (1982). In France, purveyor of off-kilter horror and skin flicks Jean Rollin had already directed *The Grapes of Death* (1978), about a farming community turned into zombies because of a dangerous pesticide (an echo of Jorge Grau's 1974 agriculture industry zombie origin story *The Living Dead at the Manchester Morgue*) and would return to the subgenre with *The Living Dead Girl* (1981), a poetic tale about a dead heiress brought back to life by a toxic chemical spill and the lover who seeks to rekindle a romance with her undead love.

By now, the zombie had become a global phenomenon. The undead would slowly shuffle across Asia during the 1980s in films such as Hwa I Hung's *Kung Fu Zombie* (Hong Kong, 1981), Ho Meng Hua and Moon-Tong Lau's *The Rape After* (Hong Kong, 1984) and Nobuhiko Obayashi's *Summer Amongst the Zombies* (Japan, 1988). From there they would even make it as far as New Zealand, as future *Lord of the Rings* director Peter Jackson would add his absurdly gory comic-horror film *Braindead* to the pantheon in 1992. This wave, this global phenomenon, had been primarily influenced not by the man dubbed "father of the zombie"[56] but by the horror directors of Europe and the filone system, which had taken Romero's blueprint and sent the shuffling zombie off in a number of new, exciting directions.

Similarly, back in the U.S., it was the success of the controversial Italian entries to the zombie film genre that had shaken up audiences and censors alike, rather than Romero's hugely impactful and imaginative second undead outing, that led to a huge increase in production of films featuring the living dead.

Nineteen eighty-five proved a banner year for the zombie, as George Romero's series of sociopolitical horrors continued with *Day of the Dead* and the Dan O'Bannon–directed *Return of the Living Dead* was also released. The two films went head-to-head, opening within a week of each other in the U.S.,[57] as both properties sought to determine which would become the defining legacy of the 1968 film that had changed everything.

Romero's third zombie film follows on from the timeline of *Dawn*, in that by the "day" the zombies have completely overrun the entire world, destroying all societies and forcing small pockets of survivors underground. In a military bunker, a group of scientists and soldiers perform experiments on a captive zombie in attempts to ascertain if the undead can be retrained or pacified. As tensions rise and cabin fever sets in, different factions form and oppose each other, of course leading the humans to become nothing more than fodder for the unemotional, inevitable march of the zombies. According to Romero himself, the film was a "tragedy about how a lack of human communication causes chaos and collapse even in this small little pie slice of society."[58] It became known for its shocking gore (with returning special effects maestro Tom Savini producing some of his very best work: this time, Savini's zombies take on elements of Fulci's creatures and others from across the filone, and set-pieces feature incredibly inventive, gore-soaked kills) and its very scathing view of modern society.

Day wasn't as well received as *Night* and *Dawn* had been, largely due to an even heavier dose of cynicism than both of the previous films combined. Janet Maslin of the *New York Times* asserted that it "recapitulates a lot of 'Dawn of the Dead' without taking the idea much further" and professed her expectation that, when the finale comes, "a large segment of the audience will wish this happened sooner."[59] Roger Ebert criticized the actors' performances and Romero's verbose script, arguing that "we are so busy listening to their endless dialog that we lose interest in the movie they occupy."[60]

The *Segnalazioni cinematografiche* waxed lyrical about the film, once more appearing to be quite invested in Romero's filmmaking even if the Holy See could never permit its content. Unlike its previous reviews of his zombie triptych, this one focused not on the social message but on the film's gore effects, stating that "lovers of the horror genre will find bread for their teeth and a feast for their eyes, with hundreds of meters of throbbing viscera, many bloody, torn and pulped livers and brains overflowing from the skull … a real collage of amputated limbs to be devoured with taste and decapitated bodies, with the variant that even in death the victims' teeth continue to gnaw and their eyeballs to spin threateningly."[61]

The Vatican's critic describes the film's impressive splatter in poetic detail, giving what appears to be high praise to Savini and Romero's gore: "the slow, frightening advance of the swaying and ravenous zombies and their hoarse cries ... resonant of certain atrocious grins of Goya and certain bodily deformations in Bosch, they are angelic things ... even those who detest the genre cannot deny the exceptional nature of the tricks and special effects used. And, however terrifying and truculent the film is, its packaging, like the acting of the performers, all have their own validity, even if, beyond the technical aspects, the judgment can only be negative."[62]

Despite delving deep into the film and sharing how impressed it was by the morbid aesthetics of *Day of the Dead* (even comparing them favorably to the art of masters such as Goya and Bosch), the *Segnalazioni cinematografiche* declared the film to be "unacceptable [and] repulsive."[63]

Something of particular interest in the review of *Day of the Dead* is that the Vatican appears to understand that its words are having less effect on the country's population than they once did. The review ends with an exasperation, a lament even, that fans of horror will continue to enjoy these films despite the Church's reservations, grieving over the fact that "you can be strong on the palate, but such tortures of the human creature are always repugnant, even to know that all this is desired (and it is an aggravating circumstance) for spectacular and commercial purposes."[64]

This is a very notable comment, in that it represents a tacit admission by the *Segnalazioni cinematografiche*'s writer that the Vatican is by now essentially powerless to stop the success of these sacrilegious films. The influence of the Church had diminished significantly over the last few years, and the warnings of the *Segnalazioni cinematografiche* were regularly failing to stop the country's cinema operators from screening sacrilegious horror content, much to the delight of genre fans who flocked to see it.

As noted by Scott[65] and White[66] the Catholic Church had, since 1960, experienced an unprecedented mass apostasy. Nineteen eighty-five was a year of introspection and reflection for the Church, as it considered just how much its influence on Italian society had waned. In 1984, the Vatican and the state of Italy had signed a concordat under which Roman Catholicism ceased to be the state religion of Italy. Prime Minister Bettino Craxi and the Vatican Secretary of State, Cardinal Agostino Casaroli, signed the document, which ended 55 years of the Vatican being recognized by the state as the official religion of Italy.[67] This concordat was signed for a number of reasons, not least of which being the Church's long and dedicated attempts to recycle its image after its complicity in fascism: in 1929, a concordat was signed between then Pope Pius XI and Mussolini, as the Vatican sought to ally with Mussolini's fascist regime.[68] The Pontiff's successor, Pius XII, subsequently signed a concordat with Hitler in 1933 that tied Roman Catholicism to the Third Reich and made all Catholic clerics have to take an oath to serve the "Fatherland" of Hitler's Germany. It was after the defeat of Hitler, the ousting of Mussolini and the collapse of fascism that the country's artists, poets and, most importantly its filmmakers began to produce art criticizing the Vatican and questioning the Church.

The historical links with fascism, and the Second Vatican Council in the early 1960s (itself assembled in attempts to "update" the Church and extricate itself from its tarnished reputation), all contributed to the mass apostasy in Italy that led to this severe diminishing of the Vatican's power over its people. The 1984 concordat, ending Roman Catholicism's "reign" as state religion, clearly felt like something of a milestone. The writers of *Segnalazioni cinematografiche*, which for 50 years had monitored cinema as an art form and done all it could to stop "harmful" content being screened in the nation's cinemas, were coming to realize that they no longer wielded the same power they once did.

Dan O'Bannon's parallel entry into the zombie canon was based on a novel written by *Night of the Living Dead* writer John Russo (who had retained the rights to the "of the Living Dead" title after he and George Romero parted ways). The film sought to distance itself from Romero's as much as possible, and in doing so became one of the most singular and original in the subgenre ever released. O'Bannon's zombies now had a new origin story, created as a result of a military chemical spill that later causes an acid rainstorm (an origin somewhat borrowed from the ecological disasters in various European filone movies). In *Return of the Living Dead*, the zombies are also fast moving, able to run, think quickly and even speak. The notion of zombies moaning "Brains!"[69] as they seek to devour their prey originated from this 1985 movie.

O'Bannon's undead creatures could not be killed by a head shot or decapitation (in fact the film's protagonists are unable to find a way to destroy them, discovering that even when chopped into pieces, those individual, dismembered limbs, heads and torsos remain in an animated state), and it is revealed that their zombified state causes them nothing but pain, from which they seek a release that will never come.

The finished film, so different from everything that had come before it, proved difficult to market. Executive in Charge of International Marketing Paul M. Sammon noted, "Tinseltown was confused ... most studio people did not know about, understand or even like horror movies"[70] and that even distributor Orion Pictures had little faith in this curious movie that was as much comedy as horror. The studio's executives "eyes would just glaze over. They'd either say I was crazy, or tell me to get lost,"[71] recounted Sammon.

Despite the cynicism at Orion, divesting from the serious, politically conscious Romero template paid off: the film found reasonable box-office returns, earning over $14 million from its $4 million budget, and was a hit with critics as well. Roger Ebert called it "a satisfactory ghoul movie, moving with precision from the funny opening scenes through the obligatory middle passages of pseudo-science, and on to the barf-bag climax"[72] and awarded it three out of four stars. O'Bannon's directorial debut birthed a new franchise, spawning four sequels over the course of two decades.

As already evidenced, the Vatican had shown that even though it had strong reservations about the zombie film and its profane resurrections, the Holy See's reviewers had at least engaged with the films, even praising the aesthetics and technical aspects of some (while still damning their repugnant content) and providing intellectual discussion on the sociopolitical messages contained in the filone's highlights. This understanding of the zombie film did not extend to *Return of the Living Dead*, which was summarily dismissed by the Holy See:

> "It wants to be a horror film but it's just a crazy and shabby film, moreover with rather painful acting,"[73] began the *Segnalazioni cinematografiche*'s review, which went on to attack the film for its "absolute lack of values, ruthlessness and cynicism without limits"[74] and appeared to be particularly mystified by the irony of Linnea Quigley's Trash, "the half-naked girl who complains about the loss of her shoe."[75] The verdict was "unacceptable [and] repellent."[76] The verdict neither deterred cinema operators from screening it nor audiences from viewing it.

Perhaps the most pertinent aspect of *Return of the Living Dead* was, as Sammon predicted, that it had blended horror and comedy perfectly. While George Romero would continue to work in the filone, directing a further three in his "of the Dead" series, ultimately it was O'Bannon's film, as it grew in cult status, that helped the filone turn another corner and continue into the new millennium. In proving that the zombie also worked as comedy, O'Bannon would inspire films such as John Elias Michalakis' *I Was a Teenage Zombie* (1987), Peter Jackson's *Braindead/Dead Alive* (1993) and, of course, Edgar Wright's *Shaun of the Dead* (2004). The zomcom as it became known would continue through the new millennium, in films such as Ruben Fleischer's *Zombieland* (2009) and its 2019 sequel, Jordan Rubin's 2014 U.S. film *Zombeavers*, and the filone would even produce a zombie comedy musical in the form of John McPhail's *Anna and the Apocalypse* (2018).

Over the decades, the humble zombie shuffled forth from an occultist and world traveler's writings, via an independent Pittsburgh filmmaker's controversial debut, to dominate the genre output of Europe and eventually outgrow its genre to become big box-office business. Even the slasher film benefited from a dose of the undead. By its sixth film, the *Friday the 13th* franchise had seen Jason Voorhees turn from unstoppable killer to zombified monster, rising from his grave to slice and dice a new batch of victims. William (Maniac) Lustig would return to the slasher with a zombie twist in his 1988 film *Maniac Cop*, which spawned a number of sequels. Zombies also became a staple of the burgeoning found footage genre, featuring in a Spanish series known as the *REC* franchise and Romero's own *Diary of the Dead* (2007). They even went mainstream, thanks to Francis Lawrence's Will Smith vehicle *I Am Legend* (2007), Marc Foster's 2013 *World War Z* and, most recently, the successful video game franchise *The Last of Us* and its television adaptation.

While the Vatican's writers would steadfastly refuse to directly acknowledge the notion of the profane resurrection in the zombie canon, its undead antagonists moved forward inexorably and refused to be stopped. By the mid–1980s, the Vatican had all but lost its power to censor and censure films effectively. Angeli's "new secularisation"[77] had been at least partly realized, Roman Catholics had become considerably less devout and Italy was a much more permissive society in general than it had been several decades earlier.

The slow, shuffling zombies of horror cinema had managed to outrun the Vatican.

In Lucio Fulci's 1969 film *Beatrice Cenci*, Francesco Cenci (Georges Wilson) preys upon his daughter Beatrice (Adrienne La Russa) as Pope Clement VIII (top right) and his Vatican prosecutors look on but do not intervene. The director (top left) looks down upon Beatrice, ready to tell her story. Illustration by the author.

7

Get Thee to a Nunnery!
(The Vatican versus ... Nunsploitation)

Throughout this book there have been examples of genre films carrying quasi-religious iconography, symbols and subtextual themes of the sacred and the profane and how the Vatican has reacted to these supposed acts of celluloid sacrilege. But there was an exploitation oeuvre, a transgressive subgenre with such potency that it needed no subtext or symbolism in order to powerfully critique and genuinely hurt Roman Catholic patriarchy in ways no other type of film could. An exploitation subgenre that was so effective precisely because it dealt *overtly* with Roman Catholicism, and its films were rooted in historical fact—an immensely powerful tool for the provocateur artists of an Italy that no longer trusted its Church and sought to express the national feeling via the medium of cinema.

This chapter's title comes, of course, from the play *Hamlet*, as William Shakespeare's conflicted, traumatized young hero makes a misogynistic outburst at Ophelia. It is used here because the line itself is a play on words that is reflective of the nunsploitation genre. In Hamlet's outburst, "nunnery" may indeed mean a convent, where Ophelia's chastity could be protected, but the word was also Elizabethan slang for "brothel" or "whorehouse."[1] Hamlet may just as well have been criticizing Ophelia for her *lack of* chastity as for a desire to keep it precious. The first recorded use of the term meaning brothel is thought to come from the 1593 Thomas Nash novel *Christ's Teares Over Jerusalem*. Nash writes of "one gentleman generally acquainted they give his admission unto sans fee, & free privilege thenceforward in their nunnery, to procure them frequentance."[2] His term is an ironic one, as he explains it is "this city—Sodoming trade"[3] rather than a Holy Convent that he refers to. Thus, the nunnery is the home of both the sacred and the profane. Were it not for the irony, it would be contradiction: where women are locked away together by the papal patriarchy to serve, they are bastions of chastity and innocence and yet also sexualized, immoral temptresses.

And so the nunnery sets the stage for the most Italian of all exploitation genres: nunsploitation, described by Thompson as "a veritable onslaught of satanic imagery, provocative nudity, righteous violence, and burgeoning feminist thought,"[4] another ironic contradiction. The nunsploitation oeuvre is, of course, brazen exploitation. The main conflict of the narratives within the subgenre is almost without exception profane by nature, carrying heavy sexual content (both consensual and abusive, but often with the line between muddied and blurred) as well as liberal helpings of torture and murder. There is, however, another side to the films in that they are inherently political—cynical, transgressive but factual historical narratives exploring stories of religious oppression under a corrupt Church.

The earliest example of the nunsploitation film was perhaps Jerzy Kawalerowicz's 1961 film *Mother Joan of the Angels*, a demonic possession film that would precede the satanic horror subgenre by several years and ask the question that those at the margins of the world would suddenly become curious about: what do all those women do behind those convent walls?

While the answer to that question would inevitably be something illicit, rebellious or heretical, the nunsploitation genre *is* based on historical fact, with real-life inspiration thought to include Marianna de Leyva, a 17th-century Italian teenager sent against her will to a convent. Once there, the girl dubbed the Nun of Monza would continue a love affair that gave her two secret children. When she was to be exposed, Marianna and her lover murdered a nun who threatened them. The pair were subsequently convicted and Marianna was sentenced to 14 years in a cramped prison cell. Her story has been told many times in Italian art, notably in Alessandro Manzoni's 1827 novel *The Betrothed* and in Eriprando Visconti's 1969 film *The Awful Story of the Nun of Monza*.

Visconti's adaptation told this story with Anne Heywood cast in the lead role and precipitated a sudden surge in nunsploitation flicks in the early 1970s. It features the darker moments of Marianna's life story told as spectacle, with the focus on scenes of rape, the subsequent scandal of her illegitimate child and her imprisonment and torture for said "crime."

The film picks up with Marianna as an adult, already known as Sister Virginia Maria, the narrative eschewing the initial controversy that her parents conspired with the Church to send her to a convent against her will. What it does show us is that Marianna's love affair begins with her rape, and that her rapist/lover Giampaolo is sent to the convent by the local priest, who wants to protect him from the Spanish. Her rapist becomes her lover, although how is never quite determined: she has him sent away but later requests his return. It is assumed that she has either been groomed or that her reaction is due to the trauma of having become institutionalized (or a combination of both).

In the film, Marianna/Sister Virginia Maria is presented as a complex character: strong-willed, passionate, adept and suspicious of the convent's priest and his machinations. She has agency, authority, and remains a strong protagonist throughout, in spite of her appalling treatment at the hands of others. As the plot progresses and she learns that she cannot count on anybody around her, she grows more resolute and refuses to be subjugated further.

Visconti's film does not appear to fit the usual exploitation mold, at least not at first. The direction; acting; production design all bear the hallmarks of a period drama (if made on a modest budget), and it is controversial only in its subject matter. There is very little transgressive content, with the focus of the story on cerebral machinations and skullduggery, at least until Marianna/Sister Virginia Maria's rape. The sequence itself is genuinely harrowing but not because it is graphic. The most upsetting aspect is that throughout, she screams for mercy, begs the other nuns for help … but they do not. The sisters are complicit, the priest Father Paolo unmoved. When Marianna needed help most, her Church and her God had forsaken her.

Anne Heywood is fantastic, her performance one of trauma and despair, as she self-flagellates and demands punishment for what has happened to her. There are several skillful red flags embedded in the performance, subtle cries for help that the character makes but that go unanswered. It is apparent in Visconti's narrative that, despite the rape, the true villain here is not considered to be Antonio Sabato's Giampaolo. Hardy Krüger's confessor Father Paolo is cold, ruthless and a sexual predator himself, using his influence to bed an impressionable young nun at one stage. It is he and Marianna's Church-based support network that are the antagonists of the story. Paolo attempts to bully Marianna into giving up her child, claiming that he is her only hope at salvation (when of course he, along with Giampaolo, is the one responsible for her predicament). Marianna not only loses her own humanity, in the trauma of her rape, but any chance she might have had to be a mother to the poor child birthed from said trauma is taken from her as well.

This was not, of course, just Marianna's fate, it was also indicative of the plight of many nuns throughout history and in the modern church as well. Goldenberg recognizes that "this pattern of behavior has been the standard for the Catholic Church since the Middle Ages. For more than a thousand years, the church has denigrated religious women when they challenged clerical abusers."[5] Goldenberg cites the Beguines, a lay religious movement for women popular throughout medieval cities in parts

In Eriprando Visconti's *The Awful Story of the Nun of Monza* (1969), Marianna de Leyva (Anne Heywood) is raped by Giampaolo (Antonio Sabàto). Father Paolo (Hardy Krüger) and Sister Benedetta (Margarita Lozano) look on dispassionately. Illustration by the author.

of the European continent. These women were "paradigms of female religiosity,"[6] caring for the sick and teaching in school, praying and meditating. However, for the sin of being independent of the Church, The Vatican targeted them, labeled them heretics, prostitutes, beggars and lesbians. Many were executed, others forced to recant and enter convents, where they would be abused by clerics.

Goldenberg asserts that "the piety of these religious women has long stood in stark contrast to the failings of the Catholic clergy,"[7] comparing the chaste, charitable and industrious lives of the Beguines to their patriarchal Catholic counterparts fathering children in secret and being responsible for massive bloodshed around the world, not least during the Crusades. She goes on to cite other examples, leading right up to the present day, and the recent #NunsToo social media movement that saw many nuns, emboldened by the success of the #MeToo movement in sharing women's stories and bringing high-profile abusers to justice, finally able to come forward and speak their truths.

The Roman Catholic Church has recently admitted that it has had a systemic problem with the rape, abuse and sexual slavery of nuns at the hands of its priests. In 2019, Pope Francis admitted to the world that many Roman Catholic nuns had been sexually abused by priests.[8] In one case made public, Francis' predecessor Pope Benedict had been forced to disperse an entire congregation of nuns who were being abused by priests and bishops, with the abuse extending not just to rape but effectively to sex slavery: "Pope Benedict had the courage to dissolve a female congregation which was at a certain level, because this slavery of women had entered it—slavery, even to the point of sexual slavery—on the part of clerics or the founder."[9]

It should be noted that this was not, in fact, a courageous act but in itself a deliberate act of cover-up. Pope Benedict did indeed put a stop to this particular instance of heinous abuse, but he did so in secrecy in order to keep word from reaching the outside world. His actions were made public years later by his successor only because Pope Francis could no longer hide the systemic abuse the Vatican was complicit in. The only act of heroism on display was that of Lucetta Scaraffia, editor of the Vatican magazine *Women, Church, World* and her 11-strong editorial team. Scaraffia exposed the sexual abuse of the nuns only for church elders to attempt to gag and delegitimize her and her team. She went ahead and published anyway, and it was only at this point, after the article was published and Scaraffia and her team all resigned from their roles, that Pope Francis publicly acknowledged the issue of widespread abuse against nuns for the first time.[10]

Pope Francis would admit that the problem was a systemic and ongoing one, but he claimed it to be one that tended to happen in "certain congregations, predominantly new ones,"[11] perhaps in an effort to play down the longevity of the Church's heinous crimes against women and children. The pontiff, while admitting this was a problem within the Church, considered that the issue was rooted not in the Church's view of its nuns but in wider society "seeing women as second class."[12]

While that is, on the surface, a fair statement, it is somewhat disingenuous of Pope Francis to attempt to separate the problem from the Church and point the finger at wider society when discussing the systemic abuse that has taken place, unchallenged, within Roman Catholic institutions for several centuries and has seen many attempts to bring it to light be buried by the Vatican.

Even prior to Scaraffia's exposé, there were other attempts to shine a light on these heinous crimes, such as that made by Sister Maura O'Donoghue, a Medical Missionary of Mary from Ireland.[13] Dedicated to revealing the suffering of so many of her peers, Sister O'Donoghue compiled a 1994 report on priests' alleged sexual abuse of nuns in more than 20 countries, only to see it buried by the Vatican. The existence of the report only emerged publicly seven years later, at which point a Vatican spokesman, Dr. Joaquin Navarro-Valls, acknowledged that "the problem is known about"[14] but insisted it was "restricted to a certain geographical area"[15] Navarro-Valls was understood to mean that these crimes only happened in Africa, a racist attempt to paint those working missions in Black countries as savages, while maintaining white, western Roman Catholicism as civilized and beyond reproach, which of course is demonstrably false.

Visconti's film (and the nunsploitation genre in general) is therefore problematic to the Church in that it challenges it in not one but two ways. First, we turn to hegemonic memory in contextualizing *The Awful Story of the Nun of Monza* and the nunsploitation subgenre as a whole. The Church has always sought to subjugate its flock with regard to the memory of its past, rather than allow the Italian people to confront the necessary truths, process them and move forward. The films covered in this chapter highlight many specific abuses carried out by the Church on its own people, often by order of the Vatican. Second, these films also shone a light on what were (and, in some cases, remain) *current* abuses and crimes, those still being perpetrated by priests upon nuns around the world, crimes that the Vatican was well aware of and sought not to rectify but to suppress. At a time when the Church was fighting for the hearts and minds of its flock in a period of mass apostasy, it sought both to establish and maintain hegemonic memory and an amnesia related to its historical abuses and to keep its ongoing abuses out of the public consciousness.

The initial reaction from the *Segnalazioni cinematografiche* is perhaps unsurprising. "From the historical documents relating to the Nun of Monza character, the author has extracted the most striking and strongest facts, treading with heavy hand on the different situations without measure, taste and respect for … historical truth."[16] The Vatican's critic is tested by Visconti's film in a way that its previous critics were not by other exploitation subgenres: the Vatican could usually point to the fantastical or the salacious content of the film as a way to dismiss it swiftly, but here, the story is a *true* story, one of a number of historical crimes committed by the Vatican.

Therefore, in an attempt to avoid addressing the Vatican's culpability in this historically factual case, the *Segnalazioni cinematografiche* is forced to critique the director's adaptation of the story, rather than the story itself. So the Vatican's reviewer reminds the public that films of this nature require "a certain formal care in the reconstruction of environments and customs"[17] before criticizing Visconti. "Having distorted a historical episode by telling it in a partisan and partial way and having deprived it of both an ever necessary study of the environment, and of human dramas and consequent note of pity for the characters themselves, is the greatest demerit (of the film)."[18]

The review ends with the comment that "the author seems to be pleased with his accurate and crude descriptions."[19] Visconti's film would be judged *inaccettabile* and Catholic audiences ordered to stay away from it. The Church accused the director of proudly presenting a partisan retelling of the story of the Nun of Monza, and urged the Italian people to take Visconti's retelling of the story with a hefty pinch of salt. In fact, one of the less salacious films in the nunsploitation subgenre is merely holding a mirror up to one of the very real crimes committed by the Church throughout history. While Visconti's film takes some liberties with the Nun of Monza's historically accurate life story, the film does not trivialize or sensationalize the seedier elements. How she ended up at the convent in the first place is not discussed, the rape scene is handled with a considerate touch, avoiding the male gaze, allowing the sound of Anne Heywood's screams to fill the scene (all of which contributes to an overwhelming sense of empathy with her). There is very little of the exploitative sex and nudity associated with exploitation cinema. The film is, at its heart, a genuine adaptation of historical fact, and historical fact that the Church would rather its flock forgot about. Perhaps this is behind the *Segnalazioni cinematografiche*'s decision to react with such guarded outrage.

By the time of *The Awful Story of the Nun of Monza*'s release, Lucio Fulci was already wrapping up his own study on exploitation, rape and Vatican corruption taking place behind the walls of a nunnery with his 1969 film *Beatrice Cenci*. It would be a decade before he found international notoriety as a director of video nasty zombie films, but in 1969 Fulci was primarily known as a writer and director of bawdy Italian comedies and was about to embark on the darkest period of his career, one in which he committed a number of criticisms of the Church to celluloid. Fulci, a tortured Catholic but also an openly critical thinker, was becoming preoccupied with his and the nation's apostasy, and it began to steadily infiltrate his work, beginning with this film. Like other directors, Fulci understood that protesting the Church's guilt in its present-day crimes was a dangerous game, one that could (indeed would) see him in court, so to turn to the crimes of the Vatican's past, already committed to the history books, was a way to shine a spotlight on the misdeeds of the Holy See.

Beatrice Cenci (played by Adrienne La Russa in the film) was a young Italian heiress, born in Rome in 1577 and deceased just 22 years later. The daughter of the authoritarian Count Francesco Cenci (George Martin appearing to relish in the excesses of the role), her controversial and tragic life story made her a proto-feminist icon and one of the most revered women in all of Italy's rich history.[20] Her father was a nobleman of papal lineage who had inherited a vast fortune, which he used to lead a life of sexual violence and depravity. Often tried for his crimes—which included multiple counts of child molestation and sodomy—by the Church, where others would have received the death penalty, he escaped this fate on multiple occasions due to his vast wealth. Rather than have him killed, the corrupt Vatican would extort his land and money from him as punishment.[21]

Francesco locked Beatrice away in a nunnery, where she could not escape his "visits" and he could easily force her to indulge in his depravity away from prying eyes. He subjected her to multiple incestuous rapes and beatings, until she and her lover Olimpio (played here by Cuban-born genre legend Tomas Milian) plotted and carried out his murder.

Pope Clement VIII authorized the torture of Beatrice and her consorts, carried out by Vatican investigators to secure their confessions. Though Beatrice proved formidable and refused to confess even under torture, the truth was discovered and, on September 11, 1599, Beatrice Cenci and her coconspirators were publicly beheaded. Beatrice was noted to have retained her steely resolve right up until the moment of her death, producing neither cries nor tears as she was executed.[22,23]

The executions sparked public outrage, not least because Beatrice had been punished with death for merely protecting herself against the vile actions of her father. The people understood that the patriarchal papal courts had allowed so many of Francesco's crimes to go without the punishment they deserved and that the Vatican's real reason for punishing Francesco's murderer was because she had put an end to the lucrative operation of fines paid by her father to the Church for his crimes. Pope Clement of course gained control of what remained of the Cenci fortune, ensuring the Vatican had successfully embezzled the entire Cenci estate over the course of several years.[24]

Beatrice Cenci was Fulci's first and only foray into historical drama, and his adaptation was quite reserved when compared with his later works. There was little in the way of salacious sexual content, and the violence and gore that Fulci would later become known for was only briefly evident in the murder of Francesco. A relatively simple historical drama was all it needed to be: the Cenci story highlighted the corruption and cover-ups of the Vatican at the dawn of the 17th century all by itself, events that we now know continued until as recently as the last decade.

Beatrice Cenci was a deliberate attack on the Vatican. Fulci's intention was to criticize the institution from a moral standpoint, to point out its hypocrisy, its intolerance and its punishment of those who question not the word of God but the word of the Church. That Beatrice Cenci was bestowed sainthood after her execution, as the Church sought to quell rising resentment at the unjust nature of her murder, offered clear evidence of the Vatican's cynicism and amorality without the need to sensationalize elements of the story.

Knowing he would face censure, the director had wrong-footed his producers and financiers by providing them with a "ringer" script: the screenplay he showed to Georgio Agliani and Filmena for their approval was a much more palatable affair, miles from the one he intended to direct. As the director himself explained: "The Producer wanted something different, more melodramatic. We gave him one script and shot another."[25] Fulci's finished film showed a director who wished to pull no punches and indeed would go on to deliver some damaging blows to Church and state alike in films such as *Don't Torture a Duckling* and *The Eroticist* (both 1972). Here, he was willing to present a historical epic in a brutal cinema verité style, shorn of the rose-tinted lenses and other accoutrements more palatable to those in authority.

Upon its release, *Beatrice Cenci* provoked great controversy. Some screenings prompted walkouts; others precipitated violence, and word soon traveled back to the Holy See through the Church's various institutional and social networks. The Vatican subsequently reviewed *Beatrice Cenci* and had much to say about Fulci's film.

"From facts handed down to us by history and popular tradition, the author has made a confusing and gross 'grand-guignolesque' drama, seizing every opportunity to exacerbate the most dark and gruesome aspects of the story,"[26] began the irate review. The *Segnalazioni cinematografiche* went on to attack Fulci's "preconceived notion of the negative attitudes of the Church"[27] (in effect, condemning the director for daring to highlight the corruption and cover-up of Francesco Cenci's crimes, and the Church's cynical reasons for the torture and execution of the young noblewoman Beatrice, who sought only to protect herself from her evil father). The film was declared a "complacent representation of the most raw and morbid elements of the murky page of history."[28] Here, the Vatican suggests the real historical events could never be truly verified, so Fulci could never truly *know* the truth and could only present what he *chose* to present: a salacious and damning indictment of the Church that may or may not be accurate.

After the Holy See censured the film, it subsequently proved a commercial flop. While this would ultimately help Fulci cultivate a reputation, and lead him to further attacks on the institution through his art, it adds yet more evidence to our understanding that the Vatican very much prefers not to have a light shone on its own corruption and complicity in the systemic rape and abuse of young women in its care, whether historical or current in nature.

In 1971, English auteur and l'enfant terrible Ken Russell released *The*

Devils, a film still considered by many the most shocking and controversial ever made. Russell's film is a dramatized account of Urbain Grandier, a French Catholic priest who was convicted of witchcraft and burned at the stake after the well-documented Loudun possessions witchcraft trial in 1634. Grandier was, it was determined, guilty of summoning the evil spirits that subsequently possessed a convent of Ursuline nuns, or so it was alleged. Russell's film focused partly on Grandier (Oliver Reed) and partly on the sexually repressed Sister Jeanne des Anges (Vanessa Redgrave), who incites the entire incident.

Russell, an apostate, had seen Jerzy Kawalerowicz's 1961 film *Mother Joan of the Angels* and had become fascinated by the tale of Loudon, using the story to deal with his own feelings with regard to his Catholic faith.[29] He saw Grandier as a sympathetic character, a man battling against his patriarchal religion and being punished for it. Russell's is a truly epic film, with grandiose sets that are almost science fiction–like in their design, actors fully immersed in their roles and some incredibly breathtaking, utterly transgressive sequences.

In January 1971, Russell showed a rough cut of the film to the BBFC and to his executives at Warner Bros. and, in what is believed to be an unusual case, both the BBFC and Warners came up with two separate (but with lots of crossover) lists of demanded cuts, with Russell having to make all of the changes before his film could be released.[30]

Cuts were made to reduce the duration of sexual elements, as well as make them less explicit (including Russell's now-infamous "Rape of Christ" sequence, which features an orgy of nuns cavorting against a life-size crucifixion tableau). A number of sequences that mixed sex and religious iconography were removed, as was some of the violence and gore. Then Russell found himself approached with yet more cuts to comply with, and it took three months to edit and further negotiate before the film could be granted an X certificate in May of 1971.[31]

Even in its (still) heavily censored version, the film is very sexually explicit, exploitative and violent, and frequently sacrilegious. Subsequently, it is one of the most widely banned films of all time (again, for emphasis—this is in its heavily censored form). Around the world the film was initially met with great praise by critics, prior to their shouts being overtaken by the much louder voice of controversy. Roger Ebert was celebratory in his discussion of the film, and even quite profound:

> Make no mistake. *The Devils* has a message for our time. For we learn from the mistakes of the past. We live in a time of violence, and it is only by looking in the mouth of the Devil that we can examine his teeth. In a time when our nation is responsible for violence on a global scale, it is only by bearing witness to violence on a personal scale that we can bring the war home.[32]

7. Get Thee to a Nunnery! 153

Roman Catholicism was, of course, outraged by *The Devils* even in its heavily censored state. The Church took exception to its graphic scenes of sexual perversions and of violence and torture, and campaigned for it to be banned in many countries (including the UK, where it was not only banned but was subsequently unavailable on home video formats until as late as 2011). In Italy, the Vatican made its voice on the film heard. The *Segnalazioni cinematografiche* "review" had much to say.

> The film, which claims to be a reconstruction of a historical fact, is inspired by a romantic literary source more than a true and obscure documentation and develops almost exclusively in a key favourable to exasperated fury and controversy. The conviction of fanaticism, superstition and, above all, of the abuse of religion for political purposes is made in vanity by a particular insistence on nauseous elements of delirium from the abundance of morbid and violent sequences.[33]

The *Segnalazioni cinematografiche*'s moral verdict was similar to that it had issued on Visconti's *The Awful Story of the Nun of Monza*, but because the tone of Russell's film was much more transgressive, so was the Church's damnation more emphatic. The Vatican's writer closed his review by accusing the filmmaker of "a systematic denigration of religious values such as to make the work completely unacceptable."[34]

Rife[35] sums up the controversy very well, dissecting the Vatican's complaints with precision and pointing out that the Roman Catholic Church hates that anyone might suggest it is infallible in its leadership. For decades, it has outright refuted certain controversies only to later be found to be complicit in them, from the deep-state cabal of Propaganda Due to widespread child abuse scandals, the systematic abuse of nuns, and the systemic cover-ups of each. Despite this, the representation of members of the clergy on-screen is damned if presented as fallible, complex or in any way prone to human seductions. Rife asserts that

> much has been made of Russell's conflation of sexual and religious frenzy in the film, particularly the infamous, largely unseen 'Rape of Christ' scene, where hysterical nuns violate a statue of Jesus. But the truly provocative— some might even say blasphemous—part of the film is its assertion that, even while preaching their rhetoric of sin and salvation, nuns and priests and cardinals are only human, and humans are nothing but animals. Filthy, power-hungry, lustful animals.[36]

The film returns to the idea of fear used as a tool by the Church, something that is explored both by *The Devils*' narrative (by suggesting this was Grandier's plight; that he was subject to those fear-driven attacks that in the end took his life) and by the film's underlying aim: to openly criticize the Church for instilling that very fear in its director. In her extensive

In Ken Russell's *The Devils*, nuns under the power of witchcraft writhe and cavort together, creating a perverse likeness of the cross. Illustration by the author.

literature review, Schroeder raises questions about religion's role in the building of human character and seeks to answer the question: "How much are mores and manners driven by fear of divine retribution versus unconditional piety?"[37] Parsons provides personal anecdotes of religious trauma to discuss their own understanding of religious fear and how it was used by predatory figures of Church authority:

> The initial friendship offered by a controlling pastor may seem very attractive and important to someone with a precarious mental history. Such individuals are however extraordinarily vulnerable to the abusive controlling techniques used by some religious leaders. Quite often there is an appeal to demonic forces as the explanation for symptoms of mental distress. If the individual buys into this explanation, the state of bondage is complete. Emotionally and psychologically they are in complete thrall to this religious leader who appears to offer them a way forward.[38]

Merritt agrees, registering the distinct ability to identify, in retrospect, psychological trauma that religion caused and recalling the "fire and damnation sermons ... [that] made me think that God's anger far outweighed God's love."[39] Merritt's final assertion is particularly telling: "Using fear, when it is already untamed in a person's mind seems (at the least) irresponsible, and (at its worst) close to torture. It can be a very traumatic experience when the adults, who are in charge of your spiritual health, exaggerate that fear in order to manipulate you."[40]

Fear works best in the house of ignorance. Where Catholic audiences' minds are drawn to the transgressions of the Catholic Church, they are drawn to its weaknesses. Fear then becomes more difficult to use as a weapon. Yet, that is what the *Segnalazioni cinematografiche* attempts to continue do with its response to these historical films that seek to shine a light on the transgressions of the Roman Catholic Church. The Holy See's verdicts on these films are often written not with careful consideration but in anger, in a further attempt to "exaggerate that fear in order to manipulate"[41] its flock.

Fear, once it has lost enough potency, no longer keeps the ignorant masses under control. The public's thirst for these transgressive exposés of Vatican behavior was beginning to outgrow its fear of the Holy See, and over the coming years many films would be added to the nunsploitation canon, often directed and produced by apostate Italians.

Sergio Bergonzelli's *Our Lady of Lust* (1972, known as *Cristiana Monaca Indemoniata* in Italy) is a simple exploitation premise of a promiscuous young woman (the titular Cristiana, played by Toti Achilli) who promises to devote her life to God when her plane does not crash. Over the course of her stay at a convent, she falls prey to a series of (expected) temptations that titillate and hopefully satiate the audience. The *Segnalazioni cinematografiche* was quick to dismiss this one, damning it as "an ignoble porno-comic"[42] and identifying its main problem as that of "insincere vocations ... the alleged constraints of religious life is only a pretext to show every kind of obscenity to the unfortunate spectator."[43]

The clearly rattled Vatican reviewer finished their piece by calling the film "a continuous insult to both the audience and the intelligence of the public, whose only opportunities for relief derive from the frequent and completely involuntary plunges into ridicule that mark the painful story."[44] The *Segnalazioni cinematografiche* deemed the film *inaccettabile*, but Italy's Catholics would instead flock to screenings in theaters that dared to exhibit it, to get a look at the latest film that had shocked the Vatican to anger.

Just over a year later, Gianfranco Mingozzi's *Flavia the Heretic* was released, to similar uproar from the Vatican as the films of Visconti and Russell had received. This time a historical epic set in 15th-century Puglia, it told the story of Flavia Gaetani (Florinda Bolkan), the passionate, rebellious young woman sent to a monastery by her noble father for her romantic interest in a Muslim traveler. At the monastery, misandrist nun Maria teaches Flavia in a proto-feminist school of thought, and as she learns and philosophizes, Flavia becomes increasingly angered by the Catholic patriarchy she sits within. After a cult attacks her convent, Flavia teams with an army of Muslims to destroy her foes.

Again, Mingozzi's movie was not particularly exploitative and followed the lead set by *Mother Joan of the Angels*, *Beatrice Cenci* and *The Awful Story of the Nun of Monza* in presenting a historical tale in a straightforward manner. The always excellent Florinda Bolkan puts on a convincing performance as Flavia, and her character's decisions make sense in the face of what she had to put up with. When Flavia rises up with outsiders against the Roman Catholic patriarchy one feels a swell of pride, only for this to deflate as Flavia comes, of course, to realize her new allies are no better than her previous ones. Rather than ramping up the sex and violence, Mingozzi's film is filled with substance, asking important questions about women being made to function inside a number of patriarchal systems that do not benefit them in any way—questions that are still resonant and relevant now.

The *Segnalazioni cinematografiche* called the film "a pseudo-historical drama on obsessive hysteria, on fanaticism, on the revolts against the subordination to which women were obliged in medieval times"[45] and criticized its story for "[serving] as an excuse to denigrate the ecclesiastical power that, in the name of the general order, would always have opposed the female personality and her just redemption."[46]

Once more presented with a historical tale, the Vatican takes a little care not to criticize the events held in the narrative directly, or attempt to refute that they happened. Instead, it critiques Mingozzi's presentation and content, which it asserts is more cynical and partisan than it appears to be to a modern viewer.

"The reconstruction, in homage more to a perverse taste of the show than to a thematic affirmation, contains scenes of rare cruelty and turpitude. Unacceptable/negative."[47] The verdict is outright, but once again the reasoning feels flimsy. Flavia is a very measured affair, with scattered nudity and sex that is not particularly gratuitous.

The visceral condemnation from the Holy See hides its discomfort, its embarrassment. Shouting in anger is its last recourse where intelligent reasoning can only force admissions of guilt. The Vatican is effectively hamstrung, impotent to do anything other than accuse these directors of sensationalizing the true stories they adapt. Yes, nunsploitation films are, at times, salacious stories that examine the relationship between the flesh and the spirit, but these are not fictional narratives, at least not entirely.

The Nun of Monza, Beatrice Cenci, Flavia ... these were real women. Young, vulnerable women, and the crimes visited upon them either by the Church or with its knowledge and complicity are factual and cannot be argued against.

When each film highlights the Vatican's historical evils, it also shines a light upon those crimes that are still going on behind closed doors, those yet to be uncovered and reported on by the likes of Sister Maura O'Donoghue and Lucetta Scaraffia, those yet to be made public via #NunsToo. When the *Segnalazioni cinematografiche* sneers at these "pseudo-historical drama"[48] films, it is clear that the real source of ire is the criticism for organized religion that courses through the narrative. The Holy See knows it is being put under fresh interrogation by these subversive filmmakers, and the attempts to censor and ban nunsploitation films are an example of its continued efforts to cover up its crimes. The Vatican cannot rewrite the history books (although it would very much like to), so instead it hopes to keep them closed, to let its flock forget. When Visconti, Fulci, Mingozzi and others put these stories to celluloid, they are presented to entirely new generations who might otherwise have remained ignorant of the Church's own acts of evil.

Domenico Paolella's *Story of a Cloistered Nun*, seeing Eleonora Giorgi's Carmela forced into a convent against her will after refusing an arranged marriage, was released the same year as Mingozzi's *Flavia the Heretic*. Carmela arrives to find sexually repressed nuns, lots of on-screen lesbian sex and a plot by the nuns that will see them murder Carmela's lover. Once again, the story tells of a young woman (possibly still a child) forced into a convent by a severe parent, then adapting to what she finds there. To this narrative arc, Paolella adds that Carmela was promised as an infant to be a particular man's wife, prompting an element of rebellion against the patriarchy that also features in *Flavia the Heretic*. At the film's end, Carmela leaves the convent and dedicates the rest of her life to helping the sick.

The *Segnalazioni cinematografiche* frames its review in what the film could have done better to satisfy the Vatican of its worth. "Inspired by real events, the film ignores Carmela's most important and significant value, which is only hinted at in a final caption—to focus on those elements, proper to the shabby conventional thread of our cinema, which wants monasteries full of poor obsessed women, devoted to clandestine loves according to and against nature."[49] The Vatican's reviewer reveres the much more powerful Christian image of Carmela as a Mother Theresa figure, inspiring hope and love through missionary work with the people of underdeveloped countries. Perhaps it is at least partially correct: had the film allowed for an additional 20 minutes of narrative, showing Carmela at peace as she undertakes charitable work despite all in the convent that showed her the ugly side of her religion, it would have provided a very strong resolution to Carmela's struggle and been a more complete dramatic film. That said, it is clear from the review that the *Segnalazioni cinematografiche*'s writer is exasperated at yet another cinematic attempt to sensationalize the transgressions of the Roman Catholic Church.

The reviewer finishes a brief but emphatic dismissal of the film with "the story is built in such a way as to induce the viewer to believe that hypocrisy and debauchery are inevitable consequences of cloistered life. Unacceptable/licentious."[50]

Nunsploitation was spreading around the globe. Nineteen seventy-four saw the release of Japanese director Norifumi Suzuki's *School of the Holy Beast*, which has young Maya (Yumi Takigawa) become a nun only to find predatory archbishops, brutal discipline and masochistic rituals. Jishū nuns had already been featured in films about feudal Japan, but now the country was learning the power of the archetype in exploitation fare. Suzuki's film would be followed by Masaru Konuma's *Cloistered Nun: Runa's Confession* (1976), Kōyū Ohara's *Sister Lucia's Dishonor* (1978) and *Wet Rope Confession: Convent Story* (1979) and Mamoru Watanabe's *Rope of Hell: A Nun's Story* (1981), among others.

In Spain, Italy's neighbor that was also largely in thrall to Catholicism, nunsploitation experiments would soon be in full flow. By the time the Japanese were experimenting with their own nunsploitation cycle, Jesús ("Jess") Franco had already delivered his entry into the canon, directing *The Demons* (1973) in an attempt to cash in on the popularity of both William Friedkin's *The Exorcist* and the polarity of Ken Russell's *The Devils*. Deighan notes that "it's going to be a fairly straightforward nunsploitation film, but dramatically veers from that path into more traditional witch-hunting territory with torture, exploitation, political machinations, and plenty of sex."[51]

Franco's film explored a dungeon of terror, where young nuns suspected of falling prey to the Devil (any hint of sexuality from the imprisoned nuns, any agency whatsoever, is attributed to demonic possession) are tortured as part of their "treatment." Franco certainly ramped up the sexual content for his release. The young nuns of the convent are seen cavorting in the throes of wet dreams. The nun who discovers them soon joins them, gripped by a disabling lust, upon which Franco's camera lingers in provocative close-up. Nuns are tested for whether they are "intact" by being sexually molested, and are then damned to very fetishistic forms of torture in efforts to force the Devil out of them. These scenes are unflinching to say the least, filmed very much with the male gaze in mind and really quite shocking on occasion.

Despite believing the film matched up more closely with the likes of Michael Reeves' 1968 *Witchfinder General* or Michael Armstrong and Adrian Hoven's *Mark of the Devil* (1970), Deighan considered that "the Devils notwithstanding, *The Demons* is probably the most erotic witch-hunting film of the period, putting far more emphasis on sex than violence."[52]

The film presented young girls essentially being used for sex and other depravities by the very people who should safeguard them, with torture "demanded" by the cowardly, superstitious belief in demonic possession and exorcism. In an act of filone magic, its story deftly walks a series of thematic tightropes between nunsploitation and satanic horror and delivers something that sees them intertwine when they need to without sacrificing plotting or suspension of disbelief. The Vatican, already familiar with Franco's transgressive eroticism and horror, was suitably incensed by his latest offering, stating that the film's "nauseating storytelling (from which the religion it has massacred is not extraneous) is treated with an adequate concoction of idiocy, unbridled eroticism, liturgical-monastic upheavals with the inevitable vernacular Latin, taste for the horrid and macabre, situations and solutions of a serene absurdity. There is no need to spend any more words on this product of degenerate cinematography."[53]

While officially falling under the guidance of the Holy See, the Roman Catholicism of Spain had often been more extremist than that of its patriarchy. Since the days of Ferdinand and Isabella, the Spanish Church had been considered more orthodox and conservative than that of Rome. The Inquisition had more power than it had anywhere else, and the 16th-century Protestant Reformation was met with such vehement opposition that it failed to take hold in the country thanks to a violent countermovement that burned its churches and killed its clerics. Over its history, as the Vatican learned (very often from its own mistakes) to become more accepting of the world beyond its walls, the Spanish church only became more extremist. As the Vatican had with Mussolini and Hitler, the Spanish Church allied itself with Francisco Franco in a marriage of convenience that remained throughout the Spanish general's rule, fearing any form of religious freedom.

It is therefore unsurprising that Spain would have its own subversive, anti–Catholic directors, and Franco was chief among them, his transgressive content often taking aim at the oppressive religion of his country. Here, in a rare break from the norm (the Holy See had, on occasions, attempted to influence the Spanish Church to move with the times and accept more liberal attitudes, most of which attempts failed dismally), the Vatican criticizes Spanish art for being *too* liberal and for its desecration of the country's religious values. Such was the Vatican's disgust for Jess

Franco's work that it would appear it failed to understand how the director's work could even exist under the regime of Francisco Franco and the Spanish Catholic Church. In truth, the director used the same tactics as many of his Italian counterparts: in seeking funding coproduction from other European countries and ensuring his scripts weren't scrutinized by Spanish backers, his films could be made far from the oppressive influence of his homeland. *The Demons* was a French/Portuguese coproduction, banned in Franco's home country and censured in Italy but finding audiences across the rest of Europe, the UK and the U.S.

With the alternative title of *La Sexorcista*, Gilberto Martinez Solares' 1975 Mexican picture *Satanico Pandemonium* might (like Franco's film) have been more at home in this book's satanic horror chapter, but it carries enough of the tropes, themes and iconography of the nunsploitation genre to be discussed here. This kaleidoscopic film used the bright color and vivid images from nunsploitation and the uneasy threat of Satan to titillate and terrify in equal measure. There are a number of titles that fit within the nunsploitation canon that could equally be called satanic horror films, and several of Spain's entries to this canon were among them. Spanish-speaking exploitation directors were just as interested in filones as the Italians and, as both subgenres tend to heavily involve the Church, they make very comfortable bedfellows.

As had already been seen by its reaction to Ken Russell's *The Devils* and Jess Franco's *The Demons*, The Vatican was no more tolerant of this kind of product from overseas. The *Segnalazioni cinematografiche* declared in the case of *Satanico Pandemonium* that the film itself was "possessed"[54] and blasted the work as "a filthy ranting under which it is impossible to recognize any theme."[55]

As one of the more salacious entries into the filone (with no apparent historical significance for the Vatican to worry about) *Satanico Pandemonium* was swiftly and summarily dismissed by the *Segnalazioni cinematografiche*: "Narratively disconnected, boring and absolutely incredible on the whole and in the aberrant details, the show is a succession of serious licentiousness and scenes bordering on the blasphemous…. Unacceptable/abhorrent."[56]

The Vatican continued to take the most rigid of stances on the nunsploitation canon, and yet it became ever more popular across Europe and beyond, with more producers at home and abroad commissioning this controversial fare. By 1980, the popularity of the filone in the grubby *terza visione* theaters of Italy, the fleapits of the UK and the drive-ins of America was rivaled only by the phenomenally successful zombie and cannibal filones.

Legendary Italian sleaze merchant Aristide Massaccesi (Joe D'Amato) released *Images in a Convent* in 1979 to instant censure by the Church, which had already criticized the director and producer and a number of his films. There was no doubt D'Amato's film would be exploitation; his entire oeuvre had consisted of pornography, horror and other subversive subgenres. It was also a sure bet that the film would be controversial; D'Amato had ruffled feathers more often than most of his peers. What arrived was the most exploitative and sexually explicit film to grace the canon yet.

D'Amato's film was clearly a product of the filone system: like the directors of *The Demons* and *Satanico Pandemonium*, D'Amato wished to capitalize on both *The Exorcist* and *The Devils*, adding the pseudo-historical context in order to poke and prod at moral guardians and censors, to inflame critics and gain the film a reputation. With the above considered, D'Amato's film was a success. The *Segnalazioni cinematografiche*'s review called out the film for its claim to authenticity in the opening credits, where it "is said to be 'freely' inspired by *La Religicluse* by Denis Diderot. In fact, even if the well-known novel is not morally acceptable, the film has nothing to do with it except for the arrivals of the aristocratic novice without a vocation and the wounded officer."[57]

The *Segnalazioni cinematografiche* would dismiss Joe D'Amato as swiftly as it could: "Joe D'Amato's nuns ... are all sexual maniacs: in the convent (rebuilt with very little credibility of environments) ... it looks like one of those pornographic nights that the director himself presumed to describe in his previous films. The story is absurd and the whole film is an erotic delusion. Unacceptable/degrading."[58]

The Vatican would yet make the acquaintance of a film that caused an even more fervent reaction from it than any in the genre so far, including Russell's *The Devils*. Directed by Walerian Borowczyk in 1978 and about to be unleashed upon an unsuspecting Italian public was a film called *Behind Convent Walls*.

Polish erotica auteur Borowczyk had already fetishized prostitution in 1976's *La Marge* (The Margin, also known as *Streetwalker*), based on the subversive novel by André Pieyre de Mandiargues. Borowczyk had also released *La Bête* (The Beast) the previous year, in which the director explored the more subversive side of the Beauty and the Beast affair—bestiality. His own convent film would be in typical Borowczyk style: a sumptuous visual feast that gives way to terrible transgressions; production design so visually arresting that it almost becomes extra-sensory; high art that just so happens to house acres of naked flesh. Borowczyk's erotic horror films had a tendency to look like Merchant Ivory productions (if Ismail Merchant and James Ivory had been pornographers) and feature the most awe-inspiring mise-en-scène, terrifically detached performances and, of course, copious amounts of visceral sex.

In Joe D'Amato's 1979 *Images in a Convent*, Isabella (Paola Senatore) fornicates before the crucified Christ. Illustration by the author.

Based on Stendhal's *Walks in Rome*, Borowczyk's film is once again pseudo-historical but is unafraid to marry this with the more sensational elements of nunsploitation. It tells the very true story of greedy families who had for centuries "given" their daughters to convents without the girls' consent. The inhabitants of these convents lived a life of punishment and torture. What *Behind Convent Walls* does is show us just how depraved these repressed, frustrated young women could become, and just how far the religious patriarchy was willing to go to control them.

The Vatican opposed the film quite staunchly and campaigned for it to be banned by the state. The combination of the high production and artistic value with the most profane content, and the accusatory finger pointed at the Church for allowing these young women to be locked away and abused, carried with it more power than the rest of the genre put together. Not only did the pages of the *Segnalazioni cinematografiche* label the film "a desecration,"[59] possibly the most damning final verdict of a film in the pamphlet's history; the pastoral evaluation was bolstered by further opinions, sought by the Vatican, from contemporary critics outside its walls. These included Giovanni Grazzini from *Il Corriere della Sera*; Alfio Cantelli, writer at *Il Giornale*; *Il Tempo*'s Carlo Trionfera. The Holy See's subsequent discussion went to several pages in length.

It would be rare for a film to have such an effect on the *Segnalazioni cinematografiche* that it sought to bring in other voices to take part in a richer discussion. It usually only happened to films the Vatican was particularly impressed by, or particularly disgusted with.

The pastoral review of the film would confirm which effect Borowczyk's film had had upon the Holy See: "Although it claims to have been inspired by Stendhal's 'Roman Walks' ... the director certainly did not obey, with this film, any historical-social concern, but pursued only vulgar interests."[60] The *Segnalazioni cinematografiche* commented: "Obsessively centered on the unbridled sexuality of a group of nuns, which the camera illustrates with obsessive insistence, a morbid mixture of obscenity and anti–Catholic liveliness, the film is unworthy of any appreciation."[61]

Giovanni Grazzini from *Il Corriere della Sera* backed up the *Segnalazioni cinematografiche*'s opinion, offering a sneering portrait of the film and its director: "Most masters want to kiss the sacred sweet breads of Borowczyk, the supreme pontiff of cinematographic eroticism. We are reluctant. I believe that... [we] live in a society in which the explicit representation of copulation, masturbation and reciprocal caresses makes a scandal—and for this reason the film is sold in cinemas, not for its poetic values."[62]

Grazzini continued, asserting that

> an artist setting off on that downhill road always runs the risk of being mistaken for a merchant. Borowczyk does not escape the rule, on the contrary it is today the bleakest example. Author of ingenuity that elegance and the smile often redeem from the suspicion of pornography, he found in the West, all the more pervasive of his native Poland, exquisite intellectuals who are willing to give him diplomas of prophet and revolutionary, his classroom audience remains that of eighteen-year-olds and octogenarians, who with their red-hot imagination, their hands in their pockets and their nostalgic memories are enhanced by these visual games.[63]

Il Giornale's Alfio Cantelli was a little milder in his critique, adding, "*Behind Convent Walls* falls flat: the erotic scenes, driven by unthinkable obscenity, remain pure erotic exercises by voyeurs and certainly do not contribute to giving us a picture [of reality]."[64] Cantelli considered that the director's strengths were on display in the nonsexual scenes: "Borowczyk's hand is noted, paradoxically, precisely in the sequences in which sexual exercises are absent, such as that of the abbess's death and funeral."[65] The review offered in favor of Borowczyk that he may indeed be an artist, just not one suited to the Italian cinema system: "It should be noted, however, that some authors (such as Borowczyk) when they go abroad, are appreciated for inspiration and measure, and as they arrive in Italy they immediately fall into a cinema whose main goal is the box office of receipts."[66]

Finally, Carlo Trionfera from *Il Tempo* was apparently disappointed in the unrealized potential of film and director and the film's lack of artistic value: "*Behind Convent Walls* seems to represent almost a second defaced and unrecognizable face of the Polish director: eroticism becomes explicit pornography, the impetus turns into iconoclastic fury, the refined form colors and burns in insane and unbalanced orgiastic atmospheres."[67] Trionfera would conclude that

> the first part, all description of environments and characters, seems to refer to the best moments of Borowczyk; affirming with fluttering choral rhythms the most celebrated stylistic vocation of the author, alongside a praiseworthy and successful intent to symbolize ... however, the starting components seem to go crazy: the figurative collections degenerate into a livid carnival, overtaken by obscure games of almost childish amusements [and] the subtle expressive language is replaced by a kind of blasphemous fury.[68]

Perhaps it was a discovery that the popularity of nunsploitation was not waning but intensifying in the face of Vatican critique that led the *Segnalazioni cinematografiche* to employ noted critics from other institutions in a bid to show the weight of critical opinion against this particular film and strengthen its bid to have it banned entirely. Perhaps it was a realization that the films produced in this canon, all being at least partly factual and shining a light on both the Vatican's failings to protect its young nuns and its complicity in covering up the scandalous crimes they were subjected to, were doing real damage to the reputation of the Holy See. As it was, the genre of nunsploitation would remain popular, both domestically and abroad, for another decade or so.

More exploitation directors would turn to the genre, such as Giulio Berruti with *Killer Nun* (1979) and Bruno Mattei, who both helmed his own adaptation of *The True Story of the Nun of Monza* (1980) and directed *The Other Hell* (1981), a film that sought to cash in not only on nunsploitation but on the baroque horror popular at the time, adding elements of Dario Argento's *Suspiria* and *Inferno*. Pedro Almodóvar would turn to the genre with *Dark Habits* (1983), and Joe D'Amato would return to nunsploitation with *Convent of Sinners* (1986).

Occasional revivals of the subgenre have taken place, from Mario Baino's 1994 film *Dark Waters* to Robert Rodriguez's *Machete* (2010), Joseph Guzman's 2010 *Nude Nuns with Big Guns*, Darren Lynn Bousman's *St. Agatha* (2018), Chris Smith's *Consecration* and Tamae Garateguy's *Auxilio* (both 2023). Despite these new additions to the pantheon, nunsploitation's popularity in the 1970s would never quite be matched—much, no doubt, to the Vatican's relief.

8

The Paradox of Memory
(*The Vatican versus ... Nazisploitation*)

In Italy, cinema has contributed to constructing a paradox of memory in which the rememberer is asked to prevent past mistakes from happening again and yet is encouraged to forget what those mistakes were, or that they ever even took place.[1]

In his 2015 research paper *Italian Cinema and the Fascist Past: Tracing Memory Amnesia*, Giacomo Lichtner discusses the complexity (and lack thereof) of fascist narratives in Italian cinema, and how they impact upon generations of Italians for whom the shadow of fascism remains at their shoulder; not necessarily just because the extreme authoritarianist and ultranationalist political ideology threatens to return to the country (thanks to the efforts of certain neofascist, populist political figures and organizations, groups and other affiliates) but because they have never been afforded a proper opportunity for reflection and closure on the darkest period of their country's modern history. There is an apparent reticence to properly discuss and lay to rest the ghosts of Mussolini's Italy, with it often becoming apparent that this is out of a sense of either embarrassment, shame or self-preservation (or a combination of the three). From the moment Il Duce's regime fell, the hierarchy of Italian society immediately began the task of consciously uncoupling from a system that they were, to varying degrees, complicit in.

Consider how Germans have dealt psychologically with their country's complex and dark history: the *Wehrmachtauskunftstelle* (a data archive about people who served in World War II) receives, on average, 200,000 requests from members of the public each year.[2] Subsequent generations of Germans have grown up with a genuine interest in understanding and processing what their ancestors did during World War II, leading to an intergenerational dialogue that has helped the German people to address and reconcile with their country's past and learn how to ensure

Director Pier Paolo Pasolini, camera in hand; his corpse lying on the beach where it was discovered; and from his *Salò, or the 120 Days of Sodom*, a kidnapped adolescent, naked and weak, and 120 scratched tally marks. Illustration by the author.

it is not repeated in the future.³ This dialog has taken close to a half century to happen, for a multitude of reasons, but it *is* happening. Germany's system of government was arguably efficacious in its efforts to repair the country from its reputation, slowly but surely garnering a reputation in the postwar world as the moral and economic compass of a united European Union.

In Italy, it at times appears as though no such progress has been made, largely because of the shame and self-preservation that shaped the collective ego: it could be argued that neither state nor Church has properly addressed its complicity in the fascist era but attempted to shroud its involvement in secrecy and pray for amnesia to wash away the sins of the past. Italy never underwent a process equivalent to Germany's de–Nazification after World War II, opting to minimize any attempts to purge power structures of fascists as it instead prioritized attempts to block the Communist Party from gaining power in the country. Since then, the country has allowed those who served under Il Duce or believed in his edicts to find ways to rebuild fascism yet at the same time refused to allow the Italian people an opportunity to address what the nation went through under their former ruler.

This has, of course, led to considerable social and political trauma and turmoil for the country, including the previously mentioned secret power cabal of Propaganda Due and, of course, the Years of Lead (1968-1988), a period of tumult that saw waves of terrorist activity (from kidnappings to bombings and massacres) perpetrated by warring far-right and far-left factions. These were followed by the rise of media tycoon Silvio Berlusconi (an alleged member of the clandestine Propaganda Due) to prime minister and his many subsequent controversies including (but not limited to) media control and conflict of interest, legislative changes made out of self-preservation, foreign relations with authoritarian leaders in Russia, Belarus and Libya, and the infamous "bunga bunga" parties involving underage prostitutes. The shadow of fascism still looms over Italy today, in the form of Prime Minister Giorgia Meloni of the neofascist Brothers of Italy party (who secured 26 percent of the vote in the country's 2022 elections).

The Vatican had, as previously noted, been complicit in the fascist regime of Benito Mussolini and sympathetic to Hitler's Third Reich, thanks largely to the actions (and inaction) of Eugenio Pacelli, the man who would become Pope Pius XII and who assisted in the legitimizations of Hitler's regime through the pursuit of the *Reichskonkordat* treaty in 1933. After Mussolini's deposition in 1943 (and execution two years later), and the fall of Hitler in 1945, the Vatican immediately began efforts to distance itself from its wartime allegiances, striking up uneasy alliances with leftist intellectuals as it attempted to clean its tarnished image.⁴

In the aftermath of the fascist era, the country's poets, journalists and filmmakers (many of whom had learned their craft at Mussolini's Centro Sperimentale di Cinematografia) created the neorealism era, a filmic movement based on and around the plight of the Italian working classes under fascism, even going so far as to hire casts of genuine working-class Italians to feature in productions (rather than established acting talent). This documentary-like style of filmmaking became a global success, with filmmakers such as Vittorio De Sica, Luchino Visconti, Roberto Rossellini and Federico Fellini becoming celebrated filmmakers and globally renowned names.

The Vatican-endorsed studios Orbis Film and Film Universalia were soon set to work on a series of cine-catechisms: modern religious education told via the medium of film, as a "language of light"[5] to ensure the Vatican could continue to shepherd the Italian flock that was becoming somewhat resistant to its influence after the reign of Mussolini and actions of Pius XII. While there were high aspirations (including films to be directed by Italian cinema's leading lights, such as Fellini), only one cine-catechism saw fruition: Mario Soldati's 1945 short film *Chi e' Dio?* (Who is God?).[6] There are a number of reasons why the Vatican's alliance with the film industry's leftist intellectuals did not work out: the neorealism films of the emerging artists were very critical of both fascism and the Church, as Roman Catholicism's reputation had indeed been compromised by its alliance with Mussolini and Hitler; ironically, the Holy See was blind to the work it needed to do to regain the trust of the people and had erred in launching straight back into its role of shepherd, expecting Catholics to remain unquestioning and subservient; the Catholics of Italy were already becoming engaged in a moral and existential debate on the primacy of art or morality in film that encouraged intellectualism and free-thinking even among the working classes.[7,8]

Thus, with its own hopes for influencing congregations through the power of cinema greatly diminished, the Vatican soon poured its efforts into censorship and criticism and became very critical of the directors of the neorealism movement. In doing so, it sought to suppress dialogues in film that dealt critically with fascism, lest they continue to remind the people of the Church's alliance with the most reprehensible political, social and genocidal movement of modern times.

So what of nazisploitation?

Not quite horror but often either horror-adjacent or featuring enough real-life horrors to justify its inclusion within the umbrella of genre film, nazisploitation is a subgenre of exploitation film that was largely popularized by the Canadian production *Ilsa, She-Wolf of the SS* (1975). The subgenre's progenitors included Roberto Rossellini's anti-fascist neorealist masterpiece *Rome, Open City* (1945) and Luchino Visconti's subversive nightmare *The Damned* (1969) as well as pictures by filmmakers across Europe such as Germany's Helmut Käutner (*The Devil's General*, 1955), France's Roger Vadim (*Vice and Virtue*, 1963) and Turkey's Muzaffer Arslan (*Ankara Express*, 1970). It would be in the 1970s that nazisploitation as a subgenre would gain popularity and notoriety, with a series of films set in Nazi-occupied Europe featuring what many considered a repugnant mix of sadism and sexual abuse meant to titillate and torment in equal measure. Thanks to their flair for exploitation, for the filone system and the way it exploited what was popular elsewhere, Italian genre filmmakers would create a domestic filone within nazisploitation: the *sadiconazista*.[9]

The nazisploitation subgenre is one of the most censured and maligned (and, in certain respects, misunderstood) of the exploitation forms. What is often considered sadistic sleaze exploiting the worst genocide mankind has ever experienced also paints a perfect picture of the Nazis and of fascism as inherently evil. The films explored in this chapter each present Nazis as irredeemable characters driven by bigotry and malice, as master paradigms of degeneracy and turpitude reveling in a system that not only condones but rewards such behavior. Resisting the urge felt elsewhere to portray rank and file Nazis as just men and women obeying orders, in the nazisploitation films the central characters are "increasingly possessed, body and soul, by Nazism."[10] In addition, it has been noted by Cline that the films also present something that was all but omitted from historical texts and recollections of Nazi-occupied Europe: that SS women (though grossly outnumbered by their male colleagues) existed; that they "experienced and implemented the Holocaust in gendered ways ... to conform to the prevailing male gender norms which governed [concentration] camp culture."[11]

Recent efforts by writers and researchers have begun the practice of redeeming the subgenre, exploring its lurid excesses in examination of how it represents Holocaust trauma and disrupts the hegemonic memory that dominates the Italian public afflicted with Lichtner's memory amnesia. It is therefore useful to consider the nazisploitation film in this context: to examine the films' "co-mingling of voyeuristic spectacle with claims to verisimilitude"[12] in an appeal to memory. It is of further interest to cross-reference with the views presented by the Vatican at the time, given that the institution was inextricably linked with Nazism and had actively sought to bury said links in memory amnesia, to regain the trust of the Italian public without ever honestly admitting its mistakes.

This chapter explores how the above elements are presented in nazisploitation films, dissects critiques of the films in the *Segnalazioni cinematografiche*, and argues that said critical reception was undertaken not in good faith but as part of ongoing efforts by the Vatican to encourage memory amnesia.

Lee Frost's *Love Camp 7* (1969) is perhaps the most widely recognized early example of a core nazisploitation film: one that codifies the narrative and visual elements that we recognize with the subgenre today: the concentration camp scenario; elements borrowed from the "Women in Prison" exploitation subgenre; the gendered violence of using female prisoners as sex slaves for Nazi soldiers; distasteful and excess sex, nudity and voyeurism; grotesque human "experiments" recalling the Nazis' desires to create a superhuman race. The film itself (which sees two female U.S. soldiers infiltrate a notorious SS "love" camp in efforts to rescue an inmate) manages a neat tightrope act, balancing drama (that borders on melodrama) with its more titillating and transgressive elements, but is nonetheless easily recognizable as an influence on the canon that followed its release. While Frost's film does feature full frontal female nudity throughout the majority of its run time, its coherent narrative effectively sees it play out as a spy film: the U.S. officers (played with some somber depth by Maria Lease and Kathy Williams) infiltrate the camp in the knowledge that they must suffer rape and abuse in order to get the information required by the war effort and rescue their quarry. The women prisoners show convincing emotion as often as they show their breasts, and the Nazi antagonists are, quite rightly, presented as the irredeemable monsters they truly were. The film ends with a climactic battle and some success on the part of the U.S. officers (but at what cost). There is arguably enough drama and conflict in *Love Camp 7* to see it function as a reasonably solid movie, as well as a progenitor to the salacious and sexually aberrant content that was to follow, which would both titillate and repulse the average incumbent of drive-ins and grind house theaters.

Love Camp 7 was not released in Italy until 1976, by which point the Italian *sadiconazista* filone was already in the process of being established, with domestic genre filmmakers churning out these films that were relatively cheap to produce and therefore could make their money back from international markets even if they were censored or banned at home. Nonetheless, *Love Camp 7* is still to be considered a strong influence on the nazisploitation subgenre and the *sadiconazista* filone, as the country's filmmakers would have been aware of the film in the development of their filone, even if their audiences were not.

"The film reveals, from the false purpose of documenting Nazi atrocities, low commercial proposals. Unacceptable/aberrant."[13] The *Segnalazioni cinematografiche* offers the briefest of damnations, making no attempt to address any of the film's content but instead pronouncing its creators

8. The Paradox of Memory

as seeking only to exploit Nazi atrocities to earn money. It is dismissive of the filmmakers' attempts to add a serious message and perhaps rightly so; this is an exploitation film after all, not a neorealism commentary on fascism such as *Rome, Open City* or *The Damned*. It is a film that had previously been banned in Italy (as well as several other territories) due to its salacious content. That the Vatican's writer chooses not to engage with any of the actual content of the film whatsoever does not therefore seem particularly pertinent in isolation, but when considered alongside the *Segnalazioni cinematografiche*'s verdicts for virtually every other nazisploitation film released in Italy, it will.

The first canon *sadiconazista* film to be released in Italy was likely *In the Folds of the Flesh*, a giallo outlier (and yet another perfect example of the filone system, as it took inspiration from both Elio Petri's psychedelic giallo *A Quiet Place in the Country* and Frost's *Love Camp 7* to exploit the popularity of both) directed and cowritten by Sergio Bergonzelli and an Italian coproduction with the nation's Catholic neighbor, Spain. A subsequently bizarre mix of crime thriller, *sadiconazista* and psychedelia, Bergonzelli's film (taken from a story by genre stalwart Mario Caiano, who would direct his own entries in the canon over the coming years) is a surprisingly layered exploration of grief and trauma as perpetrated by the Holocaust, despite its many transgressive elements. It is the tale of a family whose members have suffered a trauma so profound that it has left them with shattered psyches (as demonstrated by Bergonzelli's intrusive use of splintered kaleidoscopic images that permeate the film) and an inability to tell fiction from reality (an excellently deployed mechanism that leaves the audience with exactly the same feeling throughout). The narrative is cyclical, as the family is visited by a succession of characters from the past, each of whom torments and distresses them until they are driven to murder their intruders and dispose of their corpses in an acid bath. Each cycle brings with it a flashback to the deep psychic wounds from the family's past. The trauma comes, of course, from a Nazi concentration camp, but each replay gives a different interpretation of the events that caused the family's complex anguish. It appears as though Bergonzelli is directly challenging the hegemonic memory of fascism in Italy, willing audiences to consider that their interpretation of Italy's history (informed by the machinations of a Church and state that wished to distance them from their own complicity) may not be trustworthy. It could indeed be argued that the film's identity puzzle holds a mirror up to the memory amnesia of the Italian public. Bergonzelli's direction, filled with in-camera effects and off-kilter angles, is surrealist and expressionist, challenging what the viewer is seeing (and whether we can trust our own eyes, ears and logical thought) just as the flashback devices challenge the veracity of the central family's memories.

"A mediocre giallo that turns out to be a cumbersome mix of insolent grotesque eroticism. The film focuses exclusively on morbid situations and macabre and gruesome images."[14] Here we see the Vatican's writer dismiss the film, in its entirety, in two short sentences. While both are essentially correct (the film is filled with grotesquery and shocking images, not limited to the graphic murders but also scenes of incest), the review completely overlooks any nuance of the narrative, and does not even mention the horrors of the Holocaust (one sequence in particular revolves around the concentration camp gas chambers and makes for genuinely quite harrowing viewing). Is this a simple case of the Vatican refusing to engage with the low genres, or is there something more at play? Given the film makes a forceful point of challenging conventional narratives and disrupting the audience's sense of its own past, does the Vatican consider this to be harmful to its own attempts to color the hegemonic memory of its people?

The next nazisploitation film of note to be released in Italy was Swiss director Erwin C. Dietrich's 1973 film *She Devils of the SS* (subtitle: *Frauleins in Uniform*). Dietrich's film is an unusual entry into the canon in that it is something of a ribald comedy, rather than an exploitation horror or thriller. Set in the last days of World War II, it follows a bunch of women from across Germany who have volunteered to serve in the front lines by having sex with the "brave" Nazi soldiers. From sex workers (fed up of the lack of clientele at home) to would-be Aryan princesses who wish to offer their bodies to their führer, the women are soon stripping for every German soldier they see ... until they start to become attracted to one another. From there, the women become a distraction, leaving the Nazis vulnerable to attack from the Soviet army.

It makes complete sense that *She Devils of the SS* would find an audience in Italy. It is (in all but country of origin) a *commedia sexy all'italiana*—the very Italian brand of comedy that combined eroticism with social commentary to prove something of a firebrand filone. Though heavy on nudity, softcore sex and slapstick elements, these conventions were used by subversive directors as a Trojan horse in which to hide scathing criticism of Italy's conservative Catholic institutions.

Given the talent that worked in the phenomenally successful filone (from Mariano Laurenti to Sergio Martino, Pasquale Festa Campanile to Federico Fellini) it is something of a surprise that a *commedia sexy all'italiana* film set during the years of fascism came not from a domestic director but a Swiss filmmaker. In any case, it enjoyed success in Italy, and did so despite the Vatican's consternation: "A painful comedy, in which the inspiration cannot rise beyond monotonous scenes of erotic encounters. The story is inconsistent; the background of a useless war, conducted by the blackest fanaticism, makes even more evident the pretext of the intentions of the work, whose characters seem to be engaged only in quick sexual displays. Unacceptable/licentious."[15]

As was often the case with *commedia sexy all'italiana*, the nudity and sexual content of the work was all the Vatican saw fit to comment on to condemn the film; the *Segnalazioni cinematografiche* would rarely if ever openly comment on the political content of these bawdy comedies, in case it inadvertently opened the eyes of the Italian people to subtext they might not have otherwise understood (the Church believed the Italian people to be more naive than they were, or at least convinced itself of such).

It would, of course, be Don Edmonds' 1975 film *Ilsa, She-Wolf of the SS* that popularized the nazisploitation film and truly spawned the *filone* in Italy that lasted for half a decade. The titular Ilsa (Dyanne Thorne) is a sadistic and sexually voracious concentration camp *kommandant* who undertakes sadistic experiments on her female prisoners and uses the male ones for fleeting sexual conquests before having them castrated. Ilsa is a powerful woman who displays no weaknesses but also no real humanity beyond her basest desires. Her experiments, attempting to prove that women can endure greater suffering than men (and should therefore fight alongside the men in the war), provide the horrific content of the film, while her often naked body provides the sexual.

Ilsa was critically panned upon release, with reviewers shocked by its depravity and only too happy to say so. As has often proven the case, this did not sink Edmonds' film but rather attracted cinemagoers in their droves. *Ilsa* solidified the nazisploitation subgenre and spawned a franchise that saw Edmonds return (for 1976's *Ilsa, Harem Keeper of the Oil Sheikhs*) but also attracted the likes of Spanish sleaze king Jess Franco (*Ilsa, the Wicked Warden*, 1977) and Canadian Jean LaFleur (*Ilsa, the Tigress of Siberia*, 1977) to the sordid tales of the big bosom (and bigger appetite) of the SS *kommandant*. The Vatican: "This story of a beastly 'Kapò,' in fact uses Nazi horrors not for serious complaint, but a show based on effects of sex and sadism. Badly built and misinterpreted, the work adds feelings of hatred and revenge to the images of repugnant torture and licentious nudity. Unacceptable/aberrant."[16]

In perhaps an indication that nazisploitation was, by 1976, considered a subgenre or *filone*, the *Segnalazioni cinematografiche*'s writer clearly notes his disapproval of the use of Nazi atrocities for such exploitative, subversive content. *Ilsa* begins with a title card bearing the name of the film's producer, Herman Traeger, which declares, "The film you are about to see is based on documented fact ... because of its shocking subject matter, this film is restricted to adult audiences only. We dedicate this film with the hope that these heinous crimes will never occur again."[17] The Holy See appears to take exception to this apparently disingenuous message, though it offers no further comment on the veracity of the film's portrayal of Nazis, once again evoking Lichtner's assertion that "the rememberer is … encouraged to forget what those mistakes were, or that they ever even took place."[18]

What the *Segnalazioni cinematografiche*'s review does illustrate is something that would continue as the nazisploitation film gained popularity in Italy and inspired a filone: where it had at first refrained, the Vatican was beginning to express its disappointment that, in its view, no genuine political points were being made about the Nazis' crimes against humanity in the films of the *sadiconazista* subgenre.

The pertinence of this will come to shape the rest of this chapter, as we consider if such a criticism can be said to have been made in good faith:

The titular character (Dyanne Thorne) stands proudly in the shadow of a wolf that howls at the moon in Don Edmonds' 1975 *sadiconazista* film *Ilsa, She-Wolf of the SS*. Illustration by the author.

given the assertions made by the likes of Lichtner, Fiddler and Barwell about memory amnesia and about transgressive content's challenge of the accepted, hegemonic memory of fascism in Italy, it would not appear to be in the Vatican's best interest to specifically ask for more political content in films about the genocidal regime it had been in bed with for over a decade. If, as its critics suggest, the institution wishes to orchestrate a memory amnesia in the Italian public, it would behoove it not to point out nazisploitation filmmakers' apparent lack of sociopolitical messaging.

Following the success of *Ilsa*, a filone exploded in Italy, with several domestic agitators working in the low genres turning to the subversive content that appalled censors yet captured the imagination (and lira) of domestic audiences. The first of these would be Tinto Brass, the already infamous and acclaimed director of erotic films with a distinct political bent. His 1976 film *Salon Kitty* (based on the novel by Peter Norden) covered the real-life events surrounding the Salon Kitty brothel in Berlin, which was taken over by the Nazi intelligence service for espionage purposes, as directed by SS general Reinhard Heydrich in 1939. The spies, a group of female informants, posed as prostitutes and gained intelligence not just on visiting foreign dignitaries but also on members of the Nazi Party in order to ensure the führer maintained his iron grip around every level of life in Germany. Ultimately an upbeat story, it sees informant/prostitute Margherita (Teresa Ann Savoy) and Madam Kitty (Ingrid Thulin) use their expertise to take down the wicked SS *kommandant* Helmut Wallenberg (Helmut Berger).

Brass's uncompromising eroticism, coupled with distinctly subversive political overtones, saw the film criticized and censured (it was heavily edited for the U.S. market, removing the transgressive political content in order to successfully market it as a sex film), and yet it would lead Brass directly to the apex of his career: the 1979 erotic historical drama about the rise and fall of Roman emperor Caligula.

Salon Kitty would be followed by *Achtung! The Desert Tigers* (Luigi Batzella, 1977), a film that turned to Italy's empire in the Middle East and Africa. Lichtner considers Italy's African empire to be a crucial absence in Italy's memory, citing that "the dominant narrative of *italiana brava gente* explains popular amnesia and institutional silences that still surround the darkest and bloodiest pages in Italy's history."[19] Italy had established colonies in violent and bloody fashion in the continent over the past hundred years, from Libya to Somalia, and, as they were presented in the history books of Great Britain and France, such colonizations were presented to subsequent generations of Italians in a sanitized manner; another example of the country's institutions consciously contributing to amnesia and installing a hegemonic memory that was easier to manage in its people.

Batzella's film would be just as transgressive and disruptive to hegemonic memory as those of his predecessors; depicting the *kommandant* of a POW camp in Africa committing the same medical "experiments," sexual sadism and genocide witnessed in the European SS camps of *Ilsa*, of *Love Camp 7* and of *In the Folds of the Flesh*. Beyond the unflinching sadism present elsewhere in the subgenre, Batzella's film carries a very pointed political message in its subtext: that such atrocities were perpetrated in East Africa just as they were in occupied Europe *because* of Italy's history in the region. Batzella presents us with a parallel between Nazi-occupied Europe and the colonial empires carved out from Tunisia to Eritrea, suggesting that the efforts of the British, French and Italians of a century previous were no less worthy of condemnation than Hitler's. The genocidal bloodshed that led to a colonized Africa in the 19th century in turn allowed fascism to occupy the same countries during World War II, and continue their sadistic malpractices far from the watchful eye of the Allied forces (at least until 1940, when the North African campaign began).

The Vatican, of course, saw no such value in Batzella's filone entry:

> A sex-sadism-SS film, the result of a (not very) clever commercial operation, contains three types of material or scenes: those of assault and destruction of fuel depots, with huge fires; those of war around a Libyan oasis, with the intervention of the most disparate fighters (Bedouins, Americans, English, Germans, Italians); those of torture inside a concentration camp ... the nature of the scenes of licentious orgies and sadistic torture that have been inserted in the absurd story (are) unacceptable/licentious.[20]

Exploitation journeyman Bruno Mattei would soon be attracted to the filone, churning out *SS Experiment Love Camp* (1976), *Woman's Camp 119* and *SS Girls* (both 1977). Mattei's entries were typical filone fodder, taking the base elements of their predecessors and ramping up the sleaze factor. The Nazi experiments of Mattei's movies involved reviving the frozen corpses of Nazi soldiers via necrophilia and "curing" homosexuals by having nude women dance for them. With low-budget, poor craftsmanship and little attention to detail, Mattei's films were generally considered to be the lesser entries of the filone. This did not stop them from making money with audiences eager to lap up subversive content; nor did it stop the Vatican from denouncing them:

> [*Woman's Camp 119*] is an absurd work of the infamous 'Nazi female concentration camps' that with those that preceded it has in common the narrative scheme and an inhuman taste for horrifying and sadistic details.... In the credits it offers photographs of still living Nazis and adequate captions: instead of excusing the product, tall tales expose its aberrant nature since none of the aforementioned characters (judged, convicted and already at the end of their

sentences inflicted by legal courts) could recognize themselves in the beasts invented by this type of cinema. Unacceptable/aberrant.[21]

Once more (and with a little more fervor now that the target is an Italian filmmaker), the *Segnalazioni cinematografiche* criticizes any attempt to tie the affairs of these transgressive films to the real events that took place in SS concentration camps, suggesting that it serves not to add any political weight to these works, but purely to exploit real-life tragedies for commercial purposes.

Sergio Garrone's *SS Experiment Camp* was another of the filone's sleazier entries, dealing as it did with a Nazi colonel who had been castrated by a Russian girl and, in a form of revenge, begins sexual experiments with female prisoners of the concentration camp he runs. Garrone received a similarly cold welcome from the Holy See, as he too was accused of exploiting real tragedy for cynical gain:

> The tragic and well-known photographic documents which are the background to the opening credits, try in vain to pass this porn-sadistic comic as an indictment against Nazi madness, In reality, apart from a few scenes of fake hypnosis, the work responds to an aberrant conception of cinema in which authentic victims are ignominiously offered to men and especially women executioners armed with inhuman tastes.... Unacceptable/aberrant.[22]

As the filone took hold in Italy, it of course attracted the attention of the cinematic provocateurs of neighboring Spain; namely one Jess Franco. Nineteen seventy-seven's *Ilsa, the Wicked Warden* followed Don Edmonds' original two *Ilsa* films but was not an official entry into the franchise. Rather, it was a product of the Italian-style exploitation that would see unofficial "sequels" to popular genre films pop up regularly (the most famous of which being Lucio Fulci's *Zombi 2*, marketed as a sequel to George Romero's *Zombi/Dawn of the Dead*, and Enzo G. Castellari's *L'ultimo Squalo* (The Last Shark), which capitalized on the incredible popularity of Steven Spielberg's *Jaws*). Nevertheless, Dyanne Thorne reprised her role from the previous two films (her character's name cheekily changed to Greta or Wanda in any territories where use of the Ilsa name might attract trouble), this time serving as the warden in a psychiatric hospital for young women. Somewhat of a low-genre auteur, Franco gave the film a style and craftsmanship that elevated it (at least in aesthetic terms) from the Italian entries into Nazisploitation, and its heavy erotic content ensured the Spaniard some success across Europe and in the grind houses of the U.S.

> The usual Jess Franco [the director with a hundred pseudonyms] does not escape from the aberrant conceptions of cinema... [which] he passes from one scenario to another to propose, with ridiculous and incredible excuses, the usual and identical pornographic story about sex and sadism. This time

he invents a Nazi concentration camp in the middle of a Tarzan setting and, heedless of the splendors of tropical nature, he continues to hide in the basement of the alleged clinic-prison to alternate lesbian mating with inhumane torture.... Unacceptable/aberrant.[23]

By 1978 the filone had reached a saturation point in Italy and would soon peter out (much to the relief of the Vatican and its moral censors). Cesar Canevari's aptly titled *The Gestapo's Last Orgy* (1978) was one of the final films in the *sadiconazista* filone before its popularity waned and directors moved on to the next popular streams of zombies and cannibals. Canevari's narrative takes place across multiple times and places and centers on a relationship between a woman and man (Daniela Poggi and Adriano Micantoni), borne trauma and what would become known as Stockholm syndrome. In flashback sequences, Canevari shows us the gas chamber and oven deaths of female prisoners, as well as the rape "orgy" of a number of women at the hands of the SS soldiers. Various disgusting Nazi theories are debated, such as the notion that the Jews could be farmed and used as a food source, while Poggi's Lise is crippled with guilt and anxiety after betraying her family to the Nazis years ago. She succumbs to rape and torture at the hands of her captor (Micantoni's character) and begins an extreme sadomasochistic sexual relationship with him. Lise's trauma is carried by her into the present-day narrative, where she is reunited with Micantoni's SS *kommandant* and eventually shoots him dead.

> Some well-known and acclaimed films from the recent past (*The Night Porter, Salò, Salon Kitty*) have given rise to the new ignoble trend of Italian cinema, characterized by the hypocritical attitude towards the victims and the exploitation of prosperous and available young girls for scenes of sadism and eroticism ... in the place of the persecuting Nazis of the Jews, certain Italian directors like this were not found ingenious in their inventions of torture and sadomasochistic delights. Unacceptable/degrading."[24]

The *Segnalazioni cinematografiche* went all out in its denunciation of Canevari's film, and in doing so unwittingly revealed its own hypocrisy. In highlighting the "acclaimed films"[25] from the trend in order to compare *The Gestapo's Last Orgy* unfavorably to them, the Holy See's critics invite us to revisit their reviews of *The Night Porter, Salon Kitty* and *Salò* (to which we will turn shortly) and determine what (if any) differences the Vatican considered there to be between the apparently more accomplished films of the subgenre and what it considered the more exploitative horrors and thrillers. Given that, in retrospect, Canevari's film has been considered to have a more nuanced and complex narrative and message than many of its *sadiconazista* peers, it is interesting to note the Vatican's critique of the film which, while still arriving at the decision that *The Gestapo's Last Orgy* is an unacceptable and degrading picture, actually takes some care to dissect the various elements of the film in order to do so, rather than simply dismissing it out of hand.

And so, to the Vatican's central assertion regarding the salacious and transgressive content of the nazisploitation film (and, in particular, the Italian *sadiconazista*): the directors of such films were exploiting the real-life atrocities of the Nazis and their allies not to present a worthwhile political commentary for the Italian people to digest as they reflect upon the country's relevantly recent pas, but merely to titillate audiences with sadistic sexual content. The writers of the *Segnalazioni cinematografiche* lament the lack of any worthwhile artistic or political content in the works of Luigi Batzella, Bruno Mattei, Sergio Garrone and Cesar Canevari, and go so far as to unfavorably compare these directors to the likes of Liliana Cavani (*The Night Porter*), Tinto Brass (*Salon Kitty*) and Pier Paolo Pasolini (*Salò*).

On the surface (in the case of everyone but Canevari), this seems like a reasonable critique. The Vatican appears to recognize the importance of a political message when dealing with such a complex subject (even when that message could easily lead the national train of thought toward grasping the Holy See's own complicity in the fascist axis). In denouncing the *sadiconazista* filone, the Vatican states its disappointment that these directors have chosen the titillation of transgressive violence and sexual sadism over social commentary and political bite. This somewhat compromises the assertions of Lichtner and the memory amnesia given to the Italian people and this author's suggestion that these were efforts to placate the people and to allow those institutions that propped up fascism (both Church and state) to distance themselves from it for the sake of reputation and the history books.

At least it does *until* we take a look at the Vatican's critiques of Brass, Cavani and Pasolini, all celebrated directors who tackled the subject outside of the low genres of horror and thriller. The *Segnalazioni cinematografiche*'s critiques of *Salon Kitty*, *The Night Porter* and *Salò* paint a very different picture of the Vatican's attitudes from that the Holy See wishes itself to propagate.

To return briefly to Tinto Brass' *Salon Kitty*, it is noted that the Vatican thought very little of the director's political narrative, stating, "In the film we do not find a reasoned critique [of Nazi horrors]; but a visceral and paradoxical reduction ... the hellish smell of lust and the notes of satisfying sadism ... of those who, with the excuse of a political speech, tend to drag the viewer into an abyss of obscenity. Unacceptable/aberrant."[26] The *Segnalazioni cinematografiche*'s main criticism appears, once again, to be that the film is not concerned with critiquing the horrors of the Nazi regime and its allies but pretends to do so in order to sneak salacious and aberrant content onto the screen. This flies in the face of the Vatican's assertion elsewhere that *Salon Kitty* would be considered a more "acclaimed"[27] film than the likes of *Achtung! The Desert Tigers* or *The Gestapo's Last Orgy*. However, of all of those films that the rest of the world viewed as having higher aspirations than the majority of nazisploitation film, *Salon Kitty* remains a film made by, to all intents and purposes, a pornographer—albeit a very artistic one—so it is perhaps unsurprising that the Vatican would not look particularly favorably upon his works.

Liliana Cavani is a director who may be considered more of an intellectual than Brass. A literature and philology graduate, she trained at the Centro Sperimentale di Cinematografia, where she concentrated on documentary filmmaking, and graduated to direct films with historical concerns, as well as directing opera, and is regularly mentioned favorably alongside the likes of Bernardo Bertolucci and Pier Paolo Pasolini.

Cavani's 1974 film *The Night Porter* has long been considered "a provocative and problematic film"[28] that has garnered critical acclaim and censure in equal measure. Cavani's story tells of the relationship between Holocaust survivor Lucia (Charlotte Rampling in a star-making performance) and fugitive SS officer Max (Dirk Bogarde) when, years after Lucia conceived a Stockholm syndrome like fascination with Max as a result of a coerced, grotesque sadomasochistic relationship, they meet again in a Vienna hotel. Considered an "upper-middlebrow arthouse scandal"[29] upon release, it received a wide range of opinions from critics. Roger Ebert derided the film, calling it "a despicable attempt to titillate us by exploiting memories of persecution and suffering,"[30] while *Variety* considered it "a gritty look at concentration camp quirks … transposed to a strange drama"[31] and the *Los Angeles Free Press*' Jacoba Atlas asserted, "If you go expecting a Rorschach test for your own responses, the experience will be well worth your time."[32] In the intervening 45 years, the film has been somewhat redeemed, revisited and considered to have a greater moral value by a number of contemporary critics, such as *The Guardian*'s Peter Bradshaw, who suggests of the film: "Perhaps there is something in its very crassness, horror and tastelessness that does at least jolt us towards an acknowledgment of pure evil."[33]

In its condemnation of Canevari's *The Gestapo's Last Orgy*, and the *sadiconazista* in general, the *Segnalazioni cinematografiche* cites *The Night Porter* as one of those "acclaimed films from the recent past,"[34] a dramatic highlight among exploitation trash. And yet, as with Tinto Brass' *Salon Kitty*, Cavani's film was dismissed out of hand by the Vatican's critics upon release:

> Sequences of an exhausted formalism and some scenes of robust drama do not save a poorly organized narrative architecture supported by props of the genre in vogue today, to which a director who is usually severe and free from compromises pays homage. Gruesome scenes, … sadomasochistic situations, …

Lucia (Charlotte Rampling) in Liliana Cavani's 1974 drama *The Night Porter*. A likeness of Cardinal Eugenio Pacelli (later Pius XII), "Hitler's Pope," watches from the shadows. Illustration by the author.

> abnormal couplings, ... entertained with an attention to detail that goes well beyond the bearable, all this and more occupies so much space to make one think of a failure in the face of the unhealthy charm of the perverse matter, not unlike what happens, in this belated condemnation of Nazism, to poor Lucia. Unacceptable/negative.[35]

Here, the *Segnalazioni cinematografiche* explicitly states that the Holy See does not believe the director's technical skill is enough to lift the film out of the mire of exploitation. The Vatican's writer makes no comment about the film that might contribute to the Italian people's attempts to reconcile with their country's past; concentrating only on what it deems gruesome and sadomasochistic content and asserting that the film is perverse and not to be seen by the Roman Catholic citizens of Italy. There is no attempt made to get to grips with the narrative content, nor is there any effort on the part of the writer to search for subtext, or to examine their own response to the film as per Atlas' suggested Rorschach test. Once again, it appears as though Lichtner is correct, and in forbidding the viewing of Cavani's film, the Church wishes to rely upon memory amnesia to wash away the sins of the past.

In the case of the third *sadiconazista* film positioned by Church critics as a notable and worthwhile entry into the filone, it is at first surprising that it was mentioned within the pages of the *Segnalazioni cinematografiche* at all. Given the very problematic history between the Vatican and director Pier Paolo Pasolini, it is a wonder that *Salò, or the 120 Days of Sodom* was ever reviewed by the Vatican's writers, let alone held aloft as an exemplary when discussing nazisploitation.

Born in Bologna in 1922, Pasolini would become Italy's most significant modern poet, essayist and film director, and one of a very select group of filmmakers whose work would be featured on the Vatican best movies list: 1964's *The Gospel According to St. Matthew* was included for its service to the promotion of religion through art and was considered a cine-catechism by the Vatican. Pasolini shot his neorealist take on the Bible in black-and-white in the poor Italian district of Basilicata, with the intention of projecting the modern-day Italian South onto the source material. The director used no script, and no professional actors: Jesus Christ was played by Enrique Irazoqui, a 19-year-old Spanish economics student who never acted before or again. Dedicated to Pope John XXIII, it would be considered "the best film about Jesus ever made in the history of cinema"[36] by the Vatican's own newspaper *L'Osservatore Romano*.

Beyond his 1964 biblical adaptation, the relationship between Pasolini and the Vatican was one dominated by antagonism. Pasolini was also a radical political figure, frequently at odds with the Vatican, the Christian Democratic state and the police. Notably, he collaborated with extreme-left militant organization Lotta Continua (for whom he produced a documentary, *12 December,* about the bombing of the National Agricultural Bank, nearby to the Duomo in Milan) during Italy's infamous Years of Lead. Pasolini would often find himself in court on various charges related to his works and once served a four-month suspended prison sentence after a successful prosecution over his short film *La Ricotta* (Pasolini was found guilty of "publicly undermining the religion of the state"[37]).

On the morning of November 3, 1975, just before his latest film *Salò* was about to be released, Pasolini's corpse was discovered by police on wasteland close to Rome's Ostia beach. Within hours of the discovery, the police had arrested the man they would claim to be his murderer. Seventeen-year-old sex worker Giuseppe Pelosi confessed, claiming he beat Pasolini in self-defense (because the director wanted to sodomize him with a wooden stick) before running over him accidentally. Pelosi was convicted one year later.[38,39] During an investigation into Pasolini's demise, forensic scientist Dr. Faustino Durante had asserted that there must be others involved in the murder, yet this was later mysteriously retracted and Pelosi was found by the court (without challenge) to have acted alone. After serving nine years in prison, Pelosi himself would contradict this, stating that there were at least three others involved in the murder, men with Sicilian accents who may well have been the mafiosi that Pasolini and others had accused the Christian Democrat Party and the Vatican of being in bed with (an arrangement that later turned out to be true, as discovered during the P2 scandal).

While the truth about Pasolini's death may never be known, it is thought by many that Church and state had the agitator assassinated just as he was finishing his latest work of controversy.[40] In fact, in 2023 Italian filmmakers David Grieco and Giovanni Giovannetti asked for the case of Pasolini's murder to be reopened in order to examine and present as evidence three DNA traces found at the scene of the crime by police in 2010.[41] There are also links to a statement to the parliamentary anti-mafia commission from former gangster Maurizio Abbatino, who implied the murder was linked to the theft of the original print of *Salò*. Pasolini may have gone to the beach at the Rome seaside district of Ostia on that fateful night to try to recover the film (according to the report by the parliamentary anti-mafia commission released on December 16).[42]

Upon its release shortly after Pasolini's murder, *Salò* met with expected controversy and disgust (and some acclaim), and has ever since developed a reputation as one of the most controversial films ever made. Pasolini's loose adaptation of *The 120 Days of Sodom*, by the Marquis de Sade, was transposed to the final days of World War II and structured in homage to Dante Alighieri's *Divine Comedy*. The film focuses on four corrupt Italian libertines in the fascist republic of Salò who kidnap 18 teenage boys and girls and subject them to four months of torture, sadism and sexual violence (played out to graphic extremes on the screen, through what appears to be a cold, strangely nonjudgmental lens).

While its most common readings include a criticism of fascism and one of consumerism, there is a third reading of *Salò* bubbling just beneath the surface. The secret cabal of despots is made up of the President (Aldo Valletti), the Duke (Paolo Bonacelli), the Bishop (Giorgio Cataldi) and the Magistrate (Umberto P. Quintavalle), and these men perpetrate their evils as is their wont. They abduct teenagers to feed the morbid machinery of authoritarianism, with no extremes left unvisited by these self-styled "libertines," men of great power who exist in a hegemonic structures facilitating fascist thinking. The inclusion of men with nicknames related to state, army, church and law is very precise and instantly reminiscent of those who were found to be involved in Propaganda Due's secret state. Pasolini, like all of Italy's agitator artists at the time, was aware of the rumors, of the scandal waiting to be uncovered, about the cabal between Italy's politicians, church, army, police, bankers and mafioso, and *Salò* acts as his own cruel and grimy exposé.

In the UK, the BBFC's director James Ferman defended the film upon release, and it was because of the real world powers it criticized. Stating that *Salò* was "one of the most disgusting films ever to be seen by the board, yet … it wants us to be appalled at the atrocities of which human nature is capable when absolute power is wielded corruptly."[43] There are fewer more apt examples of absolute power being wielded corruptly than in Propaganda Due, the secret cabal that had a stranglehold on Italy for a significant period of time.

At the time, Giovanni Grazzini of *Corriere della Sera* would be one to eulogize the film, hypothesizing on Pasolini's ideology in calling *Salò* "a film devoid of erotic joy, and paradoxically also devoid of vulgarity, but where the light of Pasolini's intelligence is clouded by an ideology of defeat."[44] The final few words of Grazzini's review are particularly pertinent: not only does Pasolini's film present the long-term effects of fascism (sadistic evil perpetrated by those with power giving way to the destruction of innocence); it also comments upon the apparent apathy toward it in Italy in the subsequent decades and, to a degree, the memory amnesia that Lichtner spoke of and that the Church and state appear to be complicit in creating. Grazzini notes that Pasolini had himself called *Salò* "a film against any form of power and precisely against what I call the anarchy of power."[45] By allowing those in power to sweep the horrors perpetrated by Mussolini's regime under the collective carpet, by denying its people time to properly grieve, to reflect, and to feel all the tumultuous emotions associated with that grief, Italy has fostered a nation that does not fully understand the darkest days of its recent history and therefore has become somewhat numbed to them. This amnesia, this numbness has, in turn, perpetuated an oppressive social and political environment in the country, something marked by the Years of Lead, the state within a state of P2 and, in the decades since Pasolini's death, the scandal and corruption-laced Berlusconi years and the election of Giorgia Meloni, leader of the post-fascist Brothers of Italy party, to the office of prime minister in 2022.

Forty years after its release, the film has been both damned and redeemed and is considered both transgressive extreme horror and art house political masterpiece, described as a "painful gift"[46] that the Italian people must allow themselves to receive. The film is considered "uncomfortable, devastating, elusive of any classification, like its author…. From De Sade's book to Republican Italy, Pier Paolo Pasolini condenses in a villa in Marzabotto the graphic violence of power and its young victims, destined for three circles … of earthly Hell."[47] Barber (cited by Fiddler and Banwell) would co-opt the director's own mingling of art, politics and transgression in asserting that "the filmic material of *Salò* is one that compacts celluloid and shit, in Pasolini's desire to burst the limits of cinema, via the anally resonant eye of the film-lens."[48] In doing so, Barber speaks to the combination of gaze, obscenity and amoral pleasure in the *sadiconazista* subgenre, the "echoing of historical fact through an eroticized lens"[49] that suggests these transgressive films offer more than just a subversive peep show, instead using the strengths of the low genres to communicate a political and historical knowledge of the horrors of fascism to the Italian people that can act as a counter to Lichtner's memory amnesia. It is, by now, undoubted that this was Pasolini's intention with *Salò* and, just as a high tide raises all boats, the *sadiconazista*'s most powerful film allows us to recognize and appreciate the ideological intentions of the entire filone.

The *Segnalazioni cinematografiche* chose not to comment upon *Salò* at the time of its release, perhaps because of the death of Pasolini and the ongoing court case around his murder. The film would not be reviewed by the Vatican until March of 1977 (almost 18 months after the director's murder). The decision was apparently made out of grudging respect for the recently deceased director. The critic of the *Segnalazioni cinematografiche* had quite a lot to say about the final film of Italy's preeminent agitator artist:

> The tragic death of Pier Paolo Pasolini, more than the content of this work, leads us to commit the film to the archives. In fact, the desperate gaze and the lack of hope in humanity or in values superior to it … are the aberrant mark of this…[film] that, in addition to the categorical sentence of fascism, seeks to comment upon EMB [the early fascist movement]. But, unfortunately, the easy and known style of Precious Precious Precious … does not force us [to praise the film. The subject matter and the form used, while openly binding to the well-known social and political message of the deceased Pasolini, are the aberration and aberrant that demonstrate a personality, among other

things, deformed by a partisan vision and the absence of redemptive values. Unacceptable/aberrant.[50]

The Vatican's eventual review of the film is bullish to say the least. That it calls Pasolini's death tragic, only to then refer to him as "Precious Precious Precious"[51] in what appears to be both reference to Pasolini's poetry and open mockery of both the director and those who revered him is a contemptibly cruel and self-regarding action by the Holy See, and somewhat childish to boot. In addition, the reviewer makes note of Pasolini's "well-known social and political message,"[52] a thinly veiled reference to the agitator's accusations that the state and Church had been working in collusion with the Mafia to form a deep state via Propaganda Due. The review spends very little time discussing Pasolini's style and techniques, opting instead to repeatedly call the film aberrant without offering an explanation as to why (one can assume that this is due to its sadistic content, which, when viewed without any attempt at considering context, can certainly be considered to be aberrant in nature).

Once more, the *Segnalazioni cinematografiche* is abruptly dismissive of a film that it elsewhere considered to be an acclaimed example of the filone, and Pasolini's commentary upon fascism in Italy (and the apathy afforded it in modern Italian society that allows corrupt power cabals to continue to destroy the country's soul) is apparently unworthy of consideration or discussion. Given that, elsewhere, the Vatican laments the lack of a political message in the *sadiconazista* filone (and the nazisploitation subgenre as a whole), its unwillingness to explore the messages in some of the filone's more serious entries suggests hypocrisy at best and something more sinister at worst. It would appear as though the Vatican simply does not want these conversations to take place. That, in efforts to protect itself from reputational damage, it wants the specter of fascism in Italy not to be faced, for the Italian public not to deal psychologically with their country's dark history and have the opportunity to lay it to rest, but to simply forget the aberrant actions of state and Church and allow both to determine the country's future direction for them. It appears that, in its desire for self-preservation at a time of mass apostasy, the Vatican wishes only to indulge in memory amnesia after all.

There remains, however, a sole (but notable) exception to the pattern in the Vatican's reaction to Luchino Visconti's 1969 film *The Damned*. Considered a "magnificent failure"[53] by Roger Ebert, *The Damned* carried a typical Visconti class-war commentary, this time showing how easily fascism infiltrated the wealthy classes in Germany (and, by extension, in Italy). Visconti's film follows a rich industrialist family of munitions manufacturers, the Essenbecks. Visconti's characters quite plainly represent the Krupp family of steel industrialists (which produced Hitler's battleships, U-boats, tanks and howitzers throughout World War II) and are an amoral bunch consumed by decadence who willingly kill off their patriarch (a staunch anti–Nazi) in order to benefit from supplying the fascist war effort. In doing so, they introduce a new generation of cruel, apathetic sexual deviants who thrive on life in Nazi Germany.

Visconti's film courted controversy upon release, mainly for its depictions of homosexuality, transsexuality, rape, pedophilia and incest. Visconti was an out and proud bisexual who had been in homosexual relationships with Italy's last king, Umberto II, and with actor Helmut Berger (who played sexually deviant playboy Martin in *The Damned*). The director's lifestyle had long been at odds with the conservative Christian ideals of the Italian patriarchy, where something as human as homosexuality was viewed as being as much of an aberration as the deviant behavior of rapists and child molesters. Visconti's inclusion of the controversial sexual elements in *The Damned* may well have been in reference to two events: Mussolini's internment of Italy's homosexuals on the Tremiti archipelago under a prison regime (gay men undermined the image of Italian manhood that Mussolini wished to see projected, so he sought to remove them from public life); Hitler's destruction of the Institut für Sexualwissenschaft, the Berlin sexology clinic whose leading physician campaigned for LGBTQ+ rights and tolerance. The clinic (along with all of its research) was burned to the ground in an early act of the fascist regime as the führer tightened his grip on the country. By showing the Nazis and their familiars acting out the very depraved practices that they believed were routinely committed by homosexuals, Visconti makes a damning statement about the innocence of LGBTQ+ people just trying to live their lives and the guilt of those fascist monsters who sought to imprison and to destroy them.

Despite earning itself an X rating in the U.S., *The Damned* was also nominated for the Best Original Screenplay Oscar and was named Best Foreign Film by the National Board of Review. Ebert's opposition to the film appeared to be due partly to his seeing a 90-minute cut of Visconti's four-hour epic and partly because Visconti's filmmaking style functioned a little *too* well for the critic. Ebert discussed the dreamlike elusiveness of the film's plot, the resultant confusion it caused during his viewing experience, and the technical style that turned the film's locations into "a radically under-lighted abyss"[54] with a claustrophobic effect which the critic desperately wanted to escape. Ebert did praise Visconti's capturing of the gloom of Germany's decay but pined, "We want out. We want sun; we want light; we want to see."[55] It was a cry that Germany's wartime population and the many millions of Jews imprisoned and executed as part of the Holocaust surely would have recognized; unlike the American (Catholic) film critic, they would not have the luxury of stepping outside into the street and returning to a safe, secure existence after the final reel had played.

Martin von Essenbeck (Helmut Berger) gives a drag performance in Luchino Visconti's 1969 Nazi drama *The Damned*. He wears a Masque of Death. Illustrated by the author.

Of the film, the *Segnalazioni cinematografiche* delivered what appears to be a surprisingly positive verdict, stating, "It is the tragedy of a family, connected with that of a nation increasingly possessed, body and soul, by Nazism. In spite of some exaggerations to sadism, which border on complacency, the work achieves an unusual power of representation. Technically flawless, it is also excellently interpreted."[56] Here, the Vatican's critic heaps praise upon the power of the film's narrative, Visconti's filmmaking and the interpretation of the cast. This is the only occasion on which the *Segnalazioni cinematografiche* affords a *sadiconazista* film such consideration. The film's more salacious elements are noted, but the writer does not eschew discussion of the film's artistry and power in order to focus on them, at least not immediately.

Ultimately, Visconti's film is still censured by the Vatican, and Roman Catholic Italians were ordered not to screen or watch the film: "Despite the validity of the claims it springs from, the whole affair—the facts and the condemnation represented and their motivations, excessive delay on the most aberrant details of the story, unacceptable scenes and situations all motivate the ranking [as] unacceptable."[57]

There are perhaps reasons why the *Segnalazioni cinematografiche* would be unwilling to dismiss Visconti's film out of hand, the way it would every subsequent nazisploitation effort (including that of the revered Pasolini). First, this was a progenitor of the filone: that it would help birth one of the most transgressive, exploitative filones in the history of the nation's cinema is something only understood in hindsight. At the time of its release, the Vatican could not have known what it would inspire, and likely thought it no more than a slight detour in the career of a single director. Second, the director's heritage and standing afforded him a level of respect and deference not extended to other directors. Luchino Visconti was a nobleman; the son of Giuseppe Visconti di Modrone, Duke of Grazzano Visconti and Count of Lonate Pozzolo, and Carla Erba, heiress to Erba Pharmaceuticals. The father of postwar Italian cinema, he became highly revered as the originator of neorealism (with his 1943 film *Ossessione*, which relocated James M. Cain's noir novel *The Postman Always Rings Twice* to small-town Italy after the fall of Mussolini and featured a cast of working-class unknowns alongside its two stars, Clara Calamai and Massimo Girotti) and would become a teacher at the Centro Sperimentale di Cinematografia, training a wide range of celebrated and maligned directors including Michelangelo Antonioni, Petro Germi, Liliana Cavani and Lucio Fulci. He was one of a handful of directors grouped together by Vittorio (son of Benito) Mussolini and held as darlings of Italian cinema (a group that also included Roberto Rossellini and Federico Fellini); though he joined the Communist Party during Mussolini's regime and subsequently many of his films dealt with the decay of the aristocracy and the old values that Mussolini used to his advantage. Visconti was subsequently one of the directors considered by the Vatican to take part in its ill-fated move into movie production with Orbis Film and the cine-catechisms.

Visconti was, therefore, as close to "untouchable" as a film director could be. He was of high social standing by birthright, revered by the Italian public, to the point where a swiftly damning review of one of his films would surely have raised the eyebrows of even the most trusting Catholics; therefore, to dismiss *The Damned* out of hand may have afforded the film more attention rather than less. Subsequently, the *Segnalazioni cinematografiche*'s writer may have felt compelled to treat Visconti's film with a measure of respect not afforded to subsequent entries into the canon. The caveat to this would be that the film was still deemed unacceptable and therefore would not be widely seen and could not influence the Italian public in ways that might counteract attempts to reinforce the country's hegemonic memory and potentially cause embarrassment or harm to the Vatican. Moving forward, the *Segnalazioni cinematografiche*'s writers would conveniently manifest their own memory amnesia regarding Visconti's film; to the extent that, when in later discussion of *sadiconazista* filone's more acclaimed entries, *The Damned* is not mentioned by the Vatican's writers alongside the likes of *The Night Porter, Salon Kitty* and *Salò*. It appears to have been forgotten entirely in subsequent reviews of the *sadiconazista*.

Fiddler and Banwell disagree with the Vatican's assertions that nazisploitation has no political value, suggesting that the eroticization of violence disrupts the accepted, hegemonic memory and provokes a visceral response coined by an earlier writer as "prosthetic memory,"[58] that being a supplemental artefact that "challenges more traditional forms of memory that are premised on claims of authenticity, 'heritage,' and 'ownership'"[59] Essentially, these are memories that originate outside a person's lived experience, and yet are augmented by the individual's experiential relationships to events. They add to what the audience member already knows about the past events (in this case, fascism and the Holocaust) by providing the missing part of the puzzle; the part that the mainstream filmmakers of films about World War II were discouraged from discussing in their own treatise on said events: trauma. The scenes of sexualized violence and depravity give the audience an idea of the trauma that those who suffered through internment camps and the Holocaust experienced, leading to a more deeply ingrained "memory" of the Holocaust, of fascism and of its many evils. This of course serves to challenge and disrupt the memory amnesia that Lichtner observed through the long-term trends in cinema about the fascist period.

It could therefore be argued that such films are entirely necessary in a country where, as recently as 2013 (in his Holocaust Memorial Day statement), then Italian prime minister Silvio Berlusconi stated:

> It is difficult now to put yourself in the shoes of people who were making decisions at that time [in 1938]. Obviously the government of that time, out of fear that German power might lead to complete victory, preferred to ally itself with Hitler's Germany rather than opposing it. As part of this alliance, there were impositions, including combating and exterminating Jews. The racial laws were the worst fault of Mussolini as a leader, who in so many other ways did well.[60]

Berlusconi's statement evidences the memory amnesia propagated by the Italian state in order to play down its own complicity in the horrors of fascism. If it is difficult for the Italian people to understand the decisions of the state and the Church in 1938, it is surely because those same institutions have sought to impede necessary learning and reflection. These transgressive films, according to Fiddler and Banwell, challenge that official statement, and the memory amnesia that it serves, disrupting the accepted version of events and augmenting memory with a more visceral truth (and, in doing so, allowing the individual to develop a more empathetic sense of the horrors perpetrated and the complicity of those regimes that allied themselves with the perpetrators). Rather than just providing the scenes of licentious orgies and sadistic torture that the *Segnalazioni cinematografiche* censured them for, the films attack the sanitized, hegemonic memory of fascism endorsed by the Vatican and the Italian state, seeking to replace it with a more intuitive knowledge of the true horrors of the fascist era, something that the Italian people can use to deal with the specter of their past in much the same way as their neighbors in Germany have.

In considering this, the *Segnalazioni cinematografiche*'s brief and brutal pillorying of the *sadiconazista* filone (and the wider nazisploitation subgenre) takes on a new context. Unlike in other areas of horror and exploitation, the Vatican's reviewers did not pick out a single nazisploitation film for more detailed dissection (with the exception of *The Damned*, which came before the establishment of the filone). There would be no carefully considered critique of Cesare Canevari's *The Gestapo's Last Orgy* or Luigi Batzella's *Achtung! The Desert Tigers*... more so, the Holy See also refrained from offering constructive comment on the more celebrated films of the filone, such as Tinto Brass' *Salon Kitty*, Liliana Cavani's *The Night Porter* or Pasolini's *Salò*.

Given that the critics of the *Segnalazioni cinematografiche* complained about the apparent lack of a political message in the more salacious films of the filone yet refused to properly engage with those entries that are almost universally agreed to have contributed to the ongoing cinematic narrative concerning fascism and the Holocaust, the apparent hypocrisy leads to one conclusion: that the Vatican had no authentic interest in seeing the truth about the fascist era on-screen. Rather, those that served at the Centro Cattolico Cinematografico tasked themselves with the mission of convalescing the reputation of the Vatican: to see that memory amnesia continue, lest the Italian public be led to consider more fully the Church's complicity in the horrors of fascism.

9

The Power of Christ Compels You!
(The Vatican versus ... Satanic Horror)

In 1973, Warner Bros. and celebrated "American New Wave" director William Friedkin released a film that would have repercussions on the horror movie in more ways than one.

By the end of the previous decade, the satanic horror subgenre was already sending ripples through cinema and ruffling the feathers of critics and censors, thanks to Paramount Pictures' celebrated *Rosemary's Baby* and Hammer Studios' Dennis Wheatley adaptation *The Devil Rides Out* (1968). Now thought to be borne of Danish silent mock-doc *Häxan: Witchcraft through the Ages*, the horror-noir of Jacques Tourneur, the novels of Dennis Wheatley and the life story of noted occultist Aleister Crowley, this subgenre of horror would come to cause many controversies around the world but particularly in Roman Catholic territories.

Subsequent to the release of the Friedkin's film, those with themes of Devil-worshipping cults and the coming of the Antichrist would do good business on the drive-in circuit and city picture houses alike. The likes of Tigon British Films and their folk-horror titles *Witchfinder General* (1968) and *The Blood on Satan's Claw* (1971) would leap in to fill the void left by a Hammer misstep (the studio, despite holding the rights, did not produce a follow-up to their 1968 hit until 1976's *To the Devil, a Daughter*, by which time the ailing studio was already on its way out of business). Twentieth Century-Fox and Paul Wendkos also capitalized on the burgeoning trend with 1971's *The Mephisto Waltz* (starring Alan Alda and Jacqueline Bisset), while in Italy Liger Films would release Mario Caiano's *Shadow of Illusion* (about a cult in Egypt who make ritual blood sacrifices to the deity Osiris) in the same year. But it would be in 1973 that Friedkin's epic adaptation of William Peter Blatty's book, pitting a priest of wavering faith and self-belief against the demon Pazuzu after it possesses a young girl, changed everything.

In the U.S., *The Exorcist* became the highest-grossing R-rated film in history (a record it would hold onto for 16 years), was nominated for

In William Friedkin's 1973 film *The Exorcist*, the likeness of a pope stands at the gates to the MacNeil residence, bathed in light. Illustration by the author.

10 Academy Awards (winning two, for Best Adapted Screenplay and Best Sound Mixing) and won gold in four of seven Golden Globe nominations it received. Legend tells us it also caused heart attacks and miscarriages at screenings and elicited localized mass hysteria in packed theater houses that would inspire journal articles on "cinema neurosis" and the consternation of the religious right.

Friedkin takes what appears to be legitimate knowledge of the earnestly practiced spiritual ceremony of exorcism, intended to vanquish malevolent presences and endorsed by the Church, and mixes it with a vulnerable priest who finds his faith plunged into doubt and a little girl who masturbates with a crucifix. The sacred and the profane are at home here, along with a good helping of apostasy. It is the film's treatment of Roman Catholicism that lies at the heart of much of its praise, initiating a cultural conversation at the time that raised the film from its (initially) mixed critical reception (Vincent Canby wondered "Why the Devil Do They Dig the Exorcist?"[1] while Jon Landau decried the film as "nothing more than a religious porn film"[2]) and inspired a slew of box-office hits and grind house fare about demonic possession, the Antichrist and the Devil that would dominate the horror genre for the rest of the decade.

The Exorcist's impact on cinema is undeniable. Regularly topping critics lists of the greatest horror films ever made, making it into the American Film Institute's list of key films of the first 100 years of cinema and Steven Jay Schneider's *1001 Movies You Must See Before You Die*, Friedkin's movie has enjoyed a cultural significance that few horror movies do, and its inspiration is still felt in the genre and indeed in cinema more widely 50 years later.

When speaking of the Vatican and of the horror movie, there is perhaps no more obvious example to link the Roman Catholic Church and the darkest of cinematic genres than *The Exorcist*. On one level, it is *about* the Vatican, pulling back the curtain on one of its most controversial of practices and making sport of the ultimate battle between good and evil.

Outside of the movies, exorcisms were and remain a sacramental procedure delivered by the Catholic Church for those believed to be victims of demonic possession. Not only does the Church recognize and practice exorcism; it takes its business very seriously. Paragraph 1673 of *The Catechism of the Catholic Church* explains: "When the Church asks publicly and authoritatively in the name of Jesus Christ that a person or object be protected against the power of the Evil One and withdrawn from his dominion, it is called exorcism."[3] That the Church practices exorcisms is now common knowledge across much of the world, having become global news fodder on a number of occasions, as recently as 2018 when the Vatican was forced to declare a "pastoral emergency."[4] According to one

Sicilian priest at the time, the number of people asking to be exorcized in Italy had risen to 500,000 a year, triple the usual amount.[5] As a result the Church ramped up training courses for priests in exorcism due to increased demands for deliverance from demonic possession. The name of Father Gabriel Amorth would be most likely to bring looks of vague recognition from the layperson with little to no interest in such things as Catholic exorcisms. For thirty years, Amorth served as Exorcist of the Rome Diocese. Amorth was a member of the Italian resistance during World War II, a lawyer, and then a priest of the Roman Catholic Church, where he was inducted into the role of exorcist in 1986. Amorth carried out exorcisms on the steps where Jesus was said to have met Pilate in Jerusalem, and in the residence of the Society of St. Paul in Rome. Amorth would much later become the subject of a documentary film made by William Friedkin, who captured "genuine" exorcisms on camera and then asked others to refute the footage. Most recently he has been featured in the (fictional) movie *The Pope's Exorcist* (2023), played by Russell Crowe.[6]

By the time Friedkin's *The Exorcist* opened in Italy and was viewed by the Vatican's critics in February of 1975, the filone system had already gone into overdrive (in Italy and elsewhere). The film, a box-office behemoth and controversy magnet everywhere it opened, had been parodied by vaudevillian Ciccio Ingrassia, blaxploited by William Girdler, given a U.S. grind house/drive-in partner by Mario Bava and American International Pictures and various other imitators including Alberto de Martino, Ovidio G. Assonitis and Roberto Piazzoli. The Vatican suddenly found itself facing a slew of films that went one step further than to simply include religious themes and were actually concerned with the Vatican and its most arcane practices. In the pages of the *Segnalazioni cinematografiche*, over the space of a number of years, the Holy See would not only interrogate this burgeoning subgenre of film that threatened to sensationalize an act of spiritual rescue the Church took very seriously; it would see its own reflection in the camera lens, its supposed never-ending fight against evil through a funhouse mirror, distorted but stark and presented for all to see.

Recognizing that its more controversial practices and spiritual beliefs were becoming immortalized in narrative cinema presented a challenge to the Church, in that its response would be under a measure of public scrutiny, given that it concerned both a film from a low genre (which the *Segnalazioni cinematografiche* had, as we have seen, been locked in constant battles with since their introduction to Italy in the 1950s) and a controversial practice that the Church actively undertook, so would be perfectly placed to assess from realism and adherence to proper scripture and religious practice. Also, if handled correctly, the Church could potentially receive some positive publicity out of the controversy surrounding *The*

Exorcist and other films like it, something it desperately needed as the country's mass apostasy showed no signs of slowing down in the 1970s.

The Exorcist was released at the height of the blaxploitation movement, which saw Black creators and impresarios partnering up with financiers to make films specifically for Black audiences. These were films made in very much the filone style, exploiting the success of an existing, mainstream property. More important was the act of centering Black people in their narrative, and creating reflections of race relations and how Black people saw themselves (or, more importantly, *wanted* to see themselves but were not being catered to by the Hollywood studios) in the United States of the 1970s. Young Black moviegoers wanted representation in genre fare: action, violence, sex and horror, all featuring faces they could identify with. Horror proved a consistent hit in the blaxploitation canon, from William Crain's straightforward exploitation film *Blacula* (1972) to Paul Maslansky's zombie horror *Sugar Hill* (1974) via Bill Gunn's intellectual reimagining of the vampire mythos in *Ganja & Hess* (1973).

William Girdler's *Abby* (1974), the tale of Catholic marriage counselor Abby Williams (Carol Speed), who is possessed by an African sex spirit, came out hot on the heels of Friedkin's hugely successful horror behemoth and was somewhat inspired by it to say the least. The film grossed millions in its first month (from a $500,000 budget) and quickly earned the nickname "The Blaxorcist." It was shortly after that a Warner Bros. copyright violation lawsuit saw the American International Pictures film pulled from cinemas and buried—to this day, it remains virtually impossible to buy a legitimate release of the film.[7]

The fate of the film is a shame, as it is a well-crafted low-budget horror that appeals to a different set of ideals and values: the destructive demon in question is the god Eshu of the Nigerian Yoruba; the film gives us "hard-working, salt of the earth characters to care about, then places them in peril."[8] The power of Girdler's film is in its earnest intent: to present the popular story of the day in a way that Black audiences can identify with it. Where Friedkin's movie took a crucifix and used it in a profane manner, in *Abby*, it is a moment chopping chicken for the family meal that can suddenly become an act of self-mutilation.

Girdler surely succeeds in his efforts, creating genuinely creepy set pieces where his camera winds around Abby's humble home at night and terrifying moments where Abby's demonic persona utters guttural, terrifying groans and shows us flashes of its real face, while never becoming a pastiche of Friedkin's *Exorcist*—despite the views of Warner Bros. and their lawyers. *Abby* is its own movie, for its own audience.

Due largely to the relationships American International Pictures had established in Italy, *Abby* was released in the territory prior to the Warner

Reverend Emmett Williams (Terry Carter) attempts an exorcism of Abby Williams (Carol Speed) to free her from the West African demon Eshu, in William Girdler's *Abby* (1974). Illustration by the author.

Bros. lawsuit, and the *Segnalazioni cinematografiche* offered its verdict on Girdler's movie: "The film, directed and interpreted for Black American circles, is unquestionably one of the many imitation productions ... carbon copies of *The Exorcist*."[9]

It is of no surprise that the overwhelmingly white clerics of the Vatican do not understand that this is *The Exorcist* deliberately repurposed for otherwise marginalized and forgotten Black audiences. What is of particular interest is that this film wasn't outright forbidden by the Church. The Vatican's verdict was that *Abby* was "questionable/ambiguous,"[10] and the film was reserved for adults of a certain moral maturity. That the Vatican deemed its content permissible at all is a surprise in and of itself, given the institution's view of the horror genre ... although further analysis may be able to provide an explanation, or at least a hypothesis.

The *Segnalazioni cinematografiche* review of *Abby* goes beyond the aesthetic and beyond the censorious, as the writer considers that "the moral questionability of the coda is visibly determined by the scenes that describe the main character's perversion"[11] and is forced to contemplate the benefits and risks of the film's "ambiguous mixture of Christianity and pagan magic in the attitudes and rites of the Protestant pastor."[12]

The Vatican's critic opted to engage with Girdler's film, its content and its themes and through discourse seek to present an intelligent critique rather than impose a strict sentence. Even more interesting is that this would later become the theme of *Segnalazioni cinematografiche* reviews of this subgenre in particular. The verdict of "questionable/ambiguous" would appear again and again where we might expect to see "unacceptable" as the Vatican sought to better contemplate the intentions behind these films' use of religion and the Devil and determine how much responsibility lies with the filmmakers in their representations when spreading a Christian message through film and how much lies with the role of censor, to protect the flock from potentially distressing visions. The *Segnalazioni cinematografiche* would therefore begin to interrogate its own considerations over the course of several film reviews.

It is worth noting that the Holy See is not entirely averse to self-reflection when it comes to its treatment of cinema, just slow to put it into action. Perhaps the best example of this involves Federico Fellini's 1960 transgressive masterpiece drama *La Dolce Vita*. Upon its original release, the Vatican was outraged. It wrote passionately against the film in its own daily newspaper *L'Osservatore Romano*, while the *Segnalazioni cinematografiche* called it "morally unacceptable."[13] Fellini's film was perhaps the first where much of the Roman Catholic population of Italy ignored the ecclesiastical ban entirely and descended upon the country's cinemas to see it en masse. *La Dolce Vita* knew massive box-office success both at home and abroad and has since been named as one of the greatest films of all time. The *Segnalazioni cinematografiche* would revisit Fellini's film some 20 years later and ask Church film writers to critically reappraise both the film and the institution's 1960 review of it. In its defense, it handled this exercise with aplomb, maintaining that its earlier arguments were made in good faith and acknowledging that the effect of the movie on audiences over time was not as negative as the Vatican had feared.

It would, however, remain unusual for a *Segnalazioni cinematografiche* critic to engage so deeply with a film from one of the low genres. The decision to do so here could have been borne of censorship, of pride, or of genuine intellectual interrogation. Whether the Vatican sought to understand the films' messages or simply determine whether they presented the Church itself in a positive or negative light, it would continue to engage with satanic horror films.

L'Esorciccio would be Italian comedian Ciccio Ingrassia's contribution to the rich vein of films made in the style of *The Exorcist*. The vaudevillian comic was one half of Franco and Ciccio. A duo as formidable as any, they had loomed large in Italian comedy for decades and featured regularly in movies since 1960, notably in some 14 films directed by future genre provocateur Lucio Fulci. Here, Ingrassia writes (with Marino Onorati), directs and stars in the domestic comedy. The film's plot is exactly as you might imagine, essentially a movie-length sequence of various absurdist set pieces that English-speaking audiences might associate with the movies of Mel Brooks. Ingrassia plays the titular Italian exorcist, who despite his utter incompetence successfully exorcizes a number of people bewitched by an occult amulet, unwittingly beating Satan's evil at every turn before ultimately succumbing to it himself. The film's humor is very much family friendly, as are its faux scares, and it was a domestic success.

In bringing his parody to the screen, Ingrassia exercised the appropriate amount of caution in never explicitly mentioning the Catholic Church. He had seen his friend and former collaborator Fulci already get in much trouble with the Vatican over representations of its history in his blackly painted historical drama *Beatrice Cenci* (1969), pointed accusations at its involvement in the shady state affairs of Propaganda Due in the satirical comedy *The Eroticist*, and shining a light on the widespread abuse of children by Catholic clergy in rural giallo *Don't Torture a Duckling* (both 1972). Subsequently, Ingrassia smartly made no mention of the Catholic Church, nor was there an appearance by any supposed agent of the Church, in his film. While Ciccio played the exorcist's role in an outfit a priest might wear, he was careful to portray a man of no organized religion, a layperson with a sideline in demon hunting.

Ciccio's tactful avoidance of religion paid off, and the Vatican saw no reason that the Roman Catholic population might come to harm from watching his film. The *Segnalazioni cinematografiche* reacted kindly to Ingrassia's comedy, calling it "a funny film, better than average"[14] and asserting that such parodies (generally a very popular type of film in Italy) "harmonize with the simple environment in which they live,"[15] essentially considering the film's message uncomplicated but harmless. The Vatican's final word is typically reserved, but the review remains a positive one: "The caricature involves various aspects of modern life, unpretentious of refined irony, but also without excessive bells and whistles, sometimes arousing healthy laughs, which are rather rare goods in current productions. Acceptable/coarse."[16]

It was not far into his directorial career that former cinematographer and special effects man Mario Bava realized that he wasn't going to achieve profit or success domestically. Mario's career as a cameraman had spanned two decades and seen him work with many established directors, including silent-era legend Roberto Roberti, domestic innovators Roberto Rossellini and Steno, and even Hollywood titan Orson Welles. As noted in earlier chapters, Bava's first steps into directing were for Riccardo Freda on his 1957 gothic horror bet *I Vampiri*, and sci-fi monster movie *Caltiki: The Immortal Monster* the following year, before launching fully into infamy with the 1960 film *Black Sunday* and later creating the giallo filone with

9. The Power of Christ Compels You! 201

1963's *The Girl Who Knew Too Much* and *Blood and Black Lace* in 1964. While his offerings were innovative and shocking, they were, as a rule not particularly well received on home soil, in part due to ecclesiastical bans from the pages of the *Segnalazioni cinematografiche*.

Seeking success on foreign soil, Bava would soon form a relationship with distributor AIP, home of Roger Corman, Herman Cohen, Alex Gordon and Lou Rusoff. As part of the deal, Bava would receive production funds up front and hire a mix of Italian and U.S. cast and crew, with AIP having final say on the U.S. cut and title of the film. AIP were adept at marketing, and their sci-fi, teen monster and melodrama double bills would go on profitable runs across the U.S. drive-in circuit, sometimes playing regularly for years. Bava soon became more of a cult name in America than he ever would in Italy.

The deal between Bava and AIP didn't always go the director's way. A number of his films were retitled and recut for U.S. audiences, irrespective of Bava's preference. His 1960 sole directorial debut was originally called *The Mask of Satan*, only retitled *Black Sunday* by AIP (and censored by them to reduce the gore content) before finding success in the U.S. markets. The individual segments of 1963's anthology film *Three Faces of Fear* would be recut and rearranged, the film becoming *Black Sabbath* in the process.

With Bava's 1971 proto-slasher *Bay of Blood*, AIP had success exploiting the popularity of the film for years. When Wes Craven's debut *Last House on the Left* was released upon unsuspecting audiences across drive-in theaters, *Bay of Blood* was ready to be retitled *Last House Part 2* and put on a double bill with the film. Working hand in hand with Italian directors as well as U.S. B-movie auteurs, AIP had learned the value of the filone system, of how celluloid imitations would make money for both themselves *and* the films that inspired them.

The Exorcist was released at around the time Bava was working on his surreal horror *Lisa & the Devil*, starring Elke Sommer and Telly Savalas. After multiple successes across giallo, sci-fi, adventure and, of course, horror, the director's most idiosyncratic film yet told the story of a young American tourist who stays overnight as the guest of Spanish aristocrats on their family estate. The house is revealed to be plagued by supernatural evil and dark secrets involving necrophilia.

As *The Exorcist* became a phenomenal success, AIP of course saw the value in exploiting it. After early screenings of Bava's latest film were disastrous, it would become the project of producer Alfredo Leone to salvage. Leone hired Bava junior, Lamberto, to shoot additional scenes and reedit the movie to maximize its potential. The final product, titled *The House of Exorcism*, centers Elke Sommer's tourist as a woman possessed, recounting the tale of her ordeal to a priest as he attempts to save her from the demon inside her. In this instance, the AIP version of the film was the one released in most territories.

One thing Bava could be sure of was a swift dismissal by the *Segnalazioni cinematografiche*. The Vatican had, through its positioning during the Mussolini regime and its recognition as the true faith of Italy, known a level of success in keeping the horror genre out of Italy for several decades. There had been no horror genre to speak of, until the late 1950s and Bava's films that set off the gothic horror trend and then the giallo. Horror was, in the eyes of the Holy See, the most shocking and corrupting of all genres, and Bava was the man responsible for its sudden proliferation. Subsequently, the *Segnalazioni cinematografiche* tended to react to Bava's films in a very heavy-handed manner.

The pastoral evaluation asserted that *The House of Exorcism* was "evidently ... inspired by the recent fashion of ecclesial interventions against demonic possessions...[which] has not benefited either the spectacular values or the moral dignity of the work, which is aberrant."[17] Contemplating the same institution's views of *Abby* and *L'Esorciccio*, the *Segnalazioni cinematografiche*'s rush to damn Bava is all the more jarring.

The review did not stop at criticizing the quality of the film, but also called into question Bava's moral standing in directing it: "The succession of erotic scenes that in human madness or diabolical action find only a convenient excuse; they are also scenes that ask Satan for the patronage of dialogues of paradoxical obscenity."[18] Was Bava, in his transgressions, guilty of asking the patronage of Satan? Was he doing the Devil's work for him?

In its final damnation, the review dismissed even the resolution of the film with derision, stating: "That the priest of the story manages to prevail in extremis is entirely secondary and cannot be an element capable of 'exorcising' this indecent product; on the contrary, the presence of the religious exacerbates the immorality of the film ... just as his sacramental action makes him acquire completely incorrect doctrinal implications."[19] The *Segnalazioni*'s decision was emphatic. While the current influx of satanic horror pictures was something the Vatican appeared to see some value in, Bava's film was effectively banned: unable to be screened in any cinema owned or operated by Catholics, it would receive limited distribution in *terza visione* theaters domestically and see more success in other territories.

Similarly dismissed was Italian genre journeyman (and former spaghetti western director) Alberto de Martino's 1974 film *L'Anticristo*, which tells the story of a paralyzed young woman who has a crisis of faith and, with the help of a psychologist, unlocks her past life as a witch during the

9. The Power of Christ Compels You!   203

Inquisition. The film is perhaps the most obvious imitator of Friedkin's landmark horror, at least according to Peter Markham, who wryly noted that "admirers of carbon-copy cinema—if any exist—will be well pleased with Alberto de Martino's *The Antichrist*."[20]

In de Martino's effort, the involvement of the Church is interesting. A Vatican cardinal at first refuses to help the young woman, instead offering a secular parapsychologist. Later, when the Holy See authorizes a priest to undertake an exorcism, he is only partially successful: in the end it is the girl's father, with the help of an iron crucifix that finally defeats the demon that has possessed her.

The *Segnalazioni cinematografiche* suggested that the "rising friction of vulgar or stomach-churning scenes and, above all, the repertoire of shocks [means that] the product can be ridiculous or repulsive according to the digestive capacity of the spectator"[21] before determining the film to be "unacceptable/negative"[22] and stating that "pastorally, the film is to be estimated entirely negative, due to the licentiousness of the scenes and to the unacceptability of the subjects that are suggested."[23]

The Vatican considered de Martino's film to be actively harmful, both in its presentation of the Church and its "scoundrel concoction of vulgar or disgusting scenes, and, above all, the repertoire of filthiness and licentiousness that in blatant demonic literature…[is] a shameful homage to a corrupting power that is anything but annoying for the Evil One."[24] The film is also recognized by the Church to have "blatantly parasitic intentions,"[25] stealing its narrative and themes directly from *The Exorcist*. As it had done with Bava's *The House of Exorcism*, the Holy See came down hard on De Martino, concluding that, in his corrupting influence, he was doing the Devil's work.

To the filone in Italy we can also add Ovidio G. Assonitis and Roberto Piazzoli's 1974 offering *Chi Sei?* (Who Are You?), titled *Beyond the Door* for its U.S. release. Detailing a woman possessed by a demon, Assonitis and Piazzoli's film was successful (earning $15 million against a $350,000 budget) before the litigious Warner Bros. filed a lawsuit in August 1975 seeking an injunction and $2 million in damages, again citing copyright infringement. If Bava and de Martino's films paid deference to Satan, *Beyond the Door* appeared to be besotted by him. In the film's opening moments, the Devil himself is allowed to break the fourth wall and address the audience from behind a blank screen in an initially quite disturbing moment before the film breaks down into the derivative silliness typical of the filone.

The *Segnalazioni cinematografiche* determined the film to be "a confused mixture of psychology, papsychology and Satanism, poor in drama and often involuntarily grotesque"[26] and considered it to "induce more incredulous laughter or disgust than fruitful reflections on the presence

of Evil in life."²⁷ The filmmakers were criticized for the manner in which they dealt with the subject of demonology, leaving "a legacy of spectators in a field that is already difficult in itself and a source of misunderstandings anxiety, perplexity, discouragement."²⁸

The Vatican was further angered that *Beyond the Door*'s only agent of the Church acts not to exorcize the evil but is in league with it. Father Merrin believes the demon will allow him to cheat death, and so is an antagonist in the story. The *Segnalazioni cinematografiche* damned the film for its use of such a "malignant priest"²⁹ and considered the film to be completely unacceptable.

Finally, after imitator, parody and reimagining, the Vatican arrived at the main course: One year after it opened in box offices elsewhere, *The Exorcist*'s producers arranged a distribution deal that would bring it to the home of Roman Catholicism. Having seen the hysteria the film caused everywhere it had already opened, the Holy See's turn to influence the film's domestic reception had come, as it presented its evaluation of the most shockingly religious horror movie the world might ever see….

With the exception of Girdler's blaxploitation effort *Abby*, the *Segnalazioni cinematografiche* had been incredibly dismissive of the filone created by *The Exorcist*, censuring and damning domestic offerings in the vein of the controversial masterpiece. When it came to Friedkin's film, however, the Vatican's writer chose his words carefully. The dismissive tone that was employed for the wretched horror movies of Bava, of de Martino, Assonitis and Piazzoli was missing, in its place a serious interrogation of *The Exorcist*'s aesthetics and its deeper moralistic value.

"There is no reason to doubt the objectivity of the facts which, moreover, have numerous findings in the ancient and modern ecclesial chronicle and are preceded by rather explicit evangelical episodes on the 'freedoms' granted by Divine Providence, powers of darkness, puzzling mysteries and sometimes the perennial struggle of Good against Evil."³⁰ The Vatican affords the film far more respect than it did to not only its imitators but to your average slasher or zombie or rape-revenge movie or the films of nunsploitation and nazisploitation, discussing its apparent realism in great detail.

In the film, Friedkin and his cast played the exorcism set piece without bells and whistles, allowing the power of the situation to do the work and only resorting to a few very key special effects when the terror needed to be ramped up another level. Here, the reviewer recognizes that. In a detailed two-page review, the journal discusses "the reality of sin and evil

Opposite: **A likeness of Pope Paul VI lurks...** *Beyond the Door!* **Illustration by the author.**

in general; faith in absolute divine power and in the efficacy of sacramental rites; the difference in the scope of science and religion with the limits of the former compared to the latter; the importance of the priestly mission."[31]

The *Segnalazioni cinematografiche* continues to discuss the film as though it were a documentary, playing the role of interested intellect more than executing its paternalistic duty as moral guardian. The Vatican's writer's intent, to interrogate the work's value to the Church rather than criticize the risk it posed to the Italian public, is unusual and interesting to see.

Eventually, the writer turns to the point of the piece (his parochial duty): "On the other hand, strong reservations must be raised about the cinematographic form adopted which, in contrast to the positive substance of the themes, can induce spectators to aberrant emotional reactions and even to contrasting interpretations."[32]

From here, the *Segnalazioni cinematografiche* considers that the more visceral on-screen representations of exorcisms had contained "upsetting manifestations of Evil in all its brutality, [and] it is not admissible that excesses of fictional realism are reached such as to be disconcerting and traumatic, or such as to suggest hatred and piety together, such as to mix the obscene with the more composed and spiritual reflections, such as to instil horror and emotion together."[33] Finally the gloves come off and the Holy See seeks to exert its authority, criticizing the film from a moralistic standpoint: "As miserable as the state of a victim of Satan may be, the screen can describe it effectively even without resorting to deprecation, foul language, revolt, obscene and blasphemy. Questionable/ambiguous."[34]

Once again, the *Segnalazioni cinematografiche* voices its concerns bluntly but stops short of rendering the film as unacceptable, aberrant or morally repugnant, all decrees it made about a number of genre films. Crucially there is no outright ecclesiastical ban. The Vatican appears to understand that there is a benefit to depicting the priestly mission to vanquish evil on-screen, even in the most controversial horror film ever released. Perhaps seeking a closer connection to the public via this film (which had dominated at box offices everywhere it went), it ultimately allows its flock to make up their own minds about William Peter Blatty and William Friedkin's Oscar-winning film.

This subtly different attitude from the Holy See is hardly cause to cry "Revolution!," but it *does* show the Vatican's thinkers engaging with horror cinema in a different way. It is not that the Church considered the violence of demonic possession an acceptable sight to subject its flock to; rather, *in spite* of its critique's closing moral judgments, the Vatican is somewhat more intellectually invested in this new subgenre, which confronts the same battles that its senior clergy fights, both figuratively and literally.

In *The Exorcist*, and in at least some of the films it inspired, there are no psychosexual deviants, no chain saw–wielding monsters, vigilantes or serial killers. There is only the holy fight against Satan, and here, the priests are not patriarchal tyrants or corrupted or predators. They are the story's protagonists, its heroes ... providing they are painted in the right light.

While *The Exorcist* had only just hit Italy's shores, elsewhere the satanic horror subgenre was in overdrive. A slew of lurid titles emblazoned with pseudo-occult imagery would be released in the next couple of years, all rich with the presence of Satan, his demons, and the Antichrist: Robert Fuest would direct Ernest Borgnine and William Shatner in *The Devil's Rain*; ailing Hammer Studios and director Peter Sykes finally adapted a second Dennis Wheatley book and released *To the Devil, a Daughter*. Satanic horror movies were everywhere: fans needed only look for the *Mark of the Devil* and drink *The Blood on Satan's Claw* in order to dance *The Mephisto Waltz* and become *Satan's Slave*.

Back in Hollywood, Harvey Bernhard and Twentieth Century–Fox noted that the model observed by both *Rosemary's Baby* and *The Exorcist* shared several common elements that influenced their success. Each film combined a New Hollywood director (Roman Polanski; William Friedkin) with a visionary producer (William Castle; William Peter), hired serious talent with real acting chops (Mia Farrow, John Cassavetes; Ellen Burstyn, Max von Sydow) and an intelligent but cynical screenplay and went on to realize both critical and box-office success stories.

Bernhard's own response was *The Omen*, David Seltzer's original screenplay about an American diplomat unwittingly bringing up the Antichrist as his own son. It would be given to up-and-coming New Hollywood director Richard Donner to helm and cast Gregory Peck as diplomat Robert Thorn; Lee Remick as his wife, Katherine; and a supporting cast of established character actors such as Billie Whitelaw, David Warner and Patrick Troughton, formerly the eponymous Doctor Who of the 60s UK TV series.

Released in 1976, *The Omen* was a commercial success, earning $60 million from a budget of $2.8 million and becoming one of the year's top grossers. Its critical reception was mixed, however. Roger Ebert, so moved by both *Rosemary's Baby* and *The Exorcist*, seems suddenly jaded of the genre when he opines that the film "takes all of this [Satanism] terribly seriously, as befits the genre that gave us 'Rosemary's Baby' and 'The Exorcist' ... all of this material is approached with the greatest solemnity, not only in the performances but also in the photography, the music and the very looks on people's faces."[35]

The United States Conference of Catholic Bishops (formerly the Legion of Decency) took umbrage at the film, calling it a "slick, expensively mounted but essentially trashy horror show. Though it refers to scripture and religious beliefs, its only interest in religion is in terms of its exploitation potential."[36] It became one of only eight horror films in the modern (post–*Psycho*) era to be condemned by the organization, all of which were regarded as denigrating orthodox religious practice.[37]

The Vatican also shared a dim view of Donner's movie, noting in particular what the Holy See considered to be the absurdity of the film's plot: "The film strives to adapt a mysterious prophecy of the Apocalypse to modern circumstances. To this end it falls into obvious forcing and ridiculous details."[38]

By now, it is apparent that the *Segnalazioni cinematografiche* probes a little deeper with this subgenre than it does most horror films, presumably because of the subject matter and previous commercial successes and the positioning of the clergy as the heroes of these stories. However, unlike with *The Exorcist* and the films of its filone, what the Church finds here, it does not like. The reviewer hones in on the film's flaws in its representation of religion, commenting that "its danger lies in the presumption before the interpretation of Sacred Scripture; in the evident confusion between religion and superstition; in the caressing of morbid interests for all that is spiritual or parapsychological."[39]

Once more, it appears as though the Church is affording the satanic horror subgenre more good faith than it previously has the horror film in general. Rather than decry the film's morbid or bloodthirsty content, it seeks to interpret the ecclesiastical actions of the film's players and comment upon authenticity. Where *The Exorcist* appeared to earn the Vatican's grudging respect, *The Omen* commits the sin of presumption, of conflating religion with superstition and, in doing so, loses something from its message in the eyes of the Church.

In addition, and much like the films of de Martino, Assonitis and Piazzoli, in this film the Church *fails;* its agents taken care of by the Morningstar evil machinations, leaving the child Damien's father and Warne's photojournalist to negotiate the supernatural element without God in their hearts. As a result, they too fail, and at the end of the movie, the still alive Damien Thorne has been transferred into the care of the President of the United States of America and the First Lady, surely a sign of great success for the Devil. It is perhaps in this that the Church determines *The Omen* to have failed in its artistic and spiritual intent.

By the time of Damiano Damiani's 1982 *Amityville: The Possession*, the Vatican had further considered its position on the role of these heroic priests battling terrifying evils in the latest grimy transgressions of the horror movie. Damiano's prequel, overseen by Italian super-producer Dino De Laurentiis and focusing on the original murders that started the

In Damiano Damiani's *Amityville II: The Possession* (1982), Father Frank Adamsky (James Olson) stands outside the Amityville house, contemplating the evil he must vanquish. Illustration by the author.

legend of that Long Island house, is a battle for a single soul. The heroic Father Adamsky fights the incalculable power of Satan for possession of Sonny Montell in a film that borrows as much from Friedkin's *Exorcist* as it does from Stuart Rosenberg's 1979 original film *The Amityville Horror*.

In its review of Damiani's film, the *Segnalazioni cinematografiche* has determined that the films of this subgenre are "made with care and well interpreted"[40] where they depict priests in acts of spiritual bravery, determining that "the positive element is to present the power of Evil as a reality ... but not overdo it. The Church has the power to win."[41] This summation follows the thinking observed in the *Segnalazioni cinematografiche*'s critiques of *The Exorcist* (where the Church prevails thanks to a heroic priest who battles the demon Pazuzu even in the face of a crisis of faith) and *The Omen* (where Church intervention fails, leaving laypersons to better interpret and fight the evil). Where the Church no longer has the power to win, it is not being seen in the appropriate light. It may cause parishioners to question their faith, to doubt its power to protect them. The Vatican has been more engaged with this area of horror than it has most genre fare, suggesting the Holy See does see intellectual and spiritual merit in films that depict the battle between God (via his earthly servants) and Satan (via his demons and his unholy seed), even if it cannot fully approve of the content.

In Damiani's supernatural chiller, there is lots for the Church to approve of. Father Adamsky, while he undergoes terrible tests in his battle with the evil of Amityville, never doubts his faith and, with God beside him, is unwavering in his constant battle. Here, we see a powerful yet holy protagonist, the Church as the ultimate good. The depiction of a simple everyman-of-the-cloth is one that Roman Catholicism can at least take some pride in.

The film, like many in the subgenre, was branded "questionable"[42] and not banned outright but reserved for adults of a moral maturity, as "the climate of anguish and permanent confusion, some indecent scenes and some atrocities require moral reservations."[43] To be pronounced as questionable, rather than unacceptable, is actually a huge success for these films. The Vatican of the 1950s to the 1970s would never decree a horror film to be suitable for audiences in general, such was the observed potential for spiritual corruption when the Vatican was engaged in a battle against apostasy, a war waged to win back the hearts and spirits of the Italian people. In *The Exorcist*, and in the satanic horror subgenre, the Church finds itself as protagonist in a fantastical narrative, waging the tireless fight against an indefatigable evil, and even the most chaste must succumb to seduction. But in seeing their kind positioned almost as superheroes have the Vatican's critics become guilty of pride, one of the capital vices? Distorted, romanticized and with the benefit of special effects, do representations of the clergy as arch protagonists (as with *The Exorcist*'s Father Damien Karras and *Amityville: The Possession*'s Father Adamsky) play to the egos of the Vatican's clerics? Or do they simply learn more about themselves and the view of the public by paying attention to the way they are portrayed in fiction (as might members of any profession, let alone one with an interest in film censorship)?

Whatever the driving factor, this reflection would continue, with the Church regularly giving counsel on matters of exorcism on the silver screen and the responsibility of filmmakers to the churchgoing public. As recently as 2016, Father Francesco Bamonte, president of the International Association of Exorcists in Rome, wrote in *L'Osservatore Romano* that portraying exorcisms in the cinema "could promote greater awareness"[44] about matters of faith, if presented in the right manner. Arguing that the presentation of evil, of demonic possession and the sacrament of exorcism is often "disappointing and unacceptable"[45] and that filmmakers have a responsibility to teach that God's power wins out: "the demon, even if he doesn't want to, is forced against his will to affirm the truth of our Holy Faith."[46] This reads almost like a summarized version of the previous comments made by the *Segnalazioni cinematografiche* critics, which would suggest a coordinated message has developed over time, with the Vatican keen to see itself represented on-screen, in the battle against the Fallen Angel himself, as it serves a dual purpose: to maintain control of the population via fear, teaching cinema audiences that the evil of sin brings about God's enemies, and that they are terrifying, powerful demons that an ordinary man could not possibly fight; and to increase credibility of the institution—as Father Bamonte suggested above, Rome would prefer cinematic portrayals of exorcism to "affirm the truth of our Holy Faith."[47] Presenting demonic possession as a winnable battle for the Church helps the Church retain an element of credibility with its flock, who trust it to protect them and keep them safe from the evils of Hell, of which they are afraid.

The Vatican remains concerned about the representation of both good and evil in the films of the satanic horror subgenre. That the Devil is presented as an evil God, rather than a creation of God turned rogue, with no real power of his own, remains a source of consternation for the Church. When priests and exorcism rites are used, the Holy See expects that true spirituality will not be mixed with superstition or be easily overcome by the occult. But perhaps more than anything, it is the roles of priests as protagonists, as heroes victorious in these silver screen battles between good and evil, that sways the Church and causes its writers to look more closely at the themes and messages in these genre films presented to them for critique.

A gallery of subversive directors whose films were censured by the Church in the pages of the *Segnalazioni cinematografiche*. Top row, l to r: George A. Romero, Wes Craven, William Friedkin. Middle row, l to r: Umberto Lenzi, Lucio Fulci, Mario Bava. Bottom row, l to r: Luchino Visconti, Pier Paolo Pasolini, Liliana Cavani. Illustration by the author.

Conclusion

A lot has happened, to both cinema and the Church, since the Vatican issued its first paternalistic decree on film in 1909, forbidding members of the clergy from attending any public film screenings. The Holy See's attitude toward the cinematic medium has, on the surface at least, shifted greatly, and its influence over the form has certainly altered. Pius XI's decree in 1930 demanded Catholics "watch only virtuous films and deplore the evil of the wicked ones"[1] because cinema was "too often used as an incentive to evil passions."[2] Fast-forward to Pope John Paul's 1995 address in celebration of 100 years of cinema, which hailed that "masterpieces of the art of film making can be moving challenges to the human spirit"[3] and recognized the art form's "remarkable ability to influence public opinion and culture across all social and political frontiers."[4] As recently as 2023, Pope Francis held court with an Italian filmmakers' foundation to express that "a good movie has the power to inspire wonder and to evangelize by reflecting the beauty of God's creation"[5] and urged them to "reawaken that wonder."[6]

The reputation of the Vatican would, across the many decades spanned by these various decrees, transform substantially. It would become an official component of the Italian state's power structure with the Lateran Treaty of 1929, and later ally itself with both Mussolini and Hitler, with Cardinal Pacelli (later Pope Pius XII) signing a concordat with the Reich to proclaim Roman Catholicism its recognized religion.

As a means of spiritual renewal for the church (and an opportunity for it to try to disentangle itself from its sordid recent history), the Vatican announced the Second Vatican Council of 1962–65, seeking to relegitimize its position as the global head of the Roman Catholic faith and bring its standing in Italy up to date. Unfortunately for the Church, this would lead to what Angeli called "the new secularisation"[7] and a period of mass apostasy for the Italian people that took place across several decades since. Italians would later defy Vatican influence, including passing legislation to institute divorce in Italy in 1970[8] (reaffirmed in a referendum in 1974) and to legalize abortion in 1978.[9]

The biggest scandal in the postwar history of Italy's power structures enveloped the Vatican and the Christian Democrat Party in 1981, when anti-corruption forces closed in on members of P2 and revealed the "secret government"[10] of members of parliament, military officials, senior police officials and others, with links to both the Vatican and the Mafia.[11,12] In 1984, a new concordat was signed that ended Roman Catholicism's tenure as the state religion of Italy and, with it, effectively ended its power over matters of state. Later, in 2019, Pope Francis finally ended the Vatican's "secrecy rule"[13] with regard to child sexual abuse perpetrated by the clergy and the long-ranging, institutional abuse of nuns, including sexual slavery.

While Pope Francis is formally credited with admitting to the Vatican's complicity in institutional abuse, it will not be a hero's ending. The pontiff admitted in 2019 there was "no more an excuse"[14] for pontifical secrecy in the crimes committed upon children by 2 percent of the Church's clergy, but of course there had never been a suitable excuse to begin with, and the crimes had already been exposed by others. Exposés such as those of journalists from the *Boston Globe* who uncovered widespread abuse in their archdiocese (abuse that had been covered up at the highest level)[15] and made the sexual abuse of minors by Roman Catholic clerics a globally discussed issue led to a crisis for the Church that eventually led to Pope Francis' announcements some years later.

Before these exposés were even made, filmmakers such as Lucio Fulci, Aldo Lado and Vittorio De Sisti had published theirs, in the form of *Don't Torture a Duckling* and *Who Saw Her Die?*, gialli with murderous, abusive and deluded clergy as their black-gloved killers, taking the innocence from children in order to (in their perverted minds) preserve it. In fact, as has been highlighted in several of the chapters of this book, each of the above incidents and events surrounding the Church has been cataloged, to some degree or another, by filmmakers (often Italian ones) working in horror and exploitation genres.

Massimo Dallamano and Sergio Martino would follow in the footsteps of Lado, De Sisti and Fulci. The narratives of Dallamano's Schoolgirl Trilogy and Martino's *Suspicious Death of a Minor* introduced schoolgirl prostitution rings (very real events happening in Italy in the 1970s, where young girls were routinely enslaved, abused and murdered by the very people supposed to keep them safe) and criticized Church and state for failing to protect Italy's children and instead protecting its predators.

In the rape/revenge film, directors have tested the Church's supposed progressiveness by taking an original biblical tale in the Story of Dinah and using it to create a subversive, exploitative subgenre of horror film. Following on from Ingmar Bergman's lead, Wes Craven (who himself had a very strict, orthodox Christian upbringing) crafted a version of the Book of Genesis story for the U.S. drive-ins and grind houses, one that has been developed further by exploitation directors (including Catholics such as Abel Ferrara) and even taken on a feminist bent in more modern years. However, the Holy See's reaction has, almost uniformly, remained the same. Despite the modern teachings of the Church that "rape deeply wounds the respect, freedom, and physical and moral integrity to which every person has a right. It causes grave damage that can mark the victim for life. It is always an intrinsically evil act,"[16] the critics of the *Segnalazioni cinematografiche* repeatedly responded to these films in a way that reflects the original biblical tale, with very little consideration of the unjust and evil nature of rape, instead concentrating heavily on the negative implications of the revenge portion of these stories, as revenge is a product of the cardinal sin wrath and therefore (in the teachings of the Church) the greater threat to the souls of humankind than those inciting events that have the power to destroy a life even when they do not take it completely.

Rarely have the writers of the Vatican's film review journal considered the rape/revenge narrative from the perspective of the (usually female) survivor, although it could be argued that neither have the writers and directors of the films themselves. On the rare occasion that the rape/revenge protagonist is given complexity of character, truly empowered and offered catharsis and redemption, such as Ferrara's *Ms .45*, she has had an impact on both the audience and on the Vatican's reviewer. In reviewing that film, it is worth noting that the *Segnalazioni cinematografiche* paid far closer attention to Zoë Lund's Thana, touched by her experience and examining her condition with a care and consideration not offered to Sandra Peabody's Mari Collingwood (*Last House on the Left*) or Camille Keaton's Jennifer *(I Spit on Your Grave)*. Even as it labels the film unacceptable, the *Segnalazioni cinematografiche*'s review focuses on Thana's tragic "madness"[17] (what we would today understand to be her post-traumatic stress disorder), considers the effects of her rape on her reaction to it, and stops short of fully condemning her acts of wrath.

The *Segnalazioni cinematografiche* responds to these narratives with a greater passion than it does those of the fantastic, of the shuffling zombie or flesh-eating cannibal. Despite the overtly perverse and sacrilegious iconography and symbolism of the profane resurrection and the perverted Eucharist, it was only when directors directly involved real-life Catholic figures (such as the missionaries of Lenzi's *Cannibal Ferox*, the Templar Knights of Amando de Ossorio's *Tombs of the Blind Dead* and the Conquistadores of Fulci's *Zombi 2*) that the Vatican sought to censure films of these filones for reasons beyond the blood, gore and violent content, opting in the case of zombie filone to engage with its films on an artistic level (as long as those films weren't directed by Catholics). Even when Fulci's zombies were a product of a priest's suicide, or biblical apocalypse, the Holy See sought not to engage with the same vitriol for this apparent sacrilege and for perversions of scripture as it had when the same director took aim at pederast Catholic priests or historical pontiffs and their inquisitors.

The nunsploitation genre saw the attempts of directors such as Eriprando Visconti, Gianfranco Mingozzi and (once again) Lucio Fulci to shine a cold, clinical light on the wickedness the Church had perpetrated upon figures such as Marianna de Leyva (the Nun of Monza), Beatrice Cenci and Flavia Gaetani throughout history. These grisly historical epics presented with all the exploitation genre trappings sought not only to sensationalize and titillate but to hold the church to account—not just for the misogynistic horrors of its deep past but those that would continue right through to the directors' lifetimes (and beyond). Looking back at those films, fully aware now of the modern abuses, the sexual slavery of nuns since reported by truly heroic figures such as Sister Maura O'Donoghue, Medical Missionary of Mary from Ireland, and Lucetta Scaraffia, editor of the Vatican magazine *Women, Church, World*, and her 11-strong editorial team, it now becomes obvious that Italy's subversive directors were trying to draw the public's attention to what had not only happened hundreds of years in the Church's past but to crimes and abhorrences still ongoing in its present.

The hegemonic memory that both Church and state were so keen to install and maintain in Italy following the defeat of fascism across Europe, a collective amnesia it sought to impress upon the population, and the great lengths that the Vatican went to relegitimize its position in the hearts and minds of its flock went challenged in the *sadiconazista*, or nazisploitation film. While often maligned and censured as exploitative trash, the films of genre stalwarts stand shoulder to shoulder with those of more celebrated directors such as Liliana Cavani, Pier Paolo Pasolini and Luchino Visconti, always presenting the Nazis as irredeemable monsters driven by evil (rather than just people "carrying out their orders" out of fear for the regime they worked within), choosing to explore the Holocaust in all its lurid excesses and filling every frame with a brutal honesty. Sergio Bergonzelli, Bruno Mattei and Luigi Batzella (among others), alongside their counterparts from the U.S., Canada and other nations (such as Don Edmonds, Lee Frost, and Jess Franco) presented the Nazis as sadistic and sexually transgressive, willing to inflict every possible harm on their prisoners, and while elements of these films were created in the service of titillation, there is little doubt that the Italian directors used this as a way to tell their truths about the fascists of both Germany and of Italy, their evils displayed on the screen for all to see. Batzella in particular would focus on the Italian army in the Middle East and Africa, and the horrors they committed there (a crucial omission from much of the hegemonic memory of the era, and a pertinent one as it began before Mussolini and fascism came to power). This writer agrees with Fiddler and Banwell,[18] in that these Italian filmmakers, whether those considered poets or those deemed to be exploitative, all sought to provide an "echoing of fact through an eroticized lens,"[19] to disrupt the hegemony and replace it with a more authentic political and historical memory of fascism and the Italian institutions complicit in it.

A question mark still very much hangs over the murder of Pier Paolo Pasolini. With the three DNA traces found at the scene of the crime by police in 2010 so far not investigated, there is at the time of writing an opportunity to reopen the case of the murder of Italy's most subversive filmmaker and learn more about who really killed him. Should the filmmakers David Grieco and Giovanni Giovannetti get their way and the case be re-opened, and the suspected links to mafiosi be discovered, it suggests a connection to Propaganda Due: Italy's deep state, the secret cabal of politicians, military and police top brass, of bankers, mafiosi and clergy active throughout the 1970s. Though he was not the only director to do so, Pasolini had through his art warned the public of the existence of Propaganda Due, as well as attempted to subvert the institution's preference for hegemony via memory amnesia by presenting the most provocative on-screen narratives on the evil (and banality) of the regime that Roman Catholicism had once been formally allied with.

Throughout, the Church has been more concerned with (or at least more conscious of) cinematic sins committed against it as an institution than against the Bible or the Word of God. The sacrilege and blasphemy inherent to the iconography of the zombie film (the profane resurrection) or the cannibal filone (the subverted Eucharist) goes largely ignored by the Vatican's writers, who nonetheless condemn such films but more for their broader content than any specific crimes against scripture or deity. However, when the filmmaker's lens is pointed at the Vatican itself rather than the symbolism of the religion it governs, the Holy See sits up and takes notice, condemning those films that seek to challenge hegemony and uncover truth (such as the clergy-as-abuser/murderer trope in gialli, the historical crimes of the Vatican in nunsploitation and its dalliances with fascism in nazisploitation) with far greater passion that those which seek to subvert the sacraments or the contents of the Bible.

In an interesting twist on the Vatican's overall impression of horror and other exploitation genres, we come to a subgenre that it actually appears to (to a certain degree) approve of, or at least is less inclined to censure the messaging of.

Where horror depicts the church (and by definition its clergy) as crusading hero, fighting the good fight, the never-ending battle against Satan for the souls of humanity, the *Segnalazioni cinematografiche* celebrates and understands the potency of such imagery, even if it must still fulfill its duty to censure it. Where what the Church considers to be a real evil rather than either an element of fantasy or a direct attack on itself as in institution or, where the opportunity is given to show priests as protagonists, in acts of spiritual bravery to vanquish the foe and save a human soul, there is recognition by the Church, who note the power in being able to "present the power of Evil as a reality ... but not overdo it. The Church has the power to win."[20] The clerics of the Centro Cattolico Cinematografico do see an intellectual and spiritual merit in films that depict the battle between God (via his earthly servants, the clergy) and Satan (via his demons that possess unfortunate members of the flock), but even those narratives must fall within the boundaries of what it considers to be appropriate. Where the satanic horror subgenre mixes its spirituality with superstition or paganism, or presents the Devil as an evil God (rather than a rogue creation, ultimately powerless in the face of faith and will), it still causes the church a great deal of discomposure. In the eyes of the Vatican it remains the filmmaker's responsibility to ensure to present demonic possession or the Antichrist as a winnable battle, and that the priestly mission is carried out with "faith in absolute divine power and in the efficacy of sacramental rites; the difference in the scope of science and religion with the limits of the former compared to the latter."[21]

Cinema, like any other art form, is often used to speak truth to power, to criticize and challenge and protest in what is generally (but not always) considered a safe environment, free from any real danger of political reprisal from the police and state. In Italy, as the country's artists began to recover from years spent under the shadow of fascism, they turned to their art to interrogate a past that the state and church would not allow them to reflect upon openly and honestly. This led to an entire generation of domestic filmmakers asserting their passionate beliefs in a wide variety of cinematic offerings, often using genre film as the blunt-force tool required to express their frustration with both state and church. While this was Italian filmmakers' path to creating their feature films, they joined genre directors from around the world in working elements of the Roman Catholic faith and institution into their narratives, often acting as provocateurs in their stories' use of quasi-religious symbols and iconography and themes of the sacred and the profane, from criticism of the institution's history to its crimes of the present, from amoral retellings of the biblical story of Dinah, daughter of Jacob, to stark recollections of the Church's involvement with fascism and its complicity within the deep state of 1970s Italy.

Throughout, the Church has retained its belief that "some cinema productions merit criticism and disapproval, even severe criticism and disapproval. This is the case when films distort the truth, oppress genuine freedom, or show scenes of sex and violence offensive to human dignity. It is a fallacy for film-makers to do this in the name of free artistic expression."[22] Horror and exploitation genres certainly have the content that the Vatican considers "offensive to human dignity"[23] in abundance, and while they might not necessarily be "masterpieces of the art of film making [that] can be moving challenges to the human spirit"[24] they may still, with the right elements, have "the power to inspire wonder and to evangelize by reflecting the beauty of God's creation"[25] that Pope Francis was looking for. Where it shows the presence of faith, belief in its deity and a clergy able to battle evil, proudly displayed on the celluloid screen for audiences to see, even the horror film is able to provoke consideration and even, on rare occasions, a level of acceptability with the church. The *Segnalazioni cinematografiche*, and by extension the Vatican, appears to have learned over the years that the time of Pius XI's 1930 decree to "watch only virtuous films and deplore the evil of the wicked ones"[26] has, at least to some degree, passed, and that even a genre the Holy See has previously held as completely unacceptable may have its merit, after all.

A plethora of popes! Likenesses of pontiffs during whose papal tenures the CCC fought the distribution of horror and exploitation movies. Top row, l to r: Pius XII (2 March 1939–9 October 1958); John XXIII (28 October 1958–3 June 1963). Bottom row, l to r: John Paul I (26 August 1978–28 September 1978); John Paul II (16 October 1978–2 April 2005); Paul VI (21 June 1963–6 August 1978). Illustration by the author.

Chapter Notes

Introduction

1. Pope John Paul II (1995). Address of his Holiness John Paul II to the Plenary Assembly of the Pontifical Council for Social Communications (2) [online]. Available at: http://www.vatican.va/content/john-paul-ii/en/speeches/1995/march/documents/hf_jp-ii_spe_19950317_plen-pccs.html [Accessed 21 June 2020]
2. USCCB (no date). Vatican Best Films List [online]. Available at: https://web.archive.org/web/20120422064928/http://old.usccb.org/movies/vaticanfilms.shtml [Accessed 21 June 2020]
3. Pope John Paul II, 2.
4. Pope John Paul II, 2.
5. Pope John Paul II, 3.
6. Pope John Paul II, 3.
7. Angeli, S. (2017). Catholicism in Italian cinema in the age of "the new secularisation" (1958–1978) [online]. Available at: http://westminsterresearch.wmin.ac.uk/18419/1/Angeli_%20Silvia_thesis.pdf [Accessed 28 May 2018]
8. Brook, C. J. (2019). *Screening Religions in Italy: Contemporary Italian Cinema and Television in the Post-Secular Public Sphere*. Toronto: University of Toronto Press.
9. University of Pennsylvania (1996). The Cinema Under Mussolini [online]. Available at: http://ccat.sas.upenn.edu/italians/resources/Amiciprize/1996/mussolini.html [Accessed 22 June 2020]
10. Dowling, S. (2013). How Hitler helped make Hollywood [online]. Available at: https://theworld.org/stories/2013-02-14/how-hitler-helped-make-hollywood [Accessed 9 July 2023]
11. University of Pennsylvania.
12. Dowling.
13. Curti, R. (2015). *Italian Gothic Horror Films 1957–1969*. Jefferson, NC: McFarland, 12.
14. Guli.
15. Angeli, 59.
16. Pope Pius XI (1936). Encyclical Letter of Pope Pius XI on the Motion Picture: VIGILANTI CURA [online]. Available at: http://www.vatican.va/content/pius-xi/en/encyclicals/documents/hf_p-xi_enc_29061936_vigilanti-cura.html [Accessed 21 June 2020]
17. Sherwood, H. (2020). Unsealing of Vatican archives will finally reveal truth about "Hitler's pope" [online]. Available at: https://www.theguardian.com/world/2020/mar/01/unsealing-vatican-archive-reveal-hitler-truth-pope-pius-xii [Accessed 12 July 2020]
18. Sherwood.
19. Escrivá, J. (no date). Conversations 60 [online]. Available at: http://www.escrivaworks.org/book/conversations/point/60 [accessed 12 January 2020], 60.
20. Angeli, 55.
21. Angeli, 56.
22. Curti, 12.
23. *Segnalazioni cinematografiche* (1935), vol. 1. Rome: Centro Cattolico Cinematografico, 57. Translated from Italian by the author.
24. *Segnalazioni cinematografiche*, vol. 1, 13.
25. *Segnalazioni cinematografiche*, vol. 1, 39.
26. *Segnalazioni cinematografiche*, vol. 1, 19.
27. *Segnalazioni cinematografiche*, vol. 1, 40.
28. *Segnalazioni cinematografiche*, vol. 1, 46.

29. *Segnalazioni cinematografiche*, vol. 1, 35.
30. *Encyclopaedia Britannica* (no date). Italy from the 1960s [online]. Available at: https://www.britannica.com/place/Italy/Italy-from-the-1960s [Accessed 22 June 2020]
31. Martinelli, A., and Chiesi, A. (1999). *Recent Social Trends in Italy 1960–1995*. 1st ed. Montreal: McGill-Queen's University Press.
32. Angeli, 1.
33. carroll.edu (no date). Second Vatican Council [online]. Available at: https://www.carroll.edu/mission-catholic-identity/second-vatican-council [Accessed 12 July 2020]
34. carroll.edu.
35. carroll.edu.
36. Hitchcock, J. (2020). Was Vatican II a Mistake? [online]. Available at: https://www.crisismagazine.com/2020/was-vatican-ii-a-mistake [Accessed 12 July 2020]
37. McInerny, R. (no date). What Went Wrong with Vatican II [online]. Available at: https://www.ewtn.com/catholicism/library/what-went-wrong-with-vatican-ii-10174 [Accessed 12 July 2020]
38. Winters, M S. (2018). Hostility to Vatican II runs deep with Pope Francis' critics [online]. Available at: https://www.ncronline.org/news/opinion/distinctly-catholic/hostility-vatican-ii-runs-deep-pope-francis-critics [Accessed 12 July 2020]
39. Winters.
40. Curti, 12.
41. Glieberman, O. (2009). "Psycho": The horror movie that changed the genre [online]. Available at: https://ew.com/article/2009/08/04/psycho-the-horror-movie-that-changed-the-genre/ [Accessed 22 June 2020]

Chapter 1

1. West, A. (2015). Think of the Children! Examining "Pre-Code" Horror and its influence on cinema [online]. Available at: https://www.comingsoon.net/horror/news/747804-think-children-examining-pre-code-horror-influence-cinema [Accessed 10 November 2020]
2. West.
3. Boissoneault, L. (2018). The Nazi Werewolves Who Terrorized Allied Soldiers at the End of WWII [online]. Available at: https://www.smithsonianmag.com/history/nazi-werewolves-who-terrorized-allied-soldiers-end-wwii-180970522/ [Accessed 20 July 2023]
4. Boissoneault.
5. *Segnalazioni cinematografiche* (1945), vol. 18. Rome: Centro Cattolico Cinematografico. Translated from Italian by the author.
6. Guarneri, M. (2017). *The Gothic bet: Riccardo Freda's I vampiri (1957) and the birth of Italian horror cinema from an industrial perspective*. London: Palgrave Communications, 29. https://doi.org/10.1057/s41599-017-0030-3
7. Guarneri.
8. Abbott, S. (2002). "The vampire transformed: Riccardo Freda and Mario Bava's *I Vampiri* (1956)." *Kinoeye New Perspectives on European film* 2 (18) [online]. Available at: http://www.kinoeye.org/02/18/abbott18.php [Accessed 11 November 2020]
9. *Segnalazioni cinematografiche* (1957), vol. 41. Rome: Centro Cattolico Cinematografico, 182. Translated from Italian by the author.
10. *Segnalazioni cinematografiche*, vol. 41, 182.
11. *Segnalazioni cinematografiche* (1959), vol. 45. Rome: Centro Cattolico Cinematografico, 103 Translated from Italian by the author.
12. *Segnalazioni cinematografiche*, vol. 45, 103.
13. *Segnalazioni cinematografiche* (1960), vol. 48. Rome: Centro Cattolico Cinematografico, 199. Translated from Italian by the author.
14. *Segnalazioni cinematografiche* (1959), vol. 46. Rome: Centro Cattolico Cinematografico, 106. Translated from Italian by the author.
15. *Segnalazioni cinematografiche*, vol. 46, 106.
16. Curti, R. (2017). *Riccardo Freda: The Life and Works of a Born Filmmaker*. Jefferson, NC: McFarland, 147.
17. *Segnalazioni cinematografiche*, vol. 46, 214.
18. *Segnalazioni cinematografiche*, vol. 46, 214.
19. Paul, L. (2005). *Italian Horror Film Directors*. Jefferson, NC: McFarland, 304.

20. Curti, R. (2015). *Italian Gothic Horror Films 1957-1969*, 61.
21. *Segnalazioni cinematografiche*, vol. 48, 32.
22. *Segnalazioni cinematografiche*, vol. 48, 32.
23. *Segnalazioni cinematografiche*, vol. 46, 104.
24. *Segnalazioni cinematografiche*, vol. 48, 120.
25. Wagstaff, C. (2007). *Italian Neorealist Cinema: An Aesthetic Approach*. Toronto: University of Toronto Press, 361.
26. *Segnalazioni cinematografiche*, vol. 48, 214.
27. *Segnalazioni cinematografiche*, vol. 48, 214.
28. *Segnalazioni cinematografiche*, vol. 48, 214.
29. *Segnalazioni cinematografiche* (1961), vol. 49. Rome: Centro Cattolico Cinematografico, 138. Translated from Italian by the author.
30. Conterio, M. (2015). *Black Sunday*. Leighton Buzzard: Auteur.
31. Conterio, M. (2016). Why your favourite directors love Mario Bava [online]. Available at: https://lwlies.com/articles/why-your-favourite-directors-love-mario-bava/ [Accessed 8 September 2018]
32. Tobias, S. (2012). *Black Sunday* [online]. Available at: https://film.avclub.com/black-sunday-1798174302 [Accessed 8 September 2018]

Chapter 2

1. Conterio, M. (2016). Where to begin with Mario Bava [online]. Available at: https://www.bfi.org.uk/features/where-begin-mario-bava [Accessed 13 July 2023]
2. Conterio.
3. *Segnalazioni cinematografiche* (1961), vol. 49. Rome: Centro Cattolico Cinematografico, 192. Translated from Italian by the author.
4. *Segnalazioni cinematografiche*, vol. 49, 192.
5. *Segnalazioni cinematografiche*, vol. 48, 54.
6. *Segnalazioni cinematografiche*, vol. 48, 54.
7. *Segnalazioni cinematografiche*, vol. 48, 54.
8. Hoberman, J. (2003). Mad Scientist Seeks Flesh for Fantasy in French Scare Classic [online]. Available at: https://www.villagevoice.com/2003/10/28/mad-scientist-seeks-flesh-for-fantasy-in-french-scare-classic/ [Accessed 13 July 2023]
9. Lane, J. F. (2006) Obituary: Alida Valli [online]. Available at: https://www.theguardian.com/news/2006/apr/24/guardianobituaries.film [Accessed 13 July 2023]
10. *Segnalazioni cinematografiche* (1960), vol. 47. Rome: Centro Cattolico Cinematografico, 230. Translated from Italian by the author.
11. *Segnalazioni cinematografiche* (1963), vol. 53. Rome: Centro Cattolico Cinematografico, 161. Translated from Italian by the author.
12. Totaro, D. (2011). A Genealogy of Italian Popular Cinema: The Filone [online]. Available at: https://offscreen.com/view/genealogy_filone [Accessed 3 November 2018]
13. Koven, M. (2006). *La Dolce Morte: Vernacular Cinema and the Italian Giallo Film*. Lanham, MD: Scarecrow Press, 5.
14. Koven, 16.
15. Burfield, H. (2022). Le donne silenziate: the foundations of the Italian patriarchy [online]. Available at: https://www.thecambridgelanguagecollective.com/europe/dkmpmpfowvfek8bweriudeekjmpt1t [Accessed 22 July 2023]
16. Burfield.
17. Ellinger, K., and Deighan, S. (2016). Daughters of Darkness Episode 14: Footprints in Delirium: Exploring the Art Giallo, Part 3 [podcast], October 30. Available at: https://diaboliquemagazine.com/episode-16-footprints-delirium-exploring-art-giallo-part-3/ [Accessed 19 April 2020]
18. Janisse, Kier-La (2012). *House of Psychotic Women*. Godalming: FAB Press, 57.
19. Janisse, 16.
20. *Segnalazioni cinematografiche* (1974), vol. 76. Rome: Centro Cattolico Cinematografico, 187. Translated from Italian by the author.
21. Bonilla, T., and Hyungjung Mo, C. (2019). The evolution of human trafficking messaging in the United States and its effect on public opinion. *Journal of Public Policy* 39 (2): 201–234.

22. Bishopaccountability.org (2019). What percentage of priests were accused? [online]. Available at: http://www.bishop-accountability.org/AtAGlance/data_priests.htm [Accessed 17 May 2020]
23. Cinematografo.it (2016). Chi l'ha vista morire? [online]. Available at: https://www.cinematografo.it/film/chi-lha-vista-morire-d7bk8sql [Accessed 17 May 2020]. Translated from Italian by the author.
24. Cinematografo.it Chi l'ha vista morire?
25. Cinematografo.it (2016). Non Si Sevizia un Paperino [online]. Available at: https://www.cinematografo.it/cinedatabase/film/non-si-sevizia-un-paperino/19811/ [Accessed 13 November 2018]
26. *Segnalazioni cinematografiche* (1974), vol. 77. Rome: Cattolico Centro di Cinematografico, 201. Translated from Italian by the author.
27. *Segnalazioni cinematografiche*, vol. 77, 201.
28. Akor, L. (2011). Trafficking of Women in Nigeria: Causes, Consequences and the Way Forward. *Corvinus Journal of Sociology and Social Policy* 2:89–110.
29. *Segnalazioni cinematografiche* (1975), vol. 79. Rome: Centro Cattolico Cinematografico, 170. Translated from Italian by the author.
30. Ferre, L. (2022). P2 (Propaganda Due) [online]. Available at: https://occult-world.com/p2-propaganda-due/ [Accessed 22 July 2023]
31. Ferre.
32. BBC (1981). On This Day 26 May 1981: Italy in crisis as cabinet resigns [online]. Available at: http://news.bbc.co.uk/onthisday/hi/dates/stories/may/26/newsid_4396000/4396893.stm [Accessed 22 July 2023]
33. Thrower, S., et al. (2012). Zombie Flesh Eaters (Media notes). Arrow Films, 97.
34. Rafferty, T. (2008). Beauty, Brutality and Three Tough Mothers [online]. Available at: https://www.nytimes.com/2008/06/01/movies/01raff.html [Accessed 17 November 2020]
35. *Segnalazioni cinematografiche* (1972), vol. 72. Rome: Centro Cattolico Cinematografico, 125. Translated from Italian by the author.

Chapter 3

1. Hunter, R. (2016). "*Preferisco l'inferno*: early Italian horror cinema." In Baschiera, S., and Hunter, R. (eds)., *Italian Horror Cinema*. Edinburgh: Edinburgh University Press, 16.
2. Brueggemann, T. (2020). "Psycho" Turns 60 This Week: How the 1960 Release Created an Iconic Film [online]. Available at: https://www.indiewire.com/2020/06/psycho-turns-60-this-week-1960-release-1202237395/ [Accessed 16 June 2020]
3. Rothman, L. (2015). Read What TIME's Original Review of Psycho Got Wrong [online]. Available at: https://time.com/3907090/original-review-1960-psycho/ [Accessed 16 June 2020]
4. LeJeune, C.A. (1960). *Psycho*: Archive Review [online]. Available at: https://www.theguardian.com/film/2010/oct/22/psycho-hitchcock-archive-review-horror [Accessed 16 June 2020]
5. LeJeune.
6. LeJeune.
7. LeJeune.
8. *Segnalazioni cinematografiche*, vol. 49, 54.
9. *Segnalazioni cinematografiche*, vol. 49, 54.
10. Ebiri, B. (2018). What If Francis Ford Coppola Remade "Psycho"? [online]. Available at: https://www.villagevoice.com/2018/06/04/dementia-13-what-if-francis-ford-coppola-remade-psycho/ [Accessed 17 June 2020]
11. Ebiri.
12. *Segnalazioni cinematografiche* (1964), vol. 55. Rome: Centro Cattolico Cinematografico, 69. Translated from Italian by the author.
13. *Segnalazioni cinematografiche*, vol. 55, 69.
14. *Segnalazioni cinematografiche*, vol. 55, 69.
15. *Segnalazioni cinematografiche* (1971), vol. 70. Rome: Centro Cattolico Cinematografico, 96. Translated from Italian by the author.
16. Lowenstein, A. (2016). The *Giallo* Slasher Landscape: *Ecologia Del Delitto*, *Friday the 13th* and subtractive spectatorship. In Baschiera, S., and Hunter, R., (eds.), *Italian Horror Cinema*. 1st ed. Edinburgh: Edinburgh University Press, 130.

17. Nastasi, A. (2015). The Beyond: Mario Bava's *A Bay of Blood* [online]. Available at: http://www.shocktillyoudrop.com/news/374057-beyond-mario-bavas-bay-blood/ [Accessed 24 July 2023]
18. Lowenstein, 137.
19. Nastasi, A. (2015). The Beyond: Sergio Martino's *Torso* [online]. Available at: http://www.comingsoon.net/horror/news/745661-beyond-sergio-martinos-torso [Accessed 20 November 2020]
20. cinematografo.it (no date). I corpi presentano trace di violenza carnale [online]. Available at: https://www.cinematografo.it/cinedatabase/film/i-corpi-presentano-tracce-di-violenza-carnale/21955/ [Accessed 20 November 2020]. Translated from Italian by the author.
21. cinematografo.it *I corpi presentano trace di violenza carnale*.
22. *Segnalazioni cinematografiche* (1975), vol. 78. Rome: Centro Cattolico Cinematografico, 455. Translated from Italian by the author.
23. *Segnalazioni cinematografiche*, vol. 78, 455.
24. *Segnalazioni cinematografiche*, vol. 78, 455.
25. *Segnalazioni cinematografiche*, vol. 78, 455.
26. Weiler, A. H. (1975). "Black Christmas" (1974). Review [online]. Available at: https://www.nytimes.com/2018/12/11/movies/black-christmas-review.html [Accessed 18 June 2020]
27. *Variety* (1973). *Black Christmas* [online]. Available at: https://web.archive.org/web/20131231231035/https://variety.com/1973/film/reviews/black-christmas-1200423278/ [Accessed 18 June 2020]
28. *Segnalazioni cinematografiche* (1976), vol. 81. Rome: Centro Cattolico Cinematografico, 145. Translated from Italian by the author.
29. *Segnalazioni cinematografiche*, vol. 81, 145.
30. Ebert, R. (1979). *Halloween* [online]. Available at: https://www.rogerebert.com/reviews/halloween-1979 [Accessed 18 June 2020]
31. Arnold, G. (1978). "Halloween": A Trickle of Treats [online]. Available at: https://www.washingtonpost.com/archive/lifestyle/1978/11/24/halloween-a-trickle-of-treats/2e2bd834-3a45-4780-93a1-96cfefeb56a9/ [Accessed 18 June 2020]
32. cinematografo.it (no date). Halloween: La Notte Delle Streghe [online]. Available at: https://www.cinematografo.it/cinedatabase/film/halloween---la-notte-delle-streghe/15948/ [Accessed 18 June 2020]
33. The Numbers (2020). Box Office History for Halloween Movies [online]. Available at: https://m.the-numbers.com/movies/franchise/Halloween [Accessed 17 June 2020]
34. cinematografo.it (no date). *Venerdi 13* [online]. Available at: https://www.cinematografo.it/film/venerdi-13-kipm3y1q [Accessed 11 November 2023]
35. cinematografo.it *Venerdi 13*.
36. *Segnalazioni cinematografiche* (1980), vol. 89. Rome: Centro Cattolico Cinematografico, 218. Translated from Italian by the author.
37. *Segnalazioni cinematografiche* (1981). vol. 91. Rome: Centro Cattolico Cinematografico, 248. Translated from Italian by the author.
38. *Segnalazioni cinematografiche*, vol. 91, 218.
39. *Segnalazioni cinematografiche*, vol. 91, 305.
40. *Segnalazioni cinematografiche*, vol. 91, 305.
41. *Segnalazioni cinematografiche* (1982), vol. 93. Rome: Centro Cattolico Cinematografico, 151. Translated from Italian by the author.
42. *Segnalazioni cinematografiche*, vol. 93, 151.
43. *Segnalazioni cinematografiche*, vol. 93, 151.
44. *Segnalazioni cinematografiche* (1982), vol. 93. Rome: Centro Cattolico Cinematografico, 307. Translated from Italian by the author.
45. The Numbers (2020). Box Office History for Nightmare on Elm Street Movies [online]. Available at: https://www.the-numbers.com/movies/franchise/Nightmare-on-Elm-Street#tab=summary [Accessed 19 June 2020]
46. The Numbers.
47. *Segnalazioni cinematografiche* (1986), vol. 100. Rome: Centro Cattolico Cinematografico, 79. Translated from Italian by the author.
48. *Segnalazioni cinematografiche*, vol. 100, 79.
49. *Segnalazioni cinematografiche*, vol. 100, 79.

50. *Segnalazioni cinematografiche*, vol. 100, 79.
51. *Segnalazioni cinematografiche*, vol. 100, 80.
52. *Segnalazioni cinematografiche*, vol. 100, 80.
53. *Segnalazioni cinematografiche*, vol. 100, 80.
54. *Segnalazioni cinematografiche*, vol. 100, 80.
55. The Numbers.
56. *Segnalazioni cinematografiche* (1986), vol. 101. Rome: Centro Cattolico Cinematografico, 68. Translated from Italian by the author.
57. *Segnalazioni cinematografiche*, vol. 101, 68.
58. *Segnalazioni cinematografiche*, vol. 101, 68–69.
59. *Segnalazioni cinematografiche*, vol. 101, 69.
60. *Segnalazioni cinematografiche*, vol. 101, 69.
61. *Segnalazioni cinematografiche*, vol. 101, 69.
62. *Segnalazioni cinematografiche* (1990), vol. 109. Rome: Centro Cattolico Cinematografico, 172. Translated from Italian by the author.

Chapter 4

1. Mulvey, L. (1975). Visual Pleasure and Narrative Cinema [online]. Available at: http://www.luxonline.org.uk/articles/visual_pleasure_and_narrative_cinema%28printversion%29.html [Accessed 23 November 2020]
2. Mulvey.
3. Heller-Nicholas, A. (2011). *Rape-Revenge Films—A Critical Study.*. Jefferson, NC: McFarland, 187.
4. Billson, A. (2018). How the "rape-revenge movie" became a feminist weapon for the #MeToo generation [online]. Available at: https://www.theguardian.com/film/2018/may/11/how-the-rape-revenge-movie-became-a-feminist-weapon-for-the-metoo-generation [Accessed 6 June 2020]
5. Billson.
6. McAndrews, M. B. (2019). When The Party's Over: How Women Reclaim the Rape-Revenge Story [online]. Available at: https://www.girlsontopstees.com/read-me/2019/10/25/when-the-partys-over-how-women-reclaim-the-rape-revenge-story [Accessed 6 June 2020]
7. McAndrews.
8. Canby, V. (1971). Peckinpah's "Straw Dogs" Starring Hoffman Arrives [online]. Available at: https://www.nytimes.com/1972/01/20/archives/peckinpahs-straw-dogs-starring-hoffman-arrives.html [Accessed 6 June 2020]
9. Ebert, R. (1971). *Straw Dogs* [online]. Available at: https://www.rogerebert.com/reviews/straw-dogs-1971 [Accessed 6 June 2020]
10. *Segnalazioni cinematografiche* (1973), vol. 75. Rome: Centro Cattolico Cinematografico, 180. Translated from Italian by the author.
11. *Segnalazioni cinematografiche*, vol. 75, 180.
12. *Segnalazioni cinematografiche*, vol. 75, 180.
13. *Segnalazioni cinematografiche*, vol. 75, 180.
14. *Segnalazioni cinematografiche*, vol. 75, 37.
15. *Segnalazioni cinematografiche*, vol. 75, 37–38.
16. *Segnalazioni cinematografiche*, vol. 75, 38.
17. Ebert, R. (1972). *Last House on the Left* [online]. Available at: https://www.rogerebert.com/reviews/last-house-on-the-left-1972 [Accessed 17 May 2020]
18. Winell, M. (2018). Understanding Religious Trauma Syndrome—It's Time to Recognize It [online]. Available at: https://www.babcp.com/Review/RTS-Its-Time-to-Recognize-it.aspx [Accessed 19 May 2019]
19. Zinoman, J. (2011). *Shock Value—How a few eccentric outsiders gave us nightmares, conquered Hollywood and invented modern horror*. London: Penguin Books, 70.
20. Zinoman, 82.
21. Ebert, R. (1972), *Last House on the Left*.
22. BBFC (no date). Case Studies: *Last House on the Left* [online]. Available at: https://www.bbfc.co.uk/case-studies/last-house-left [Accessed 17 May 2020]
23. *Segnalazioni cinematografiche*, vol. 79, 127.
24. *Holy Bible* (2012). *New International Version*. London: Hodder & Stoughton. Matthew 5, 38:39.

25. *Segnalazioni cinematografiche*, vol. 79, 127.
26. *Segnalazioni cinematografiche*, vol. 78, 537.
27. Withnall, A. (2014). Pope Francis: "One in 50" Catholic priests, bishops and cardinals is a paedophile [online]. Available at: https://www.independent.co.uk/news/world/europe/pope-francis-one-50-catholic-priests-bishops-and-cardinals-are-paedophiles-9602919.html [Accessed 6 June 2021]
28. Hobbs, V. (2018). "Rape culture in sermons on divorce." In Blyth, C., Colgan, E., and Edwards, K. (eds.), *Rape Culture, Gender Violence, and Religion: Interdisciplinary Perspectives*. London: Palgrave Macmillan, 87–110.
29. Hobbs, 87.
30. Saunders, Fr. W. (no date). Ethical Treatment After Rape [online]. Available at: https://www.catholiceducation.org/en/culture/catholic-contributions/ethical-treatment-after-rape.html [Accessed 6 July 2023]
31. Serpa, Fr. V. (no date). Does the Church teach that it is better to die than to be raped? [online]. Available at: https://www.catholic.com/qa/does-the-church-teach-that-it-is-better-to-die-than-to-be-raped [Accessed 6 July 2023]
32. Saunders.
33. Hobbs.
34. Serpa.
35. Saunders.
36. Hobbs.
37. *Segnalazioni cinematografiche*, vol. 75, 38.
38. *Holy Bible* (2012). *New International Version*. London: Hodder & Stoughton. Romans 12:19.
39. Saunders, Fr. W. (2003). What are Capital Sins? [online]. Available at: https://www.catholiceducation.org/en/culture/catholic-contributions/what-are-capital-sins.html [Accessed 23 June 2023]
40. *Holy Bible* (2012). *New International Version*. London: Hodder & Stoughton. Genesis 34:1–31.
41. Saunders, What are Capital Sins?
42. *Segnalazioni cinematografico*, vol. 81, 264.
43. *Segnalazioni cinematografico*, vol. 81, 264.
44. *Segnalazioni cinematografico*, vol. 81, 264.
45. *Segnalazioni cinematografico*, vol. 81, 264.
46. *Segnalazioni cinematografico*, vol. 81, 264.
47. *Segnalazioni cinematografico*, vol. 81, 264.
48. Ebert, R. (1974). *Death Wish* [online]. Available at: https://www.rogerebert.com/reviews/death-wish-1974 [Accessed 24 May 2020]
49. Slenfsrud, J. (1974). What Do They See in "Death Wish"? [online]. Available at: https://www.nytimes.com/1974/09/01/archives/what-do-theysee-in-death-wish-women-applaud-the-vigilante-actions.html [Accessed 24 May 2020]
50. Canby, V. (1974). "Death Wish" Exploits Fear Irresponsibly [online]. Available at: https://www.nytimes.com/1974/08/04/archives/death-wish-exploits-fear-irresponsibly-death-wish-exploits-our-fear.html [Accessed 6 June 2020]
51. Clarke, D. (2010). Re-release of I Spit on Your Grave banned by Film Body [online]. Available at: www.irishtimes.com/news/re-release-of-i-spit-on-your-grave-banned-by-film-body-1.653261%3Fmode=amp [Accessed 21 May 2020]
52. Ebert, R. (1972). *I Spit on Your Grave* [online]. Available at: https://www.rogerebert.com/reviews/i-spit-on-your-grave-1980 [Accessed 17 May 2020]
53. BBFC (no date). Case Studies: *I Spit on Your Grave* [online]. Available at: https://www.bbfc.co.uk/case-studies/i-spit-your-grave [Accessed 21 May 2020]
54. Heller-Nicholas, A. (2011). "The Violation of Representation: Art, Argento and the Rape-Revenge Film." *FORUM: University of Edinburgh Postgraduate Journal of Culture & The Arts*, no. 13 (December). http://www.forumjournal.org/article/view/676
55. McAndrews, M. B. (2019). [Through Her Eyes] The History of Rape-Revenge Films and the Importance of Female Directors [online]. Available at: https://bloody-disgusting.com/editorials/3586210/eyes-history-rape-revenge-films-importance-female-directors/ [Accessed 20 May 2020]
56. *Segnalazioni cinematografiche* (1984), vol. 97. Rome: Centro Cattolico di Cinematografico, 379. Translated from Italian by the author.

57. *Segnalazioni cinematografiche*, vol. 97, 379.
58. *Segnalazioni cinematografiche*, vol. 97, 379.
59. *Segnalazioni cinematografiche*, vol. 97, 379.
60. *Segnalazioni cinematografiche*, vol. 97, 379.
61. *Segnalazioni cinematografiche*, vol. 97, 379.
62. Preziosi, P. (2020). The faith-haunted, stomach-churning cinema of Abel Ferrara [online]. Available at: https://www.americamagazine.org/arts-culture/2020/03/03/faith-haunted-stomach-churning-cinema-abel-ferrara [Accessed 9 July 2023]
63. Burke, D. (2019). Amid uproar, Vatican clarifies Pope's comments on "sexual slavery" of nuns [online]. Available at: https://edition.cnn.com/2019/02/06/world/pope-nuns-slavery/index.html [Accessed 9 July 2023]
64. Saunders, Ethical Treatment After Rape.
65. Grey, C. (2014). The spiritual side of Abel Ferrara [online]. Available at: https://www.dazeddigital.com/artsandculture/article/22491/1/the-spiritual-side-of-abel-ferrara [Accessed 8 July 2023]
66. Preziosi.
67. Preziosi.
68. Preziosi.
69. Preziosi.
70. Grey.
71. Grey.
72. Time Out (1981). *Ms. 45* [online]. Available from: https://www.timeout.com/london/film/ms-45 [Accessed 26 May 2020]
73. Time Out, *Ms. 45*.
74. The Editors, RogerEbert.com (2013). On "Ms. 45" and Revenge Movie Feminism [online]. Available at: https://www.rogerebert.com/features/on-ms-45-and-revenge-movie-feminism [Accessed 26 May 2020]
75. The Editors, RogerEbert.com (2013). On "Ms. 45" and Revenge Movie Feminism [online] Available at: https://www.rogerebert.com/features/on-ms-45-and-revenge-movie-feminism [Accessed 26 May 2020]
76. The Editors, RogerEbert.com (2013) On "Ms. 45" and Revenge Movie Feminism [online] Available at: https://www.rogerebert.com/features/on-ms-45-and-revenge-movie-feminism [Accessed 26 May 2020]
77. *Segnalazioni cinematografiche* (1982), vol. 92. Rome: Centro Cattolico di Cinematografico, 91. Translated from Italian by the author.
78. *Segnalazioni cinematografiche*, vol. 92, 91.
79. *Segnalazioni cinematografiche*, vol. 92, 91.
80. *Segnalazioni cinematografiche*, vol. 92, 91.
81. *Segnalazioni cinematografiche*, vol. 92, 91.
82. *Segnalazioni cinematografiche*, vol. 92, 91.
83. *Segnalazioni cinematografiche*, vol. 92, 91.
84. Segnalazioni cinematografiche, vol. 92, 91.

Chapter 5

1. *Holy Bible* (2012). *New International Version*. London: Hodder & Stoughton. Luke 22:19.
2. Morgan, J. (2021). Why Were the Early Christians Accused of Cannibalism? [online]. Available at: https://clarifyingcatholicism.org/articles/why-were-the-early-christians-accused-of-cannibalism/ [Accessed 19 June 2023]
3. Morgan.
4. Silver, S. K. (2000). "'And the Word Became Flesh . . .': Cannibalism and Religious Polemic in the Poetry of Desportes and d'Aubigné." *Renaissance and Reformation / Renaissance et Réforme* 24 (1): 45–56.
5. Catt, C. (2022). 13 + Mondo Films & Shockumentaries: Twisted Portrayals of Life and Death [online]. Available at: https://creepycatalog.com/mondo-films-shockumentaries/ [Accessed 18 June 2023]
6. Goodall, M. (2019). Critics hated the forgotten "mondo" genre, but their influence can be seen in Oscar-winning films today [online]. Available at: https://theconversation.com/critics-hated-the-forgotten-mondo-genre-but-their-influence-can-be-seen-in-oscar-winning-films-today-923310 [Accessed 18 June 2023]

7. *Segnalazioni cinematografiche* (1962), vol. 52. Rome: Cattolico Centro di Cinematografico, 12. Translated from Italian by the author.
8. *Segnalazioni cinematografiche*, vol. 52, 12.
9. Thomson, Ian (2013). Pier Paolo Pasolini: No Saint [online]. Available at: https://www.theguardian.com/film/2013/feb/22/pier-paolo-pasolini [Accessed 19 June 2023]
10. Thomson.
11. *Segnalazioni cinematografiche* (1969), vol. 67. Rome: Cattolico Centro di Cinematografico, 190. Translated from Italian by the author.
12. *Segnalazioni cinematografiche*, vol. 67, 190.
13. *Segnalazioni cinematografiche*, vol. 67, 190.
14. *Segnalazioni cinematografiche*, vol. 52, 12.
15. *Segnalazioni cinematografiche*, vol. 79, 163.
16. *Segnalazioni cinematografiche*, vol. 79, 163.
17. *Segnalazioni cinematografiche*, vol. 79, 163.
18. *Segnalazioni cinematografiche*, vol. 79, 163.
19. Doubt, M. (2018). Monsters of the Wild Frontier—1970s Horror [online]. Available at: https://www.longlivethevoid.com/news/monstersofwildfrontmark [Accessed 9 December 2023]
20. *Segnalazioni cinematografiche*, vol. 79, 21.
21. *Segnalazioni cinematografiche*, vol. 79, 21.
22. Doubt, Monsters of the Wild Frontier—1970s Horror.
23. Zinoman, 71.
24. Davis, C. (2015). 6 times Wes Craven reinvented horror [online]. Available at: https://archive.kitsapsun.com/news/6-times-wes-craven-reinvented-horror-ep-1253001544-354509251.html/?page=1 [Accessed 9 December 2023]
25. *Segnalazioni cinematografiche* (1978), vol. 85. Rome: Cattolico Centro di Cinematografico, 80. Translated from Italian by the author.
26. *Segnalazioni cinematografiche*, vol. 85, 80.
27. *Segnalazioni cinematografiche*, vol. 85, 80.
28. *Segnalazioni cinematografiche*, vol. 85, 80.
29. *Segnalazioni cinematografiche*, vol. 85, 80.
30. Peeke, D. (2020). Cannibal Holocaust was banned in the UK until 2001—but why was the horror movie so shocking? [online]. Available at: https://www.gamesradar.com/cannibal-holocaust-anniversary-shocking-movies/ [Accessed 18 June 2023]
31. Sohrabi-Shiraz, A. (2020). Banned horror film was so realistic the director was charged with murder [online]. Available at: https://www.dailystar.co.uk/showbiz/banned-horror-film-realistic-director-2211131148 [Accessed 18 June 2023]
32. Sohrabi-Shiraz.
33. McCreesh, L (2022). Director of graphic horror film so disturbing it was banned for 21 years dies [online]. Available at: https://www.dailystar.co.uk/showbiz/director-graphic-horror-film-disturbing-2101035813 [Accessed 18 June 2023]
34. *Segnalazioni cinematografiche* (1985), vol. 99. Rome: Centro Cattolico Cinematografico, 223. Translated from Italian by the author.
35. *Segnalazioni cinematografiche*, vol. 99, 223.
36. *Segnalazioni cinematografiche*, vol. 99, 223.
37. Bitel, A. (2018). Discover the grainy depravity of this notorious cannibal horror [online]. Available at: https://lwlies.com/articles/cannibal-ferox-review/ [Accessed 20 June 2023]
38. *Cannibal Ferox* (1981) [film]. Umberto Lenzi. dir. Italy: Dania Film.
39. *Segnalazioni cinematografiche*, vol. 100, 183.
40. *Segnalazioni cinematografiche*, vol. 100, 183.
41. *Segnalazioni cinematografiche*, vol. 100, 183.
42. Southall, R. (no date). Amazonia: The Catherine Miles Story (aka Cannibal Holocaust II). (1985). [online]. Available at: https://www.starburstmagazine.com/reviews/amazonia-catherine-miles-story/ [Accessed 9 December 2023]
43. *Segnalazioni cinematografiche*, vol. 100, 95.
44. Goodwin, D. (no date). *Green Inferno* (1988) [online]. Available at: https://www.

starburstmagazine.com/reviews/green-inferno-1988/ [Accessed 10 December 2023]

45. Woods, P. (2019). *The Green Inferno*—Antonio Climati (88 Films) [online]. Available at: https://avenoctum.com/2019/03/07/the-green-inferno-antonio-climati-88-films/ [Accessed 10 December 2023]

46. *Segnalazioni cinematografiche* (1989), vol. 107. Rome: Cattolico Centro di Cinematografico, 68. Translated from Italian by the author.

47. *Segnalazioni cinematografiche*, vol. 107, 68.

48. *Segnalazioni cinematografiche*, vol. 107, 68.

49. *Segnalazioni cinematografiche*, vol. 107, 68.

50. *Segnalazioni cinematografiche*, vol. 107, 68.

Chapter 6

1. The History of the Zombie in Popular Culture (2006) [online]. Available at: https://u.osu.edu/abel118eng4563/the-history-of-the-zombie-in-popular-culture/ [Accessed 25 June 2023]

2. Sage, V. (2009). "The Gothic, The Body, and the Failed Homeopathy Argument." In Baxter, J. (ed.,) *J. G. Ballard: Contemporary Critical Perspectives*. 1st ed. London: Bloomsbury Publishing, 37

3. Thrower et al., 23.

4. Thrower et al., 23.

5. *Dawn of the Dead* (1978) [film]. George A. Romero, dir. USA: Laurel Group Inc.

6. DeCou, J. (2012). "The Living Christ and the Walking Dead: Karl Barth and the Theological Zombie." In Paffenroth, K., and Morehead, J. W. (eds.), *The Undead and Theology*. Eugene, OR: Pickwick Publications, 79–100.

7. LaMothe, K. L. (2004). *Between Dancing and Writing: The Practice of Religious Studies*. New York: Fordham University Press, 230

8. LaMothe, 230.

9. Variety Staff (1968). Film Review: *Night of the Living Dead* [online]. Available at: https://variety.com/1967/film/reviews/night-of-the-living-dead-1200421603/ [Accessed 25 June 2020]

10. Variety Staff.

11. Variety Staff.

12. The Numbers (2023). *Night of the Living Dead (1968)*. [online]. Available at: https://www.the-numbers.com/movie/Night-of-the-Living-Dead-(1968)#tab=-summary [Accessed 25 June 2023]

13. *Segnalazioni cinematografiche*, vol. 70, 189.

14. *Segnalazioni cinematografiche*, vol. 70, 189.

15. *Segnalazioni cinematografiche*, vol. 70, 189.

16. Russell, J. (2005). *Book of the Dead: The Complete History of Zombie Cinema*. Godalming: FAB Press.

17. *Segnalazioni cinematografiche* (1976), vol. 80. Rome: Centro Cattolico Cinematografico, 87. Translated from Italian by the author.

18. *Segnalazioni cinematografiche*, vol. 80, 87.

19. *Segnalazioni cinematografiche*, vol. 80, 87.

20. *Segnalazioni cinematografiche*, vol. 80, 75.

21. *Segnalazioni cinematografiche*, vol. 80, 75.

22. *Segnalazioni cinematografiche*, vol. 80, 75.

23. Navarro, M. (2019). "The Living Dead at Manchester Morgue" Remains One of the Best Zombie Films [online]. Available at: https://bloody-disgusting.com/editorials/3595447/living-dead-manchester-morgue-remains-one-best-zombie-films/ [Accessed 26 June 2020]

24. *Segnalazioni cinematografiche*, vol. 78, 100.

25. Russell, 131.

26. Hochgesang, J., Lawyer, T., and Stevenson, T. (no date). The Psychological Effects of The Vietnam War [online]. Available at: https://web.stanford.edu/class/e297c/war_peace/media/hpsych.html [Accessed 26 June 2020]

27. Hochgesang et al.

28. American Film Institute (no date). *Dead of Night* (1974). [online]. Available at: [Accessed 26 June 2020]

29. *Segnalazioni cinematografiche* (1978), vol. 84. Rome: Centro Cattolico Cinematografico, 55 Translated from Italian by the author.

30. *Segnalazioni cinematografiche*, vol. 84, 55.

31. *Segnalazioni cinematografiche*, vol. 84, 55.
32. *Segnalazioni cinematografiche*, vol. 84, 55.
33. Mulligan, R. (no date). Legacy of the Dead: The Revolution Will be Militarized—Part 1 [online]. Available at: https://www.library.cmu.edu/about/news/2017-10/legacy-dead-revolution-will-be-militarized-part-1 [Accessed 17 September 2023]
34. *Lucio Fulci—Genre Terrorist* (2007). Video Recording, Box Office Spectaculars, Inc., Italy.
35. Larkin, B. (2019). Christianity Converted. *Christian History Magazine* [online], vol. 130. Available from: https://christianhistoryinstitute.org/magazine/article/christianity-converted [Accessed 1 July 2023]
36. Weidenkopf, S. (2023). The Real Story of the Conquistadors [online]. Available at: https://www.catholic.com/magazine/online-edition/the-real-story-of-the-conquistadors [Accessed 11 December 2023]
37. Weidenkopf.
38. Weidenkopf.
39. Russell, 130.
40. Thrower et al., 23.
41. Thrower et al.
42. *Segnalazioni cinematografiche* (1980), vol. 88. Rome: Centro Cattolico Cinematografico, 123–124. Translated from Italian by the author.
43. *Segnalazioni cinematografiche*, vol. 91, 262.
44. *Segnalazioni cinematografiche*, vol. 91, 262.
45. *Segnalazioni cinematografiche*, vol. 91, 262.
46. *Segnalazioni cinematografiche*, vol. 91, 262.
47. *Segnalazioni cinematografiche*, vol. 91, 262.
48. Kay, Glenn (2008). *Zombie Movies: The Ultimate Guide*. Chicago: Chicago Review Press, 111.
49. *Segnalazioni cinematografiche*, vol. 92, 98.
50. *Segnalazioni cinematografiche*, vol. 92, 98.
51. *Segnalazioni cinematografiche* (1981), vol. 90. Rome: Centro Cattolico Cinematografico, 31
52. *Segnalazioni cinematografiche*, vol. 90, 31.
53. *Segnalazioni cinematografiche*, vol. 91, 262.
54. *Segnalazioni cinematografiche*, vol. 91, 262.
55. *Segnalazioni cinematografiche*, vol. 91, 262.
56. Rawat, K. (2022). How George A. Romero became the father of the zombie with *Night of the Living Dead* [online]. Available at: https://indianexpress.com/article/entertainment/hollywood/how-george-a-romero-became-the-father-of-the-zombie-movie-with-night-of-the-living-dead-7755165/ [Accessed 16 September 2023]
57. Ebert, R. (1985). *Return of the Living Dead* [online]. Available at: https://www.rogerebert.com/reviews/return-of-the-living-dead-1985 [Accessed 28 June 2020]
58. Nichrelay, A. (2019). RIP: "Day of the Dead" Icon Joseph Pilato Has Passed Away [online]. Available at: https://apsari.com/joseph-pilato-day-of-the-dead-george-romero-actor-passed-away-dead-70-in-his-sleep-zombie [Accessed 28 June 2020]
59. Maslin, J (1985). *Day of the Dead* [online]. Available at: https://www.nytimes.com/1985/07/03/movies/film-day-of-the-dead.html [Accessed 28 June 2020]
60. Ebert, R. (1985). *Day of the Dead* [online]. Available at: https://www.rogerebert.com/reviews/day-of-the-dead-1985 [Accessed 28 June 2020]
61. *Segnalazioni cinematografiche*, vol. 100, 285.
62. *Segnalazioni cinematografiche*, vol. 100, 285–286.
63. *Segnalazioni cinematografiche*, vol. 100, 286.
64. *Segnalazioni cinematografiche*, vol. 100, 286.
65. Scott, Emmet (2016). The Decline and Fall of the Roman Catholic West [online]. Available at: https://www.newenglishreview.org/Emmet_Scott/The_Decline_and_Fall_of_the_Roman_Catholic_West/ [Accessed 7 September 2018]
66. White, H. (2010). Italy's Last Catholic Generation? Mass Attendance in "Collapse" among Under 30s [online]. Available at: https://www.lifesitenews.com/news/italys-last-catholic-generation-

mass-attendance-in-collapse-among-under-30s [Accessed 13 September 2018]

67. Kamm, H. (1984). Italy Abolishes State Religion in Vatican Pact [online]. *New York Times*, 19 February. Available at: https://www.nytimes.com/1984/02/19/world/italy-abolishes-state-religion-in-vatican-pact.html [Accessed 1 July 2023]

68. Kamm.

69. *Return of the Living Dead* (1985) [film]. Dan O'Bannon, dir. USA: Orion Pictures.

70. Sellars, C., and Smart, G. (2016). *245 Trioxin: The Story of* The Return of the Living Dead. Burntwood: Cult Screenings UK Ltd., 165.

71. Sellars and Smart, 165.

72. Ebert, R. (1985). *Return of the Living Dead* [online]. Available at: https://www.rogerebert.com/reviews/return-of-the-living-dead-1985 [Accessed 28 June 2020]

73. *Segnalazioni cinematografiche*, vol. 99, 128.

74. *Segnalazioni cinematografiche*, vol. 99, 128.

75. *Segnalazioni cinematografiche*, vol. 99, 128.

76. *Segnalazioni cinematografiche*, vol. 99, 128.

77. Angeli, 1.

Chapter 7

1. British Library (no date). First use of the word "nunnery" to mean "brothel," 1593 [online]. Available at: https://www.bl.uk/collection-items/first-use-of-the-word-nunnery-to-mean-brothel-1593?mobile=off [Accessed 10 June 2020]

2. Nashe, Tho. (1593). Christ's Teares Over Jerusalem. [online]. Available at: http://www.oxford-shakespeare.com/Nashe/Christs_Tears_1.pdf [Accessed 5 July 2023]

3. Nashe.

4. Thompson, R. (2018). Sisters of Perpetual Aberration: A Nunsploitation Watchlist [online]. Available at: https://www.rue-morgue.com/sisters-of-perpetual-aberration-a-nunsploitation-watchlist/ Accessed 10 June 2020]

5. Goldenberg, L. R. (2019). #NunsToo: How the Catholic Church has worked to silence women challenging abuse [online]. Available at: https://www.washingtonpost.com/outlook/2019/04/17/nunstoo-how-catholic-church-has-worked-silence-women-challenging-abuse/ [Accessed 10 July 2023]

6. Goldenberg.

7. Goldenberg.

8. BBC News (2019). Pope admits clerical abuse of nuns including sexual slavery [online]. Available at: https://www.bbc.co.uk/news/world-europe-47134033 [Accessed 6 June 2021]

9. BBC News.

10. Giuffrida, A. (2019). The Vatican editor who exposed the sexual abuse of nuns—and took on the Pope [online]. Available at: https://www.theguardian.com/lifeandstyle/2019/may/08/vatican-editor-sexual-abuse-lucetta-scaraffia-nuns-misogyny [Accessed 23 June 2023]

11. BBC News.

12. BBC News.

13. McGarry, P. (2019). The Irish woman who exposed abuse of nuns by priests 25 years ago [online]. Available at: https://www.irishtimes.com/news/social-affairs/religion-and-beliefs/the-irish-woman-who-exposed-abuse-of-nuns-by-priests-25-years-ago-1.3788555 [Accessed 2 July 2023]

14. McGarry.

15. McGarry.

16. *Segnalazioni cinematografiche* (1969), vol. 66. Rome: Centro Cattolico Cinematografico, 154. Translated from Italian by the author.

17. *Segnalazioni cinematografiche*, vol. 66, 154.

18. *Segnalazioni cinematografiche*, vol. 66, 154.

19. *Segnalazioni cinematografiche*, vol. 66, 154.

20. Allyn, R., and Gorgone, R. (2018). Beatrice Cenci, Victim, Murderer and Proto-Feminist Icon in 1599 in Rome [online]. Available at: https://www.througheternity.com/en/blog/history/beatrice-cenci-life-death-rome.html [Accessed 9 July 2023]

21. Harper, E. (2014). The Femme Fatale Whose Tragic End Festers in the History of Rome [online]. Available at: https://www.atlasobscura.com/articles/beatrice-cenci-haunts-rome [Accessed 23 September 2018]

22. Allyn and Gorgone.

23. Harper.
24. Craner, O. (2011). *Beatrice Cenci* (Lucio Fulci, 1969) [online]. Available at: https://kirkpatrickmission.wordpress.com/2011/12/01/beatrice-cenci-lucio-fulci1969/ [Accessed 23 September 2018]
25. *Lucio Fulci—Genre Terrorist* (2007). Video Recording, Box Office Spectaculars, Inc., Italy.
26. *Segnalazioni cinematografiche* (1970), vol. 68. Rome: Centro Cattolico Cinematografico, 71. Translated from Italian by the author.
27. *Segnalazioni cinematografiche*, vol. 68, 71.
28. *Segnalazioni cinematografiche*, vol. 68, 71.
29. Righetti, J. (2016). *The Devils*: Sex, Hysteria and Censorship [online]. Available at: https://filmschoolrejects.com/the-devils-sex-hysteria-and-censorship-75711ba3e015/ [Accessed 12 June 2020]
30. BBFC (no date). *Case Studies: The Devils* [online]. Available at: https://www.bbfc.co.uk/case-studies/devils [Accessed 12 June 2020]
31. BBFC.
32. Ebert, R. (1971). The Devils [online]. Available at: https://www.rogerebert.com/reviews/the-devils [Accessed 12 June 2020]
33. *Segnalazioni cinematografiche* (1971), vol. 71. Rome: Centro Cattolico Cinematografico, 105. Translated from Italian by the author.
34. *Segnalazioni cinematografiche*, vol. 71, 105.
35. Rife, K (2016). In this banned masterpiece, the evil is real but the witches are not [online]. Available at: https://film.avclub.com/in-this-banned-masterpiece-the-evil-is-real-but-the-wi-1798244378 [Accessed 12 June 2020]
36. Rife.
37. Schroeder, S. (2015). Faith or Fear? [online]. Available at: https://www.psychologicalscience.org/observer/faith-or-fear [Accessed 13 June 2020]
38. Parsons, S. (2015). Fear and control in church-understanding Spiritual Abuse [online]. Available at: http://survivingchurch.org/2018/02/22/fear-and-control-in-church-understanding-spiritual-abuse/ [Accessed 13 June 2020]
39. Merritt, C. H. (2014). Fear, anxiety, and Christian community [online]. Available at: https://www.christiancentury.org/blogs/archive/2014-06/fear-anxiety-and-christian-community [Accessed 13 June 2020]
40. Merritt.
41. Merritt.
42. *Segnalazioni cinematografiche*, vol. 75, 138.
43. *Segnalazioni cinematografiche*, vol. 75, 138.
44. *Segnalazioni cinematografiche*, vol. 75, 138.
45. *Segnalazioni cinematografiche*, vol. 77, 231.
46. *Segnalazioni cinematografiche*, vol. 77, 231.
47. *Segnalazioni cinematografiche*, vol. 77, 231.
48. *Segnalazioni cinematografiche*, vol. 77, 231.
49. *Segnalazioni cinematografiche*, vol. 77, 163.
50. *Segnalazioni cinematografiche*, vol. 77, 231.
51. Deighan, S. (2014). *Les démons* aka *The Demons* (U.S. Blu-ray Review) [online]. Available at: https://diaboliquemagazine.com/les-demons-aka-demons-us-blu-ray-review/ [Accessed 14 June 2020]
52. Deighan.
53. *Segnalazioni cinematografiche*, vol. 76, 136.
54. *Segnalazioni cinematografiche*, vol. 81, 202.
55. *Segnalazioni cinematografiche*, vol. 81, 202.
56. *Segnalazioni cinematografiche*, vol. 81, 202.
57. *Segnalazioni cinematografiche* (1980), vol. 86. Rome: Centro Cattolico Cinematografico, 268 .Translated from Italian by the author.
58. *Segnalazioni cinematografiche*, vol. 86, 268.
59. *Segnalazioni cinematografiche*, vol. 84, 332.
60. *Segnalazioni cinematografiche*, vol. 84, 332.
61. *Segnalazioni cinematografiche*, vol. 84, 332.
62. *Segnalazioni cinematografiche*, vol. 84, 333.
63. *Segnalazioni cinematografiche*, vol. 84, 333.

64. *Segnalazioni cinematografiche*, vol. 84, 333.
65. *Segnalazioni cinematografiche*, vol. 84, 333.
66. *Segnalazioni cinematografiche*, vol. 84, 333.
67. *Segnalazioni cinematografiche*, vol. 84, 334.
68. *Segnalazioni cinematografiche*, vol. 84, 334.

Chapter 8

1. Lichtner, G. (2015). Italian Cinema and the Fascist Past: Tracing Memory Amnesia [online]. Available at: https://brill.com/view/journals/fasc/4/1/article-p25_2.xml?language=en [Accessed 13 December 2020]
2. Tietzel, N. (2005). Germany and Post-War Trauma [online]. Available at: https://dartcenter.org/content/germany-and-post-war-trauma [Accessed 13 December 2020]
3. Tietzel.
4. Gennari, D. T., and Vanelli, M. (2010). "Did Neorealism start in church? Catholicism, cinema and the case of Mario Soldati's *Chi è Dio?*" *New Review of Film and Television Studies* 8 (2): 198–217.
5. Gennari and Vanelli.
6. Gennari and Vanelli.
7. Gennari and Vanelli.
8. Vanelli, M. (2017). Italian Cinema and Catholicism: From Vigilanti cura to Vatican II and Beyond. In *Companion to Italian Cinema*, ed. F. Burke. Oxford: Wiley.
9. *Segnalazioni cinematografiche*, vol. 68, 97.
10. *Segnalazioni cinematografiche*, vol. 68, 97.
11. Cline, S. (2014). Women at Work: SS Aufseherinnen and the Gendered Perpetration of the Holocaust. Ph.D. thesis, University of Kansas, iii.
12. Fiddler, M., and Banwell, S. (2019). "Forget about all your taboos: transgressive memory and Nazisploitation." *Studies in European Cinema* 16 (2): 141.
13. *Segnalazioni cinematografiche*, vol. 81, 7.
14. *Segnalazioni cinematografiche*, vol. 70, 112.
15. *Segnalazioni cinematografiche*, vol. 81, 172.
16. *Segnalazioni cinematografiche*, vol. 81, 236.
17. *Ilsa: She-Wolf of the SS* (1975) [online]. Don Edmonds. Canada: Aeteas Filmproduktions / Cinépix Film Properties. [Accessed 14 December 2020]. Vimeo.
18. Lichtner.
19. Lichtner.
20. *Segnalazioni cinematografiche* (1977), vol. 82. Rome: Centro Cattolico Cinematografico, 422. Translated from Italian by the author.
21. *Segnalazioni cinematografiche*, vol. 82, 403.
22. *Segnalazioni cinematografiche*, vol. 82, 300.
23. *Segnalazioni cinematografiche*, vol. 84, 39.
24. *Segnalazioni cinematografiche*, vol. 82, 379.
25. *Segnalazioni cinematografiche*, vol. 82, 379.
26. *Segnalazioni cinematografiche*, vol. 81, 121.
27. *Segnalazioni cinematografiche*, vol. 82, 379.
28. Insdorf, A. (2000). *The Night Porter* [online]. Available at: https://www.criterion.com/current/posts/66-the-night-porter [Accessed 21 December 2020]
29. Bradshaw, P. (2020). *The Night Porter* review—descent into sex and Nazism still chills [online]. Available at: https://www.theguardian.com/film/2020/nov/27/the-night-porter-review-dirk-bogarde-charlotte-rampling-liliana-cavani [Accessed 21 December 2020]
30. Ebert, R. (1975). *The Night Porter* [online]. Available at: https://www.rogerebert.com/reviews/the-night-porter-1975 [Accessed 21 December 2020]
31. Variety Staff (1973). *The Night Porter* [online]. Available at: https://variety.com/1973/film/reviews/the-night-porter-1200423141/ [Accessed 21 December 2020]
32. Atlas, Jacoba (1974). *The Night Porter* [online]. Available at: https://voices.revealdigital.org/?a=d&d=BGJFHJH19741108.1.39&e=-------en-20--1--txt-txIN--------------1 [Accessed 21 December 2020
33. Bradshaw.
34. *Segnalazioni cinematografiche*, vol. 82, 379.

35. *Segnalazioni cinematografiche*, vol. 77, 117.
36. Ansa (2014). Osservatore Romano,"Vangelo secondo Matteo" di Pasolini il miglior film su Gesù [online]. Available at: https://www.ansa.it/sito/notizie/cultura/cinema/2014/07/21/osservatore-romano-vangelo-secondo-matteo-di-pasolini-il-miglior-film-su-gesu_79bfe83d-49a1-4d61-a0f4-d1494f5b6eec.html [Accessed 22 December 2020]
37. Andrews, G. (2005). The life and death of Pier Paolo Pasolini [online]. Available at: https://www.opendemocracy.net/arts-Film/pasolini_2982.jsp [Accessed 15 September 2018]
38. Thomson, I. (2014). Did Pasolini predict his own murder? [online]. Available at: https://www.telegraph.co.uk/culture/film/11155034/Did-Pasolini-predict-his-own-murder.html [Accessed 22 December 2020]]
39. Schiru, R. and Egan, L. (2016). The violent death of "inconvenient" intellect, Pier Paolo Pasolini [online]. Available at: http://ilglobo.com.au/news/33313/the-violent-death-of-inconvenient-intellect-pier-paolo-pasolini/# [Accessed 22 December 2020]
40. Vulliamy, E. (2014). Who really killed Pier Paolo Pasolini? [online]. Available at: https://www.theguardian.com/world/2014/aug/24/who-really-killed-pier-paolo-pasolini-venice-film-festival-biennale-abel-ferrara [Accessed 22 December 2020]
41. ANSA (2023). Plea to reopen Pasolini murder file presented [online]. Available at: https://www.ansa.it/english/news/lifestyle/arts/2023/03/03/plea-to-reopen-pasolini-murder-file-presented_823996a4-df79-4d90-be86-434d0010017a.html [Accessed 22 June 2023]
42. ANSA.
43. BBFC (no date). Education/Case Studies: *Salò/120 Days of Sodom* [online]. Available at: https://www.bbfc.co.uk/education/case-studies/salo-120-days-of-sodom [Accessed 10 September 2023]
44. cinematografo.it (no date). Salò o le 120 giornate di Sodoma [online]. Available at: https://www.cinematografo.it/cinedatabase/film/sal-o-le-120-giornate-di-sodoma/14720/ [Accessed 22 December 2020]
45. cinematografo.it.
46. cinematografo.it.
47. cinematografo.it.
48. Fiddler and Banwell, 149.
49. Fiddler and Banwell, 149.
50. *Segnalazioni cinematografiche*, vol. 82, 163–164.
51. *Segnalazioni cinematografiche*, vol. 82, 164.
52. *Segnalazioni cinematografiche*, vol. 82, 164.
53. Ebert, R. (1970). *The Damned* [online]. Available at: https://www.rogerebert.com/reviews/the-damned-1970 [Accessed 22 December 2020]
54. Ebert, *The Damned*.
55. Ebert, *The Damned*.
56. *Segnalazioni cinematografiche*, vol. 68, 97.
57. *Segnalazioni cinematografiche*, vol. 68, 97.
58. Fiddler and Banwell, 142.
59. Fiddler and Banwell, 141.
60. Lichtner.

Chapter 9

1. Canby, V. (1974). Why the Devil Do They Dig "The Exorcist?" [online]. Available at: https://www.nytimes.com/1974/01/13/archives/why-the-devil-do-they-dig-the-exorcist-why-they-dig-exorcist.html [Accessed 7 June 2020]
2. Travers, P., and Reiff, S. (1974). *The Story Behind The Exorcist*. New York: Signet Books, 160.
3. The Catholic Truth Society (2012). *The Catechism of the Catholic Church*. London: The Catholic Truth Society, 1673.
4. Sherwood, H. (2016). Vatican to hold exorcist training course after "rise in possessions" [online]. Available at: https://www.theguardian.com/world/2018/mar/30/vatican-to-hold-exorcist-training-course-after-rise-in-possessions-exorcism-priests [Accessed 8 June 2020
5. Sherwood.
6. Pacatte, Sr. Rose (2018). New film documents famous exorcist Fr. Gabriele Amorth [online]. Available at: https://www.ncronline.org/news/media/new-film-documents-famous-exorcist-fr-gabriele-amorth [Accessed 8 June 2020]
7. Doubt, M. (2018). [#WiHM] Feb 22nd (Black History Month). Abby 1974 [online]. Available at: https://www.longlivethevoid.com/news/wihm9feb22mark [Accessed 08 June 2020]

8. Doubt.
9. *Segnalazioni cinematografiche*, vol. 81, 195.
10. *Segnalazioni cinematografiche*, vol. 81, 195.
11. *Segnalazioni cinematografiche*, vol. 81, 195.
12. *Segnalazioni cinematografiche*, vol. 81, 195.
13. *Segnalazioni cinematografiche*, vol. 47, 120.
14. *Segnalazioni cinematografiche* (1975), vol. 78, 461.
15. *Segnalazioni cinematografiche* (1975), vol. 78, 461.
16. *Segnalazioni cinematografiche* (1975), vol. 78, 461.
17. *Segnalazioni cinematografiche* (1975), vol. 78, 467.
18. *Segnalazioni cinematografiche* (1975), vol. 78, 467.
19. *Segnalazioni cinematografiche* (1975), vol. 78, 467.
20. Markham, P. (1976). The Antichrist (L'Anticristo). *Monthly Film Bulletin* 43 (504): 75. British Film Institute.
21. *Segnalazioni cinematografiche* (1975), vol. 78, 186.
22. *Segnalazioni cinematografiche* (1975), vol. 78, 186.
23. *Segnalazioni cinematografiche* (1975), vol. 78, 186.
24. *Segnalazioni cinematografiche* (1975), vol. 78, 186.
25. *Segnalazioni cinematografiche* (1975), vol. 78, 186.
26. *Segnalazioni cinematografiche* (1975), vol. 78, 185.
27. *Segnalazioni cinematografiche* (1975), vol. 78, 185.
28. *Segnalazioni cinematografiche* (1975), vol. 78, 185.
29. *Segnalazioni cinematografiche* (1975), vol. 78, 185.
30. *Segnalazioni cinematografiche* (1975), vol. 78, 77.
31. *Segnalazioni cinematografiche* (1975), vol. 78, 77.
32. *Segnalazioni cinematografiche* (1975), vol. 78, 78.
33. *Segnalazioni cinematografiche* (1975), vol. 78, 78.
34. *Segnalazioni cinematografiche* (1975), vol. 78, 78.
35. Ebert, R. (1976). *The Omen* [online]. Available at: https://www.rogerebert.com/reviews/the-omen-1976 [Accessed 8 June 2020]
36. McCarthy, L. M. K. (2016). Your God Had His Chance and He Blew It: Modernity, Tradition and Alternative Religion in 1960s and 1970s Horror. Ph.D. Diss., University of East Anglia. Available at: https://ueaeprints.uea.ac.uk/id/eprint/63060/1/Your_God_Had_His_Chance_and_He_Blew_It__Modernity,_Tradition_and_Alternative_Religion_in_1960s_and_1970s_Horror_Final_Edit3_2.pdf (Accessed 6 August 2023), 8.
37. McCarthy, 8.
38. *Segnalazioni cinematografiche*, vol. 82, 95.
39. *Segnalazioni cinematografiche*, vol. 82, 95.
40. *Segnalazioni cinematografiche* (1983), vol. 94. Rome: Centro Cattolico Cinematografico, 258. Translated from Italian by the author.
41. *Segnalazioni cinematografiche*, vol. 94, 258.
42. *Segnalazioni cinematografiche*, vol. 94, 258.
43. *Segnalazioni cinematografiche*, vol. 94, 258.
44. Glatz, C. (2016). Exorcist films should teach how God always conquers evil, exorcist says [online]. Available at: https://www.catholicnews.com/services/englishnews/2016/exorcist-films-should-teach-how-god-always-wins-over-evil.cfm [Accessed 8 June 2020]
45. Glatz.
46. Glatz.
47. Glatz.

Conclusion

1. Passannanti, E. (2014). Italian Cinema and Censorship by Religion. Ph.D. thesis, Brunel University. Available at: https://bura.brunel.ac.uk/bitstream/2438/13863/1/FulltextThesis.pdf [Accessed 9 September 2023]
2. Pope Pius XI (1930). Divini Illius Magistri [online]. Available at: https://www.vatican.va/content/pius-xi/en/encyclicals/documents/hf_p-xi_enc_31121929_divini-illius-magistri.html [Accessed 9 September 2023]
3. Pope John Paul II, 2.
4. Pope John Paul II, 2.

Notes—Conclusion

5. Mares, C. (2023). Pope Francis encourages filmmakers to "reawaken wonder" [online]. Available at: https://www.catholicnewsagency.com/news/253688/pope-francis-encourages-filmmakers-to-reawaken-wonder [Accessed 9 September 2023]
6. Mares.
7. Angeli, 1.
8. Friendly, Jr., A. (1970). Italy's First Divorce Law Is Approved by Parliament [online]. Available at: https://www.nytimes.com/1970/12/01/archives/italys-first-divorce-law-is-approved-by-parliament.html [Accessed 9 September 2023]
9. Havránek, F. (1979). Abortion Law in Italy [online]. Available at: https://pubmed.ncbi.nlm.nih.gov/445601/ [Accessed 9 September 2023]
10. Spence, R. (2020). Secret Societies in Italy: Origins of Propaganda Due [online]. Available at: https://www.wondriumdaily.com/secret-societies-in-italy-origins-of-propaganda-due/ [Accessed 9 September 2023]
11. Spence.
12. Mathiason, N. (2003). Who killed Calvi? [online]. Available at: https://www.theguardian.com/business/2003/dec/07/italy.theobserver [Accessed 9 September 2023]
13. Reuters (2019). Pope ends "secrecy" rule on child sexual abuse in Catholic church [online]. Available at: https://www.theguardian.com/world/2019/dec/17/pope-francis-ends-pontifical-secrecy-rule-child-sexual-abuse-catholic-church [Accessed 9 September 2023]
14. Reuters.
15. Henley, J. (2010). How the *Boston Globe* exposed the abuse scandal that rocked the Catholic church [online]. Available at: https://www.theguardian.com/world/2010/apr/21/boston-globe-abuse-scandal-catholic [Accessed 12 September 2023]
16. Saunders, Ethical Treatment After Rape.
17. *Segnalazioni cinematografiche*, vol. 92, 91.
18. Fiddler and Banwell.
19. Fiddler and Banwell, 149.
20. *Segnalazioni cinematografiche*, vol. 94, 258.
21. *Segnalazioni cinematografiche*, vol. 78, 78.
22. Pope John Paul II, 2.
23. Pope John Paul II, 2.
24. Pope John Paul II, 2.
25. Mares.
26. Pope Pius XI (1930). Divini Illius Magistri.

Bibliography

Abbott, Stacey. The vampire transformed: Riccardo Freda and Mario Bava's *I Vampiri* (1956). http://www.kinoeye.org/02/18/abbott18.php 2002.
Akor, Linus. Trafficking of Women in Nigeria: Causes, Consequences and the Way Forward. *Corvinus Journal of Sociology and Social Policy* 2 (2011): 89–110.
Allyn, R. and Gorgone, R. Beatrice Cenci, Victim, Murderer and Proto-Feminist Icon in 1599 in Rome. https://www.througheternity.com/en/blog/history/beatrice-cenci-life-death-rome.html 2018.
American Film Institute. *Dead of Night* (1974). https://catalog.afi.com/Catalog/moviedetails/55333.
Andrews, Geoff. The life and death of Pier Paolo Pasolini. https://www.opendemocracy.net/en/pasolini_2982jsp/ 2005.
Angeli, Silvia. Catholicism in Italian cinema in the age of "the new secularisation" (1958–1978). Ph.D. diss., University of Westminster, 2017.
Ansa. Osservatore Romano, "Vangelo secondo Matteo" di Pasolini il miglior film su Gesù. https://www.ansa.it/sito/notizie/cultura/cinema/2014/07/21/osservatore-romanovangelo-secondo-matteo-di-pasolini-il-miglior-film-su-gesu_79b-fe83d-49a1-4d61-a0f4-d1494f5b6eec.html 2014.
ANSA. Plea to reopen Pasolini murder file presented. https://www.ansa.it/english/news/lifestyle/arts/2023/03/03/plea-to-reopen-pasolini-murder-file-presented_823996a4-df79-4d90-be86-434d0010017a.html 2023.
Arnold, Gary. "Halloween": A Trickle of Treats. https://www.washingtonpost.com/archive/lifestyle/1978/11/24/halloween-a-trickle-of-treats/2e2bd834-3a45-4780-93a1-96cfefeb56a9/ 1978.
Atlas, Jacoba. "The Night Porter." *Los Angeles Free Press* 12, no. 556 (1975).
BBC. On This Day 26 May 1981: Italy in crisis as cabinet resigns. http://news.bbc.co.uk/onthisday/hi/dates/stories/may/26/newsid_4396000/4396893.stm 1981.
BBC News. Pope admits clerical abuse of nuns including sexual slavery. https://www.bbc.co.uk/news/world-europe-47134033 2019.
BBFC. Case Studies: *I Spit on Your Grave*. https://www.bbfc.co.uk/case-studies/i-spit-your-grave.
BBFC. Case Studies: *Last House on the Left*. https://www.bbfc.co.uk/case-studies/last-house-left.
BBFC. Case Studies: *Salò/120 Days of Sodom*. https://www.bbfc.co.uk/education/case-studies/salo-120-days-of-sodom.
BBFC. Case Studies: *The Devils*. https://www.bbfc.co.uk/case-studies/devils/
Billson, Anne. How the "rape-revenge movie" became a feminist weapon for the #MeToo generation. https://www.theguardian.com/film/2018/may/11/how-the-rape-revenge-movie-became-a-feminist-weapon-for-the-metoo-generation 2018.
Bishopaccountability.org. What percentage of priests were accused? http://www.bishop-accountability.org/AtAGlance/data_priests.htm 2019.

Bitel, Anton. Discover the grainy depravity of this notorious cannibal horror. https://lwlies.com/articles/cannibal-ferox-review/ 2018.
Boissoneault, Lorraine. The Nazi Werewolves Who Terrorized Allied Soldiers at the End of WWII. https://www.smithsonianmag.com/history/nazi-werewolves-who-terrorized-allied-soldiers-end-wwii-180970522/ 2018.
Bonilla, Tabitha, and Hyungjung Mo, Cecilia. "The evolution of human trafficking messaging in the United States and its effect on public opinion." *Journal of Public Policy* 39, no. 2 (2019): 201–234.
Bradshaw, Peter. *The Night Porter* review—descent into sex and Nazism still chills. https://www.theguardian.com/film/2020/nov/27/the-night-porter-review-dirk-bogarde-charlotte-rampling-liliana-cavani 2020.
British Library. First use of the word "nunnery" to mean "brothel," 1593. https://www.bl.uk/collection-items/first-use-of-the-word-nunnery-to-mean-brothel-1593?mobile=off.
Brook, C J. *Screening Religions in Italy: Contemporary Italian Cinema and Television in the Post-Secular Public Sphere*. Toronto: University of Toronto Press, 2019.
Brueggemann, Tom (2020). "Psycho" Turns 60 This Week: How the 1960 Release Created an Iconic Film. https://www.indiewire.com/2020/06/psycho-turns-60-this-week-1960-release-1202237395/ 2020.
Burfield, Hannah. Le donne silenziate: The foundations of the Italian patriarchy. https://www.thecambridgelanguagecollective.com/europe/dkmpmpfowvfek8bweriudeekjmptlt 2022.
Burke, Daniel. Amid uproar, Vatican clarifies Pope's comments on "sexual slavery" of nuns. https://edition.cnn.com/2019/02/06/world/pope-nuns-slavery/index.html 2019.
Canby, Victor. "Death Wish" Exploits Fear Irresponsibly. https://www.nytimes.com/1974/08/04/archives/death-wish-exploits-fear-irresponsibly-death-wish-exploits-our-fear.html 1974.
Canby, Victor. Peckinpah's "Straw Dogs" Starring Dustin Hoffman Arrives. https://www.nytimes.com/1972/01/20/archives/peckinpahs-straw-dogs-starring-hoffman-arrives.html 1971.
Canby, Victor. Why the Devil Do They Dig "The Exorcist"? https://www.nytimes.com/1974/01/13/archives/why-the-devil-do-they-dig-the-exorcist-why-they-dig-exorcist.html 1974.
Carroll College. Second Vatican Council. https://www.carroll.edu/about/history/catholic-history-heritage/vatican-ii.
The Catholic Truth Society. *The Catechism of the Catholic Church*. London: The Catholic Truth Society, 2012.
Catt, Chris. 13 + Mondo Films & Shockumentaries: Twisted Portrayals of Life and Death. https://creepycatalog.com/mondo-films-shockumentaries/ 2022.
Cinematografo.it. Cinedatabase. https://www.cinematografo.it/trova-film 2016.
Clarke, Donald. Re-release of *I Spit on Your Grave* banned by Film Body. https://www.irishtimes.com/news/re-release-of-i-spit-on-your-grave-banned-by-film-body-1.653261 2010.
Cline, Shelly Marie. Women at Work: SS Aufseherinnen and the Gendered Perpetration of the Holocaust. Ph.D. diss., University of Kansas, 2014.
Clover, Carol. *Men, Women and Chainsaws: Gender in the Modern Horror Film*. Princeton, NJ: Princeton University Press, 1992.
Conterio, Martyn. *Black Sunday*. Leighton Buzzard: Auteur, n.d.
Conterio, Martyn. Where to begin with Mario Bava. https://www.bfi.org.uk/features/where-begin-mario-bava 2016.
Conterio, Martyn. Why your favourite directors love Mario Bava. https://lwlies.com/articles/why-your-favourite-directors-love-mario-bava/ 2016.
Cowan, Douglas E. *Sacred Terror: Religion and Horror on the Silver Screen*. Waco: Baylor University Press, 2008.
Craner, Oliver. *Beatrice Cenci* (Lucio Fulci, 1969). https://kirkpatrickmission.wordpress.com/2011/12/01/beatrice-cenci-lucio-fulci1969/ 2011.
Curti, Roberto. *Italian Gothic Horror Films 1957–1969*. Jefferson, NC: McFarland, 2015.

Bibliography 241

Curti, Roberto. *Mavericks of Italian Cinema: Eight Unorthodox Filmmakers, 1940s-2000s*. Jefferson, NC: McFarland, 2018.
Curti, Roberto. *Riccardo Freda: The Life and Works of a Born Filmmaker*. Jefferson, NC: McFarland, 2017.
Davis, Clint. 6 times Wes Craven reinvented horror. https://archive.kitsapsun.com/news/6-times-wes-craven-reinvented-horror-ep-1253001544-354509251.html/?page=1 2015.
DeCou, Jessica. "The Living Christ and the Walking Dead: Karl Barth and the Theological Zombie." In *The Undead and Theology*, edited by Paffenroth, K., and Morehead, J. W. Eugene, OR: Pickwick Publications, 2012.
Deighan, Samm. *Les démons* aka *The Demons* (US Blu-ray Review). https://diaboliquemagazine.com/les-demons-aka-demons-us-blu-ray-review/ 2014.
Doubt, Mark. Monsters of the Wild Frontier—1970s Horror. https://www.longlivethevoid.com/news/monstersofwildfrontmark 2018.
Doubt, Mark. [#WiHM] Feb 22nd (Black History Month) Abby 1974. https://www.longlivethevoid.com/news/wihm9feb22mark 2018.
Dowling, Siobhan. How Hitler helped make Hollywood. https://theworld.org/stories/2013-02-14/how-hitler-helped-make-hollywood 2013.
Ebert, Roger. *The Damned*. https://www.rogerebert.com/reviews/the-damned-1970 1970.
Ebert, Roger. *Day of the Dead*. https://www.rogerebert.com/reviews/day-of-the-dead-1985 1985.
Ebert, Roger. *Death Wish*. https://www.rogerebert.com/reviews/death-wish-1974 1974.
Ebert, Roger. *The Devils* [online]. Available at: https://www.rogerebert.com/reviews/the-devils 1971.
Ebert, Roger. *Halloween*. https://www.rogerebert.com/reviews/halloween-1979 1979.
Ebert, Roger. *I Spit on Your Grave*. https://www.rogerebert.com/reviews/i-spit-on-your-grave-1980 1980.
Ebert, Roger. *Last House on the Left*. https://www.rogerebert.com/reviews/last-house-on-the-left 1972.
Ebert, Roger. *The Night Porter*. https://www.rogerebert.com/reviews/the-night-porter-1975 1975.
Ebert, Roger. *The Omen*. https://www.rogerebert.com/reviews/the-omen-1976 1976.
Ebert, Roger. *Return of the Living Dead*. https://www.rogerebert.com/reviews/return-of-the-living-dead-1985 1985.
Ebert, Roger. *Straw Dogs*. https://www.rogerebert.com/reviews/straw-dogs-1971 1971.
Ebiri, Bilge. What if Francis Ford Coppola Remade "Psycho"? https://www.villagevoice.com/2018/06/04/dementia-13-what-if-francis-ford-coppola-remade-psycho/ 2018
Editors, RogerEbert.com. On "Ms. 45" and Revenge Movie Feminism. https://www.rogerebert.com/features/on-ms-45-and-revenge-movie-feminism 2013.
Ellinger, Kat. *All The Colours of Sergio Martino*. Shenley: Arrow Film Distributors, 2018.
Ellinger, Kat and Deighan, Samm. Daughters of Darkness Podcast Episode 14: Footprints in Delirium: Exploring the Art Giallo, Part 3. https://diaboliquemagazine.com/episode-16-footprints-delirium-exploring-art-giallo-part-3/ 2016.
Encyclopaedia Brittanica. Italy from the 1960s. https://www.britannica.com/place/Italy/Italy-from-the-1960s.
Escriva, Josemaria. Conversations 60. http://www.escrivaworks.org/book/conversations/point/60
Ferre, L. P2 [Propaganda Due]. https://occult-world.com/p2-propaganda-due/ 2022.
Fiddler, Michael, and Banwell, Stacey. "'Forget about all your taboos': transgressive memory and Nazisploitation." *Studies in European Cinema* 16, no. 2 (2019).
Friendly, Alfred, Jr. Italy's First Divorce Law Is Approved by Parliament. https://www.nytimes.com/1970/12/01/archives/italys-first-divorce-law-is-approved-by-parliament.html 1970.
Gennari, Daniela Treveri, and Vanelli, Marco. "Did Neorealism start in church? Catholicism, cinema and the case of Mario Soldati's *Chi è Dio?*" *New Review of Film and Television Studies*, 8, no. 2 (2010): 198–217.

Giuffrida, Angela. The Vatican editor who exposed the sexual abuse of nuns—and took on the Pope. https://www.theguardian.com/lifeandstyle/2019/may/08/vatican-editor-sexual-abuse-lucetta-scaraffia-nuns-misogyny 2019.

Glatz, Carol. Exorcist films should teach how God always conquers evil, exorcist says. https://www.occatholic.com/exorcist-films-should-teach-how-god-always-conquers-evil-exorcist-says/ 2016.

Glieberman, Owen. "Psycho": The horror movie that changed the genre. https://ew.com/article/2009/08/04/psycho-the-horror-movie-that-changed-the-genre/ 2009.

Goldenberg, Lila Rice. #NunsToo: How the Catholic Church has worked to silence women challenging abuse. https://www.washingtonpost.com/outlook/2019/04/17/nunstoo-how-catholic-church-has-worked-silence-women-challenging-abuse/ 2019.

Goodall, Mark. Critics hated the forgotten "mondo" genre, but their influence can be seen in Oscar-winning films today. https://theconversation.com/critics-hated-the-forgotten-mondo-genre-but-their-influence-can-be-seen-in-oscar-winning-films-today-923310 2019.

Goodwin, Daniel. *Green Inferno* (1988). https://www.starburstmagazine.com/reviews/green-inferno-1988/.

Grant, Michael. "Cinema, horror, and the abominations of hell: Carl-Theodor Dreyer's *Vampyr* (1931) and Lucio Fulci's *The Beyond* (1981)." In *The Couch and the Silver Screen: Psychoanalytic Reflections on European Cinema*, edited by Andrea Sabbadini. New York: Brunner-Routledge, 2003, 145–155.

Greer, John Michael. *The Element Encyclopedia of Secret Societies*. New York: Harper Element, 2006.

Grey, Carmen. The spiritual side of Abel Ferrara. https://www.dazeddigital.com/artsandculture/article/22491/1/the-spiritual-side-of-abel-ferrara 2014.

Guarneri, Michael. The Gothic bet: Riccardo Freda's *I vampiri* (1957) and the birth of Italian horror cinema from an industrial perspective. https://doi.org/10.1057/s41599-017-0030-3 2017.

Guli, Roberto. Film Censorship During Fascism. http://cinecensura.com/wp-content/uploads/2014/04/Film-censorship-during-Fascism_Guli.pdf 2014.

Harper, Elizabeth. The Femme Fatale Whose Tragic End Festers in the History of Rome. https://www.atlasobscura.com/articles/beatrice-cenci-haunts-rome 2014.

Havránek, F. (1979) "Abortion Law in Italy." *Cesk Gynekol* 44, no. 3 (1979).

Heller-Nicholas, Alexandra. *Masks in Horror Cinema: Eyes Without Faces*. Cardiff: University of Wales Press, 2019.

Heller-Nicholas, Alexandra. *Rape-Revenge Films—A Critical Study*. Jefferson, NC: McFarland, 2011.

Heller-Nicholas, Alexandra. "The Violation of Representation: Art, Argento and the Rape-Revenge Film." *FORUM: University of Edinburgh Postgraduate Journal of Culture & The Arts*, no. 13 (December). http://www.forumjournal.org/article/view/676 2011.

Henley, Jon. How the *Boston Globe* exposed the abuse scandal that rocked the Catholic church. https://www.theguardian.com/world/2010/apr/21/boston-globe-abuse-scandal-catholic 2010.

Hitchcock, James. Was Vatican II a mistake? https://www.crisismagazine.com/2020/was-vatican-ii-a-mistake 2020.

Hobbs, Valerie. "Rape culture in sermons on divorce." In *Rape Culture, Gender Violence, and Religion: Interdisciplinary Perspectives*, edited by Blyth, C., Colgan, E., and Edwards, K. London: Palgrave Macmillan, 2018, pp. 87–110.

Hoberman, J. Mad Scientist Seeks Flesh for Fantasy in French Scare Classic. https://www.villagevoice.com/2003/10/28/mad-scientist-seeks-flesh-for-fantasy-in-french-scare-classic/ 2003.

Hochgesang, Josh, Lawyer, Tracye, and Stevenson, Toby. The Psychological Effects of The Vietnam War. https://web.stanford.edu/class/e297c/war_peace/media/hpsych.html 2014.

Holy Bible. New International Version. London: Hodder & Stoughton, 2012.

Hunter, Russ. "*Preferisco l'inferno*: early Italian horror cinema." In *Italian Horror Cinema*,

Bibliography 243

edited by Baschiera, Stefano, and Hunter, Russ. Edinburgh: Edinburgh University Press, 2016, pp. 15–29.
Insdorf, Annette. *The Night Porter.* https://www.criterion.com/current/posts/66-the-night-porter 2000.
Janisse, Kier-La. *House of Psychotic Women.* Godalming: FAB Press, 2012.
Kamm, Henry. Italy Abolishes State Religion in Vatican Pact. https://www.nytimes.com/1984/02/19/world/italy-abolishes-state-religion-in-vatican-pact.html 1984.
Kay, Glenn. *Zombie Movies: The Ultimate Guide.* Chicago: Chicago Review Press, 2008.
Koven, Mikel J. *La Dolce Morte: Vernacular Cinema and the Italian Giallo Film.* New Jersey: Scarecrow Press, 2006.
LaMothe, Kimerer L. *Between Dancing and Writing: The Practice of Religious Studies.* New York: Fordham University Press, 2004.
Lane, John Francis. Obituary: Alida Valli. https://www.theguardian.com/news/2006/apr/24/guardianobituaries.film 2006.
Larkin, Brian. Christianity Converted. https://christianhistoryinstitute.org/magazine/article/christianity-converted 2019.
LeJeune, C. A. *Psycho*: Archive Review. https://www.theguardian.com/film/2010/oct/22/psycho-hitchcock-archive-review-horror 1960.
Lichtner, Giacomo. Italian Cinema and the Fascist Past: Tracing Memory Amnesia. https://brill.com/view/journals/fasc/4/1/article-p25_2.xml?language=en 2015.
Lowenstein, Adam. "The *Giallo*/Slasher Landscape: *Ecologia Del Delitto, Friday the 13th* and subtractive spectatorship." In *Italian Horror Cinema*, edited by Baschiera, Stefano and Hunter, Russ. Edinburgh: Edinburgh University Press, 2016, pp. 127–144.
Lucio Fulci—Genre Terrorist. Rome: Box Office Spectaculars, 2007.
Mares, Courtney. Pope Francis encourages filmmakers to "reawaken wonder." https://www.catholicnewsagency.com/news/253688/pope-francis-encourages-filmmakers-to-reawaken-wonder 2023.
Markham, P. (1976). "The Antichrist (L'Anticristo)." *Monthly Film Bulletin* 43, no. 504 (1976). British Film Institute.
Martinelli, Alberto, Chiesi, Antonio, and Stefanizi, Sonia. *Recent Social Trends in Italy 1960–1995.* Montreal: McGill-Queen's University Press, 1999.
Maslin, Janet. Day of the Dead. https://www.nytimes.com/1985/07/03/movies/film-day-of-the-dead.html 1985.
Mathiason, Nick. Who killed Calvi? https://www.theguardian.com/business/2003/dec/07/italy.theobserver 2003.
McAndrews, Mary Beth (2019). [Through Her Eyes] The History of Rape-Revenge Films and the Importance of Female Directors. https://bloody-disgusting.com/editorials/3586210/eyes-history-rape-revenge-films-importance-female-directors/ 2019.
McAndrews, Mary Beth. When The Party's Over: How Women Reclaim The Rape-Revenge Story. https://www.girlsontopstees.com/read-me/2019/10/25/when-the-partys-over-how-women-reclaim-the-rape-revenge-story 2019.
McCallum, Lawrence. *Italian Horror Films of the 1960s.* Jefferson, NC: McFarland, 1998.
McCarthy, Linda Mary Kathleen. Your God Had His Chance and He Blew It: Modernity, Tradition and Alternative Religion in 1960s and 1970s Horror. Ph.D. diss., University of East Anglia, 2016.
McCreesh, Louise. Director of graphic horror film so disturbing it was banned for 21 years dies. https://www.dailystar.co.uk/showbiz/director-graphic-horror-film-disturbing-2101035813 2022.
McGarry, Patsy. The Irish woman who exposed abuse of nuns by priests 25 years ago. https://www.irishtimes.com/news/social-affairs/religion-and-beliefs/the-irish-woman-who-exposed-abuse-of-nuns-by-priests-25-years-ago-1.3788555 2019.
McInerny, Ralph. What Went Wrong with Vatican II. https://www.ewtn.com/catholicism/library/what-went-wrong-with-vatican-ii-10174
Merritt, Carol Howard. Fear, anxiety, and Christian community. https://www.christiancentury.org/blogs/archive/2014-06/fear-anxiety-and-christian-community 2014.
Morgan, Jackson. Why Were the Early Christians Accused of Cannibalism? https://

clarifyingcatholicism.org/articles/why-were-the-early-christians-accused-of-cannibalism/ 2021.
Mulligan, Rikk. Legacy of the Dead: The Revolution Will be Militarized—Part 1. https://www.library.cmu.edu/about/news/2017-10/legacy-dead-revolution-will-be-militarized-part-1 2017.
Mulvey, Laura. Visual Pleasure and Narrative Cinema. http://www.luxonline.org.uk/articles/visual_pleasure_and_narrative_cinema%28printversion%29.html 1975.
Nashe, Thomas. *Christ's Teares Over Jerusalem*. London: Scolar Press, 1970.
Nastasi, Alison. The Beyond: Mario Bava's *A Bay of Blood*. http://www.shocktillyoudrop.com/news/374057-beyond-mario-bavas-bay-blood/ 2015.
Nastasi, Alison. The Beyond: Sergio Martino's *Torso*. http://www.comingsoon.net/horror/news/745661-beyond-sergio-martinos-torso 2015.
Navarro, Meagan. "The Living Dead at Manchester Morgue" Remains One of the Best Zombie Films. https://bloody-disgusting.com/editorials/3595447/living-dead-manchester-morgue-remains-one-best-zombie-films/ 2019.
Nichrelay, Apeksha. RIP: "Day of the Dead" Icon Joseph Pilato Has Passed Away [online]. Available at: https://apsari.com/joseph-pilato-day-of-the-dead-george-romero-actor-passed-away-dead-70-in-his-sleep-zombie 2019.
The Numbers. Box Office History for Halloween Movies. https://m.the-numbers.com/movies/franchise/Halloween 2020.
The Numbers. Box Office History for Nightmare on Elm Street Movies. https://www.the-numbers.com/movies/franchise/Nightmare-on-Elm-Street#tab=summary 2020.
The Numbers. *Night of the Living Dead* (1968). https://www.the-numbers.com/movie/Night-of-the-Living-Dead-(1968)#tab=summary 2023.
Ohio State University. The History of the Zombie in Popular Culture. https://u.osu.edu/abell118eng4563/the-history-of-the-zombie-in-popular-culture/ 2006.
Pacatte, Sister Rose. New film documents famous exorcist Fr. Gabriele Amorth. https://www.ncronline.org/news/media/new-film-documents-famous-exorcist-fr-gabriele-amorth 2018.
Parsons, Stephen. Fear and control in church -understanding Spiritual Abuse. http://survivingchurch.org/2018/02/22/fear-and-control-in-church-understanding-spiritual-abuse/ 2015.
Passannanti, Erminia. Italian Cinema and Censorship by Religion. Ph.D. diss., Brunel University, 2014.
Paul, Louis. *Italian Horror Film Directors*. Jefferson, NC: McFarland, 2005.
Peeke, Dan. *Cannibal Holocaust* was banned in the UK until 2001—but why was the horror movie so shocking? https://www.gamesradar.com/cannibal-holocaust-anniversary-shocking-movies/ 2020.
Pope John Paul II. Address of his Holiness John Paul II to the Plenary Assembly of the Pontifical Council for Social Communications. http://www.vatican.va/content/john-paul-ii/en/speeches/1995/march/documents/hf_jp-ii_spe_19950317_plen-pccs.html 1995.
Pope Pius XI. Divini Illius Magistri. https://www.vatican.va/content/pius-xi/en/encyclicals/documents/hf_p-xi_enc_31121929_divini-illius-magistri.html 1930.
Pope Pius XI. Encyclical Letter of Pope Pius XI on the Motion Picture: *VIGILANTI CURA*. http://www.vatican.va/content/pius-xi/en/encyclicals/documents/hf_p-xi_enc_29061936_vigilanti-cura.html 1936.
Preziosi, Patrick. The faith-haunted, stomach-churning cinema of Abel Ferrara. https://www.americamagazine.org/arts-culture/2020/03/03/faith-haunted-stomach-churning-cinema-abel-ferrara 2020.
Rafferty, Terrence. Beauty, Brutality and Three Tough Mothers. https://www.nytimes.com/2008/06/01/movies/01raff.html 2008.
Rawat, Kshitij. How George A Romero became the father of the zombie with *Night of the Living Dead*. https://indianexpress.com/article/entertainment/hollywood/how-george-a-romero-became-the-father-of-the-zombie-movie-with-night-of-the-living-dead-7755165/ 2020.
Reuters. Pope ends "secrecy" rule on child sexual abuse in Catholic church. https://

www.theguardian.com/world/2019/dec/17/pope-francis-ends-pontifical-secrecy-rule-child-sexual-abuse-catholic-church 2019.
Rife, Katie. In this banned masterpiece, the evil is real but the witches are not [online]. Available at: https://film.avclub.com/in-this-banned-masterpiece-the-evil-is-real-but-the-wi-1798244378 2016.
Righetti, Jamie. *The Devils:* Sex, Hysteria and Censorship. https://filmschoolrejects.com/the-devils-sex-hysteria-and-censorship-75711ba3e015/ 2016.
Romagnoli, Michele. *L'occhio del testimone: il cinema di Lucio Fulci*. Ferrara: Kappalab, 2015.
Rothman, Lily. Read What TIME's Original Review of *Psycho* Got Wrong. https://time.com/3907090/original-review-1960-psycho/ 2015.
Russell, Jamie. *Book of the Dead: The Complete History of Zombie Cinema*. Godalming: FAB Press, 2005.
Sage, V. "The Gothic, The Body, and the Failed Homeopathy argument." In *J. G. Ballard: Contemporary Critical Perspectives*, edited by Baxter, J. London: Bloomsbury Publishing, 2009.
Saunders, Father William. Ethical Treatment After Rape [online]. Available at: https://www.catholiceducation.org/en/culture/catholic-contributions/ethical-treatment-after-rape.html.
Saunders, Father William. What are Capital Sins? https://www.catholiceducation.org/en/culture/catholic-contributions/what-are-capital-sins.html 2003.
Schiru, Riccardo, and Egan, Laura. The violent death of "inconvenient" intellect, Pier Paolo Pasolini. https://web.archive.org/web/20200811183745/https://ilglobo.com/news/the-violent-death-of-inconvenient-intellect-pier-paolo-pasolini-33313/ 2016.
Schroeder, Sarah. Faith or Fear? https://www.psychologicalscience.org/observer/faith-or-fear 2015.
Scott, Emmet. The Decline and Fall of the Roman Catholic West. https://www.newenglishreview.org/Emmet_Scott/The_Decline_and_Fall_of_the_Roman_Catholic_West/ 2016.
Segnalazioni cinematografiche, vol. 1, 17, 20, 22–28, 30, 35–36, 41, 43–50, 52–59, 63–73, 75–82, 84–85, 88, 90, 91–97, 99–109, 111–112, 118. Rome: Centro Cattolico Cinematografico, 1935–1994.
Sellars, Christian, and Smart, Gary. *245 Trioxin: The Story of* The Return of the Living Dead. Burntwood: Cult Screenings UK Ltd., 2016.
Serpa, Father Vincent. Does the Church teach that it is better to die than to be raped? https://www.catholic.com/qa/does-the-church-teach-that-it-is-better-to-die-than-to-be-raped.
Shakespeare, William. *Hamlet*. New York: Simon & Schuster, 2012.
Sheppard, Dr. L. M. K. "'I don't know if we've got the heir to the Thorn millions here or Jesus Christ himself': Catholicism, Satanism and the Role of Predestination in *The Omen* (1976)." In *Scared Sacred*, edited by Booth, Rebecca, Griffiths, Valeska, and Thompson, Erin. London: House of Leaves Publishing, 2021.
Sherwood, Harriet. Unsealing of Vatican archives will finally reveal truth about "Hitler's pope." https://www.theguardian.com/world/2020/mar/01/unsealing-vatican-archive-reveal-hitler-truth-pope-pius-xii 2020.
Sherwood, Harriet. Vatican to hold exorcist training course after "rise in possessions." https://www.theguardian.com/world/2018/mar/30/vatican-to-hold-exorcist-training-course-after-rise-in-possessions-exorcism-priests 2016.
Shipka, Danny. *Perverse Titillation: The Exploitation Cinema of Italy, Spain and France, 1960–1980*. Jefferson, NC: McFarland, 2011.
Silver, Susan. K. "'And the Word Became Flesh...': Cannibalism and Religious Polemic in the Poetry of Desportes and d'Aubigné." *Renaissance and Reformation / Renaissance et Réforme* 24, no. 1 (2000): 45–56.
Slenfsrud, Judy. What Do They See in "Death Wish?" https://www.nytimes.com/1974/09/01/archives/what-do-theysee-in-death-wish-women-applaud-the-vigilante-actions.html 1974.
Sohrabi-Shiraz, Ariane. Banned horror film was so realistic the director was charged with

murder. https://www.dailystar.co.uk/showbiz/banned-horror-film-realistic-director-2211131148 2020.
Southall, JR. Amazonia: The Catherine Miles Story (aka Cannibal Holocaust II) (1985). https://www.starburstmagazine.com/reviews/amazonia-catherine-miles-story//.
Spence, Richard. Secret Societies in Italy: Origins of Propaganda Due. https://www.wondriumdaily.com/secret-societies-in-italy-origins-of-propaganda-due/ 2020.
Thompson, Erin. "The Last Temptation: Demonic Warfare, and Supernatural Sacrifice in *The Amityville Horror* (1979) and *When The Lights Went Out* (2012). In *Scared Sacred*, edited by Rebecca Booth, Valeska Griffiths and Erin Thompson. London: House of Leaves Publishing, 2021.
Thompson, Rocco. Sisters of Perpetual Aberration: a Nunsploitation Watchlist [online]. https://www.rue-morgue.com/sisters-of-perpetual-aberration-a-nunsploitation-watchlist/ 2018.
Thomson, Ian. Did Pasolini predict his own murder? https://www.telegraph.co.uk/culture/film/11155034/Did-Pasolini-predict-his-own-murder.html 2014.
Thomson, Ian. Pier Paolo Pasolini: No Saint. https://www.theguardian.com/film/2013/feb/22/pier-paolo-pasolini 2013.
Thrower, Stephen. *Beyond Terror: The Films of Lucio Fulci*. Godalming: FAB Press, 2015.
Tietzel, Nina. Germany and Post-War Trauma. https://dartcenter.org/content/germany-and-post-war-trauma 2005.
Time Out. *Ms.45*. https://www.timeout.com/london/film/ms-45 1981.
Tobias, Scott. *Black Sunday*. https://film.avclub.com/black-sunday-1798174302 2012.
Totaro, Donato. A Genealogy of Italian Popular Cinema: The Filone. https://offscreen.com/view/genealogy_filone 2011.
Travers, Peter, and Reiff, Stephanie. *The Story Behind* The Exorcist. New York: Signet Books, 1974.
University of Pennsylvania. The Cinema Under Mussolini. http://ccat.sas.upenn.edu/italians/resources/Amiciprize/1996/mussolini.html 1996.
USCCB. Vatican Best Films List. https://web.archive.org/web/20120422064928/http://old.usccb.org/movies/vaticanfilms.shtml.
Vanelli, Marco. "Italian Cinema and Catholicism: From *Vigilanti cura* to Vatican II and Beyond." In *Companion to Italian Cinema*, edited by Burke, F. Oxford: Wiley, 2017, pp. 104–120.
Variety Staff. *Black Christmas*. https://web.archive.org/web/20131231231035/https://variety.com/1973/film/reviews/black-christmas-1200423278/ 1973.
Variety Staff. *Night of the Living Dead*. https://variety.com/1967/film/reviews/night-of-the-living-dead-1200421603/ 1968.
Variety Staff. *The Night Porter*. https://variety.com/1973/film/reviews/the-night-porter-1200423141/ 1973.
Vulliamy, Ed. Who really killed Pier Paolo Pasolini? https://www.theguardian.com/world/2014/aug/24/who-really-killed-pier-paolo-pasolini-venice-film-festival-biennale-abel-ferrara 2014.
Wagstaff, Christopher. *Italian Neorealist Cinema: an Aesthetic Approach*. Toronto: University of Toronto Press, 2007.
Weidenkopf, Steve. The Real Story of the Conquistadors. https://www.catholic.com/magazine/online-edition/the-real-story-of-the-conquistadors 2023.
Weiler, A. H. *Black Christmas* (1974). https://www.nytimes.com/2018/12/11/movies/black-christmas-review.html 1975.
West, Alexandra. Think of the Children! Examining "Pre-Code" Horror and its influence on cinema. https://www.comingsoon.net/horror/news/747804-think-children-examining-pre-code-horror-influence-cinema 2015.
White, Hilary. Italy's Last Catholic Generation? Mass Attendance in "Collapse" among Under 30s. https://www.lifesitenews.com/news/italys-last-catholic-generation-mass-attendance-in-collapse-among-under-30s 2010.
Winell, Marlene. Understanding Religious Trauma Syndrome—It's Time to Recognize It. https://www.babcp.com/Review/RTS-Its-Time-to-Recognize-it.aspx 2018.

Winters, Michael Sean. Hostility to Vatican II runs deep with Pope Francis' critics. https://www.ncronline.org/news/opinion/distinctly-catholic/hostility-vatican-ii-runs-deep-pope-francis-critics 2018.

Withnall, Adam. Pope Francis: "One in 50" Catholic priests, bishops and cardinals is a paedophile. https://www.independent.co.uk/news/world/europe/pope-francis-one-50-catholic-priests-bishops-and-cardinals-are-paedophiles-9602919.html.

Woods, Pete. *The Green Inferno*—Antonio Climati (88 Films). https://avenoctum.com/2019/03/07/the-green-inferno-antonio-climati-88-films/ 2019.

Zinoman, Jason. *Shock Value—How a few eccentric outsiders gave us nightmares, conquered Hollywood and invented modern horror.* London: Penguin Books, 2011.

Index

Abbatino, Maurizio 183
Abbott & Costello Meet Frankenstein 24
Abby 197-198, 202, 205
abortion 17, 67, 86, 213
abstract 44, 46, 61
The Abyss of the Living Dead 136
Achilli, Toti 155
Achtung! The Desert Tigers 175, 180, 191
Adamsky, Father 209-210
Africa 46-47, 117, 148, 175-176, 197, 198, 217
"aggiornamento" 17
Agliani, Georgio 151
Agren, Janet 110
Airoldi, Conchita 64-65
Aitkenhead, Melanie 78
Alarcón, Pedro Antonio de 16
Alda, Alan 193
Alighieri, Dante 11, 183
Almodóvar, Pedro 164
Amazonia: The Catherine Miles Story 112-113
ambiguity 60, 127
American Film Institute 126
American International Pictures 36, 83, 201-202
American Psycho 62
The Amityville Horror 209
Amityville: The Possession 208-210
Amorth, Gabriel, Father 196
Anders, Luana 60
Andress, Ursula 106
Angel of Vengeance 88, 93
Angeli, Sylvia 14, 17, 141, 213
Anges, Sister Jeanne des 152
Ankara Express 169
Anna and the Apocalypse 140
Anthropophagus 2
Antichrist 35, 193, 195, 203, 207, 218
Antonioni, Michaelangelo 110, 189
Apocalypse Now 109
apostasy 6-8, 17, 19, 49, 74-75, 82, 97, 99, 101, 112, 118, 126, 138-139, 148-149, 152, 155, 186, 195, 197, 210, 213
April Fool's Day 67
Argento, Claudio 128

Argento, Dario 2, 53-54, 57, 64-66, 68, 71, 128-129, 132, 164
Armstrong, Michael 159
Arnold, Gary 68
Arnold, Jack 29, 31
Arslan, Muzaffer 169
Artaud, Anton 120
Assonitis, Ovidio G. 196, 203, 205, 208
Atlas, Jacoba 180
attitudes 9, 17, 18, 22, 29, 84, 85-87, 97, 151, 179, 198
Audray, Elvire 112
Australia 102-103, 107
Auxilio 164
avarice 87
Avati, Pupi 136
Axe 60, 78
Aztec Empire 129

Bad Lieutenant 94
Baino, Mario 164
Baise Moi 78
Bamonte, Francesco, Father 210-211
Band, Charles 60
banned 5, 12, 15, 22, 26, 36, 62, 76, 78, 90, 103, 107, 152-153, 160, 162, 164, 170-171, 202, 210
Banwell, Stacy 185, 190-191, 217
Baptist 3, 82
The Barbarians 109
Barber 185
Barcelona 131
Barilli, Francesco 43, 45-47
Basilicata 182
Báthory, Countess Elizabeth 26-27
Batzella, Luigi 175-176, 179, 216
Bava, Lamberto 201
Bava, Mario 2, 13, 20, 26-29, 33-37, 42-45, 48, 53-54, 57, 61-66, 68, 71, 83, 196, 200-205, 212
A Bay of Blood 2, 61-63, 66, 69, 83, 201
Bazzoni, Luigi 45
BBFC (British Board of Film Classification) 5, 83, 152, 184
The Beast in Heat 78

249

Index

Bean, Alexander "Sawney" 105
Beatty, Ned 81
Beauty and the Beast 74, 161
Bécquer, Gustavo Adolfo 123–124
Bedlam 118
The Beguines 145–146
Behind Convent Walls 161–164
Belarus 167
Benedict, Pope 147
Berger, Helmut 175, 187–188
Bergman, Ingmar 9, 76, 78–79, 82–83, 105, 214
Bergonzelli, Sergio 155, 171, 216
Berlusconi, Silvio 167, 185, 191
Bernhard, Harvey 207
Berruti, Giulio 164
Bertarelli, Massimo 69
Bertolini, Francesco 11
Bertolucci, Bernardo 50, 180
bestiality 99, 161
La Bête 161
The Betrothed 144
The Beyond 134–135
Beyond the Door 203, 205
Bianchi, Andrea 136
The Bicycle Thieves 34
Billson, Ann 78
The Bird with the Crystal Plumage 54
birth control 17
bisexual 65, 187
The Bishop (*Salò*) 184
Bisset, Jacqueline 193
Bitel, Anton 111
Black Christmas 66–67
Black Magic Rites 31
Black Narcissus 39
Black Sabbath (Three Faces of Fear) 201
Black Sunday (The Mask of Satan) 20, 34,-35 37, 44, 201
Blacula 197
Blatty, William Peter 193, 206–207
Blaxploitation 196–197, 205
Blood and Black Lace 44–45, 61–62, 84, 201
The Blood on Satan's Claw 193, 207
The Bloodstained Butterfly 45
Blount, Lisa 108
Blumhouse 57
Bogarde, Dirk 180
Bolkan, Florinda 38, 49, 155–156
Bologna 182
Bonacelli, Paolo 184
Bones and All 115
Bonilla, Tabitha 48
The Book of Exodus 84
The Book of Genesis 87, 91, 215
The Book of Matthew 84, 182
The Book of Revelation 134
Boorman, John 81, 84, 87
Borgnine, Ernest 79, 207
Borowczyk, Walerian 161, 164

Bosch, Hieronymus 138
The Boston Globe 214
Bousman, Darren Lynn 164
Bowles, Ann 129
Bradshaw, Peter 180
Braindead (Dead Alive) 136, 140
Brass, Tinto 175, 179–180, 191
Brazil 23, 103
Brigante, Elisa 129
Bronson, Charles 85, 88–89
The Bronx 93
Brooks, Andy 126–127
Brooks, Mel 200
Brothers of Italy 167, 185
Brueggemann, Tom 57, 66
Bryant, Carolyn 118
Bundy, Ted 103
Burial Ground 136
Burstyn, Ellen 207
Burton, David 15
Burton, Tim 36

The Cabinet of Dr. Caligari 22
Caiano, Mario 171, 193
Cain, James M. 189
Calamai, Clara 190
Caligula 175
Caltiki: The Immortal Monster 29–31, 34, 200
Camerini, Mario 16
Campanile, Pasquale Festa 83, 88, 172
Canada 66, 69, 126, 217
Canby, Vincent 89, 195
Canevari, Cesar 178, 180, 191
Cannibal Ferox 110–111, 132, 215
Cannibal Holocaust 2, 98, 107–113
cannibalism 47, 97–100, 107, 110–112, 115, 122, 125, 215
canon 46, 55, 57, 64, 69, 86, 92, 107, 119, 124, 131, 139, 141, 155, 158, 160–161, 164, 170–172, 190, 197
Cantelli, Alfio 163
Caribbean 129, 130, 134
Carpenter, John 55–56, 68, 70–71
Casaroli, Agostino C. 140
Cassavetes, John 207
Cassinelli, Claudio 51–52
Castellari, Enzo G. 129, 177
Castle, William 59, 207
Cat O' Nine Tails 54
Cat People 117
Cataldi, Giorgio 184
Catalonia 105
The Catechism of the Catholic Church 86, 168, 182, 195
Catherine of Siena, Saint 88
Cavani, Liliana 179–182, 189, 191, 212, 216
Cavara, Paolo 99, 103
Cenci, Beatrice 134, 142, 149–151, 156–157, 200, 216

Index

Cenci, Count Francesco 142, 149–151
Centro Cattolico Cinematografico 6–7, 14, 54, 122, 192
Centro Sperimentale di Cinematografia 12, 18, 22, 50, 110, 168, 180, 189
"cheerful and reassuring dreams" 12, 14
Chi e' Dio? 168
child abuse 49–52, 71, 84, 150, 153, 187, 214
Children Shouldn't Play with Dead Things 126
Chimbu tribe 99, 199
The Christian Democrat Party 25, 182, 184, 214
Christie, Agatha 45, 60
Christ's Teares Over Jerusalem 143
Cinecittà Studio 12, 54
cinéma vérité 89, 103, 109, 111, 151
cisgender 65
City of the Living Dead 116, 133–134
Clark, Bob 66–68, 126
Clark, David 102
Clement VIII, Pope 142, 150
Clémenti, Pierre 100
Cleopatra 15
clergy 11, 14, 48–49, 51, 53, 84, 93–94, 146, 153, 200, 204, 208, 210, 213–214, 217–219
Climati, Antonio 101–103, 106, 109, 112–114
Cline, S. 169
Cloistered Nun: Runa's Confession 158
Clover, Carol 76
Cocytus 134
coda 48, 57–58, 61, 63, 65, 67–68, 71, 198
Cohen, Herman 201
Collingwood, Mari 82, 215
Colombia 110, 112
Columbia Pictures 15
Commedia all'italiana 30
commedia sexy all'italiana 30, 171–173
communion 3–5
communism 18, 136, 167, 190
concordat 13, 138
confession 4, 32, 150, 158
confirmation 6
controversy 39, 57, 59, 76, 79, 90, 100, 107, 144, 151–153, 183, 187, 196
conquistadors 130, 134
Consecration 164
Convent of Sinners 164
Coppola, Francis Ford 60–61, 67
Corman, Roger 28–29, 37, 59–61, 67, 201
Il Corriere della Sera 163, 184
Cortés, Hernán 139
coup d'état 11
Crain, William 197
Craven, Wes 63, 70–72, 79, 81–83, 88, 89, 93, 96, 102, 103, 105, 109, 201, 212, 214
Craxi, Bettino 138
Crime Without Passion 15
Crowe, Russell 196
Crowley, Aleister, 193

crucifixion 3, 23, 72, 105, 109, 195, 197, 203, 134, 135, 136, 152, 195, 199, 203
cruelty 61, 63–64, 66, 100, 102, 106–109, 111, 114, 120, 156, 184, 186–187
Culp, Robert 79
Cunillés, José María 131
Cunningham, Sean S. 63, 64, 69, 71, 82, 83
Curtis, Jamie Lee 69, 56

Dallamano, Massimo 50–52, 66, 214
D'Amato, Joe (Aristide Massaccesi) 2, 106, 160–162, 164
Damiani, Damiano 5, 208–210
The Damned 169, 171, 185–188, 190–191
Darabont, Frank 117
Dark Habits 164
Dark Waters 164
Davis, Gloria 110
Dawn of the Dead (Zombi 2) 116, 118–119, 123, 128–132, 137, 177
Day of the Dead 118, 137–138
The Day the Earth Stood Still 27
Dead & Buried 133
de Angelis, Fabrizio 129
Death Wish 85, 88–89, 92–93
Deathdream 126–127, 131
Decournau, Julia 115
Deighan, Samm 47, 158–159
dehumanization 103, 127
De Liguoro, Giuseppe 11
Delirium 31
Deliverance 81, 84, 87
de Mandiargues, André Pieyre 161
De Martino, Alberto 196, 202–203, 205, 208
Dementia 13 60, 67
de Mille, Cecil B. 15
The Demons 158–161
Deodato, Ruggero 5, 17, 83, 98, 107–114
de Ossorio, Amando 123, 215
De Sade, Marquis 183, 185
De Selle, Lorraine 110–111
De Sica, Vittorio 18, 23, 34, 42, 76, 168
De Sisti, Vittorio 49–50, 214
Despentes, Virginie 78
destruction of innocence 48, 51–52, 83, 184
Devil Hunter 106
The Devil Rides Out 193
The Devils 152–154, 158–161
The Devil's General 169
The Devil's Rain 207
Diary of the Dead 141
Diderot, Denis 161
Dietrich, Erwin C. 172
di Laurentiis, Dino 70, 88, 208
Di Leo, Fernando 101
Dinah, daughter of Job 76, 77, 79, 81, 83, 85, 87, 89, 91, 93, 95, 214, 218
Direzione Generale per la Cinema 12, 14
Dirty Harry 88
The Divine Comedy 183

252 Index

Divini Illius Magistri 13
divorce 17, 30, 47, 86, 213
Dr. Jekyll and Mr. Hyde 22, 31
documentary 12, 16, 32, 42, 99, 107, 109, 111, 112, 114, 132, 168, 180, 182, 196, 206
La Dolce Vita 26, 42, 199
Doll 45, 60, 65, 103
Donner, Richard 207-208
Don't Torture a Duckling 38, 49-50, 134, 151, 200, 214
Dracula 24, 26-28, 30, 36-37, 55, 117
Dream Warriors (A Nightmare on Elm Street Part 3) 75
Dreyer, Carl Theodor 31-32
Driller Killer 2
drive-in 29, 36, 63-64, 68, 78, 81-82, 124, 132, 160, 170, 193, 196, 201, 215
The Duke (Salò) 184
Dunne, Eithne 60
Dunwich 133
Duomo 182
Durante, Dr.Faustino 183

East Lothian 105
Eaten Alive! 110
Ebert, Roger 68, 82, 89-90, 128, 137, 140, 152, 180, 186-187, 207
Edmonds, Don 173-174, 177, 216
Egypt 193
Eklöf, Isabella 78
Ellinger, Kat 47
Emmanuelle and the Last Cannibals 106
Enabling Act of 1933 13
envy 87
Erba, Carla 189
Erba Pharmaceuticals 189
Eritrea 176
eroticism 30-31, 33, 113, 159, 163-164, 172, 175, 178
The Eroticist 53, 134, 151, 200
Eshu 197-198
L'Esorciccio 199, 202
The Eucharist 97, 99-100, 107, 110-111, 125, 213, 217
European Union 167
evil 2, 6, 9, 13, 27, 29, 35-36, 48, 52-53, 68, 73-75, 78, 82, 84, 86, 92, 94, 102, 118, 151, 152, 157, 169, 180, 184, 195-196, 200-201, 203, 205, 208-211, 213, 215-219
Evil Dead 2, 78
The Exorcist 158, 161, 193-201, 203, 205, 207-210
exploitation 6-8, 18, 30, 51-53, 78, 82-84, 89-90, 92, 96, 99, 101, 103, 107-110, 112, 115, 117, 129, 143-145, 148-149, 155, 158, 160-161, 164, 168-172, 176-178, 180, 182, 191, 197, 208, 214-217, 219-220
Exposé (House on Straw Hill) 78
expressionist 9, 22, 27, 31, 33, 39, 43, 57, 171
Eyes Without a Face 41-42, 44

Fargeat, Coralie 78
Farrow, Mia 207
Farrow, Tisa, 129
fascism 11-12, 16-17, 22-23, 25, 27, 42, 46, 53, 75, 83, 89, 100-101, 126, 138-139, 165, 167-169, 171-173, 176, 179, 183-187, 190-192, 216-218
Faster, Pussycat! Kill! Kill! 79
Father 4-5, 8, 34, 37, 39-42, 76, 87, 100, 128, 136, 139, 145-146, 150-151, 156, 189, 196, 203, 205, 208-209, 210-211
Fellini, Federico 18, 23, 26, 42, 168, 172, 189, 199
Fennell, Emerald 78
Ferdinand II of Aragon, King 159
Ferman, James 184
Ferrara, Abel 77, 92-96, 215
Ferroni, Giorgio 32
fetish 31, 63, 94, 118, 158, 161
Fiddler, Michael 185, 190, 217
Film Universalia 168
Filmena 151
filone 44-45, 48, 51-54, 57, 60, 63, 69, 79, 83, 88-89, 106, 108, 110, 113-115, 124-125, 128, 131-133, 136-137, 139-140, 150, 160-161, 169-179, 182, 185-186, 189-191, 196-197, 200, 201, 203, 205, 208, 215-217
Final Girl 61, 63, 67, 68
Finland 103
Firefly Funhouse 60
First Apology 97
Fisher, Terence 28, 31, 35
Flavia the Heretic 155-157, 216
Fleischer, Ruben 140
Fleming, Victor 15
Florey, Robert 15
Footprints on the Moon 45
Ford, John 105
Forlani, Arnaldo 53
Foster, Marc 141
Four Flies on Grey Velvet 54
Fragasso, Claudio 131
France 23, 29, 41, 123, 136, 169, 175
Francis, Pope 147, 213, 214, 219
Franco, General Francisco 159-160
Franco, Jesús 106, 136, 158-160, 173, 177, 216
Franju, Georges 37, 41-42, 44
Frankenstein 12, 24-28, 37, 55, 117-118
Freaks 22
Freda, Riccardo 13, 25-27, 29-32, 34-36, 37, 200
Freddie, Luigi 12
Freddy's Revenge (A Nightmare on Elm Street Part 2) 73
The French Connection 88, 90
Friday the 13th 62-63, 67, 69, 141
Friedkin, William 5, 88, 90, 158, 193-197, 203, 206-207, 209, 212
Frost, Lee 170-171, 216
Frozen Scream 133

Index 253

Fuest, Robert 207
Fulci, Lucio 2, 5, 18, 38, 49–53, 66, 110, 128–137, 142, 149–151, 157, 177, 189, 199–200, 212, 214–216

Gacy, John Wayne 103
Gaetani, Flavia 155–157, 216
Galatea Films 34
Ganja & Hess 197
Garateguy, Tamae 164
Garfield, Brian 88
Gariazzo, Mario 45, 112–113
Garrone, Sergio 177, 179
Gastaldi, Ernesto 30, 52
Gates of Hell 129, 134, 167
Gein, Ed 102
generation X 124
George, Susan 80
Germany 139, 169, 172, 175, 186, 187, 191, 216
Germi, Pietro 30, 52, 110, 189
The Gestapo's Last Orgy 78, 178, 180, 191
Ghost Ship 118
giallo 7, 18, 37–38, 43–54, 57, 61–69, 71, 110, 129, 134, 171–172, 200–202, 214, 217
Giorgi, Eleonora 157
Il Giornale 163
Il Giorno 50
Giovannetti, Giovanni 183, 217
Girdler, William 196–197
The Girl Who Knew Too Much 43–45, 48, 61, 201
Girotti, Massimo 189
gluttony, 87
God 3–4, 6, 8, 29, 33, 46, 55–75, 82, 87–88, 92–94, 97, 99–101, 106, 119, 133, 135, 145, 150, 155, 168, 197, 208, 210–211, 213, 217–219
Godzilla 27
The Golden Globes 195
Goldenberg, Lila Rice 145–146
Good Friday 129
Goodwin, Daniel 114
Gordon, Alex 201
Gordon, Richard 32
The Gospel According to St. Matthew 182
gothic 7, 14, 18, 21, 25, 27–28, 29, 30–32, 34–37, 42, 45, 60, 118, 200, 202
Goya, Francisco 138
grand guignol 25, 40–41, 79, 120, 122–123, 130, 151
Grandier, Urbain 152–153
Grandmother 1, 3
The Grapes of Death 136
Grau, Jorge 124–126, 133, 136
Grazzini, Giovanni 163, 184
Great Britain 103, 175
Greek, Janet 78
Green Inferno 113–114
Gregory the Great, Saint 87
Grieco, David 183, 217
grind house 33, 71, 76, 82, 105, 170, 195–196

grotesque 64, 101, 129, 170, 172, 180, 203
Guadagnino, Luca 115
guardian 73, 206
The Guardian 180
Gunn, Bill 197
Guzman, Joseph 164

Haiti 117, 123–124
Halperin, Edward 117, 129
Halperin, Victor 117–118, 129–130
Hamlet 143
Hammer Studios 27–30, 34, 37, 193, 207
Hannibal Brooks 88
Hannie Caulder 79
Happy Death Day 65
Hard Times for Vampires 30
Harlin, Renny 75
Harron, Mary 62
Hatchet for the Honeymoon 61–62
Haviv, Yuri 91
Häxan: Witchcraft through the Ages 193
Hays Code 13, 21–22, 37
He Knows You're Alone 62
hegemony 148, 169, 171–172, 171, 176, 184, 190–191, 217–217
heinous 69, 92, 106, 109, 119, 147, 173
Heller-Nicholas, Alexandra 76, 90
Herzog, Werner 114
heteronormative 64
Heydrich, General Reinhard 175
Heywood, Anne 144–146, 149
Hill, Debra 68
Hills, Jennifer 91–93
The Hills Have Eyes 105–106, 115
Hitch Hike 83
Hitchcock, Alfred 18, 37, 39–45, 53, 57, 58–61, 64–68
Hitler, Adolf 11–14, 139, 167–168, 176, 181, 186–187, 191, 213
Hivite 87
Hobbs, Valerie 86
Hoffman, Dustin 80
holiday 67–69
Holiday 78
Hollywood 12, 14–15, 18, 21–22, 25, 42, 81, 88, 117, 197, 200, 207
The Holocaust 13–14, 17, 169, 171–172, 180, 187, 190–192, 216
Homer 112
homogenous 36
homophobia 64
homosexuality 74, 81, 87, 100, 176, 187
Hooper, Tobe 102–106, 109
Horror Film Academy 106
House by the Cemetery 133
House of Dracula 24
The House of Rothschild 15
House on 56th Street 15
House on Straw Hill 78
The House on the Edge of the Park 78

Index

Hoven, Adrian 159
Hua, Ho Meng 136
Hugo, Victor 37
Hung, Hwa I 136
Hunter, Russ 55
Hussey, Olivia 66–67
hypocrisy 5, 16, 19, 87, 94, 150, 158, 178, 186, 192

I Am Legend 141
I Spit on Your Grave 76, 78, 90–93, 96, 213, 215, 217
I Walked with a Zombie 118
I Was a Teenage Zombie 140
Iceland 103
iconography 5–7, 18, 94, 135, 143, 152, 160, 218
I'll Never Forget What's'isname 88
Ilsa, Harem Keeper of the Oil Sheikhs 173
Ilsa, She-Wolf of the SS 168, 174, 273
Ilsa, the Tigress of Siberia 173
Ilsa, the Wicked Warden 173, 177
Images in a Convent 160, 162
In the Folds of the Flesh 171, 176
inaccettabile 57, 149, 155
Incan Empire 129
incest 72, 150, 172, 187
Indigenous 101, 103, 107, 110, 112, 113, 114, 115, 129–130
L'Inferno (1911 film) 12, 25
Inferno (1980 film) 164
Inferno (poem) 7, 11, 24, 134
Inferno in Diretta (Cut and Run) 108
Ingrassia, Ciccio 196, 199–200, 202
Institut für Sexualwissenschaft 187
International Association of Exorcists 210
Inuit 103
The Invisible Man 15
Irazoqui, Enrique 182
Isabella I of Castile, Queen 159
Island of Death 78
Italy 7, 9, 11–18, 22–30, 32, 34, 36–37, 39, 41–42, 44–49, 51–52, 54, 57, 59, 61, 64, 69, 75, 79, 83, 92, 94, 97, 99–101, 103, 106–107, 109–110, 118, 120, 124–125, 128, 131–132, 134, 136, 138–139, 141, 143, 150, 153, 155, 158, 160, 16165, 167, 169, 170–178, 182, 184–187, 189, 193, 196–197, 200–203, 207, 213–214, 216–218

Jackson, Michael 119
Jackson, Peter 136, 140
Jacob 76–96
Jacopetti, Gualtiero 99
Janisse, Kier-La 47
Japan 27, 31, 136, 158
Jefferson, Thomas 58
Jerusalem 143, 196
Jesus Christ 3, 84, 97–116, 130, 133, 135, 153, 182, 195–196
John the Baptist, Saint 3

John XXIII, Pope 17, 33, 182, 220
John Paul II, Pope 8, 10, 220
Jolie, Angelina 94
Jones, Duane 120, 122
Jonestown 110
Joseph Brenner Associates 64
Judaism 84
Judgment Day 3, 5, 119, 133–136
Julius II, Pope 129
Jungle Holocaust 107
Jupiter Clan 105

kaleidoscopic 160, 171
Karras, Father Damien 210
Käutner, Helmut 169
Kawalerowicz, Jerzy 144, 152
Keaton, Camille 91, 215
Keitel, Harvey 94
Kendall, Suzy 63
Kennedy, Burt 79
Kent, Jennifer 78
Kersey, Paul 85, 88–89
Kidder, Margot 66–67
killer in the house 66
Killer Nun 164
Kirkman, Robert 117
Kitrosser, Martin 63
Kitty, Madam 175
Klimovsky, León 123–124
Knights Templar 123, 129, 215
Knowles, Paul John (the Casanova Killer) 102
Konuma, Masaru 158
Korean War 88
Koven, Mikel 45
krimi 45
Krueger, Freddy 48, 70–73, 75
Krüger, Hardy 145–146
Krupp (family) 186
Kung Fu Zombie 136

The Ladies' Club 78
Lado, Aldo 45, 49–52, 83–84, 88, 214
LaFleur, Jean 173
LaMothe, K.A. 119
Landau, John 195
Landis, John 119
Landon, Christopher 65
Lang, Fritz 43, 45
La Russa, Adrienne 142, 149
Lassander, Dagmar 61
The Last House on the Beach 83
The Last House on the Left 2, 62, 78, 83–84, 92–93, 103, 105, 124, 201, 215
The Last of Us 141
Lateran Treaty of 1929 213
Lau, Moon-Tong 136
Laurenti, Mariano 172
Lawrence, Francis 141
Lease, Maria 170

Index

Léaud, Jean-Pierre 100
Leite, Natalia 78
LeJeune, C.A. 58
Lenzi, Umberto 5, 18, 110–115, 132–133, 212, 215
Leone, Alfredo 201
The Leopard Man 118
lesbian 64–65, 146, 157, 178
Let's Fall in Love 15
Lewton, Val 118, 129
LGBTQ+ 187
libertines 183–184
Libya 167, 175–176
Lichtner, Giacomo 165, 169, 174–175, 179, 182, 184–185, 190
Liger Films 193
Lisa & the Devil (House of Exorcism) 201–203
The Living Dead at the Manchester Morgue (Let Sleeping Corpses Lie) 124, 133, 136
The Living Dead Girl 136
Los Angeles Free Press 180
Lotta Continua 182
Louisiana 135
Love Camp 7 78, 170–171, 176
Lowenstein, Adam 62
Lugosi, Bela 28, 117–118
Lumet, Sidney 88
Lumière brothers 9
Lund, Zoë 77, 93, 215
Lustig, William 71, 141
lynching 72, 118, 122

Machete 164
The Mafia 53, 183–184, 186, 214, 217
Magee, Patrick 60
The Magic Island 117
The Magistrate (Salò) 184
Majano, Anton Giulio 31–32
male gaze 64, 76, 78, 90, 149, 158
A Man Called Horse 110
The Man from Deep River 110
The Man Who Knew Too Much 37
Manchester 124–125, 133, 136
Manhattan 129
Maniac 141
Maniac Cop 141
Manzoni, Alessandro 144
La Marge 161
Mark of the Devil 159, 207
Markham, Peter 203
Martin, George 149
Martino, Sergio 52–54, 57, 63–66, 68, 71, 106, 172, 208, 214
martyr 93
Martyr, Justin 97
Marzabotto 185
Maslansky, Paul 197
Maslin, Janet 137
Massacre in Dinosaur Valley (Natura Contro) 113

Mastroianni, Armand 62
Mattei, Bruno 131–133, 164, 176, 179, 216
Mayes, Wendell 88
McAndrews, Mary-Beth 78, 90–91
McCormick, Nelson 69
McCrann, Charles 133
McCulloch, Ian 129
McKendrick, Leah 78
McPhail, John 140
Meloni, Giorgia 167, 185
The Mephisto Waltz 193, 207
Merchant Ivory Productions 161
Merrin, Father 205
Merritt, Carol Howard 154–155
Metaphor 24, 79, 115, 126, 131
#MeToo 146
Meyer, Russ 79
Mexico 129
M.F.A. 78
MGM Studios 15, 22
Micantoni, Adriano 178
Michalakis, John Elias 140
Milan 107, 182
Milian, Tomas 150
Milioni, Enzo 45
Mill of the Stone Women 32, 36
Millor, Victor 63
Mingozzi, Gianfranco 155–158, 216
Miraglia, Emilio 45
missionaries & missions 46, 50, 99, 103, 107, 110, 114–115, 130, 134, 147–148, 156–157, 192, 206, 215–216, 218
Mo, Cecilia Hyunjung 48
Monaco 58
mondo 99, 100–103, 106, 108–110, 114
Mondo Cane 99, 101–102, 108
Mondo Cannibale 106
Monicelli, Mario 29–30
monogamy 64
Monroeville Mall, Pennsylvania 128
The Monster of the Opera 31
Montell, Sonny 209
Morandini, Morando 50
Morra, Mario 101–103, 106, 109, 112–114
Mother Joan of the Angels 144, 152, 156
Motor Psycho 79
The Mountain of the Cannibal God 106
Ms .45 77, 93, 95–96, 215
MTV 72, 73
Mulvey, Laura 76, 90
Murnau, F.W. 45
Murphy, Stephen 83
Mussolini, Benito 11–18, 22–24, 42, 53, 138–139, 159, 165, 167–168, 184, 187, 189–191, 202, 213, 217
Mussolini, Vittorio 189

Namibia 101
Nash, Thomas 143
Nastasi, Alison 62–63

Index

National Agricultural Bank 182
National Board of Review 187
National Viewers and Listeners Association 1, 74
Nationalsozialistische Deutsche Arbeiterpartei 11
Navarro, Meagan 123
Navarro-Valls, Dr. Joaquin 148
Nazis 165, 167, 181–191, 216–217
Negrin, Alberto 51
neorealism 9, 18, 22–23, 27, 30, 34, 168, 171, 189
New Hollywood/New American Wave 81, 88, 193, 207
New Line Cinema 70–72
The New Secularization 6, 17, 75, 141, 213
The New York Times 67, 89, 137
New Zealand 136
Nielsen, Leslie 69
Nietzsche, Friedrich, 100
The Night Evelyn Came Out of the Grave 45
Night of the Bloody Apes 78
Night of the Demon 78
Night of the Living Dead 118, 120–122, 125, 126, 128, 131–132, 139
The Night Porter 178–182, 190–191
Night Train Murders 83
The Nightingale 78
Nightmare City 132
A Nightmare on Elm Street 4, 48, 70–74
Nixon, Richard 103
Norden, Peter 175
Norman, Leslie 27
North by Northwest 58
Norway 103, 107
Nosferatu 9–10
Nude Nuns With Big Guns 164
Nun of Monza (Marianna de Leyva; Sister Virginia Maria) 144–146, 148–149, 153, 156–157, 164, 216
nunnery 143–164
nunsploitation 7, 18, 93, 134, 143–144, 149, 156–160, 162, 164, 216, 217
#NunsToo 146, 157
nymphomaniac 51

O'Bannon, Dan 137, 139–140
Obayashi, Nobuhiko 136
occult 117, 123–124, 140, 193, 200, 207, 211
O'Dea, Judith 120
O'Donoghue, Sister Maura 147, 157, 216
Ohara, Kōyū 158
O'Malley, Sheila 95
The Omen 207–209
Onorati, Marino 199
Ophelia 143
Opus Dei 14
Orbis Film 168, 190
Orion Pictures 139–140
Ormsby, Alan 126
The Oscars 18, 187, 195, 206

L'Osservatore Romano 34, 182, 199, 210
Ossessione 22, 189
Ostia 183
The Other Hell 164
Our Lady of Lust 155

Padovan, Adolfo 11
Pagan 124, 130, 198, 218
Paolella, Domenico 157
Paolo, Father 145
Papua New Guinea 131
parable 87
Paramount Studios 15, 22, 193
Parsons, Stephen 154
Partito Nazionale Fascista 11
Pasolini, Pier Paolo 17, 92, 101, 110, 112, 166, 179, 180, 182–186, 189, 191, 212, 216–217
patriarchy 1–2, 46–47, 51, 59, 89, 93, 119, 143, 146, 150, 152, 156–157, 159, 162, 187, 207
Patton, Bart 60
Peabody, Sandra 82, 215
Peck, Gregory 207
Peckinpah, Sam 79, 80
Peeping Tom 39–41, 44, 54
Pelosi, Giuseppe 183
The Perfume of the Lady in Black 43, 45–46
Petri, Elio 18
Philip IV, King 123
philosophy 81–82
Piazzoli, Roberto 196, 203, 205, 208
Pilate, Pontius 196
Pinhead 8
Pius XI, Pope 13, 17, 138, 213, 219
Pius XII, Pope (Pacelli, Eugenio; "Hitler's Pope") 13–14, 20, 167–168, 181, 213, 220
Pizarro, Francisco 129
Play Motel 45
The Playgirls and the Vampire 32–33
Plenary Assembly 9–10
Pliny 112
Poggi, Daniela 178
Polanski, Roman 207
poliziotteschi 48, 51
Polselli, Renato 30–33
polyamory 65
The Pope's Exorcist 196
Porcile 100–101
pornography 4, 45, 64, 92, 106, 120, 122, 161, 163–164, 177, 180
Portugal 123
The Postman Always Rings Twice 189
POV 63–64
"Poverty Row" 117
Powell, Michael 37, 39–42, 44, 54
The President (*Salò*) 184
Pressburger, Emeric 39
Price, Vincent 28, 59
pride 5, 87, 156, 199, 210
profane 5–6, 19, 117–141, 143–144, 162, 195, 197, 215, 217–218

Profondo Rosso 64–66
promiscuity 51, 63, 155
Promising Young Woman 78
Propaganda Due (P2) 53, 75, 113, 153, 167, 183–186, 200, 214, 217
Prosperi, Franco E. 83, 88, 99, 103
prostitution 49–50, 146, 161, 167, 175, 214
Protestant 3, 97, 159, 198
Psycho 18, 37, 39–43, 57–61, 66–68, 208
psychoanalytical 37, 39–42, 44–45, 47, 52, 57, 63, 65–66, 73, 76, 79, 95–96, 103, 126, 154, 165, 186, 202–203, 207, 208
PTSD (Post-Traumatic Stress Disorder) 82, 95, 126, 215
Puglia 155
Puppet Master 60
Puzzle 45

The Quatermass Xperiment 27, 29, 30, 33
queer 65
A Quiet Place in the Country 171
Quigley, Linnea 140
Quintavalle, Umberto P. 184

racism 101, 120, 122
Rader, Dennis (The BTK Killer) 103
Rains, Claude 15
Rampling, Charlotte 180
rape 7, 18, 76, 78, 80–96, 105, 108, 133, 144–146, 149–153, 159, 170, 178, 187, 205, 214–215
The Rape After 136
"Rape of Christ" 152–153
rape/revenge 7, 18, 76, 78, 82–83, 87–88, 90, 92, 96, 105, 133, 214–215
Raw (2017) 115
REC 141
Reckless 15
The Red Queen Kills Seven Times 45
The Red Rings of Fear 50
Red Roses for the Führer 101
The Red Shoes 39
Redgrave, Vanessa 152
Reed, Oliver 152
Reeves, Michael 159
Regnoli, Piero 32–34, 132
La Religicluse 161
religious iconography 5–7, 18, 94, 135, 143, 152, 160, 215, 217–218
Religious Trauma Syndrome 6, 82, 154
Remick, Lee 207
resurrection 5, 8, 35, 72, 75, 117–141, 215, 217
Return of the Living Dead 137, 139–140
Revenge (2017) 78
Revenge Ride 78
La Ricotta 100, 183
Rife, K. 153
RKO 117
Roach, Frank 133
Roberti, Roberto 200
Rochdale 1, 3

Rodriguez, Robert 164
Ro.Go.Pa.G 100
Rollin, Jean 136
Rome, Open City 169, 171
Romero, George A. 2, 177, 212
Rope of Hell: A Nun's Story 158
Rosemary's Baby 193, 207
Rossellini, Roberto 23, 42, 110, 168, 189, 200
Rubin, Jordan 140
Rusoff, Lou 201
Russell, Chuck 75
Russell, Jamie 125
Russell, Ken 5, 151–155, 158, 160–161
Russia 12, 167, 177
Russo, John 120, 139

Sabato, Antonio 145
Sacchetti, Dardano 129
sacrament 3, 4, 6, 97, 99, 195, 202, 206, 210, 217–218
sacred 5–6, 19, 119, 126, 143, 163, 195, 208, 218
sadiconazista 169–171, 174, 178–180, 182, 185–186, 189–191, 216
sadism 28, 42, 50, 66, 68, 71, 103, 120, 169, 173, 176–171, 177–179, 183–184, 186, 189, 191, 216
St. Agatha 164
Salò, or the 120 Days of Sodom 166, 178–179, 182–185, 190
Salon Kitty 175, 178–180, 190–191
same sex relationships 17
Sammon, Paul M. 139–140
San Girolamo 112
Satan and Satanism 7, 12, 18, 20, 31, 34–35, 74, 134, 144, 152, 158–160, 193–211, 218
Satanico Pandemonium 160–161
Savage Man, Savage Beast 101–102
savagery 24, 46, 79, 100, 102–103, 105, 107, 111–112, 148
Savalas, Telly 201
Savini, Tom 118, 130, 137–138
Savoy, Teresa Ann 175
Saxon, John 66
scandal 1, 19, 84, 94, 103, 113–114, 133, 144, 153, 163–164, 180, 183–185, 214
Scaraffia, Lucetta 147–148, 157, 216
She Devils of the SS 172
Schindler's List 9
School of the Holy Beast 158
Schrader, Paul 90
Schroeder, Sarah 154
Schweick 134–135
Scob, Edith 41
Scorsese, Martin 88, 90
Scott, Emmet 138
Seabrook, William 117–118, 120, 129
The Searchers 105
The Second Coming 3, 133, 134
Second Vatican Council 17, 18, 97, 139, 213
Seddok: Erede Di Satana 31–32
Segnalazioni Cinematografiche 6, 8, 13–19,

24–25, 27–28, 34, 35, 40–42, 47, 50–54, 57, 59–61, 64–75, 79, 81, 83–84, 86, 89–90, 92, 95–96, 99–103, 109–110, 112–114, 120, 122–127, 130–132, 137–140, 148–149, 151, 153, 155–158, 160–164, 170–171, 173–174, 177–180, 182, 185–186, 189–191, 196, 198–203, 205–206, 208–209, 211–212, 215, 218–219
Seltzer, David 207
the seven deadly sins 87
The Seven Doors Hotel 134
The Seventh Seal 9
sex 11, 17, 21, 30, 32, 39–40, 43–48, 51, 60, 65, 74, 81, 84, 86, 95, 100, 115, 118, 143–144, 149–150, 152, 156, 159, 161, 163, 170, 172–173, 175, 179, 183, 187, 189, 197, 216, 219
sex trafficking 48–49, 52, 93, 147, 179, 214, 216
sexual violence 31, 35, 48–49, 52, 63, 68, 71, 76, 81, 84, 86–88, 90, 93–94, 96, 107, 113, 144–145, 147–148, 150, 152–153, 156–158, 161, 169, 173, 176–177, 179–180, 183, 187, 190, 197, 214, 216
sfruttamento 83
Shadow of Illusion 193
Shakespeare, William 143
Shatner, William 207
Shaun of the Dead 140
Shaye, Bob 71–72
Shelley, Mary Wollstonecraft 12, 25, 118
Sherman, Gary 113
Sholder, Jack 73–74
Short Night of Glass Dolls 45
The Siege of Trencher's Farm 79
Siegel, Don 88
Silverstein, Elliot 110
sin 3–4, 7, 21, 39, 48, 50, 81, 86–88, 90, 95, 99, 104, 119, 146, 153, 164, 167, 182, 205, 208, 211, 217
Singapore 103, 107
Siodmak, Curt 24
The Sister of Ursula 45
Sitges International Fantastic Film Festival 105–106
slasher 7, 18, 54–57, 59, 61–63, 65–69, 71, 74–75, 103, 140, 141, 201, 205
Slenfsrud, Judy 89
sloth 87
Smith, Will 141
snuff 107
Solares, Gilberto Martinez 160
Soldati, Mario 68
Somalia 175
Society of St. Paul 196
Sommer, Elke 201
Spain 106, 123–126, 128, 136, 158–160, 171, 177
Spanish Inquisition 159, 203
Speed, Carol 197–198
Spielberg, Steven 9, 177
The Spirit of St. Louis 88
SS Experiment Camp 177
SS Experiment Love Camp 176

SS Girls 176
The Stations of the Cross 3, 4, 100
Steele, Barbara 20, 33–35
Stendhal 162–163
Stevenson, Robert Louis 37
Stoker, Bram 36–37
Story of a Cloistered Nun 157
Strabo 112
Straw Dogs 79–80, 84–85, 92–93
subtext 7–8, 24, 47, 53, 72–73, 79, 83, 88, 110, 118, 120, 122, 131, 143, 173, 176, 182
subversive 5, 7, 16, 18–19, 21–22, 30, 44, 53, 57, 59, 60, 66, 78, 82, 89, 101, 131, 157, 159, 169, 172, 175, 176, 185, 212
Sugar Hill 197
Summer Amongst the Zombies 136
surrealism 31–32, 171, 201
suspense 39–40, 47, 50, 54, 67, 69–70, 88, 121, 134
suspicion 11, 37, 49–50, 52–53, 82, 95, 102, 107, 145, 163 214
The Suspicious Death of a Minor 52, 214
Suspiria 65, 164
Suzuki, Norifumi 158
Sweden 103
Sweet and Savage 101
Sykes, Peter 207

Taipei 99
Takigawa, Yumi 158
Tarantini, Massimo 113
Taxi Driver 88, 90
Il Tempo 163–164
Ten Little Indians 60
Tenebrae 78
terror 24, 39, 65, 68, 102, 105, 112, 128, 158, 205
terrorism 129, 131, 134, 167
Tessari, Duccio 45
The Texas Chain Saw Massacre 102–104, 106, 115, 124
Thana 77, 215
Theater of Cruelty 120
Thi, Coralie Trinh 78
the Third World 99, 107
Thorn, Damian 208, 210
Thorn, Katherine 207
Thorn, Robert 207
Thorne, Dyanne 174, 277
The Three-Cornered Hat 16
Thriller 119
Thrower, Stephen 118, 119, 125
Thulin, Ingrid 173
Tigon British Films 193
Till, Emmett 118
Time Out 95
To Catch a Thief 58
To the Devil, a Daughter 193
Töres döttrar i Wänge 76
Torso 63–66, 68

torture 3, 20, 38, 49–50, 82, 92, 102, 107, 108, 111, 114, 115, 134, 138, 144, 149–151, 155, 158, 159, 162, 173, 176, 178, 183, 191, 200, 214
Tourneur, Jacques 34, 118, 129, 130, 193
Toxic Zombies (Forest of Fear) 133
transgender 65, 187
Trash 140
trauma 2, 6, 39, 43, 46–47, 50, 51, 63, 82, 90, 93, 95–96, 103, 126, 143, 145, 154–155, 167, 169, 171, 178, 190, 206, 213
Tremiti archipelago 187
Trionfera, Carlo 163–164
Troughton, Patrick 207
Tunisia 176
Twentieth Century-Fox 15, 193, 207

L'Ultimo Squalo (The Last Shark) 177
Umberto II 187
L'Unione Cinematografica Educativa (LUCE) 12, 54
United Artists 117
The United States Conference of Catholic Bishops (the Legion of Decency) 21, 207
United States of America 21–22, 28, 49, 66, 94, 102, 118, 120, 197, 208
Universal Monsters 27, 72
Ursuline Nuns 152

Vadim, Roger 169
Valletti, Aldo 184
Valli, Alida 41–42
The Vampire and the Ballerina 30
I Vampiri 13, 25–29, 30–32, 34–36, 200
Vampyr 31–32
Vanzina, Stefano "Steno" 29,-30, 200
Variety 67, 90, 120, 180, 218
Vatican best movies list 9, 182
Vengeance of the Zombies 123
Veracruz, Mexico 129
Vertigo 37
Vice and Virtue 109
Victor Emmanuel IV (King) 11
video nasties 1–2, 4–5, 62, 74, 76, 83, 90, 98–99, 103, 107–108, 115, 133, 149
Video Recordings Act 62, 76, 83, 90, 133
Vienna 180
Vietnam 82–83, 88, 103, 105, 120, 122, 126–128, 131
Vigilanti Cura 13
This Violent World 101
The Virgin Spring 76, 78, 82, 105
Virus (Hell of the Living Dead) 133
Visconti, Eriprando 144–146, 148–149, 153, 155, 157, 216
Visconti, Luchino 22, 23, 42, 50, 110, 168–169, 186–190, 212, 216
Visconti di Modrone, Giuseppe 189
Von Essenbeck, Martin 186, 188
Von Sydow, Max 207
voodoo 47, 117, 128, 130

Voorhees, Jason 69, 141
Voorhees, Pamela 63, 69

Walks in Rome 162
Wallace, Edgar 45
Wallenberg, SS kommandant Helmut 175
Wan, James 65
Warhol, Andy 93
Warner, David 207
Warner Brothers 15, 152, 193, 197, 203
The Washington Post 68
Watanabe, Mamoru 158
Watergate 103
Watts, Carl "Coral" Eugene (The Sunday Morning Slasher) 103
Wehrmachtauskunftstelle 165
Weiler, A.H. 67
Welch, Raquel 79
Welles, Orson 100, 200
Wendkos, Paul 193
Werewolf 24
Werker, Alfred L. 15
West, Peter 129
West Germany 103
Wet Rope Confession: Convent Story 158
What Have They Done to Your Daughters? 50–52
What Have You Done to Solange? 50
Wheatley, Dennis 193, 207
White, Hilary 138
White Jesus 110
White Zombie 117, 130–131
Whitehouse, Mary 1
Whitelaw, Billie 207
Whitworth, James 105
Who Saw Her Die? 49, 50, 214
The Wild Bunch 79
Wilder, Billy 88
Williams, Gordon 79
Williams, Kathy 170
Winner, Michael 85, 88–90
Witchfinder General 159, 193
Wloszcyna, Susan 95
The Wolf Man 24–25
Woman's Camp 119
Women, Church, World 147, 216
Women in Prison 170
Woods, Pete 114
World War II 18, 21, 165, 167, 172, 176, 183, 186, 190, 196
World War Z 141
wrath 6, 87–90, 92–93, 96, 215
Wright, Edgar 140
WWE 60
Wyatt, Bray 60

X—The Unknown 27

Years of Lead 113, 167, 182, 184
The Young Racers 60

Index

Zarchi, Meir 76, 90–92, 96
Zeder 136
Zinoman, Jason 105
Zombeavers 140

Zombie Flesh Eaters (Zombi 2) 116, 128, 133
Zombie Jesus 130
Zombieland 140

www.ingramcontent.com/pod-product-compliance
Lightning Source LLC
Chambersburg PA
CBHW032035300426
44117CB00009B/1069